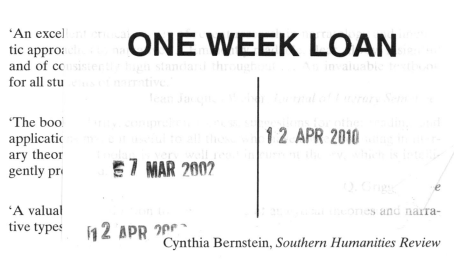

# ONE WEEK LOAN

'An excel...ent...ual... approa... and of co...sistently high standard throughout... An invaluable textbook for all stu...ents of narrative.'

Jean Jacques ...

'The boo... ...rly, comprehe... ...se suggestions for othe... ...din... ...d applicatio... ...use it useful to all these wh... ...dving in ...r ary theor... ...oolan is very well read in everything...is...tails gently pro...

1 2 APR 2010

E 7 MAR 2002

'A valual... ...tion to... ...eories and narrative types

Cynthia Bernstein, *Southern Humanities Review*

*Narrative* explores a range of written, spoken, literary and non-literary narratives. It shows what systematic attention to language can reveal about the narratives themselves, their tellers, and those to whom they are addressed. Topics examined include plot structure, time manipulation, point of view, oral narratives and children's stories.

This classic text has been substantially rewritten to incorporate recent developments in theory and new technologies, and to make it more usable as a course book. New material includes sections on film, surprise and suspense, and online news stories. The section on children's narrative has been updated, and the discussion of newspaper stories incorporates contemporary examples. There are new exercises which relate closely to chapter content and new sections on further reading.

**Michael Toolan** is Professor of Applied English Linguistics at the University of Birmingham. His previous books include *Language in Literature* (1998), *Language, Text and Context: Essays in contextualized stylistics* (1993) and *The Stylistics of Fiction* (1990).

# The INTERFACE Series

**The Series Editor**
Ronald Carter is Professor of Modern English Language at the University of Nottingham and was National Coordinator of the 'Language in the National Curriculum' Project (LINC) from 1989 to 1992.

# Narrative
## A critical linguistic introduction

Second Edition

**Michael Toolan**

London and New York

**In loving memory of
Margaret 'Mac' McAloren
who told such stories,
and never told on us.**

First published 1988
Reprinted 1991, 1992, 1994, 1995, 1997

Second edition first published 2001
by Routledge
11 New Fetter Lane, London EC4P 4EE

Simultaneously published in the USA and Canada
by Routledge
29 West 35th Street, New York, NY 10001

*Routledge is an imprint of the Taylor & Francis Group*

© 1988, 2001 Michael Toolan

Typeset in Times by Wearset, Boldon, Tyne and Wear
Printed and bound in Great Britain by University Press, Cambridge

*British Library Cataloguing in Publication Data*
A catalogue record for this book is available from The British
Library

*Library of Congress Cataloging in Publication Data*
Toolan, Michael J.
  Narrative : a critical linguistic introduction / Michael Toolan. –
2nd ed.
    p.  cm. – (Interface)
  Includes bibliographical references and indexes.
  1. Discourse analysis. Narrative. I. Title. II. Interface (London,
England)

  P302.7 .T66 2001
  401'.41–dc21
                                                          2001019304

ISBN 0–415–23174–4 (hbk)
ISBN 0–415–23175–2 (pbk)

# Contents

# Preface

Narratives are everywhere, performing countless different functions in human interaction; therefore the area of inquiry of this book must be delimited rather strictly. As the subtitle indicates, it is intended as a critical introduction, and I hope to be genuinely critical and genuinely introductory. More narrowly still, this critical introduction is specifically concerned with language-oriented or linguistically-minded perspectives on narrative: ways of looking at narrative that attend systematically to the language of stories, and models of narrative-analysis that focus on the linguistic form of narratives or their linguistically-describable structure. The basic rationale for such an emphasis is the conviction that systematic analytical attention to the logic and dynamics of language behaviour can shed light on any sub-domain or mode of language behaviour. The mode spotlighted here is narrative.

What is it about narrative that makes it such a pervasive and fascinating phenomenon? And how can one begin to answer such a question without entering into a narrative of one's own? The fact is, as my opening sentence announces, narratives are everywhere. Or are potentially so. Everything we do, from making the bed to making breakfast to taking a shower (and notice how these combined – in any order – make a multi-episode narrative), can be seen, cast, and recounted as a narrative – a narrative with a middle and end, characters, setting, drama (difficulties resolved), suspense, enigma, 'human interest', and a moral. (The moral of the story of my making breakfast this morning could be stated as 'Don't try to clean the toaster while cooking porridge'.) From such narratives, major and minor, we learn more about ourselves and the world around us. Making, apprehending, and then not forgetting a narrative is making-sense of things which may also help make sense of other things.

Just how pervasive and important oral and written narratives are to our lives becomes startlingly clear if we stop to think of the forms of narrative we depend on as props and inspirations: biographies and autobiographies; historical texts; news stories and news features in many media; personal letters and diaries; novels, thrillers and romances; medical case histories; school records; curricula vitae; police reports of 'incidents'; annual performance reviews; and, often most crucially, the stories we tell about ourselves and others – stories of triumphs and disasters, pleasure and pain – in the course of our everyday lives. These are only some of the materials shaping our lives that are palpably narrative in form and function.

But we might also consider many other preoccupations which, as a means of assisting comprehension, we 'narrativize'. Law students struggling to grasp and retain the ramifications of the law concerning theft may well, as a sense-making procedure, cast the law(s) as a developing story shaped by attendances to and departures from precedent, and by statutory revisions. And the criminal law in its entirety can be seen as a revisable story: the story is about socially impermissible conduct and the means of redress available when such conduct is exposed. This all-embracing 'story of the law' subsumes an infinite number of more specific episodes (actual and hypothetical), with probable but contestable outcomes: if you do this, in those circumstances, then you may be liable to such and such penalties.

Science, too, may at first glance look very different from narrative. We often think of it as an expanding storehouse of incontestable facts, the hallowed repository of objective knowledge of how things in the world work: a rich but static description, quite remote from 'storytelling'. But that turns out to be mistaken in both theory and practice. In theory, the emphasis on scientific enquiry as an ongoing revisable narrative (with revisions made on the rational grounds that the revised account brings enhanced descriptive or explanatory power, and greater generalizability) is now commonplace. And in practice, too, one has only to think of how science is taught in schools to see the centrality of narrative to understanding.

For instance, the concepts of fuel, energy and work might be taught in the primary school by telling stories about eating breakfast before running around, and putting fuel in the car before going on a long trip. If the child doesn't get the point of these stories, and see the logical connections between the stages within each story as well as the analogical parallels across the stories, they won't begin to understand the concepts involved. At secondary school the presentation may be less informal and more theorized, but narrative methods persist. Any laboratory exercise in physics, chemistry or biology, for example, is a planned and guided story in which the child is an essential participant. Testing for the hydrogen that is released when copper filings are added to sulphuric acid is, for teacher and lab assistant, an old, old story (ah, they don't make them like that any more!). But it's a new story, a narrative of enforced personal experience if you like, for the child, the moral of which is to be learned. And afterwards, in the passive voice style that tries to keep human interest out of the picture, they must 'write up' the experiment.

If the above is a reminder that narrative is a mode that, directly or more indirectly, may inform almost every aspect of human activity, I must now stress that the following chapters are concerned almost entirely with narratives in a narrower sense: literary narratives, folktales, stories by and for children, conversationally-embedded spoken narratives, and news stories in the media. There are linguistic similarities between these types of stories which I hope, rather than leading to a boring sameness, will be thought-provoking, and linguistic differences, too, which are yet not so great as to make for unmanageable heterogeneity.

For this second edition, I have made many minor revisions and rephrasings, some cuts and several additions or expansions. The expansions have been kept in check by the need to keep the book to a manageable length, and the requirement that something linguistic and introductory could be relevantly said about each topic. The substantially new sections include ones on narrativity (1.3), modes of narration (3.8), surprise and suspense (4.7), film narration (4.8), Labov applied to literature (6.11), systemic story genres (7.6), the structure and analysis of hard news stories in print and online (8.2–8.4, 8.6), and gender (8.7). All the Further Reading and Notes and Exercises sections, at the end of each chapter, have been radically revised and brought up to date.

On the other hand, I have sometimes retained from the first edition particular demonstration analyses even where these use approaches that may have developed further in very recent years. The more recent work often builds on the earlier work, so that the latter remains both important and truly introductory.

In the following chapters, particularly the earlier and more literary-minded ones, presentation and discussion of models and theories often involves detailed reference to one or more of a few celebrated literary texts which I have taken as exemplary. So the best way to read these chapters is with those narratives both firmly in memory and close to hand for direct consultation. This special collection comprises the following stories: James Joyce's 'Eveline' and 'The Dead', from *Dubliners*; William Faulkner's 'That Evening Sun' and 'Barn Burning'; Katherine Mansfield's 'Bliss'; and Vladimir Nabokov's novel, *Pnin*. Many other narratives, short and long, oral and written, literary and non-literary, will be discussed in the course of the book. But those six are especially relevant to the first five chapters.

A linguistic introduction can hardly avoid the occasional use of more technical terms that may at first seem off-putting to those who have taken no linguistics courses. I have tried to keep specialist jargon to a minimum, explaining terms as the discussion proceeds.

# Acknowledgements

Nearly all the work on the first edition of this book was done while I was a member of the Department of English Language and Literature of the National University of Singapore, while any better thoughts that have emerged in the second edition arose at my next academic home, the English department of the University of Washington, Seattle, or my present one, the Department of English of the University of Birmingham. Much of the material presented here has been used on courses in Stylistics or Narrative at all three institutions, and all kinds of small debts are owed to students on those courses. I still owe thanks to all those listed in the first edition, friends, colleagues and students, together with a goodly number of scholars who have one way or another influenced or unwittingly contributed to the second edition: Anneliese Kramer-Dahl, Betty Samraj, Brian Ridge, Carmen-Rosa Caldas-Coulthard, Carol Marley, Charles Owen, Chris Heffer, David Birch, David Butt, Gail Stygall, George Dillon, George Wolf, Hayley Davis, Heidi Riggenbach, Jim Martin, K. P. Mohanan, Malcolm Coulthard, Michael Halliday, Michael Hoey, Monika Fludernik, Nigel Love, Norman Macleod, Paul Hopper, Paul Simpson, Peter Verdonk, Peter White, Phil Gaines, Roy Harris, Ruth Page, Sandy Silberstein, Talbot Taylor, Thara Mohanan, Thiru Kandiah, Tony Hung, and Victor Li. Thanks also to Ms Gouri Uppal for permitting me to reproduce conversational data from her National University of Singapore MA thesis (1984).

Special thanks remain due to Rukmini Bhaya Nair, with whom I first co-taught courses on Narrative Structure.

Very special thanks to Ronald Carter, general editor of the Interface series, for entrusting this project to me in the first place and for being a powerful advocate for literary linguistics these twenty years and more; and to Louisa Semlyen at Routledge who was unfailingly supportive when the second edition turned out to be harder and longer work than I had expected.

Mega special thanks to Julianne Statham, who has again gone above and beyond the proverbial in reading through chunks of this in draft, helping me absent the most turgid bits. And a verbal hug, too, for Roisin, Patrick, and Miriam, teenagers with attitude; Chapter 7 was first written when only Roisin was old enough to enjoy *Burglar Bill*, and Miriam's story had not even begun. Now all three are old enough and smart enough to explain the new narratives to me.

The author and the publisher also wish to thank the copyright holders for their permission to reproduce the following material in this book:

'Hague links Labour with murder rise', by Philip Webster and Tom Baldwin, © Times Newspapers Limited, 19 December 2000.

'Race and Policing: Hague's defiance inflames the anger', by Paul Waugh and Andrew Grice, 19 December 2000, © The *Independent*/Syndication.

'Hague race jibe angers ministers', by Nicholas White and Nick Hopkins, 19 December 2000, © The *Guardian*.

'Tory Leader "won't be gagged on crime"', by George Jones, 19 December 2000, © The *Telegraph*.

'Crazy Hague defies Dami dad's plea', 19 December 2000, © The *Mirror*.

# 1 Preliminary orientations

## 1.1 Teller, tale, addressee

What is narrative? What do we mean by 'narrative structure'? Where does a linguistic approach come in, and how helpful can it really be? The following are introductory notes on these and other basic issues, which should at least indicate the terrain to be covered, and why it is significant.

Commentators sometimes begin by stating the truism that any tale involves a teller, and that, therefore, narrative study must analyse two basic components: the tale and the teller. But as much could be said of every speech event: there is always inherently a speaker, separable from what is spoken. What makes narratives different, especially literary or extended spoken ones, is that the teller is often *particularly* noticeable. Tellers of long narratives can be surprisingly present and perceptible even as they unfold a tale that ostensibly draws all our attention, as readers or listeners, to other individuals who are within the tale. As a result we may feel that we are dividing our attention between two objects of interest: the individuals and events in the story itself, and the individual telling us about these. Thus when we read Coleridge's 'Rime of the Ancient Mariner' or Bronte's *Wuthering Heights* or listen to the rambling anecdote of a friend, part of the experience is the activity of 'reading' or scrutinizing the character of the teller: the returned mariner, Lockwood, the friend. Already the two literary examples cited involve an enriching complication. In both texts mentioned, there is more than one teller: besides the mariner, for instance, is a 'higher' teller who writes, 'It is an ancient Mariner/And he stoppeth one of three'. But we can address such complications later, and should concentrate here on narrative's dual essential foci, teller and tale.

The possibility of achieving this effect of divided attention exploits a basic characteristic of narrative. Narrative typically is a recounting of things spatiotemporally distant: here's the present teller, seemingly close to the addressee (reader or listener), and there at a distance is the tale and its topic. This selection of effects of closeness and distance can be represented graphically:

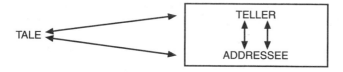

But since the present teller is the sole access to the distant topic, there is a sense, too, in which narrative entails making what is distant and absent uncommonly present: a three-way merging rather than a division. Diagrammatically this merging-and-immediacy can be represented as:

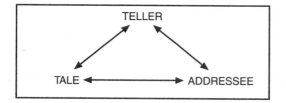

However, since tellers can become intensely absorbed in their self-generated sense of the distant topic they are relating, addressees sometimes have the impression that the teller has withdrawn from them, has taken leave, so as to be more fully involved in the removed scene. This third type of relation between tale, teller, and addressee (a withdrawing and merging) might be cast thus:

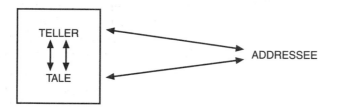

In short, narratives always involve a Tale, a Teller, and an Addressee, and these can be 'placed', notionally, at different degrees of mutual proximity or distance. Hawthorn (1985) broaches these same issues, taking a painting by Millais, *The Boyhood of Raleigh*, as capturing something central to narrative. In that painting an old seaman, with his back to the viewer, appears to be addressing two young boys who are evidently fascinated and absorbed by what he tells them. The old man is using his whole arm to point out to the sea, visible in the distance. But the boys' eyes are on the man and his gesturing arm, not any distant scene he may be designating.

Narrative focusses our attention on to a story, a sequence of events, through the direct mediation of a 'telling' which we both stare at and through, which is at once central and peripheral to the experience of the story, both absent and present in the consciousness of those being told the story. Like the two young boys we stare at the 'telling' while our minds are fixed upon what that telling points towards. We look at the pointing arm but our minds are fixed upon what is pointed at.

(Hawthorn, 1985: vii)

One of the distinctive characteristics of narrative concerns its necessary source, the narrator. We stare at the narrator rather than interacting with him as we would if we were in conversation; at the same time, in literary narratives especially, that narrator is often 'impersonalized', and attended to as a disembodied voice.

Thus there is a teller in every tale to a far greater degree than there is a speaker *in* any ordinary turn at talk. Because narratives are, relative to ordinary turns of talk, long texts and personalized or evaluated texts, there is a way in which, while your conversational remarks *reflect* who you are (your identity and values), in the course of any narrative the narrator's text *describes* that narrator. In brief snatches of conversation, a person may be able, through accent-mimicry for example, to 'pass' for someone of a different class or gender or ethnic identity; but to take on another's identity in a sustained fashion, across a number of personal narratives, is ordinarily very difficult, and may even imply disabling confusion or a personality disorder. The reflection/description contrast may be chiefly a matter of degree, but it is arguably an important contrast with far-reaching consequences – e.g. even for assessments of mental health or illness.

This brings us to another important asset of narrators: narrators are typically trusted by their addressees. In at least implicitly seeking and being granted rights to a lengthy verbal contribution, narrators assert their authority to tell, to take up the role of knower, or entertainer, or producer, in relation to the addressees' adopted role of learner or consumer. To narrate is to bid for a kind of power. Sometimes the narratives told crucially affect our lives: those told by journalists, politicians, colleagues, employers assessing our performance in annual reviews, as well as those of friends, acquaintances, enemies, parents, siblings, children – in short, all those which originate from those who have power, authority or influence over us. Any narrator then is ordinarily granted, as a rebuttable presumption, a level of trust and authority which is also a granting or asserting of power. But this trust, power and authority can be exploited or abused, as is reflected in literary critical discussion of 'unreliable narration'. Narrative misrepresentation is a complex process, difficult to unravel. One exemplification of it arises far from literature: in criminal cases of serious fraud. Where, after having pleaded not guilty, a defendant is found guilty, the sentencing judge often refers to the obfuscating detailed deception that has been uncovered as 'a complex tissue of systematic distortion and fabrication', or uses a similar revealing description.

Even before we attempt a working definition of narratives, it is clear

ese are typically 'cut off' in some respects from surrounding co-
ıd context (their verbal and non-verbal environment, respectively:
rmer comprises any language that precedes or follows the narra-
uvc, .he latter includes anything non-verbal of relevance, including the
situation and the identities of teller and addressee). Narratives often
appear to stand alone, not embedded in a larger frame, without any
accompanying information about the author or the intended audience:
they're just 'there', it seems, like pots or paintings, and you can take
them or leave them. They differ, at least in degree, from more transac-
tional uses of language, as when someone asks you a question, or makes
a request or a promise or warning: in such cases there is strong expectation that the addressee will respond or act in predictable ways. So some
of the normal constraints on how we make sense of discourse seem to be
suspended. And it seems we do not always have to relate narratives
directly and immediately to their authors, or socio-historical backgrounds.

## 1.2 Typical characteristics of narratives

We can begin to define narrative by noting and inspecting some of its
typical characteristics:

1   A degree of artificial fabrication or constructedness not usually appar-
    ent in spontaneous conversation. Narrative is 'worked upon'.
    Sequence, emphasis and pace are usually planned (even in oral narra-
    tive, when there has been some rehearsal – previous performance – of
    it). But then as much could be said of, for example, elaborate descrip-
    tions of things, prayers, scholarly articles.
2   A degree of *pre*fabrication. In other words, narratives often seem to
    have bits we have seen or heard, or think we have seen or heard,
    before (recurrent chunks far larger than the recurrent chunks we call
    words). One Mills and Boon heroine or hero seems much like another
    – and some degree of typicality seems to apply to heroes and heroines
    in more elevated fictions too, such as nineteenth-century British
    novels. Major characters in the novels of Dickens, Eliot, Hardy, etc.,
    seem to be thwarted (for a time at least) in roughly comparable ways.
    And the kinds of things people do in narratives seem to repeat them-
    selves over and over again – with important variations, of course.
    Again, prefabrication seems common in various types of writing and
    visual spectacle besides narrative, although the kinds of things men-
    tioned above seem particularly to be prefabricated units of narrative.
3   Narratives typically seem to have a 'trajectory'. They usually go some-
    where, and are expected to go somewhere, with some sort of develop-
    ment and even a resolution or conclusion provided. We expect them
    to have beginnings, middles, and ends (as Aristotle stipulated in his
    *Poetics*). Consider the concluding words of children's stories:

And they all lived happily ever after;
since then, the dragon has never been seen again.

and notice the finality and permanence conveyed by the *ever/never* pair. Or consider the common story-reader's exit-line:

And that is the end of the story.

which has near-identical counterparts in the closing sequences of radio and television news bulletins. All these examples mark this attention to the expectation of closure and finality, itself just one aspect of the broader underlying expectation of narrative trajectory. Relatedly, the addressee is usually given to understand, and does so assume, that even embarking on their story the teller knows how it ends up (not the precise wording, but the event-based or situational gist). Exceptions to this might include Dickens's serialized novels, and the bedtime story that a parent makes up for a child, *impromptu*. Even these, along with more planned-outcome narratives, can be distinguished from both diaries and live commentaries, in that in the latter new intervening acts, beyond the control of the witness/reporter, can dictate the shape and content of the report. In true narratives, arguably, the teller is always in full control although, like Dickens and the bedtime story-teller, they may not fully foresee at the outset that material which they will control.

4   Narratives have to have a teller, and that teller, no matter how back-grounded or 'invisible', is always important. In this respect, despite its special characteristics, narrative is language communication like any other, requiring a speaker and some sort of addressee.

5   Narratives are richly exploitative of that design feature of language called displacement (the ability of human language to be used to refer to things or events that are removed, in space or time, from either speaker or addressee). In this respect they contrast sharply with such modes as commentary or description. Arguably there has to be *some* removal or absence, in space or time, for a discourse to count as a narrative. Thus if I listen in my car to a radio running commentary on a simultaneously-occurring football match or funeral, this approaches the status of narrative by virtue of spatial displacement (it is not a narrative at all if I am at the football match directly witnessing, and listening to the radio commentary). But live commentaries, like real diaries, breach characteristic 3 above, and are arguably not narratives at all. More borderline are edited TV highlights of sports and other events (interestingly, one rarely finds edited highlights of matches and events on radio).

6   Narratives involve the recall of happenings that may be not merely spatially, but, more crucially, temporally remote from the teller and his audience. Compare our practices with those of the honeybee,

whose tail-wagging dance overcomes spatial displacement, in that it communicates about distant sources of nectar, but cannot encompass temporal displacement. Thus it can only signal to its chums back in the hive immediately upon its return from the nectar-source. Accordingly, the honeybee's tail-wagging is no proper narrative in our sense, but merely a kind of reflex observation. As Roy Harris has remarked:

> Bees do not regale one another with reminiscences of the nectar they found last week, nor discuss together the nectar they might find tomorrow.

> (Harris, 1981: 158)

This is a lovely image (or narrative), partly because in fact it is something that (as far as we know) we humans alone do, and no other animals – even those with simple language systems.

A first attempt at a minimalist definition of narrative might be:

a perceived sequence of non-randomly connected events

This definition recognizes that a narrative is a sequence of events. But 'event' itself is really a complex term, presupposing that there is some recognized state or set of conditions, and that something happens, causing a change to that state. The emphasis on 'non-random connectedness' means that a pure collage of described events, even given in sequence, does not count as a narrative. For example, if each member of a group in turn supplies a one-paragraph description of something or other, and these paragraphs are then pasted together, they will not count as a narrative unless someone comes to perceive a non-random connection. And by 'non-random connection' is meant a connectedness that is taken to be motivated and significant. This curious transitional area between sequential description and consequential description is one of the bases for the fun of a familiar party game in which people around a table take turns to write a line of a 'story', the other lines of which are supplied, in secret, by the other participants.

The important role of 'change of state' has been celebrated in the more linguistic term *transformation* by the structuralist Tzvetan Todorov (1977: 233):

> The simple relation of successive facts does not constitute a narrative: these facts must be organized, which is to say, ultimately, that they must have elements in common. But if all the elements are in common, there is no longer a narrative, for there is no longer anything to recount. Now, transformation represents precisely a synthesis of

differences and resemblance, it links two facts without their being able to be identified.

The one-line definition of narrative also suggests that consequence is not so much 'given' as 'perceived': narrative depends on the addressee seeing it as narrative – the circularity here seems inescapable. While most would agree that the traditional novel is a narrative, there can be legitimate disagreement as to the status, as narrative, of less familiar and complex structures. For example, imagine you enter a cartoonist's studio and find three frames, on separate pieces of paper, on his desk. They have quite different characters, settings, furniture, etc., and seem to be about quite unrelated topics. They seem to be rough drafts, because on the corner of one is a coffee-ring, where the cartoonist has carelessly left a cup, and on the second one there's a food stain in the top corner, while the third has some cigarette ash *and* a coffee ring on it! You think you see a narrative before you – though the cartoonist hotly denies this.

That example, however whimsical, tries to touch on a fundamental but problematic feature of narrative study. Perceiving non-random connectedness in a sequence of events is the prerogative of the addressee: it is idle for anyone else (e.g. a teller) to insist that here is a narrative if the addressee just does not see it as one (see 7.3). In this respect at least, the ultimate authority for ratifying a text as a narrative rests not with the teller but with the perceiver or addressee.

But, in practice, we expect and demand much more complex connectedness, non-randomness, and sequentiality in the events of narratives. In the terms first highlighted by Aristotle, we expect *ends* as well as beginnings and middles (something not commented upon in the quotation from Todorov above). In more twentieth-century terminology, we expect complex *motivations* and *resolutions* – even in quite 'simple' tales such as folktales. Thus Benjamin Colby has written:

> Folk narrative in its simplest form is the verbal description of one or more concern-causing events and of the way in which the concern is eliminated or diminished.

> (Colby, 1970: 177)

As we shall see in the next chapter, this definition is similar to that of the pioneer Russian narratologist Vladimir Propp. Propp studied the overarching structure of the Russian fairytale, identifying it as one in which an initial state of equilibrium is disturbed by various forces of turbulence. This turbulence brings disequilibrium and upheaval before some sort of action (perhaps an intervention) leads to the restoration of a modified version of the original equilibrium.

My skeletal definition emphasizes the role of the perceiver, but not that of an independent teller. This is because the two roles are not entirely separate. I have already suggested that the activity of perceiving consequential relatedness of states is the enabling condition for narrative: we might in addition speculate that it is an activity necessarily to be performed by all tellers and addressees, at least if they intend to be tellers or addressees.

## 1.3  Narratives and non-narratives

If a slightly less minimal definition were proposed, it might run something like this:

> A narrative is a perceived sequence of non-randomly connected events, typically involving, as the experiencing agonist, humans or quasi-humans, or other sentient beings, from whose experience we humans can 'learn'.

This definition introduces (1) one or more foregrounded individuals as experiencers, and (2) the idea of addressees 'learning' from narratives – i.e. the factor of human interest without which intended recipients might well not be willing listeners. And if one wished to elaborate this one step further, it might be to specify that our preference is often for the sequence of connected events to take shape around a state or period of turbulence or crisis, subsequently resolved. That is, while a sequence of events entails some sort of change of state, a sequence containing a resolved crisis or problem entails a pronounced change of state.

All these more contentious elaborations of the initial minimalist definition are useful when one attempts to distinguish narratives from all kinds of non-narrative texts. For *if* a narrative is a sequence of logically and chronologically related events, bound together by a recurrent focus (which may not be constant or exclusive) on one or more individuals ('characters') in whom the reader becomes interested (positively or negatively); and if the narrative is in addition that kind of chronological sequence in which a period of turbulence, crisis or uncertainty is superseded by a later stage of calm, solution or closure; and if these are indeed defining criteria of narratives; *then* texts which display few or none of the above features will not be narratives. And texts which have some of the above features, or all of the above but only weakly or barely perceptibly, should feel 'marginal', or 'semi-narrative'. We can summarize those three chief or defining features as:

- sequenced and interrelated events;
- foregrounded individuals;
- crisis to resolution progression.

Now consider a literary text such as Michelle Roberts' novella – if that is what it is – entitled *Une Glossaire/A Glossary*. This comprises a series of alphabetized glosssary entries, with French headword and English-language commentary, which offer brief (typically one-page) glimpses or recollections of the rural Norman childhood that the narrator, with French mother and English father, had access to. Cumulatively the text amounts to an act of recovery, of beachcombing for fragments, and of memorializing, all made the more poignant since the narrator's cherished French aunt, Brigitte, is dying of cancer as this glossary-compilation proceeds.

Is *Une Glossaire/A Glossary* (as a whole, not in its separate entries) a narrative, by the foregoing criteria? Certainly a conventional glossary would lack all three core desiderata listed above. And initially, at least, *Une Glossaire/A Glossary* appears to lack them too – unlike indisputably narrative texts, like 'Barn Burning' and *Pnin*, where the reader can almost immediately find indicators of the onset of an event-sequence, the beginning of a foregrounding of one or more individuals, and even the first sketching of conditions that may lead to a crisis. But is this 'glossary' in fact more a journal than a glossary? If it were genuinely a journal then, like a genuine diary, it would lack the possibility of mapping-out a before and after, one already known and past to the teller, who is now in a controlling position from which to recount them.

But the very first section of *Une Glossaire*, titled *Absence*, ends by asserting that in writing a sort of geography the writer aims 'to reclaim the past'; and s/he 'set(s) myself to remembering'. Both these suggest some activity of narrative recall may be what is going to be undertaken. Even this, however, can be removed from orthodox narrative if a number of *distinct* past scenes, objects, feelings, are recalled (just as an old person relating all their wartime memories may not integrate these into a unified story). Now consider Roberts' second section, *Artichauts*. There is very little in the way of narrative in this brief section: it is quasi-encyclopaedic, with only two sentences about how 'we' and Grandpère eat artichokes, individualizing the text. However, in subsequent sections, we do gradually learn more of particularly cherished or focussed-upon individuals: Grandpère and Brigitte and, indirectly but perhaps most crucially, the maturing narrator herself. A further feature suggestive of narrative status is the fact that the glossary terminates at the letter P (*Plage*). We can take this as an indication that the text is not really or merely a true glossary at all. The plage or beach of course is a place of termination, of profound transition, the end of one situation or status and the beginning of a very different one. So, an 'objective correlative' for narrative change, or resolution. And on the beach at low tide the narrator finds a kind of glossary of 'semiotic' fragments. And when the narrator says, 'I must put them [the fragments, the memories?] into some sort of order. Make a list,' we are reminded of course that she has done just that, in the foregoing text. An alphabetized list is sharply non-narrative. But since this is such an annotated and embellished list, one in which the whole becomes clearer as the later items on the list are reached, we still have grounds for saying that here is a narrative, albeit of a non-traditional kind. The decision in all such borderline cases is really based on what the reader takes the ultimate purpose of the text to be: narrative, or hortatory, or persuasive, or informative, or argumentative, and so on.

## 1.4 Story – text – narration

In the next four chapters we shall look at some of the most influential linguistically-informed discussions of narrative as verbal art: written or oral, traditional and collective, or innovative and individual. These chapters thus review what has been suggested about the poetics of narrative. By this I mean the relatively abstract and theoretical commentary on the more systematic and recurrent aspects of stories and storytelling. The poetics of any type of verbal performance (revenge tragedies, sonnets, diaries, whatever) is the study of the ground rules that shape all the productions within that type. And most of these ground rules are not logical requirements at all, but conventional norms in the production of revenge tragedies, sonnets, and so on. Thereafter, Chapters 6 to 8 explore narratives in various societal manifestations: in the social world of conversation, by and for children, and in the public worlds of storytelling in the media, the courts, and identity-construction.

Some warnings are in order concerning the way theorists of narrative poetics have split the subject of study into two, and more recently three, major domains or levels of inquiry. Thus the early-twentieth-century Russian formalists (Propp, Tomashevsky, etc.) spoke of *fabula* and *sjuzhet*, roughly equivalent to the more recent French (Benveniste, Barthes) terms *histoire* and *discours*. These are roughly equivalent in turn to Chatman's English terms, *story* and *discourse*. By the first term of each of these pairs is meant a basic description of the fundamental events of a story, in their natural chronological order, with an accompanying and equally skeletal inventory of the roles of the characters in that story.

> A *fabula* [story] is a series of logically and chronologically related events that are caused or experienced by actors.
>
> (Bal, 1985: 5)

This is the level at which we may expect the possibility of 'total transfer' from one medium to another: everything at the level of story in, say, *A Christmas Carol*, can and perhaps should appear as easily in a film or cartoon version, or a ballet, as in the original written version. It may be worth applying the linguistic terms 'paradigmatic' and 'syntagmatic' here. A linguistic paradigm is a set or class of words (or other elements) that are especially related to each other in that they amount to alternatives, in contrast with each other, usable at the same point in the verbal sequence, without any regard for matters of sequence or progression. So the paradigmatic axis of language is a 'vertical' or static column cutting through the 'chain' of speech or writing: every 'link' in the chain relates to a distinct paradigm, and at each point whatever has been chosen to fill the link or slot is tacitly contrasted with all the other members of the set or paradigm that might have been used but were not. The syntagmatic axis of language is the horizontal one, and concerns all our possible syntactic or usage options in chaining words and phrases together, fully focussed on the onward sequencing of items and paying no attention to the contrastive identity of those items. In a story outline all the events and characters are presented synoptically, with the minimum attention to, for example, complexities of sequence, as if we're getting the paradigmatic raw materials or ingredients; the syntagmatic dimension – the linear distribution of event and character presentation, disclosure, elaboration, and so on – is severely attenuated.

Above, I used the term 'version' to refer to actual cinematic or dance realizations of the core story of *A Christmas Carol*. And 'version' is as good a word as any to refer to the business of distinctive and creative working on a story to produce the discourse we actually encounter. In other words, *sjuzhet* or *discours* roughly denotes all the techniques that authors bring to bear in their varying manner of presentation of the basic story. As far as literary-minded people are concerned, discourse is much the more interesting area of narrative poetics. Story seems to focus on the pre-artistic, genre- and convention-bound basic event-and-character patterns of narrative, with scarcely any room for evaluative contrasts or discriminations – a level at which authorship seems an irrelevant concern. Discourse looks at the artistic and individualized working with and around the genres, the conventions, the basic story patterns, in the distinctive styles, voices, or manners of different authors.

For good or ill – as will become clear, I have my doubts – the above binary picture (of *histoire* versus *discours*, *fabula* versus *sjuzhet*, or *story* versus *discourse*) has in recent discussions been complicated by the argument that we need to posit three levels, not two. As I understand it, this rearrangement does not involve adjustment of both the binary categories outlined above, but rather is simply a bifurcation of the second one, discourse. In the accounts of poetics of Genette (1980; 1988), and in several of the books I will recommend as supporting textbooks in this area (e.g. Bal, 1985; Rimmon-Kenan, 1983), the business of technical manipulation and presentation of the basic story is said to involve two levels. That is to say, if we think of *histoire/story* as level 1 of analysis, then within *discourse* we have two further levels of organization, those of text and of narration. At the level of text, the teller decides upon and creates a particular sequencing of events, the time/space spent presenting them, the sense of (changing) rhythm and pace in the discourse. Additionally, choices are made as to just how (with what detail, and in what order) the particularity of the various characters is to be presented, together also with choices as to whose perspective or viewpoint will be adopted as the lens through which particular events or descriptions or characters are seen and reported (the business of focalization – to be discussed in Chapter 3). At the level of narration, the relations between the posited narrator and the narrative she tells are probed. An obvious contrast is that between a stretch of narrative embedded within a novel and told by a character, on the one hand, and a narrative told as if by a detached, external and omniscient onlooker, on the other. This is also the level at which speech presentation (the mimetic effects of pure dialogue, the deliberate ambiguities of free indirect discourse) can be analyzed.

This distinction between what we will call text and narration comes principally from Bal. It amounts to an attempt to separate a layer at which a narrative agent *relates* the text (a level of narration) from all the other aspects of text manipulation (involving choices over how the story is presented). So text presents story in a certain manner, and in the narration an agent relates that presentation. However, this latter separation is still a source of controversy, and we may well want to question this confident separation of narration from presentation. Two-level analysts, who find the story/discourse bifurcation complicated enough, will always counter with the claim that types of narration, and strategies of speech and thought-presentation, are aspects of the manner of presentation, part of a single domain of discourse.

These complex arguments will be returned to in passing but for now the chief thing to keep in mind is the disparity in terminology used. Latterly, in place of:

STORY – DISCOURSE

we have:

STORY – TEXT – NARRATION (as in Rimmon-Kenan, 1983)

with the added complication that these three terms are translated in Bal (1985) as, respectively:

FABULA – STORY – TEXT

In general I shall use the same terms as Rimmon-Kenan wherever possible, even though reference will also be made to Bal's study.

## Further reading

Studies containing interesting general reflections on the nature of narrative and its typical or defining features, from a range of literary and linguistic perspectives, include: Bal (1985); Chatman (1978); Georgakopoulou and Goutsos (1997); Hoey (2001); Longacre (1983); Schiffrin (1994); and Scholes and Kellogg (1966).

# Notes and exercises

1 There have been many proposals as to how to make fundamental distinctions between types of discourse. One such is presented in Longacre (1983), who suggests that discourses may be first distinguished from each other depending on whether or not they involve 'contingent temporal succession' and orientation to a particular agent. These yield four broad discourse categories: Narrative, Procedural (both +succession, but only the former is +agent), Behavioural, and Expository (both −succession, but only the former is +agent). Examples of the three non-narrative types include cookbooks and car manuals (Procedural), opinion-editorial exhortations and self-help books (Behavioural), budget proposals and scientific papers (Expository). Longacre's scheme, which forms a backcloth to further generic description of narrative elements, can be usefully applied to 'borderline' narratives.

2 A really strong sense of narrativity is often derived from contemplating (coherent) texts which are in sharp structural contrast with narratives. Chapter 5 of Hoey (2001) offers an informative account of the structure of 'discourse colonies': overlooked or 'Cinderella' written texts which Hoey suggests comprise elements which accumulate or combine rather like ants in an ant colony (and *not* like the non-interchangeable organs in a human body). Consider the items set out on a shopping list, or the entries in a phone book, or an encyclopaedia; or the distribution of distinct news items on the Sports page of a newspaper, or someone's listing of 'my favourite links' on their personalized web pages: each of these (the shopping list, the phone book) is a discourse colony. The 'texts' that make up a discourse colony may be one word long (e.g. the items in a shopping list), or many thousands of words long (e.g. essay-length articles in an encyclopaedia). So the texts *within* a discourse colony may well have their own kind of internal structure, which may be worth further study in their own right (e.g. the internal 'grammar' of the short film notices in the 'What's On' sections of many weeklies and weekend newspapers). Hoey's discussion of the 'discourse colony' as a neglected type of written text may be compared with Schiffrin's commentary on 'the list', as a 'nearly' narrative extended turn at talk, to be found often in everyday conversations (Schiffrin 1994: 291–315). See also Eggins and Slade (1997), on non-narrative genres in everyday conversation.

3 The idea of change (of state) is so crucial to narrative, and to the status of narrative as a definingly human activity, because without the recording of change that narrative enables, the *enactment* of further changes would be considerably hampered. In other words *talking to each other about changes/developments in the past* assists us in coming up with plans in which we initiate (or respond to) present or future changes – and this amounts to a profound resource with which to 'master' one's environment. (Cf. the discussion of narrative control in this chapter: 'master' needs to be put in hedging quotation marks here to acknowledge that attempted mastery by no means ensures success.) But notice that this reverses our everyday way of thinking about narrative: in everyday thinking, first something happens, and then you report it in a narrative. I am suggesting here that our enormous propensity for narrative (or narrativization of experience) is cognitively enabling: it helps us shape or present and plan futures to a degree far beyond the scope of other animals. In effect, first we make a narrative, and then we are able to make or adapt to real-world changes. An 'after the fact' activity, as soon as humans reflexively recognized it as such, must have equally become a 'before-the-fact' activity, of planning and projection.

4 None of this addresses death, which is perhaps the deepest human fact or anxiety underlying our narrative drive. Like a life terminated by death, narratives have endings but – perhaps more satisfyingly than we fear our lives and

deaths sometimes are – narratives also very typically *make sense* (that is to say, usually they are coherent, they resolve or explain something). So while we live with the anxiety that our lives may have one of these key attributes but not the other (they come to an end, but they do not make sense), we comfort ourselves with narratives, which have both these desiderata: they have beginnings, middles and ends, and they make sense.

# 2    Basic story structure

## 2.1 Story/*fabula*/*histoire*

Narrative poeticians have long worked with a theoretical division of their subject-matter into the domains of story (or *fabula*, or *histoire*) and discourse (or *sjuzhet*, or *discours*). Story is the basic unshaped story material, and (with qualifications) comprises events, characters and settings. The relations between these three are remarkably variable, but examples of all three are nearly always present in narrative, although it is possible to dispense with any explicit establishing of setting. Simply within the novel canon, compare the relative emphasis on event in an adventure novel with the relative emphasis on character in a Henry James novel, and the relative emphasis on setting in an historical novel. If events, characters and settings are all-important elements of story, the first of these three has nevertheless always been treated as pre-eminent and foundational by theorists of plot. For many theorists, the expressions 'basic story structure' and 'event structure' seem virtually synonymous. And a similar preoccupation with events and event structure, especially to the neglect of character, will be apparent throughout this chapter. Character and setting will be examined, however, in Chapter 4.

In order to describe story we have to adopt a medium of communication such as language. But the notion of unshaped, uncrafted, 'unaestheticized' story, underlying every organized, shaped narrative we encounter, is one that tends to treat the basic stuff of narrative as medium-independent. Terminology introduced by Chomsky (1957; 1965) to explain syntactic relations between basic sentences and more complex ones, and how the latter are derived from the former, may be of some use here. Chomsky argued that beneath or behind the 'superficial' differences between such pairs of sentences as *John fed the cat* and *The cat was fed by John*, native speakers know there is structural relatedness and an identical meaning: the two surface structures differ, but these are minor rearrangements of a single deep structure. More generally, 'deep structure' has come to mean the underlying and core format of one or more texts (or other cultural product), out of which, with enrichments and transformations that do not *displace* that deep format, particular texts are produced. The idea of deep structure as the encapsulation of the essential elements and operations of a phenomenon, before or beneath all elaborations and refractions by culture and interpretation, lives on in a range of disciplines. And in narrative study, it is the unshaped or pre-shaped story that has been equated with deep structure. Story has been thought of as a chronologically-ordered deep structure representation of all the primary and essential information concerning characters, events and settings, without which the narrative would not be well formed. The important point here is that this representation, or 'bald version', is abstract but structured. We may then think of the teller of a narrative (the creative artist, the eye-witness, or whoever) as generating a concrete 'finished product', the presented discourse.

Here the Chomskyan analogy is weakest, since clearly most narrative transformations are not so much transformations as elaborations and enrichments, a fleshing-out of the basic story stuff. Reordering transformations, however, in which events which would happen in the real world in a particular sequence ABCD are reordered so that they are encountered in the discourse in the order BACD, are very widespread. An extreme form of reordering transformation, in which crucial explanatory information is withheld until the very end of a narrative, is common in crime and detective fiction, where significant information and clues, known to the author and sometimes even the fictional detective whose enquiries are portrayed, are withheld from the reader. Such withheld information is common in 'high' fiction, too: consider the withheld information as to who Pip's benefactor is in *Great Expectations*, or as to who Esther's parents are in *Bleak House*.

The flourishing of abstraction in various humanistic academic disciplines is perhaps what underwrites the assumption that there is an abstract level of story from which all concrete narratives, embellished by variations of content, are derived. But this is untenable. All narratives involve the report of some state and some change or changes to that state, and even as we attempt to specify the allegedly core events and characters of stories (the core 'types' of which events and characters in particular narratives are 'tokens') we find that content still remains. It has not and cannot be wholly removed. If we look at what Vladimir Propp (the pioneer Russian analyst of story structure) and others actually did, we find that, in search of basic story structure, they started – inevitably – with the rich performed narrative, and tried to 'sift through' that material, discarding all but the most basic patterns. And yet even those patterns – as we shall see with Propp – are quite clearly at best (as he conceded) genre-specific, at worst corpus-specific. We need to see the implications of saying that certain identified patterns in fact hold only for a particular genre, or, more limitedly, hold only for the small collection of narratives actually analyzed.

## 2.2  Propp's morphology of the Russian fairytale

The starting point of Propp's famous study (Propp, 1968; originally published in Russian in 1928) would seem to be very much the sort of minimalist definition of narrative introduced in Chapter 1 – a text in which
there is recounted a change from one state to a modified state. As noted
earlier, we can label the actual change of state an 'event'. Thus 'event', or
'change of state', is the key and fundamental of narrative. And Propp's
morphology of the Russian fairytale is basically an inventory of all and
only the fundamental events (which he calls 'functions') that he identifies
in his corpus, which comprises 115 Russian fairytales.

In other words, Propp analyzed his collection of fairytales, looking
particularly for recurring elements or features (constants), and random or
unpredictable ones (variables). He concluded that, while the characters or
personages of the tales might superficially be quite variable, yet their
functions in the tales, the significance of their actions as viewed from the
point of view of the story's development, were constant and predictable.
Both the number and sequence of the functions are asserted to be fixed:
there are just thirty-one functions, and they always appear in the same
sequence.

> Functions of characters serve as stable, constant elements in a tale,
> independent of how and by whom they are fulfilled. They constitute
> the fundamental components of a tale.
>
> (Propp, 1968: 21)

Here, for convenience in subsequent analytical tasks, is a full list of
Propp's set of thirty-one key, fairytale-developing actions (functions),
which bring sequential changes to a specified initial situation:

1  One of the members of a family absents himself from home. (An
   extreme exponent of this function of 'absenting' is where the parents
   have died.)
2  An interdiction is addressed to the hero.
3  The interdiction is violated.
4  The villain makes an attempt at reconnaissance.
5  The villain receives information about his victim.
6  The villain attempts to deceive his victim in order to take possession
   of him or of his belongings.
7  The victim submits to deception and thereby unwittingly helps his
   enemy.
8  The villain causes harm or injury to a member of a family (defined as
   'villainy').
8a One member of a family either lacks something or desires to have
   something (defined as 'lack').
9  Misfortune or lack is made known; the hero is approached with a
   request or command; he is allowed to go or he is despatched.

10   The seeker agrees to or decides upon counteraction.
11   The hero leaves home.
12   The hero is tested, interrogated, attacked, etc., which prepares the way for his receiving either a magical agent or helper.
13   The hero reacts to the actions of the future donor.
14   The hero acquires the use of a magical agent.
15   The hero is transferred, delivered, or led to the whereabouts of an object of search.
16   The hero and the villain join in direct combat.
17   The hero is branded.
18   The villain is defeated.
19   The initial misfortune or lack is liquidated.
20   The hero returns.
21   The hero is pursued.
22   The rescue of the hero from pursuit.
23   The hero, unrecognized, arrives home or in another country.
24   A false hero presents unfounded claims.
25   A difficult task is proposed to the hero.
26   The task is resolved.
27   The hero is recognized.
28   The false hero or villain is exposed.
29   The hero is given a new appearance.
30   The villain is punished.
31   The hero is married and ascends the throne.

Propp notes some internal patterning within this sequence. Certain functions, for example, clearly go together as pairs, such as a prohibition and its violation (2 and 3), struggle and victory (16 and 18), and pursuit and deliverance (21 and 22). And clusters of functions are grouped under general headings. Thus functions 1–7 are potential realizations of the preparation, 8–10 are the complication, and later general groups include transference, struggle, return and recognition.

In addition to the thirty-one functions, Propp identifies seven basic character types or roles:

| | |
|---|---|
| villain | dispatcher |
| donor/provider | helper |
| hero (seeker or victim) | princess (+ father) |
| | false hero |

Note that an actual character may fill more than one character role (for example, some individual in the tale may be both villain and false hero) and of course one role might be filled by several individuals (there could be several people functioning as helper or villain). Demonstrating the application of this descriptive apparatus to his corpus of stories in meticulous detail, Propp concludes:

Morphologically, a tale ... may be termed any development proceeding from villainy ... or a lack ... , through intermediary functions to marriage ... or to other functions employed as a denouement. Terminal functions are at times a reward ... a gain or in general the liquidation of misfortune ... an escape from pursuit ... etc. Each new act of villainy, each new lack creates a new move. One tale may have several moves, and when analyzing a text, one must first of all determine the number of moves of which it consists. One move may directly follow another, but they may also interweave; a development which has begun pauses, and a new move is inserted.

(Propp, 1968: 92)

I will not spend time summarizing just how Propp applies this morphology to the particular tales in his corpus, since my main purpose here is to outline what he means by 'function', 'role', and 'move', so that we can identify similar elements in other stories. And the striking thing is that certain fictions rather remote from the Russian fairytale do seem to lend themselves to Proppian analysis without too much strain (see the 'Notes and exercises' section at the end of this chapter). To take an example from popular culture, consider the *Star Wars* film trilogy: without itemizing all the Proppian functions and moves, the characters filling six of the seven core roles are easy to list:

Villain: Darth Vader
Dispatcher: Luke's uncle
Donor/provider: Obi Wan Kenobi (magical power provided is the Force)
Helper: Yoda
Hero (seeker or victim): Luke Skywalker
Princess (+ father): Leia

You can apply the Proppian categories to any composed narrative, across the whole range from *The Iliad* and the Bible to Hollywood action movies, to TV series like *Buffy the Vampire Slayer*, and children's stories.

The following story written by a seven-year-old child, with Proppian functions appended on the left, may serve to demonstrate how easily and appropriately Propp's grammar can fit simple tales.

| Initial situation | 1 | Once upon a time there was a bunny named Benjie |
|---|---|---|
| + magical agent | 2 | and she had magic powers. |
| | 3 | One day she was walking in the woods |
| Departure | | and a |
| | 4 | bunny boy appeared |
| Translation | 5 | and they went together for a walk |
| Reconnaissance | 6 | and a man appeared with a big net |

|            |    |                                              |
|------------|----|----------------------------------------------|
| Villainy   | 7  | and he got the two bunnies and went in a big ship. |
|            | 8  | Poor bunnies.                                |
|            | 9  | They were caught now.                        |
| Struggle   | 10 | But right then the girl bunny tripped the man |
| Villainy nullified | 11 | and they got free once again.         |
| Reward     | 12 | So the boy bunny thanked the girl bunny for saving him. |
| ? Equilibrium (Wedding) | 13 | The boy bunny asked the girl bunny to marry him |
|            | 14 | and she said yes.                            |
|            | 15 | So they had six bunny babies                 |
|            | 16 | and they lived happily ever after.           |

(text and analysis from *King and Rentel*, 1982.
See Christie *et al.*, 1984)

If Propp's schema fits the above story with eloquent ease, we might now put it to work on a far more complex tale, that of 'Eveline', from Joyce's *Dubliners* collection. (I will be discussing this story in future chapters in relation to a number of issues.) Propp's very first function seems almost uncannily relevant:

One of the members of a family absents [himself] from home.

Relevant, but not applicable mechanically. We might say, for instance, that the 'action' of 'Eveline' is a dramatization (chiefly a mental dramatization) of a stage *within* that first function:

One of the members of a family reconsiders a decision to absent herself from home.

While Propp's fairytales proceed through developmental *actions*, 'Eveline' is very largely a mental projection, both forward to possible future events and backward to actual past ones: remembered before-events and imagined after-events. Notice how her opening revery, up to sentence 24, is a conspectual review of past circumstances as they impinge on Eveline's present situation. As Propp notes, a story has to begin with an initial situation, one into which an element of disequilibrium is introduced by the function of absentation or another of the seven preparatory functions. But in 'Eveline', it is the situation itself that is extensively dwelt upon, and none of the first 23 sentences appears to constitute a narrative-propelling function. Nor does this tendency lapse with sentence 24. It is just that with sentence 24 comes confirmation that introspective indirect discourse – the processes of thinking about living out a narrative of functional departure from the current and continuing situation – is the chief narrative mode adopted in this story (a mode I will discuss further in Chapter 4). But the emphasis on elaboration of the multiple habitual circumstances that comprise the initial situation, mere prologue to a story, remains.

However, we can do some reconstruction of a simple developmental story when Eveline's thoughts turn to Frank. She meets him, is taken out by him, at first finds this merely 'an excitement' but later begins to like him. All of that, one imagines, would count as simply one function in Proppian terms – 'The heroine meets with a (benevolent?) stranger.' Eveline's liking for Frank seems related, not wholly ironically perhaps, to the latter's implied story-tellings, which themselves form a skeletal story: He had started as a deck boy, had sailed through the Straits of Magellan, had fallen on his feet in Buenos Aires, and had returned to the old country for a holiday.

If the heroine's association with Frank is a first function, the second and third must be her father's discovery of that association and interdiction of its continuance: '[he] had forbidden her to have anything to say to him'. But subsequently (function 4?) 'she had to meet her lover secretly', so that now (function 5?) she was to go away with him to Buenos Aires to be his wife.

At this point in the text it seems that the gap between the story outlined in the two paragraphs above and the character's current reflections closes, for the next series of thoughts that are reported, incidents of family life (centred on her mother) both happy and grim, are the direct trigger of the 'sudden impulse of terror' she feels – a psychological impulse to act ('Escape! She must escape!') quite as real and compelling as an encounter with any forest-dwelling villain. Of course in this psychological story impulses are not pure and simple, but complex and clashing – a counter-impulse is to stay, keep her promise to her mother, and submit to a 'life of commonplace sacrifices'. The final paragraphs are all about that clash of impulses, the 'maze of distress' that renders her helpless and inert, unable to respond in any way to Frank's summons.

But while, in one light, Eveline's refusal to leave at the story's close can be designated as helpless failure, as an abortive move or episode or, worse, a succumbing to the villainy of oppression at home and at work; in another light, with Frank as the villain, her rejection of him may be viewed as 'manipulation resisted', as a positive act of sisterhood uniting Eveline with her mother. We shall find the pattern of these contrary readings neatly highlighted by Greimas' typology of character roles (which he calls *actants*), to be discussed in Chapter 4.

But now, and not for the last time, we may want to raise the question of reductivism. Is not Propp's bold anatomy of fairytales a procedure which hopelessly distorts, since it sets aside the important and necessary cultural context in which these tales occur, and also ignores the varying details of stories? Propp might retort to this that a structuralist/morphological approach *has* to 'reduce', and quite explicitly sets out to shear off the detail, the non-essential. 'Essential (and non-essential) with regard to what?', we might ask. Essential to the meaning, or rather, to meaning, would come the reply! For just as the phonologist, in positing all the core and distinct sound units of a language, the phonemes, deliberately discounts all the phonetic variation which does not constitute a meaning-bearing, word-changing variation, so the story structuralist will argue that he is identifying the basic narrative units of a mini-language, here the language of Russian fairytales, and in so doing is identifying the essential conditions within which story meanings can arise.

How tenable is the analogy? The strength of the phoneme case is that language use is something it's hard to stand outside of: we have strong intuitive judgments about what are and are not English sounds, English words, and so on. It's less easy to see, or insist upon, a sharp boundary to any set of stories supposedly covered by a Proppian analysis – although the boundary was sharp enough as far as Propp himself was concerned, since his corpus was quite specific: just those 115 stories. And, relatedly, we might ask why thirty-one functions? Why not thirty or thirty-two? Because, Propp implicitly answers, just thirty-one functions are needed – for the given corpus. But what, we might still ask, are the grounds of this 'need'?

The thirty-one functions identified (with neither duplication nor unjustified merging of types) are claimed, largely intuitively, to be the only functions necessary to specify the essential action structure of the stories in the corpus. The question is whether such intuitionism is defensible, or whether the whole descriptive apparatus is invalidated. But we need also to keep in mind just what the goals and expectations of a Propp or Barthes-based analysis are. The business of really getting at our intuitive judgments (rather than our public and conditioned ways of *talking about* plots and plot structures) will always present difficulties. But we do readily find groups of readers (even whole communities) disclosing substantial agreement over what is essential and non-essential in plot, characterization and so on – disclosing, in short, a common grasp of structure. This generality of agreement and commonality of grasp are the essential justification for the inductive speculations of Propp, Barthes, and others.

## 2.3 Barthes on narrative

Entirely appropriately, Barthes' famous 'Introduction' (1977; first published in French in 1966) begins with an argument about inductive versus deductive methods (in linguistics and narrative study), and defends the latter, despite the inevitable provisionality entailed in moving from the particular observations to the general hypothesis. Barthes writes:

> Narrative analysis is condemned to a deductive procedure, obliged first to devise a hypothetical model of description (what American linguists call a 'theory') and then gradually to work down from this model towards the different narrative species which at once conform to and depart from the model.

(1977: 81)

He suggests that linguistics 'seems reasonable' as a founding model for narrative analysis, but notes that discourse study will require a 'second linguistics' going beyond the sentence. But he does posit a homological relation between sentence and discourse, at least as far as semiosis – 'message-bearingness' – is concerned:

> A discourse is a long 'sentence' . . . just as a sentence . . . is a short 'discourse'.
>
> (Barthes, 1977: 83)

More particularly, Barthes emphasizes the need to separate different levels of analysis, and the need for a hierarchical typology of units, in this early essay. He proposes three major levels of narrative structure:

1  functions (as in Propp, Bremond);
2  actions (by which he refers to 'characters', rather as Greimas – discussed below – refers to them as *actants*);
3  narration (equivalent to what we have termed discourse, *discours*, or *sjuzhet*).

What follows is almost entirely to do with the first level, that of function, that by which narrative is 'driven'. The essence of a function is 'the seed that it sows in the narrative, planting an element that will come to fruition later – either on the same level or elsewhere, on another level' (1977: 89). Thus function is teleological, by which we mean it is concerned with the long-term goals or purpose (intellectual and moral as well as actional) of a narrative. Where we assume that a narrative is thus teleological, we tend to look for (and find) material dispersed through the narrative that is designed to support, sustain, and *lead to* that goal. Function is the means of achieving this overarching coherence in a narrative, rather than any merely local or adjacent cause-and-effect logic.

Barthes proceeds to distinguish two types of functions: (a) functions proper (which we might call 'Propp-type functions'); and (b) indices, which are a unit referring

> not to a complementary and consequential act but to a more or less diffuse concept which is nevertheless necessary to the meaning of the story.
>
> (Barthes, 1977: 92)

They include indices to characters' psychological states, notations of 'atmosphere', and so on. While functions proper are distributional, sequential, 'completed' further on in the story – and so have a kind of syntagmatic ratification, indices are said to be integrational, hierarchically-oriented, realized by relating them to some higher, integrated level, a paradigmatic ratification. On a broad continuum, Barthes suggests, there are heavily functional narratives such as folktales, to be contrasted with heavily indicial ones such as psychological novels.

A further cut is now introduced. Functions proper are of two types:

(a)1    Cardinal functions or nuclei or, to use Chatman's useful term, 'kernels' (in Chatman, 1969): these are real hinge-points of narratives, moments of *risk* (when things can go 'either way'); they occur consecutively and entail important consequences.

(a)2    Catalysers (not the best of terms): these fill in the narrative space between nuclei, and are described as parasitic and unilateral by Barthes, areas of safety and rest. For example, a ringing telephone or a delivered letter may herald a real nucleus in a story – and a preliminary 'hinge' would be whether the summons is answered or not, the letter opened – but all sorts of 'business', prevarications and accompaniments may surround that action as catalysers.

Indices, too, can be sub-classified as:

(b)1    Indices proper (charged with implicit relevance);

(b)2    Informants (depthless, transparent, identificatory data).

> Indices involve an act of deciphering, the reader is to learn to know a character or an atmosphere; informants bring ready-made knowledge . . . their functionality is weak.
>
> (Barthes, 1977: 96)

Finally Barthes notes that a unit can be a member of more than one class at a time: one could be both a catalyser and an index, for example. And he notes that in a sense nuclei (kernels) are the special group, with the other three unit types being expansions of nuclei. Nuclei provide the necessary framework, the other three fill it out.

Barthes goes on to appeal for descriptive study not merely of the 'major articulations of narrative' but of the organization of the smallest segments, which he sees as combining into coherent sequences:

> A sequence is a logical succession of nuclei bound together by a relation of solidarity: the sequence opens when one of its terms has no solidary antecedent and closes when another of its terms has no consequent.
>
> (1977: 101)

For example, 'having a drink' is suggested as a closed sequence with the following nuclei: order a drink, obtain it, drink it, pay for it. (But is paying as obligatory and integrated as the other three nuclei?) Now the business of seeing a sequence in such a string of reported events, and labelling it as 'having a drink' (rather than, say, 'quenching one's thirst' or 'making oneself socially available') is, for Barthes, the kind of projective interpretive activity readers are always doing in their narrative processing. It's what he later subsumes under his proaieretic code (Barthes, 1970). Naming is a key act of mental processing, under the assumption that the reader does not remember everything they read, but remembers selectively, largely on the basis of events' importance. The reader registers, and may even verbalize, the broad scenario, the main threads, in a narrative – a kind of incremental and revisable précis-making and paraphrasing. It does not appear that Barthes drew on psycholinguistic evidence in his assumptions and theorizing of 'sequence naming', but there are some interesting parallels between his proposals here and more recent psycholinguistic research on narrative (see the brief mention in the 'Further reading' section of Chapter 7).

An invaluable critical demonstration of the Barthesian machinery applied to a text is Chatman (1969), which sets it to work on the same story, 'Eveline', that I discuss extensively in this chapter. Chatman identifies just eight core narrative functions or kernels in the story; I list these below, with Chatman's interpretive labellings appended:

1   She sat at the window watching the evening invade the avenue. (SITTING AND LOOKING)
2   One time there used to be a field there in which they used to play ... (REMINISCING)
3   Now she was going to go away ... to leave her home. (REHEARSING THE DECISION TO GO)
4   Was that wise? (QUESTIONING)
5   She stood among the swaying crowd in the station at the North Wall. (PREPARING TO EMBARK)
6   Out of a maze of distress, she prayed to God to direct her, to show her what was her duty. (INDECISION CHANGING TO ANXIETY)
7   She felt [Frank] seize her hand. (FRANK'S URGING HER TO GO)
8   No! No! No! (REFUSAL)

This skeletal structure certainly tells a story, with the required connectedness of stages or moves. And Chatman's capitalized glosses of the kernels or functions proper reflect the story's attention to mental activity rather than physical change: the story is structured around reflection, reminiscence, thinking about doing something, and getting ready to do something, rather than on actions themselves. In addition, there is ample evidence that indices and informants of the character Eveline, and catalysers accompanying the narrative development that is principally 'driven' by the functions proper, all contribute to an integrated presentation. Even the smallest textual details, we might argue, play a role. Notice, for example, the words *swaying* and *maze* that are used in the course of functions 5 and 6 above. Besides their specific application in these sentences, they are also indexical, with reference to the entire story, of indeterminacy and vacillation, and encircling confusion, respectively. Many readers, casting the interpretive net wider, will proceed to extract dominating indices, informants, and so on, as they build up a sense of the basic structure of the *Dubliners* narrative as a whole. Among the indices that many generalize from 'Eveline' are qualities of dependence, submission to duty, and ineffectuality.

Despite the attractions of Barthes' basic four-way categorization of narrative material, problems remain concerning the replicability of Barthes' model, and in particular over how (by what criteria) we can confidently judge what is and is not a nucleus, a catalyser, an index proper and an informant. Some of these problems can be outlined by examining Chatman's explanation of the difference between kernels (i.e. nuclei) and catalysers. Kernels are said to be hinges, alternative path openings, and so on, while catalysers (better, 'satellites') are non-essential actions ('business') accompanying the kernels, but of no larger prospective consequence. In the extract below, Chatman italicizes the alleged kernels:

> *One of the telephones rang in the dark room.* Bond turned and moved quickly to the central desk and the pool of light cast by the green shaded reading lamp. *He picked up the black telephone* from the rank of four.

What we might question here is the assumption that the phone-ringing and answering are inherently nuclei, that Bond's moving across the room is inherently secondary. Such decisions can only be made retrospectively, it seems, in the light of a fuller scanning and assessment of adjacent text. But if the categorization is only retrospective, then it did not *guide* our reading and is of lesser psychological validity. If structuralist analysis (in terms of kernels or functions) is to be of value, we clearly need a robust explanation of the kind of interest or question that a kernel provokes, an explanation that sets out the bases of our stronger and weaker impressions of kernel-hood. I will presently propose that we can initially work 'longitudinally', like a reader, through a narrative text's grammar (in a broad sense of that term), in pursuit of more local and grammatically-cued marks of the core narrative events. Ultimately, however, when we offer a determination of what the kernel narrative utterances are, we have to operate holistically and teleologically. And this assumption is necessary in order to apply any criterion of well-formedness.

An analogous truism is that you can't parse a sentence until you've read it. Notice, however, that you can *start* to parse a sentence before you have finished reading it – I think we typically do. But we know that the analysis is provisional, may not 'go through' if we find a configuration of relations that is out of the ordinary, the unmarked form. We know, then, not to put too much trust in our parsing until the reading is complete, and we've seen all the structure there is to see. Thus as we read:

It was John who

we expect that John is the 'underlying subject', the 'doer', made the focus through a clefting device. But if we read on and find John is in fact the underlying object, the 'done to' –

*It was John who the boys attacked.*

– we are not at all troubled by the need for revision. Amending the truism, then:

> You can begin to parse a sentence or text before you've finished reading it, but you know you may need to revise your analysis.

The well-formedness test mentioned above is related to the grammatical distinction between obligatory and deletable material. In narrative 'grammar', there is a similar assumption: while catalyser and indexical material on character and setting are deletable, the functional kernels are obligatory material which, on their own, constitute a coherent 'bare' narrative (and recognizably related to the full version) – the discarded bits would constitute no sort of coherent narrative at all.

The upshot of these qualifications and reservations should be that we see more clearly that kernels and catalysers are not so much textual 'givens' as analytical constructions; and as Culler explains using a Saussurean phrase, they are 'relational terms only':

> What is a kernel in one plot or at one level of description will be a satellite at another. ... In 'Eveline', for example, the actions of the past which the heroine recalls could be organized into kernels and satellites, but within the story they become satellites or expansions of a kernel such as 'weighing the evidence'. ... We must accept that we recognize kernels only when we identify the role of an action in the plot or, to put it another way, promote an action to a constituent of plot. ... One cannot determine the role or function of an action without considering its consequences and its place in the story as a whole.
>
> (Culler, 1975b: 135–6)

In this retrospective process of sense-making and plot-determination, Barthes' notion of 'sequence-naming', or something similar, must be crucially involved. Thus as we read through 'Eveline' we must be constructing a model or scheme into which the disparate propositions (sitting at the window, leaning her head, listening to the man's footsteps, thinking about childhood days) can somehow fit. Much of this model-building will be heavily guided by our cultural background, by what we think – and what we think the writer thinks – is important in life, about what is 'normal' behaviour, and so on. When we do any text-interpreting, it is not done *in vacuo*, a truly solitary and private interrogation of the text.

Both texts and readers are inescapably shaped or framed by prior (but not fixed or eternal) cultural assumptions as to what is significant, salient. It is because there is always this context of cultural significances and saliences 'around' all our involvements with narratives that Barthes says we have 'a language of plot' within us even before we approach any particular story.

An outward sign of having made sense of the textual data is the production of reasonable paraphrase, i.e. a paraphrase that neither we nor other readers find incongruous or absurd. The paraphrase could be very long, many times the length of the original (as most literary critical articles on 'Eveline' are), or it could be single-proposition length, or just a single word. The opening paragraphs of 'Eveline' could be paraphrased as:

A young woman reflects on her past life

or as:

Reflection

But (and here the analyst's dilemma begins to look remarkably like that of those who attempt to identify the structure of spoken discourse) does it make sense to work 'from the bottom up', as Barthes and Chatman claim to be doing? Do we not have to work 'from the top down', i.e. first setting up some broad hypothesis as to what happens in the story as a whole, thus specifying the top-level constituents of story, then trying to move down the hierarchy, analysing so as to separate out the bits that have been complexly bound together? Or is this dramatic opposition of top-down and bottom-up itself a misdirection? Culler's objection to Barthes' model is quite simple but fundamental:

> [It] remains strangely atomistic, through the lack of any specification of what one is moving towards as one collects kernels and satellites and groups them into sequences. ... [And] Chatman is able to pick out [the sentence *One time there used to be a field there*] as a kernel only because he has some sense of an abstract structure towards which he is moving. .... What the reader is looking for in a plot is a passage from one state to another – a passage to which he can assign thematic value.
>
> (Culler, 1975b: 138–9)

Again, we are back to a linked before and after. The before and the after can be labelled, if we like, oppositionally as problem and solution, or logically as cause and effect. Or more neutrally, we might simply label them as situation 1 and situation 2, linked by one or multiple experiences.

## 2.4 Plot-summarizing: modelling intuitions

In his paper on 'Defining narrative units', which focusses on problems of generalizability and adequacy in certain proposed models of plot analysis, Jonathan Culler concludes:

> Competing theories of plot structure can only be evaluated by their success in serving as models of a particular aspect of literary competence: readers' abilities to recognize and summarize plots, to group together similar plots, etc. This intuitive knowledge constitutes the facts to be explained.
>
> (Culler, 1975b: 127)

To this characterization we should add a couple of caveats. The first is that, even more immediately apparent than in relation to the notion of linguistic competence on which it is loosely based, literary competence seems to be very largely learned rather than innate, and markedly culture-specific. Thus when we talk of 'readers' abilities' we have to keep clearly in mind that we are talking only of the acquired and developed ability of a group of readers, rather than some universal mental ability, comparable to the near-universal ability to walk or subtract.

The second related point is that what it means to call these culture-specific abilities 'intuitive knowledge' remains unclear. People can be better or worse at plot-summarizing, and can get better at it: does this suggest an intuitive faculty? I would be inclined to take a far more behavioural approach and argue that we get good at plot-summarizing largely because, in our kind of world, constructing and communicating summarized plots is a valued skill. By 'our kind of world' I mean a world in which children and adults frequently face examinations; in which we often have our recall of events put to various kinds of test; in which it is common to share 'at second hand' a narrative whose performance one's addressee has missed; and in which there is particularly sharp awareness of the universal constraint that influences the shape of so much of our behaviour, namely, limitation of time. Would plot-summarizing be such a valued skill in a settled, integrated oral community, where a set time and social space was reserved for storytelling? There, to précis a plot might be regarded as either incomprehensible or, worse, proof that one was a very poor storyteller.

Thus we need to qualify the idea of 'intuitive competence' in relation to narratives. It is clear that people, with their various non-universal cultural predispositions, can and do become adept at producing and understanding plot summaries. This amounts to saying that they develop community-validated skills in specifying the more important characters and events in narratives. Most crucially of all, they get good at identifying what, relative to their own frameworks of world knowledge and cultural assumptions, is the 'main point' of a story. One of the questions we need to try to answer is how on earth they do this. That they should do it is surely no great surprise:

it is merely an instance of the process of ranking or ordering things that we do all the time in all sorts of activities, making rational decisions about what things most need our attention – again, given our limited resources of time, money, and energy.

How does all this apply to 'Eveline'? Of this story, Culler suggests that readers can construct and agree on hierarchies of appropriate plot summaries, from very succinct to rather detailed ones. Indeed, if a culturally homogeneous group of people is set the task of summarizing a short story, in 100, or 40, or just 20 words, the degree of agreement over what to mention and what to discard is often gratifyingly strong (sharp disagreement may be due either to weak skills of summarizing or some covert subcultural clash). In 'Eveline' Culler notes how various potentially important plot incidents are eventually rejected by us as not central to plot, more an indirect description of Eveline's consciousness: for example, the man out of the last house going home, Eveline watching from her window. But 'She had consented to go away. . . . Was that wise?' is different:

> [This] is immediately recognized as an important structuring element which enables us [to re-interpret preceding material] . . . and to structure the material.
>
> (Culler, 1975b: 130)

Culler concludes his discussion making reference to an implicit three-level hierarchy of actions (characterizing, attributive, and plot-determining), listed in reverse order of importance:

> As we move through 'Eveline' we must decide which actions serve only to characterize her and the situation in which she has placed herself, which of these are crucial attributes involved in the change compassed by the plot, and which actions are in fact crucial as actions.
>
> (134)

Perhaps we must. But in addition most readers reading 'Eveline' know that it was written by James Joyce, that it is therefore 'Literature', and that failure to nominate or attend to a clear developmental plot, in such fiction, has its own cultural warrant. In other words, perhaps 'Eveline' is too category-marginal, too de-automatizing of plot logic, to be a suitable exemplification of our standard ability to summarize. (A rather more straightforward story, also about leaving home and the familiar, is supplied in the first exercise appended to this chapter.) When asked what happens in 'Eveline' it is not absurd to reply 'I'm not entirely sure', although such an account of the plot of, say, a James Bond novel, would be felt to be defective. In the case of literary narrative fiction, perhaps more than elsewhere, the force of James's famous observation seems especially telling:

What is character but the determination of incident? What is incident but the illustration of character?

(1963: 80)

We can follow Culler, then, in accepting Propp's teleological conception of plot structure – a conception in which evaluation of acts is held in abeyance until their significance within the encompassing sequence is perceived. Such retrospective definition of units relies very much on internalized cultural models shared by readers (thus, Eveline's sitting by a window and recollecting the past needs to be recognized as a cultural index – a cliché even – signalling introspection, serious reflection, and often also entrapment and longing). And on another level, readers need to see leaving home (as Eveline contemplates doing) as emotionally and culturally significant (with, perhaps, a special resonance for Joyce and readers of Joyce).

Propp is the first of many to be structuralist in certain of his procedures of analysis, outlined above, but quite intuitive in his grounds for asserting particular similarities or differences. He is intuitive, for example, in asserting that various characters in various stories are mere variant concrete realizations of a single abstract role (no replication test using informants was ever used by him to support his judgments); and he seeks our intuitive assent to those claims. His study remains a pathbreaking exploration of the narrative 'competence' that readers seem to share: we do have quite definite ideas about the basic plots of the narratives we read or hear; we do have an ability to summarize plots; we can often agree in identifying what is not essential to plot; and we can identify 'transformationally-related' plots.

## 2.5 In search of the grammaticization of plot structure

To restate the complication that 'Eveline' presents: as we read this story we're not entirely sure whether we should – as normally – be looking for incidents, or, instead, attend to character. But let us proceed by trying to see why, as many readers claim,

> She had consented to go away, to leave her home. (sentence 24)

is one of the more important disclosures of plot structure in the story. In doing so, we should always remember that 'importance to plot' is a co-text-relative criterion: in some sorts of stories, the fact that an individual had consented to leave home might be of slight importance given an array of more dramatic and immediate events: cf.:

> She had consented to go away, to leave her home, while the place was being redecorated.

This example is a reminder of the importance, already emphasized, of the teleological status of events in narratives. On the other hand it is fair to say that 'permanently leaving home' seems a significant and 'tellable' event in most cultures.

In probing the high plot-structuring status of sentence 24, we should first compare it to the 23 text sentences that precede it. When we come to look at things more holistically or teleologically, we must relate sentence 24 to all that follows it as well as all that precedes it, but it should be worth first approaching the sentence the way a first-time reader would, 'from the left', seen in the textual light only of those sentences that precede it. And what we find, in those sentences, are various grammatical cues that deflect or argue against treatment of them as carrying crucial narrative events. We may begin by looking at the finite verbs of the opening sentences (my emphasis of the finite verbs):

> She <u>sat</u> at the window watching the evening invade the avenue.(1) Her head <u>was leaned</u> against the window curtains and in her nostrils <u>was</u> the odour of dusty cretonne.(2) She <u>was</u> tired.(3)

All are distinguished by being either *stative* verbs, or at least verbs of static description, with no intrinsic implication of change. Stative verbs – *be, know, realize, suppose* – contrast with dynamic verbs – *sit, leave, go* – grammatically, in that the former resist progressivization while the latter progressivize freely: compare *\*She was being tired* with *She was leaving home*. Stative verbs describe states of affairs, and 'passive' processes of cognition or perception (*he knew Spanish*); dynamic verbs depict events and active processes, and 'active' mental processes (*he was learning Spanish*). In the extract from 'Eveline' above, even the dynamic verbs (sit, lean) are used in static ways.

One questionable assumption made here is that, in looking for the reporting of narrative events, we should look particularly but not exclusively at finite verbs. Almost any major part of the clause can express change-of-state, including non-finite verbs (underlined):

> (a) Chick watched the men <u>confront</u> McAndrew, <u>shoot</u> him, <u>carry</u> his body on the back of a pack-mule out to the bottom piece, and <u>bury</u> him.

And narrative events can also be expressed through *nominalizations* (explained more fully in 8.5), here underlined:

> (b) Chick saw a <u>confrontation</u> between the men and McAndrew, the latter's <u>death</u> by <u>shooting</u>, the <u>transportation</u> of the body by mule to the bottom piece, and its <u>burial</u>.

But I think most of us would agree that, for most purposes, (a) works and feels better than (b) as a narrative, and that a third alternative which reported the confrontation and shooting and so on through finite main verbs would probably be preferable to either. In making those judgments we are justifying the argument for looking for narrative events *particularly* in finite verbs. The finite verb, in short, is the unmarked, preferred and unexceptional vehicle for expression or realization of plot events, while the other forms I have mentioned are two of the marked and noticeable alternatives. Accordingly, and while mindful that our assessment is probabilistic and corrigible in the light of later text and other circumstances, we calculate that, for example, the embedded clause 'the evening invade the avenue' (embedded under *sat*, a verb of static condition) does not express a crucial plot event.

The text continues:

> Few people passed.(4) The man out of the last house passed on his way home; she heard his footsteps clacking along the concrete pavement and afterwards crunching on the cinder before the new red houses.(5) One time there used to be a field there in which they used to play every evening with other people's children.(6)

What of sentence 4? Are there any intrinsic grounds for doubting this clause's plot-structuring importance? Perhaps only if we compare it with the nearly synonymous

> A few people passed.

The latter could be used to describe the passage of a particular group of pedestrians (e.g. 'A few nuns passed'), where we respond by wondering 'What sort of people?'. This is not true of the textual alternative without the indefinite article, which lacks the required sense of deictic (explained at 3.4) or spatiotemporal specificity; it is, rather, a summative comment, retrospective and hence descriptive, rather than narrative. And non-specific to the point of carrying a null or negative implication: compare *He invited a few people over for dinner* [=specific people on a specific occasion] and *He invited few people over for dinner* [=almost none, in general]. And the term denoting the participants here, *people*, is one of a group of noticeably general, all-purpose items (others include *thing, person, stuff*) noted in Halliday and Hasan (1976). In sum, we are likely to demote (rather than promote) sentence 4 as a candidate for kernel or function status, in spite of its finite dynamic verb, because of the overtly non-specific nature of its only participant.

By contrast the next sentence (sentence 5) does exhibit the kind of identificatory specificity I am positing as a preferred characteristic of narrative clauses, particularly in its definite description of a specified individual:

> The man out of the last house passed on his way home.

This incident *could* be crucial in the plot, even in the face of the following two counter-signals:

1   In none of the following sentences is the man named, though he is apparently known: characters crucial to plots are usually denoted (by name, profession, distinguishing characteristics) rather more specifically than is done here.

2   Important characters and their important denoted actions are not usually mentioned and immediately discarded as discourse topics. There is usually a 'follow-up principle', such that one or more following clauses maintain either the prominent character or his/her action as some inner clausal element (subject, predicate, object), with the preferred option being to maintain the character as *subject* and *theme* (theme denotes whatever is the first major constituent in a sentence, hence the starting-point of the sentence's message and what the writer chooses the message to be about; various interesting effects can arise – e.g. when theme and subject diverge). Here, overriding the typical option, there is an immediate switch (to <u>*she*</u> *heard his footsteps*), itself then discarded as an extendable topic in the following sentences, which revert to the distant past:

> One time there used to be a field there in which they used to play every evening with other people's children.(6) Then a man from Belfast bought the field and built houses in it not like their little brown houses but bright brick houses with shining roofs.(7) The children of the avenue used to play together in that field – the Devines, the Waters, the Dunns, little Keogh the cripple, she and her brothers and sisters.(8)

There are basically two grounds for discounting most of this material as crucial to story development: one is the frequent emphasis on the events reported as habitual and recurrent, an emphasis that becomes excessive in the following sentence:

> Her father used often to hunt them in out of the field ... but usually little Keogh used to keep *nix*...(10)

The second ground suggesting plot non-salience is the pervasive use of distancing deictic or spatiotemporal markers, reinforcing the relative remoteness of the events and situation from the speaker's (or, in this case, the thinker's) present. Distal deictics (*one time*, *there*, *then*, *that*, and so on) are remarkably prominent:

> Still they seemed to have been rather happy then.(11) Her father was not so bad then; and besides, her mother was alive.(12)

The above sentences are of course inherently non-event-implicating anyway since their main verbs are stative and *intensive* (verbs like *be* and *appear*, which link a following description – which is not a grammatical Object – with the preceding Subject: e.g. *Bill appeared angry*, *Helen became an accountant*). But the observation that follows recapitulates the 'extradiegetic' nature of these reflections: 'That was a long time ago'. (The term 'extradiegetic' will be properly introduced in the next chapter.) The text continues:

> That was a long time ago; she and her brothers and sisters were all grown up; her mother was dead.(13) Tizzie Dunn was dead, too, and the Waters had gone back to England.(14) Everything changes.(15) Now she was going to go away like the others, to leave her home.(16)
> Home! She looked round the room ...

Again, we have a series of stative relational descriptions in sentences 13 and 14, closing with a distant, past perfect verb, and a timeless (i.e. deictically unanchored) generic sentence in 15.

Only with sentence 16 do we encounter an utterance grammatically quite distinct from all those preceding. Introduced by the proximal deictic 'Now', in striking contrast to all the previous instances of 'then', it is oriented to the speaker/thinker's narrative present, with an explicitly dynamic verb in progressive aspect (progressivizability of a verb is the very test of dynamic status). Not only is the utterance oriented to the thinker's present, it also has futuritive force, expressing an intended future course of action. The links between sentence 16 and the surrounding text are plentiful; some of these may be briefly listed, making reference to phrases here shown in italic:

*Now* she was going to *go away* like *the others*, to leave her *home*.

The 'Now' links by contrast with the 'then' of times past, recounted in the foregoing sentences; the 'go away' is lexically related to the 'gone back' of sentence 14; the 'others' in 'like the others' is linked to the previously-mentioned brothers and sisters, or the Waters, or possibly even her dead mother and Tizzie Dunn, or any combination of these; and the mention of 'home' at the close is echoed in the exclamatory 'Home!' that follows. All such cohesive ties do nothing to detract from the narrative distinctness of sentence 16 in terms of its deixis, aspect, futuritive force, dynamic verb expressing a clear change of state, and use of an already textually-prominent participant ('she', Eveline) as sentential subject and theme.

What I have done, perhaps a little laboriously, for these first two paragraphs could be done for the third paragraph, leading up to sentence 24 – 'She had consented to go away, to leave her home' – which analysts agree is important to plot. Briefly, paragraph 3 displays many of the same non-narrative characteristics as the previous two, particularly either stative main verbs or at least ones implying no change of state:

> She looked round the room … Perhaps she would never <u>see</u> again those familiar objects … He had <u>been</u> a school friend … 'He <u>is</u> in Melbourne now'.

habitual or iterative processes

> which she had <u>dusted</u> once a week for so many years. … Whenever he <u>showed</u> the photograph … her father <u>used</u> to pass it.

or both

> from which she had never <u>dreamed</u> of being divided … during all those years she had never <u>found</u> out the name of the priest.
>
> (underlining added)

Again, by sharp contrast with all these, and now with the additional impact of being a near-repetition of sentence 16, comes sentence 24:

> She had consented to go away, to leave her home.

But it is, note, an iteration with some differences which make it all the more salient to plot. For while sentence 16 can be read as the expression of the subject's own purely personal decision to act, it now emerges that another party is involved, and has proposed a specified course of action to which Eveline has agreed. And if we compare sentence 24 with:

> She had decided to go away.
> She had agreed to go away.

the subtle semiotic overtones of the verb *consent* – so prominently used in quasi-legal discussion of sexual matters – seem quite evident.

In this final section of the chapter I have offered some simple principles which may guide a reader's 'real time' processing of text in the search for plot. In this way I have tried to uncover links between grammar and plot-structure, in the conviction that such links quite typically do exist. But I repeatedly argue in terms of preferences, expectations, and tendencies (we expect main events to come in main verbs, we expect main characters to be designated – recurrently – in individualizing ways, and so on). The procedure is necessarily fuzzy and provisional, but not haphazard. There is little that is arbitrary or haphazard about the grammar of a language or the grammar of stories. And as conceded earlier, this whole exercise of provisional plot-assessment sometimes needs radical recasting after the fact and act of reading, when a synoptic and teleological perspective is adopted.

## Further reading

On basic story structure the seminal works to which I have referred are: Propp (1968) and Barthes (1977). And for a powerful critique of formalism, see Jameson (1972). Later, Barthes turned away from structural analysis to a more content-oriented approach, postulating five 'codes' that he saw as invoked and integrated in the creation of story texture (hermeneutic, semic, proairetic or actional, referential or cultural, and symbolic); his *S/Z* (1970) shows him applying the codes in an analysis of Balzac's story *Sarrasine* (see Fowler, 1981: 96–129 for discussion). Chatman (1969) is both a sympathetic overview of the early story-structuralist work of Barthes and Todorov, and a source of numerous narratological insights into the story 'Eveline', while Culler's *Structuralist Poetics* (1975a) contains lucid critique of structuralist theories of plot. Fowler (ed.) (1975), has several valuable papers, including ones by Chatman and Culler. Prince (1982; 1991) are reliable guides to the key elements and proposals in narratological theory, and can be used in conjunction with the present and subsequent chapters; see also Onega and Garcia (1996). Chapter 2 of Rimmon-Kenan (1983) covers some of the same ground as this chapter, and students might like the 'bivocal' effect of having two introductions to the same topic; Rimmon-Kenan also includes many apposite literary examples. I particularly admire and recommend Chapter 1 ('Fabula: Elements') of Bal (1985) – an advanced and authoritative introduction to both theory and practice. This text (a translation) requires attentive reading, but is rigorous and insightful. Also important are the opening chapters of Chatman (1978); Chapter 4 of Simpson (1997) – see exercise 8, below – presents and applies an exercise that is simple and extremely effective theoretically and pedagogically, particularly on very short literary narratives. From within the British text-linguistic tradition, see Chapters 4 and 6 of Hoey (2001); the latter chapter sets out a 'matrix' approach to sequencing in narrative and non-narrative texts. For reflection on narrative structuring and competence from outside literary narratology, Bruner's work is particularly to be recommended, focussing on narrative competence as an enabling resource in infancy (Bruner, 1986; 1990).

## Notes and exercises

1 Below is part of the written text of a text-and-pictures story for children by Nigel Snell entitled *Julie Stays the Night* (London: Hamish Hamilton, 1982):

> One morning the telephone started to ring.
> Mummy answered it. She said, 'It's Sally's Mummy. She has invited you to go and stay. Would you like to go?'
> 'Oh yes,' said Julie. 'I'd love to.' And she ran to tell Alexander, her pet beetle.
> The days went by and soon it was time to pack. Julie began to feel scared.
> She was going away from her Mummy and Daddy and her toys, her bed and her home.
> Julie started to cry. 'Don't be sad,' said Mummy. 'You will love it when you get there.'
> Julie wasn't so sure.
> She decided to take Alexander along in a matchbox, just in case.

Mummy took her to Sally's house by train. Julie felt very homesick.
But when they got to Sally's, her mother was very kind.
They had a big tea and played with lots of toys.
That night Julie and Sally were both allowed to stay up an extra half hour.
When they went to bed Julie showed Sally her beetle, Alexander, but he crawled out of the matchbox and went down a crack.
'He seems quite at home here,' thought Julie.

Attempt an analysis of this story, labelling events and states in terms of one, two, or all three of the following: Propp's functions; Barthes' functions and indices; my proposal about the grammaticization of core narrative clauses. Which method or combination of methods seems to you to highlight basic story structure most effectively?

2 Some of the ways we can use Propp, or a Proppian approach, are noted in Dundes's introduction to the *Morphology*. If structural analysis is not to be an end in itself, it seems vital to relate the forms Propp found to the culture (Russian, Indo-European) out of which they emerged. Dundes speculates pertinently:

> Does not the fact that Propp's last function is a wedding indicate that Russian fairy-tale structure has something to do with marriage? Is the fairy tale a model, a model of fantasy to be sure, in which one begins with an old nuclear family ... and ends finally with the formation of a new family? ... Propp's analysis should be useful in analyzing the structure of literary forms (such as novels and plays), comic strips, motion-picture and television plots, and the like.... Do children become familiar enough with the general nature of fairy-tale morphology to object to or question a deviation from it by a storyteller? ... Finally, Propp's scheme could also be used to generate new tales.

> (Dundes, 1968: xiv–xv)

Apply Dundes's questions to the next episode of any television series that you watch. How predictable is the villainy or lack that is grappled with, and what form does the resolving 'marriage' typically take? Compare these predictabilities with the functions (villainy, 'marriage', etc.) of a rather less formulaic series.

3 Taking Propp's 31 functions and 7 roles, attempt to apply them to one or two literary narratives you know well. Determine how much adjustment of the scheme is needed for it to capture the basic story of one of the following: a medieval morality play; one of Chaucer's Canterbury Tales – e.g. 'The Wife of Bath's Tale'; one of Shakespeare's comedies or problem plays; any Dickens novel, though *Oliver Twist*, *A Tale of Two Cities* and *Bleak House* seem particularly manageable candidates; Pope's 'The Rape of the Lock'; Melville's *Moby Dick*.

In fact the narratives you choose to analyze could be of any type. It might be your grandmother's oft-rehearsed story of her pursuit and courtship by your grandfather (perhaps there's no villain here, but presumably it concludes with marriage), or you could look at any simple children's story you might have to hand. But if even these narratives look at first glance unmanageably different from Propp's stories and morphology, you could certainly begin with a story which, intuitively, you feel is not too unlike those examined by Propp, e.g. a Grimm or Hans Andersen folktale.

How well does the Propp 'grammar' fit your chosen text? Where do the problems and difficulties lie? As you move away from traditional oral-based folktales, you should expect that the kinds of functions and roles involved in the basic story structure will be rather removed from those of Propp: removed, but not unrelated. And that's the point: in looking for the kinds of functions and roles from which multifarious stories are generated, we are indeed committed to identifying relatedness of structure.

4  Are the blurbs that accompany books of fiction – the brief fliers or advertisements for books that appear somewhere on their jackets – plot summaries? If not, what are they? Analyze the blurbs of three books of fiction, thinking about this question in particular. Whatever differences of detail you find, it will become newly apparent to you just how structured, carefully-worded and important such blurbs are. In a bookshop, taking a quick glance at the merchandise, the blurb may be the only part of the text that the critical potential purchaser has time to read. You might move on to compare your fiction blurbs with the blurbs that accompany popular non-fiction, academic literary criticism, linguistics textbooks, science textbooks, biographies, etc.

5  Look analytically at two or three newspaper reviews of new novels. Do these reviews contain a full summary of the plot, or only an incomplete one? Is there any discernible pattern to this variation, with certain types of fiction getting fairly full summaries, others almost none at all? Why might it be that certain reviews start a story summary (often identifying the characters and setting but only the first few events to occur) but do not complete it? Compare and contrast the reviews, in a range of publications, of a current notable fiction. Where in the review does the plot summary come, if it appears at all? Does it come all in one chunk, or intermittently? How much agreement does there seem to be over what to put into the summary, and where do there seem to be differences of emphasis? What possible grounds might there be for those differences? How might all this relate to the idea raised in this chapter that plot perception may be culturally relative?

6  In her review of Fowler (ed.) (1975) Smith challenges its seeming assumption of 'substantial agreement' over plot summaries:

> The extent to which we produce comparable plot summaries may have a good deal to do with who 'we' are and how we learned both what 'plots' are and also what it means to 'summarize' them. It is doubtful, for example, that a South American tribesman would produce the same plot summary of one of his myths as would Claude Levi-Strauss. Or to put it another way, wouldn't our explaining to the tribesman (or, of course, to a child) what we wanted when we asked for a 'plot summary' be the same as telling him how to 'process' the story the way 'we' have learned to?
>
> (Smith, 1978: 183)

Take any narrative familiar to you and your friends (it doesn't have to be highly literary), and attempt a summary of the story which is not a plot summary but still seems to you to be a fair summary in some respects (e.g. of the mood or tone). Now present your summary to one or more of those friends and ask them their opinion of it as a summary of the story. Your problems in producing a non-plot summary, and their reactions to it, should be instructive.

7  There are other approaches to the 'basic grammar' of stories than those discussed in this chapter, perhaps most notably the work of Prince (1973; 1982); and a vast body of psycholinguistic research into our mental modelling of story format. This research hypothesizes that we construct schemas, or frameworks, of archetypal stories, which we 'internalize' and use as a mental aid when we attempt to comprehend or recall particular stories. Space limitations forbid review of the theory and its assumptions, but some references to relevant literature are included in the 'Further reading' section of Chapter 7.

8  Chapter 4 of Simpson (1997) presents a very effective exercise that can be used to stimulate detailed discussion and reflection on the precise choices an author has made in composing narrative text – choices in the ordering of reported

events and states, and in the wording of those reports. Discussants are given all the sentences of a short narrative text, separated and jumbled (typically, typed on strips of paper); they are then asked, working individually or in groups, to set out these sentences in the order in which they originally appeared. Thereafter, solutions are compared and evaluated. Simpson's article reports what happens when this exercise is performed on a very short story – just 11 sentences – by Ernest Hemingway, which he based on a newspaper report of the execution of six Greek cabinet ministers in Athens in 1922. When compositors' solutions are subsequently compared with the Hemingway original, it is found that there are particular descriptive sequences of sentence in the Hemingway version that *all* groups have avoided. The Hemingway sequences 'dwell' on certain details (here, of rain and sodden-ness) which informants seem to avoid as repetitive or obsessive (he does something similar elsewhere – e.g. at the opening of his story 'Cat in the Rain'). In these ways the exercise forces us to examine not merely event-ordering in a narrative, but also the nature and ordering of accompanying descriptions – i.e. the entire *texture* of the text –in terms both of coherence or logic, and of effect. I have adopted and applied this exercise to 'scrambled' short stories by writers such as Raymond Carver ('Little Things'), Donald Barthelme ('The Baby' and 'The New Owner'), and Charles Reznikoff ('The shoemaker sat in the cellar's dusk beside his bench'). The solutions and discussions are always illuminating; the inventive unorthodoxy of writers' text-sequencing decisions is made newly apparent and, after reconsideration, newly understandable.

# 3 The articulation of narrative text I
## Time, focalization, narration

## 3.1 Narrative text: a single level of analysis

In this and the following chapter we turn from characterization of the 'elementary particles' of narratives, grouped under the label 'story', to the various expansions and individualizations of those elements that go on in the production of text. We can think of the move from the abstract level of story components to the concrete level of textual realizations as both a process and an articulation. The main processes or articulations involved are listed by Bal as the following (I have replaced her terms 'fabula' and 'story' by 'story' and 'text' respectively, to avoid confusion):

1  The events are arranged in a sequence which can differ from the chronological sequence.
2  The amount of time which is allotted in the text to the various elements of the story is determined with respect to the amount of time which these elements take up in the story.
3  The actors are provided with distinct traits. In this manner, they are individualized and transformed into characters.
4  The locations [settingsl where events occur are also given distinct characteristics and are thus transformed into specific places.
5  In addition to the necessary relationships among actors, events, locations, and time, all of which were already describable in the layer of the story, other relationships (symbolic, allusive, etc.) may exist among the various elements.
6  A choice is made from among the various 'points of view' from which the elements can be presented.

(Bal, 1985: 7)

This chapter concentrates on items 1, 2 and 6 on this list (i.e. time and focalization), before concluding with a discussion of narration – the complex different ways of narrating or being a narrator. The next chapter will focus on items 3 and 4 (character and setting) together with suspense and surprise, and the chapter after that (Chapter 5) on the subtle techniques for disclosing characters' words or thoughts, including free indirect discourse. Item 5 on Bal's list will not be addressed adequately in this book, due partly to space-limitations and partly to its less developed analysis by narratologists and discourse linguists.

## 3.2 Text and time

Time itself, in the sense of the systematic measurement of what separates particular past states from our present one, is itself a structuring and structuralist notion. Structuring, because it asserts and articulates relations between particular states or changes of state, and structuralist, in so far as it relies on our recognition of particular similarities and particular differences between specified states. What we call 'a year' must have been first perceived as a single full cycle of the warmer and colder seasons and of the natural world, matching a full cycle of the sun's movements towards and away from one's earthly location. Similarly, the perceived recurring succession of day and night gives rise to the introduction of temporal measurement in just those terms ('last night', 'in two days' time'). So:

Time is perceived repetition within perceived irreversible change.

In addition we must remember that there is something unreal and heavily convention-laden about so-called story time and text time. In neither case are we referring to actual temporal progression, but the *linear verbal representation* of temporality. A kind of artifice is at work, in which we look for a match between the 'real-world' intervals and sub-intervals of time that the narrative implies, and our sense of time passing during our experience of reading that narrative. Whether we regard a particular match as appropriate or not is a judgment largely guided by our prior reading experience, our familiarity with the particular genre that the text belongs to, and the seriousness of the events depicted.

Because text time is inescapably linear, there is an obvious and immediate disruption of any neat correlation of real time to text time as soon as the narrative involves more than one storyline: that is to say, as soon as there is more than one set of developing circumstances affecting different sets of characters. But even when we compare text time to what Rimmon-Kenan calls 'an ideal natural chronology' (1983: 45), we rarely find that the standard of steady correspondence is maintained. Even, say, when a story is purely direct speech (monologue or dialogue), it is likely that we spend considerably longer reading that written 'transcript' than would be spent in any actual speaking.

The most influential modern theorist of text time has been Gerard Genette, who isolates three major aspects of temporal manipulation or articulation in the movement from story to text:

1   Order: this refers to the relations between the assumed sequence of events in the story and their actual order of presentation in the text.

2   Duration: for Genette this chiefly concerns the relations between the extent of time that events are supposed to have actually taken up, and the amount of text devoted to presenting those same events.

3   Frequency: how often something happens in story compared with how often it is narrated in text.

As may be apparent from the foregoing discussion, the most potentially problematic of these aspects is that of duration, and I shall devote rather greater space to this aspect.

### 3.2.1 Order

Any departures in the order of presentation in the text from the order in which events evidently occurred in the story are termed by Genette **anachronies**. An anachrony is any chunk of text that is told at a point which is earlier or later than its natural or logical position in the event sequence (i.e. what we postulate by reconstruction to be the story sequence). Strictly speaking, we can find anachrony even within a single sentence. In *The king died of grief because the queen had died*, the subordinate reason clause is an anachrony, presented after the report of the king's death even though it contains the report of an event which logically and naturally – in the story – preceded his death.

But anachronies in extended narratives are more complex than that example. They naturally divide into flashbacks and flashforwards, or what Genette calls **analepses** and **prolepses**. An analepsis is an achronological movement back in time, so that a chronologically earlier incident is related later in the text. A prolepsis is an achronological movement forward in time, so that a future event is related textually 'before its time', before the presentation of chronologically intermediate events (which end up being narrated later in the text). Any delayed disclosure is thus analeptic (the reader expected, on the basis of chronological sequence, to be told of this event or episode earlier), while any premature disclosure is proleptic (the reader did not expect to be told this until later, if strict chronology had been maintained). Incidentally, Bal's useful terms for the two types of anachrony are retroversions and anticipations.

An analepsis may be either homodiegetic or heterodiegetic, depending on whether it carries information about the same character, event or storyline as has been presented in the immediately-preceding text, or about some different character or event. Examples of homodiegetic analepsis are easy to find. We could cite the second paragraph of 'Eveline', with its movement back in time to the games of Eveline's childhood days; other more complex analepses in 'Eveline' will be discussed later.

Or consider the very effective brief analepsis in 'The Dead', where Gabriel falls into a revery while trying *not* to listen to Mary Jane's complex, unmusical piano-playing. A photograph of his mother brings back to him how she always acted to ensure his advancement. But the text continues:

> A shadow passed over his face as he remembered her sullen opposition to his marriage. Some slighting phrases she had used still rankled in his memory; she had once spoken of Gretta as country cute and that was not true of Gretta at all. It was Gretta who had nursed her during all her last long illness in their house at Monkstown.

As well she might (the flint-hearted reader using hindsight might add), racked with guilt at having failed to nurse Michael Furey. Gabriel's snobbish mother is surely wrong about Gretta, but the analeptic insertion of her assessment, so much at odds with Gabriel's, steers the reader towards seeing (or being unsurprised later to see) Gretta as a rounded character, not a flat or historyless one.

If we turn now to Nabokov's *Pnin* (1957), we find many clear cases of homodiegetic analepsis dotted throughout its opening pages. The following is the novel's second paragraph, describing the middle-aged Pnin's appearance as he travels by train to an engagement as a guest lecturer:

> His sloppy socks were of scarlet wool with lilac lozenges; his conservative black Oxfords had cost him about as much as all the rest of his clothing (flamboyant goon tie included). Prior to the 1940s, during the staid European era of his life, he had always worn long underwear, its terminals tucked into the tops of neat silk socks, which were clocked, soberly coloured, and held up on his cotton-clad calves by garters. In those days, to reveal a glimpse of that white underwear by pulling up a trouser leg too high would have seemed to Pnin as indecent as showing himself to ladies minus collar and tie; for even when decayed Mme Roux, the concierge of the squalid apartment house in the Sixteenth Arrondissement of Paris where Pnin, after escaping from Leninized Russia and completing his college education in Prague, had spent fifteen years – happened to come up for the rent while he was without his *faux col*, prim Pnin would cover his front stud with a chaste hand. All this underwent a change in the heady atmosphere of the New World. Nowadays, at fifty-two, he was crazy about sunbathing, wore sport shirts and slacks, and when crossing his legs would carefully, deliberately, brazenly display a tremendous stretch of bare shin. Thus he might have appeared to a fellow passenger; but except for a soldier asleep at one end and two women absorbed in a baby at the other, Pnin had the carriage to himself.

Here is analepsis within analepsis. From the story's present time, the text jumps back to a description of Pnin's 'staid European era' and his relations with Mme Roux. But then during that description, there is a further jump back to youthful Pnin's escape from Russia. Thus we see a simple demonstration of how complex transformations of temporal order, in the articulation of story as narrative text, make that text more entertaining, engrossing, and character-expressive. Nowhere in *Pnin* do we get a plodding, blow-by-chronological-blow account of Pnin's youth in revolutionary Russia, his escape to Prague, his fifteen years there, and so on. That important background only emerges 'naturally', as it were, when, as part of Pnin's ongoing narrative present, his past briefly ceases to be distant background and becomes currently experienced foreground, as in Pnin's grieving recollection of a girl he had loved in pre-revolutionary Russia who was subsequently murdered at Buchenwald (see p. 110ff.).

In fact the recollection is remarkably intense, more like a living-through. Middle-aged Pnin is taking a vacation, along with assorted other Russian emigrés and their children, in an upstate country retreat. But when the name of Mira Belochkin crops up in conversation, Pnin withdraws into an intense memory of his youth: of country house summers at a Baltic resort, of his father and Mira's father engrossed in their chess game in a corner of the verandah.

> Timofey Pnin was again the clumsy, shy, obstinate, eighteen-year-old boy, waiting in the dark for Mira – and despite the fact that logical thought put electric bulbs into the kerosene lamps and reshuffled the people, turning them into ageing *emigrés* ... my poor Pnin, with hallucinatory sharpness, imagined Mira slipping out of there into the garden and coming toward him among tall tobacco flowers whose dull white mingled in the dark with that of her frock.
>
> (111)

Later in the same revery it is disclosed that

> In order to exist rationally, Pnin had taught himself, during the last ten years, never to remember Mira Belochkin ... One had to forget – because one could not live with the thought that this graceful, fragile, tender young woman with those eyes, that smile, those gardens and snows in the background, had been brought in a cattle car to an extermination camp and killed.... And since the exact form of her death had not been recorded, Mira kept dying a great number of deaths in one's mind, and undergoing a great number of resurrections, only to die again and again, led away by a trained nurse, inoculated with filth, tetanus bacilli, broken glass, gassed in a sham shower-bath with prussic acid, burned alive in a pit on a gasoline-soaked pile of beech-wood.
>
> (112–13)

As such passages show, grief and trauma are powerful triggers (perhaps the most powerful) of character-based analepsis, while the willed 'not-remembering' that is Pnin's means of coping with them amounts to a powerful suppression of analeptic tendencies in a character, reflected in our clichéd injunctions to the grief-stricken to 'live in the present' and 'look to the future'.

An example of heterodiegetic analepsis, offered by Genette, is the focus on Swann as protagonist of certain events in section 2 of Proust's *À la recherche du temps perdu*: events that clearly occurred long before the quite different focus of section 1, Marcel's boyhood. To return to *Pnin*, consider the extraordinary final chapter of that novel, in which the narrator himself, whom we gradually realize is the 'old friend' and academic rival whose appointment at Waindell College causes Pnin's departure, steps forward to give his own account of events. That account begins with heterodiegetic analepsis: a reversion to the narrator's own youth in Russia in 1911.

All these examples are also external analepses, moving back to a time prior to the opening of the text. Internal analepses are a textual moving-back in the story, but not such a radical moving-back as to involve crossing the text's opening, and notably include any repetitions of incidents previously narrated in their proper chronological place. Of course an analepsis could straddle or overlap the previously-established start of the narrative, in which case Genette labels the analepsis 'mixed'. As for the function of analepses, a first observation can be that they seem to be designed to 'fill gaps' in stories, though these gaps may themselves be the contrivance of the writer, and may not be perceived as gaps until after the analepsis has appeared.

But what of those analepses which cover events previously reported? On such repetitive analepsis, Bal makes some valuable observations:

> The repetition of a previously described event usually serves to change, or add to, the emphasis on the meaning of that event. The same event is presented as more, or less, pleasant, innocent, or important than we had previously believed it to be. It is thus both identical and different: the facts are the same, but their meaning has changed. In Proust, such internal retroversions form a part of the famous and specifically Proustian interruption of the linearity in searching for, and recovering of, the elusive past. But in much simpler literature too, frequent use is made of possibilities such as these. Detective novels and all kinds of texts which are constructed around mysteries, masquerades, and puzzles adopt this technique as an important structural device.
>
> (Bal, 1985: 61)

Prolepses – which are much rarer than analepses – undercut or remove suspense, since they reveal future circumstances to the reader long before any chronological imperative dictates that they be told. They foster a different kind of engaged puzzlement: the reader is made aware of their own bafflement as to how characters and events might get from the current situation to the future one prematurely revealed, and is all the more intrigued to learn of the intervening happenings. Prolepsis is common in first-person narratives, where it seems natural for the narrator to jump forward occasionally to subsequent events which are closer to that narrator's own present. Like analepses, prolepses can be homo- or heterodiegetic, depending on whether they entail a switch of focus to a different character or storyline; and they are internal, external or mixed, depending on their chronological relation to the endpoint of the basic narrative.

One qualification may be made concerning certain examples of prolepsis, such as this one from Muriel Spark's *The Prime of Miss Jean Brodie*:

> 'Speech is silver but silence is golden. Mary, are you listening? What was I saying?'
>
> Mary Macgregor, lumpy, with merely two eyes, a nose and a mouth like a snowman, who was later famous for being stupid and always to blame and who, at the age of twenty-three, lost her life in a hotel fire, ventured, 'Golden'.

Examples such as this one are better thought of as proleptic 'traces' inscribed in a narrative, rather than the full-fledged shift of temporal orientation where an extended stretch of text – a chapter, or a section – reports distantly future events. Similarly, my first example of homodiegetic analepsis in *Pnin* might be regarded as fleeting tracery rather than structural temporal reordering (in Barthesian terms, more an index than a function). Thus there seems to be a continuum of different kinds of anachrony, performing different functions, with 'fleeting tracery' and 'wholesale temporal dislocation' at opposite endpoints. The former is a contribution to dense narrative texture, but is often more a local insight into a character, or the narrator, than a manipulation of the event line; the latter is more substantially a contribution to narrative structure, sometimes requiring the reader to revise their assumptions as to just what the story is that is being told. In characterizing anachronies Genette also suggests we can distinguish their chronological distance from the present moment in the story (which I will call their 'reach', and Bal calls 'distance'), and their chronological duration (which I will call their 'extent', and Bal calls 'span').

Before leaving the topic of 'order' it is worth reiterating that in discriminating the types of anachronistic deviations that a narrative text makes from the underlying story, all our observations are relational. That is, we proceed not with the goal of simply unravelling the sequential jumble of a Faulkner or Joyce novel, restoring the wholesome chronology that might satisfy a historian or detective. Certainly unravelling is involved and is important, but so too is a sense of the relations between the various chunks of the text, where chunks told in one order (B–C–D–A–E) in fact denote events that must be assumed to have occurred in a different order (A–B–C–D–E), perhaps with considerable gaps or ellipses between A and

B and C, temporal contiguity of D and E, and so on: a potentially quite elaborate network of temporal relations. (The picture is yet more complex if we find that any two or more textual chunks report events that must have occurred at the same point in time in the reconstructible story.) Anachronies may also differ in scale. Thus an external analepsis that reaches back twenty years with a story extent of one month, embedded in a story whose extent otherwise is just twenty-four hours, should be distinguished from an analepsis identical in extent and reach but embedded in a story of year-long extent.

### 3.2.2  *Duration*

What is text duration? Can it be reduced simply to the reading time of a narrative? But readers read at different speeds, decide to break off from reading at different places (or not at all), so that every reader will have a different reading time for a narrative. On the other hand, granted absolute differences of reading pace, we might still want to argue that there are relative similarities of reading time, for fluent native speakers, for particular types of text. The application of such posited norms of reading duration, against which one would then compare the likely temporal duration of the events that the text relates, apply chiefly to scenic passages reporting monologues, dialogues, sequences of physical actions which are punctual or of short duration, and short journeys. So much genre fiction these days seems to be aimed at the travelling reader – the person travelling alone by train or plane, on a journey lasting several hours – that one imagines some powerful effects might be achieved by contriving that both the reading time and the text duration of such a book approximated, say, five hours.

Some such pan-textual norms of reading time are sometimes invoked in stylistic commentaries on effects of (variation of) pace, but this is not the approach adopted by Genette. Genette opts for an intra-textual strategy, where textual pace at any particular place in a narrative is assessed relative to pace elsewhere in that same narrative, and that pace is then expressed as a ratio between the indicated duration of the story (in minutes, hours, days) and the extent of text (in pages) devoted to its telling. This leads to identifying a norm of pace for a particular narrative, against which accelerations and decelerations can be perceived. The norm is thus text-bound, and a constancy of pace would emerge if the ratio between story-duration and extent of textual presentation were invariable – e.g. a page for every month of a character's life.

Genette's ratio is very often far more mechanical than actual texts are. For example, suppose there were a chapter for every year of a character's life, but those chapters were of rather different lengths: is this constancy of pace or variation of pace? And how should we reformulate this ratio for application to oral narratives? Presumably we would be back to hypothesizing a norm for the 'duration of delivery' – although we could alternatively take an intra-performance perspective, and make judgments about pace relative to just a particular performance of a narrative. Rather simplistic, too, is the assumption that event or story time is easy to deduce or infer from the narrative, as if the heading of each page of the text carried a digital read-out of the time elapsed. For example, just how long, in story time, is Eveline's revery? It could be anything from a few minutes to several hours: it takes place between early and late evening (when the mail-boat goes). Since we can't be sure about the pace of the revery presentation, neither can we be sure as to whether the later scene at the quayside is a presentational acceleration or deceleration.

Maximum speed is said to constitute **ellipsis**, where no text space is spent on a piece of story duration; the opposite situation is **descriptive pause**: text without story duration (for example, the descriptive openings of *A Passage to India*, or Ellison's *Invisible Man*, or Hardy's *The Return of the Native*). An example of ellipsis cited by Chatman is that between the close of Chapter 5 of Hemingway's *The Sun Also Rises*, where Jake has finished lunch and sets off for his office, and the opening of Chapter 6, when he is waiting for Brett at five o'clock. Such ellipses, Chatman argues, are widespread in modernist fiction, where a series of detailed scenic presentations are linked by abrupt spatio-temporal jumps. However, it seems worth distinguishing this sort of ellipsis, which is simply an exploitation of the temporal discontinuity we not only tolerate but probably prefer in our narratives (so we do not have to read every dull thing a character does), from the accelerations of presentation to the sharply abbreviated summary, which are perceived as involving change of pace. For we surely do not feel any change of pace, any acceleration, at the junction of Chapters 5 and 6 of *The Sun Also Rises*. I would suggest, then, that ellipsis, in the form of a spatiotemporal gap or aporia, is a narrational strategy of varying importance (depending on just what gets left out) but is not really a type of narrative pace, if we conceive of the latter as dependent on our judgments about the rapidity *of the telling* of story events. In other words I am arguing for a view of pace as the rapidity of the telling of what does get told.

### 3.2.3 Summary and scene

But more common and interesting than these are the relatively accelerated and the relatively decelerated presentation, known since Lubbock's interpretive account of Jamesian poetics as **summary** and **scene** respectively (Lubbock, 1973 [1921]). In summary, the pace is accelerated through a textual compression of a given story period into a relatively short statement of its main featutes. Rimmon-Kenan (1983: 53) cites an amusing example of Nabokovian summary, a foregrounded and conscious play with our conventional expectations both of novel duration and of what Barthes calls catalysers (satellites), indices and informants:

> Once upon a time there lived in Berlin, Germany, a man called
> Albinus. He was rich, respectable, happy; one day he abandoned his

wife for the sake of a youthful mistress; he loved, was not loved; and his life ended in disaster.

This is the whole story and we might have left it at that had there not been profit and pleasure in the telling, and although there is plenty of space on a gravestone to contain, bound in moss, the abridged version of a man's life, detail is always welcome.

(Nabokov, *Laughter in the Dark*)

In scene, story and text duration are conventionally considered identical (e.g. passages of seemingly verbatim dialogue). But there is a pace of telling that is more sharply counterposed to summary, in which things move more slowly than in scene: the situation in which text is more extended than story, which Chatman terms 'stretch'. Again, in discussing scenic pace, naturalistic assumptions and a covert comparison with the pace of real interaction creep back in. Hitherto I have been stressing that the pace of any portion of a text (the rapidity of presentation of time and events passing) is relative to the pace in other portions of that text, or relative to the pace of the text as a whole, or relative to the pace of other texts. But when we start thinking about scene, and especially the representation of direct speech exchanges between characters, something revealing happens. We tend not to assess the pace of a scene in relation to co-textual standards, but rather in relation to real-world standards.

This is a telling reminder of how our usual unquestioning view of fictional dialogue is that it is the most complete and mimetic representation of real dialogue. We tend to assume that reading direct speech dialogue 'amounts to the same thing' as being a witness to actual spoken interaction, so that to talk of the 'pace' of such written-up scenes – as if they could go faster or slower – barely makes sense to us: obviously, scenes go at just the pace of the actual interaction. But what has come to seem obvious and commonsensical is not a necessary and unavoidable feature of fictional dialogue, but a convention and an *effect*. The fictional direct speech representation of any dialogue can go faster or slower, and we neglect the artifice in fictional dialogue (e.g. all the ways in which it is not a transcription), to the detriment of our appreciation of narrative poetics. We will return to the natural and the conventional in speech representation when examining free indirect discourse in Chapter 5.

When the reader encounters relative acceleration or deceleration of presentation, they will often interpret the shift in pace as an authorial or narratorial indication of the marginality (on the one hand) or the centrality and importance (on the other) of what is being presented. More important events and conversations are usually given in scenic detail, less important or background ones in summary précis. But again, these are norms from which writers often depart for good reasons. A writer may play with our conventional expectations, a narrator-character may attempt to suppress or retreat from certain important but distasteful events, and so on. Shock and irony can be created by disclosing a central event briefly, following detailed presentation of trivial events.

Chatman (1978: 76–8) also notes the contrast between narratorial summary common in the traditional novel, and what goes on in many modern novels, where *characters* provide summaries in their own recollections of past events (as in Woolf's *Mrs Dalloway*). Hence we are really witnessing scenes here, if the duration of character-derived remembered events, and the extent of text devoted to their presentation, are commensurate with ratios for reflection-cum-presentation elsewhere in the narrative. The puzzle hinges on what counts as a story event, the presentational duration of which is to be compared with comparable events elsewhere in the novel. Is the story event 'Clarissa reminisces one day, from morning shopping to evening party'; or is there here a *series* of story events, the various incidents from her past that Clarissa reviews in memory? Perhaps the best answer to give is 'both'; we see the framing narrative, one day in the life of Clarissa Dalloway (and some other Londoners), a narrative within which the reminiscence is just a single event among many. We also see, as the reminiscence unfolds, that an embedded story is being disclosed, spanning a much greater period of time than the framing one ('a life in one day of Clarissa Dalloway').

In saying this we can maintain a dual characterization, just as, in sentence grammar, we can say that a particular embedded nominal clause (*she loved life*) counts simply as an object relative to the clause in which it is embedded (*Clarissa realized she loved life*), but has its own internal structural logic when viewed independently of the embedding clause. Thus we can now say that as a unit within the framing narrative the reminiscence maintains normal order, text-normal duration (allegedly), and singulative frequency. But as a separate narrative embedded *within* the framing narrative, we encounter the text of a story (of thirty years of Clarissa's earlier life) which involves various anachronies (many of the events are analeptically recollected, and their normal order of occurrence is departed from), variations of duration (some material is sharply summarized), and some instances of repetitive frequency (see 3.2.4).

But even this dual characterization, arguably, leaves unremarked certain effects that merit comment. A dual perspective seems all that is strictly required, distinguishing the embedded story of incidents-remembered-by-Clarissa-Dalloway from the superordinate story of incidents-on-the-day-of-Mrs Dalloway's-party. Thus, two stories at different levels: two distinct configurations of order, duration and frequency. But while this account of order can say things about that dimension in the two separate stories, it fails to identify our *experience* of retroversion as we find Clarissa's thoughts jumping back to moments in her youth. As readers processing the linear unfolding of the text, it seems we do not keep levels and stories quite as separate as the analytical approach outlined above does. In sophisticated ways that resist analytical unravelling, we unite the story of things-happening with that of things-remembered-as-having-happened, and understand Mrs Dalloway's recollected experience to be both timely and achronistic, utterly past in actuality, wholly present to consciousness. Nor are these the only stories that we unite or hold in view as we read this novel. There are the ongoing and remembered stories of Lucrezia Warren Smith, of her husband, of Peter Walsh, and others. All these stories we hold in view, unable to integrate them into a single 'macro' story, but also unable to separate them out as distinct: the textual form denies us that solution. In the reading, our requirements of chronology and causal relation in narrative are subordinated to attention to the logic (in Clarissa Dalloway and all the rest) of human reaction, whether physical or mental.

My conclusion, then, is that in a many-storied novel like *Mrs Dalloway* our experience of the temporal order resists analysis – at least analysis in terms of chronology. We seem to recognize and overlook anachronies at the same time; we neither merge (in the sense of assimilate) nor unravel these separable story sequences, but hold them in a complex enigmatic suspension. These claims may be worth recalling when we come to examine free indirect discourse in Chapter 5, for it seems that a very similar unmergeable duality, resistant to analytical dissection, operates there too. Hence the above paragraphs can be viewed as related both to the current topic and, proleptically, to that of speech and thought reporting – the embedding of voice within voice.

I have described Mrs Dalloway's reminiscence as *allegedly* of normal duration: but the strict test is to find other cases of reminiscing in the novel, of apparently similar 'real time', and compare how much text is used up in the different cases – a fairly rough and ready reckoning. And perhaps an inappropriate one. There still seem to be several problems with Genette's notion of duration – it does not always seem to be addressing what readers are responding to when they say one passage is pacey, another passage is slow. And it seems that there is an underpinning of text-internal vraisemblance (the means adopted in a text to convince the reader that the text is a true and faithful representation of reality) or verisimilitude in Genette's approach. In other words, there is an unspoken reliance on what we recognize as realistic and reasonable lengths of text to spend on particular incidents, given some sense of the overall pace of a narrative. In linguistic terminology, we could complain that his simple calculation of duration leans too far towards assuming a natural fit, at least within the narrative, and too far away from acknowledging that the norms of text-extent in the presentation of various kinds of salient incidents may be quite arbitrary and conventionalized.

In analyzing pace, supratextual comparisons are one interesting area that calls for more study. For instance, we could usefully assess the pace of Mrs Dalloway's reminiscences relative to similar reveries in other Woolf novels, in other modernist novels of the period, and in other British novels of that time (James, Hardy, Galsworthy and Bennett). For it does seem we become accustomed, as experienced readers, to certain kinds of duration linked with certain kinds of culturally-salient narrative incident. We get used to a certain kind of length of presentation of the details of a hero's early childhood in novels by Dickens and Thackeray, a certain degree of extendedness in their presentations of love scenes and death scenes and murders, so that our perceptions of duration must be not only intratextual but partly intertextual (sensitive to author, period, and genre) as well. And intratextually, as in the case of narrative discontinuity in *The Sun Also Rises* cited earlier, we accept all sorts of ellipses related to cultural taboo or tellability: no one has sex or goes to the bathroom in Austen or Dickens – or more precisely, such actions are not narrated, being taboo or felt to be uninteresting. This is no longer true when we get to Joyce and Lawrence. But, as I have argued earlier, by duration we should mean something more than the selectivity and discontinuity that can always be ascribed to a narrative (we can always think of things that must have happened but haven't been reported).

### 3.2.4 Frequency

By the term 'frequency' we denote the business of repeated textual telling of a single story incident. If the norm is 'singulative' frequency (telling $n$ times what happened $n$ times), 'repetitive' frequency is exemplified in Faulkner's *Absalom, Absalom!*, in which the murder of Charles Bon by Henry Sutpen is told thirty-nine times, by various tellers. Sometimes singulative presentation would strike us as strangely redundant and verbose: where there are multiple occurrences of an incident of a single type. An option in such cases is 'iterative' frequency – telling once what happened $n$ times. This is what happens in Faulkner's 'Barn Burning', where one of the wretched Snopes family's hurried decampings from one farm to another is narrated, but we are told that this is just the latest of a dozen such moves that the young boy Sartoris Snopes (from whose viewpoint events are told) remembers:

> To-morrow they were there. In the early afternoon the wagon stopped before a paintless two-room house identical almost with the dozen others it had stopped before even in the boy's ten years, and again, as on the other dozen occasions, his mother and aunt got down and began to unload the wagon, although his two sisters and his father and brother had not moved.
>
> (Faulkner, 'Barn Burning', 8–9)

The same story appears to embark upon an erroneous singulative telling when the boy, Sartoris, finds that his father is in court a second time, before a Justice of the Peace, and assumes that, like last time, it is to face and deny (falsely) a charge of arson. The boy accordingly bursts out, 'He ain't done it! He ain't burnt . . .' before his father silences him. Actually it would be truer to say, 'He ain't done it *yet*', for Snopes is indeed a compulsive barn-burner, and before long he has torched the property of his present landlord, Major de Spain. It is so as to break free from the awful singulative 'again and again' of relocation, confrontation, barn-burning and flight, that Sartoris alerts de Spain with the result that de Spain catches Snopes in the act, and kills him.

## 3.3  Temporal refractions in text: Nabokov's *Pnin*

So much for theorizing. We now need to return to some text, of manageable length, and see just how insightful the Genettian model can be. And here it is important to remember that, although it seemed best to present order, duration and frequency separately, in the practice of text-articulation they are parameters that reinforce or interact with each other in significant ways. Creativity or abnormality in one parameter may give rise to exceptionality in the others: an event or episode told with repetitive frequency will inevitably involve anachronisms in terms of order, and more complex oddities in duration. But we should also keep in view the possibility that other, non-Genettian methods – such as stylistic ones focussing on a narrative's patterns of tense and aspect in the verb, adverbials of temporal qualification – and an appeal to readers' norms (rather than the textual norm) may be more in tune with our judgments of textual reorderings, pace and frequency. As attractive a text as any for these purposes of demonstration is Nabokov's *Pnin*. In what follows I will focus on temporal processes in the first section of the first chapter of that novel.

Chapter 1, section 1 of *Pnin* recounts part of middle-aged Russian emigré, US-naturalized, university professor Pnin's mishap-ridden journey to a women's college where he is due to present a guest lecture. The first paragraph is almost purely descriptive (I will return to this 'almost'), with, therefore, no scope for temporal classifications. It consists of two sentences: the first locates and names Professor Timofey Pnin (and hence concerns character and setting, not event), the second supplies a brief evaluation of the prominent features of his appearance:

> The elderly passenger sitting on the north-window side of that inexorably moving railway coach, next to an empty seat and facing two empty ones, was none other than Professor Timofey Pnin. Ideally bald, sun-tanned, and clean-shaven, he began rather impressively with that great brown dome of his, tortoise-shell glasses (masking an infantile absence of eyebrows), apish upper lip, thick neck, and strong-man torso in a tightish tweed coat, but ended, somewhat disappointingly, in a pair of spindly legs (now flannelled and crossed) and frail-looking, almost feminine feet.

The second paragraph, which I have already quoted in full in 3.2.1, has an early trivial anachrony:

His Oxfords *had* cost him as much as all the rest of his clothing ... (my emphasis)

But, as we have seen, more significant homodiegetic analepses follow. Are these – the references to his European era, and its several stages (Russia, Prague, Paris) – internal or external to the basic story? That, of course, depends entirely on what we take to be the basic story; since the whole Genettian exercise is an uncovering of *relations* between parts, it is quite reasonable, in principle, for different analysts to adopt different – but congruent – solutions.

Thus if we adopt the implied time point of paragraph 1 (October 1950) as the opening of the *story* sequence as well as that of the text, then the European references in paragraph 2 are clearly analepses (of varying reach and extent), of sharply summarized duration and – at this stage at least – of singulative frequency. Such a working hypothesis is, I think, supported by the content of the rest of the novel: I take the novel's basic story to be an account of Pnin's last few months as a professor at Waindell College, 1950–1 (an account interspersed with analepses providing retrospective glimpses of Pnin's earlier life).

But one could, alternatively, see the basic story as about and including Pnin at all the stages of his life. There are several reasons why such a solution, in this case at least, seems unattractive. Broadly, it casts the novel in its entirety as a very oddly formed narrative: some fairly full presentations of parts of Pnin's childhood and adolescent experiences, often of brief temporal extent and repeatedly interrupted by extremely lengthy 'prolepses' concerning Pnin in 1950–1, with – and this is oddest of all – very few references to developments during a huge chronological span from *c.* 1920 to *c.* 1950. And more specifically, tense and temporal qualification in the opening pages compel us to treat the Pnin of 1950, on the train, as the Pnin of the narrative present –

Nowadays, at fifty-two, he was crazy about sunbathing, wore sports shirts and slacks ...

– while the Pnin of earlier days is the pre-story Pnin.

The third paragraph confirms our preferred hypothesis of the temporal structure of the novel, with amusing retrospective explanations as to Pnin's current, unrecognized, error:

Now a secret must be imparted. Professor Pnin was on the wrong train. He was unaware of it, and so was the conductor, already threading his way through the train to Pnin's coach. As a matter of fact, Pnin at the moment felt very well satisfied with himself. When inviting him to deliver a Friday-evening lecture at Cremona – some two hundred versts west of Waindell, Pnin's academic perch since 1945 – the vice-president of the Cremona Women's Club, a Miss Judith Clyde, had advised our friend that the most convenient train left Waindell at 1.52 p.m., reaching Cremona at 4.17.

But Pnin, we are told, consults his timetable and boards what he takes to be a more convenient train:

> Unfortunately for Pnin, his timetable was five years old and in part obsolete.

Now, and only now, do we see the point, in the first sentence of the novel, of the unexpected adverbial 'inexorably'; and the occurrence of that word is the single indicator of story temporal sequence in the first paragraph. 'Inexorably' implies something already begun, continuing, and impossible to stop or cancel before its own predetermined and unwelcome conclusion: a proleptic announcement of misfortune. *En passant* let us note the word *secret*, used at the third paragraph's opening ('Now a secret must be imparted'). Who is intentionally keeping the 'secret' of Pnin's mistake hidden from him, and are we readers, now in the know, complicit? Who, in the circumstances, could possibly expose this 'secret'? What kind of teasing, darkly humorous, mildly sadistic narrator are we grappling with here? Out of the accumulation of turns of phrase such as that one, we readers build a picture of the kind of narrator we are being addressed by in a novel or story, about which more is said towards the close of this chapter.

There follow several pages of description of Waindell College, of Pnin's handful of students (each briefly characterized with the aid of deadly analeptic commentary; e.g. 'languid Eileen Lane, whom somebody had told that by the time one had mastered the Russian alphabet one could practically read "Anna Karamazov" in the original'), and of Pnin's bizarre teaching style. This latter is heavily dependent on digressions, personal anecdotes, and the reading of comic passages from books.

> But since to appreciate whatever fun those passages still retained one had to have not only a sound knowledge of the vernacular but also a good deal of literary insight, and since his poor little class had neither, the performer would be alone in enjoying the associative subtleties of his text. The heaving we have already noted in another connexion would become here a veritable earthquake. Directing his memory, with all the lights on and all the masks of the mind a-miming, toward the days of his fervid and receptive youth ... Pnin would get drunk on his private wines as he produced sample after sample of what his listeners politely surmised was Russian humour. Presently the fun would become too much for him; pear-shaped tears would trickle down his tanned cheeks. Not only his shocking teeth but also an astonishing amount of pink upper-gum tissue would suddenly pop out, as if a jack-in-the-box had been sprung, and his hand would fly to his mouth,

while his big shoulders shook and rolled. And although the speech he smothered behind his dancing hand was now doubly unintelligible to the class, his complete surrender to his own merriment would prove irresistible. By the time he was helpless with it he would have his students in stitches . . .

Here, emphatically, we see the significance of the two essential components of narrative noted in Chapter 1: the teller and the tale. For while Pnin himself is absorbed in the seemingly devastating humour of the texts, his student audience's amusement is entirely derived from the absorbing spectacle of the teller. And framing these two is the reader's amusement at the artful telling of the students' amusement at Pnin's amusement: a warming feeling of togetherness in humour, all the more poignant for our awareness of the different kinds of estrangement that separate Pnin from his students, and both of them from us. The practical irrelevance of what the passage-content is that sets Pnin off is underlined by the fact that we neither seek nor require any details about it whatsoever.

The other great attraction of this stylistic tour de force is its use of the modal of iterated or habitual activity (*would*). The stages of physical collapse in Pnin's performance, culminating with the sudden emergence of his false teeth, seem so detailed and specific as to make their recurrence all the more extraordinary and laughable. And given the light-hearted nature of what is told, such iterative-frequency narration – telling once what happened often – itself enhances the spirit of recognizability and empathy that such incidents promote.

But if such a spirit were to render the reader too relaxed, the terse one-sentence paragraph that follows ensures otherwise:

All of which does not alter the fact that Pnin was on the wrong train.

The point about Pnin's habitual performance, described above, is that while iterative in frequency, and of uncertain duration, it is, being habitual, both analeptic and proleptic, a *potential* event at numerous points in time. It cannot arise during this train journey of Pnin's, to be sure, since his students are not present with him: we may thus designate its textual position, its being told here, as an achrony. (In a sense, then, 'this is not the time', here on this train journey, for one of Pnin's reading-comic-passages laughing fits; but this is precisely where we readers are told of them.) But being habitual events, these are not very firmly anchored to any particular point or points in time: the only delimitation is the obvious one that these hysterics can only arise during Pnin's classes. (The habit is rather less of a constant recurrence than, say, giving a little cough every time one begins to speak.)

The reminder that in 'our' present-time Pnin is 'still' on the wrong train is, in turn, followed by a long paragraph of characterization (again, a descriptive pause in terms of duration, not tied to any point in terms of order) concerning his fatal attraction to gadgetry. This, too, is followed by a terse reminder of the situation in the ongoing basic story:

> And he still did not know that he was on the wrong train.

The running joke continues, with a lengthy account of his eccentric command of the English language followed by yet another resumption of the story proper –

> The conductor ... had now only three coaches to deal with before reaching the last one, where Pnin rode.

– before we are treated to the lovely ramifications of a 'Pninian quandary' as to where, on his person, he should store his lecture manuscript:

> If he kept the Cremona manuscript ... on his person, in the security of his body warmth, the chances were, theoretically, that he would forget to transfer it from the coat he was wearing to the one he would wear. On the other hand, if he placed the lecture in the pocket of the suit in the bag now, he would, he knew, be tortured by the possibility of his luggage being stolen. On the third hand (these mental states sprout additional fore-limbs all the time), he carried in the inside pocket of his present coat a precious wallet ...; and it was physically possible to pull out the wallet, if needed, in such a way as fatally to dislodge the folded lecture.

Pnin's quandary is an acute form of the kind of anxiety we all feel over unwelcome possible future consequences of our present actions, proleptic imaginings all the more ironical since we know Pnin is already in a mess (no need for him to imagine one). Incidentally, the detached conditional 'if needed', towards the close of the quoted extract, indicates how very skilled is Nabokov's use of the English language. On an unexceptional reading it qualifies 'the wallet'. But on a more bizarre – but appropriately bizarre – reading it would qualify 'pulling out the wallet so as fatally to dislodge the lecture'. That is, if the wallet needed to be pulled out in such a way as fatally to dislodge and lose the lecture, then Pnin could be relied on to do the job!

The first section closes with further complex temporal reflections and projections, as Pnin learns he is on the wrong train and is redirected by the conductor. But I hope enough has been shown of just how widespread and complex the manipulations of time-lines can be, even in quite short passages. To repeat, the point of such close analyses is not to unravel a text, to return to some underlying singulative, steady-paced, linear chronology, but rather to understand more fully how, in our narratives as in our lives, we constantly demand and draw upon potential complexities of pace, iteration, and reordering.

## 3.4 Focalization

Faulkner's 'That Evening Sun' begins:

> Monday is no different from any other weekday in Jefferson now.

Readers familiar with Faulkner will know that Jefferson is his fictionalized version of Oxford, Mississippi, and that we are back in a fictionalized deep South; but we do not yet know, even roughly, when this *now* is, or how long ago the contrasted old-style Mondays were. Is the narrator contrasting the 1950s with the 1930s, or the 1930s with the 1900s? We need to know more about the viewpoint from which the story is being told. A reader must – over the succeeding sentences of the story – come up with answers to such questions, and in doing so will get an approximate 'fix' on both the place and time *from which* the teller must have composed that sentence, and the identity (insofar as this is disclosed) of the teller.

These are matters of orientation, and the linguistic term for all those elements in a language that have a specifically orientational function is deixis. The very presence in any discourse of features such as *I* and *you*, of *yesterday*, *today* and *tomorrow*, of tense choices, and of contrastive adverbs and adjectives such as *here* and *there*, *this* and *that*, *now* and *then*, means that that discourse is consequently interpreted as grounded, or anchored, as coming from a particular speaker at a particular place at a particular time. Any text, then, that contains deictic information is thereby understood as oriented from the spatiotemporal position that those deictics imply. But the paradox is that the dedicatedly orientational words (*this*, *now*, *here*, etc.) cannot be properly interpreted without information about the speaker's spatiotemporal location derived from elsewhere. Compare *It's wonderfully hot here today* (lots of deixis, but ambiguous without co-text or context) and *Friday 11 August 2000 was wonderfully hot in Brittany* (little or no deixis, largely unambiguous).

What applies to discourses in general applies particularly importantly to narratives. In the process of telling a narrative, with its almost inevitable and copious specifications of time and place, some perspective or another has to be adopted as the vantage point from which the spatiotemporally determinate events are related. Even

> Once upon a time in a distant land there lived a beautiful princess

signals, through the emphasis on *Once*, *distant* and past tense *lived*, that the perspective adopted in the telling assumes teller–listener proximity, and a spatiotemporal remoteness, in the past, of the events to be narrated. But, very importantly, the telling of a narrative does not have to maintain, throughout, a *single* perspective or orientation. Simpler narratives will tend to, and this orientation can be straightforwardly assumed to be the narrator's; but in the more complex literary and film narratives, the viewpoint of the telling may move around, from narrator to one character to another character.

'Focalization' is Gerard Genette's term (the notion was further developed by Bal) for this inescapable adoption of a (limited) perspective in narrative, a viewpoint from which things are *implicitly* seen, felt, understood, and assessed. By this is meant the angle from which things are seen – where 'seen' is interpreted in a broad sense, not only (though often most centrally) in terms of visual perception. As Rimmon-Kenan comments (1983: 71), this term does not entirely shake off the optical–photographic connotations that have made its Anglo-American critical equivalent, point of view, problematic. I hesitate to offer another variant term to compete with those we already have, but I do think orientation is a usefully wider, less visual, term than 'focalization', and would help us to remember that 'cognitive, emotive and ideological' perspectives, in addition to the simply spatiotemporal one, may be articulated by a narrative's chosen focalization. Accordingly, though I will mostly retain Genette's term 'focalization' in what follows, the reader is welcome to substitute 'orientation' if this is any help.

The great and continuing nuisance perpetuated by the term 'point of view' is that it does nothing to discourage the conflation and confusion of two distinct aspects of narrative practice:

1    The orientation we infer to be that from which what gets told is told.
2    The individual we judge to be the immediate source and authority for whatever *words* are used in the telling.

These can be summarized in two distinct questions: 'Who sees?' and 'Who speaks?'

As noted, in many narratives, orientation and discourse-authorship are sourced in a single individual. But speaking/thinking and seeing do not have to come from the same agent. There are many cases where a narrator 'undertake[s] to tell what another person sees or has seen' (Rimmon-Kenan, 1983: 72). In the early chapters of *Great Expectations*, for example, the narrator is Pip the adult, with an adult's extended vocabulary, a different person from the focalizer, who is Pip the child. An inevitable corollary of the notion of focalizer or subject-of-the-focalization is that there must also be someone or something that is the object of the process, i.e. the focalized. In the following section the different types of focalizer and focalized identified by Bal are outlined.

### 3.4.1 Types of focalization

The basic contrast is between external and internal focalization. External focalization occurs where the focalization is from an orientation outside the story (the orientation is not associable with that of any character within the text). In such cases the narrator/focalizer separation is neutralized, so that the focalization is of no particular interest, independent of the narration. Internal focalization occurs inside the setting of the events, and almost always involves a character-focalizer, though some unpersonified position or stance could be adopted. Thus in Faulkner's 'Barn Burning', the boy Sartoris is often the focalizer, but he is not the narrator (the vocabulary in sentence 2 below is emphatically not Sarty's). The story is told largely from his orientation, but he is not directly responsible for the words used, as this extract from the opening shows:

> The store in which the Justice of the Peace's court was sitting smelled of cheese.(1) The boy, crouched on his nail keg at the back of the crowded room, knew he smelled cheese, and more: from where he sat he could see the ranked shelves close-packed with the solid, squat, dynamic shapes of tin cans whose labels his stomach read, not from the lettering which meant nothing to his mind but from the scarlet devils and the silver curve of fish – this, the cheese which he knew he smelled and the hermetic meat which his intestines believed he smelled coming in intermittent gusts momentary and brief between the other constant one, the smell and sense just a little of fear because mostly of despair and grief, the old fierce pull of blood.(2) He could not see the table where the Justice sat and before which his father and his father's enemy stood, but he could hear them . . .(3)

Here, sentence 1 is not exclusively the boy's perspective, but that of anyone inside the store: only someone who was present in the makeshift courtroom at that time, or was later told what the room had been like by someone else who had been present, can make this report. Much more specifically, sentence 2 emphatically expresses the boy's orientation and sentence 3 mixes the boy's focalization ('he could hear') with information about the relative positions of the Justice and his father and the table, which cannot be through the boy's eyes since the text explicitly states he could not see these things.

Like the two types of focalizers, there are also two types of focalized, where the distinction is between viewing from outside or from within. In the former, only the external, literally visible phenomena are reported; in the latter, facts about the feelings, thoughts and reactions of a (or several) character(s) are reported, so that a penetrating intrusive portrayal is achieved. Molly Bloom in *Ulysses* is both internal focalizer and focalized from within, while in Hemingway what is focalized is very commonly viewed from without. Focalization may remain fixed, tied to a single focalizer, throughout a novel, as in *What Maisie Knew*. Of this novel Bal (1985: 104–5) writes: 'The difference between the childish version of the events [focalized by Maisie] and the interpretation that the adult reader gives them determines the novel's special effect.' But the focalizing may vary between two or more positions, as in Faulkner's *The Sound and the Fury*.

The interest in focalization stems from the fact that it highlights the 'bi-directionality' of narrative: the fact that the focussing *on* a particular object in a particular way reveals that object but also must reveal (or try not to reveal) the perspective and ideology from which that subject is seen. Furthermore, such revelatory focalization goes on regardless of whether the object focalized really exists. In this respect it is useful to distinguish between focalizeds that we as readers accept actually exist in the world of the narrative from those we take to be dreams, fantasies or other figments of one character-focalizer's imagination. We might label this distinction actual versus imagined focalizeds (a distinction slightly different from and more difficult than Bal's one between 'perceptible' and 'non-perceptible' focalizeds). Some narratives trade heavily on our uncertainty as to whether what is focalized is actual and potentially 'public experience', or imagined and perhaps an index of psychosis (a magnificent example is James's *The Turn of the Screw*).

### 3.4.2  *Facets of focalization?*

Bal (1985) seems to prefer not to attempt a detailed discrimination of *types* of focalization, emphasizing rather the levels involved. But Rimmon-Kenan (1983), evidently considerably influenced by Uspensky (1973), does attempt a typology of what she calls the facets of focalization, the major ones being perceptual, psychological and ideological, each of which permits great variation in the power or breadth of the focalizing. For example, with regard to the perceptual dimension of focalization, the focalizer may enjoy (and relay to us from) a panoramic perspective which allows holistic descriptions of large scenes, and even of several distinct but simultaneous scenes; this obviously entails an external focalizer. On the other hand, where the focalizer is a character within the narrative, the limited view of that spatiotemporally limited observer is to be expected. A similar broad contrast between the constrained and unlimited perspectives (actually with many intermediate degrees of limitedness) applies also to time focalization.

In addition to variation in spatiotemporal orientation, there is psychological variation, which Rimmon-Kenan separates into the cognitive (e.g. the internal focalizer's limited knowledge versus the external focalizer's theoretical omniscience) and the emotive (neutrality versus involvement in presentation). And in involved emotive focalization, for example, scenes are represented in a noticeably idiosyncratic way, such as seems best attributed to the mood and personal evaluations of a character. The focalized's mind and emotions, too, are open to either external or penetrative/internal treatment (assuming the focalized is human or quasi-human).

A final facet of focalization variation is the ideological. Often, it seems, one ideology or world-view, of an external narrator–focalizer, is the dominating norm, and any characters' ideologies that deviate from this standard are at least implicitly (and sometimes explicitly) censured. On the other hand, there may be a juxtaposition of different ideological orientations without any overt adjudication between them, so that the reader is torn between different views of certain events in particular and (by extension) of the world in general. On this topic, Bakhtin (1981) is particularly relevant. Insofar as both the psychological and the ideological facets of focalization are a matter of how things are evaluated, there seems to be plenty of room for overlap between these two. (Spatiotemporal perceptual focalizing, by contrast, is not inherently evaluative, being merely a disclosing by implication of the when and where of the witnessing.) In a typical situation, it may well be that, as analysts, we talk of a deviant main character as revealing weird psychology in their focalizations, this being highlighted and counteracted by the orthodox and 'reasonable' ideology of an external narrator, focalizing elsewhere; the effect of this, for the reader, is often that the character's ideology appears to be 'corrected' by the narrator's.

## 3.5  Perceptual focalization as primary

While it may be accepted, in light of the foregoing examples, that narration always entails focalization, it is debateable whether we need to posit a focalizer *position* distinct from the narratorial one in all texts, and whether we should typically work on the assumption that we can identify a focalizer's spatiotemporal, psychological and ideological orientations as distinct from those of the narrator. Quite often theorists' examples of psychological or ideological focalization (e.g. those in Rimmon-Kenan) seem easily accommodated within more orthodox characterizations of the particular narrator as naïve or childlike or self-conscious or paranoid. Orientational limitation attributed to a particular character's perspective does seem to make the best sense in relation to spatiotemporal matters; in the areas of psychology and ideology it seems far less easy to resolve that a particular emphasis is not that of the narrator – except, of course, where we are faced with the speech or thought of a character, directly or indirectly rendered, but that is another matter. In focalization the essential question remains: 'Who sees?' More fully, the question to ask in determining spatiotemporal focalization is:

> Who is the immediate seer here, and whose is the 'zero-point' for time measurement here, to whom we attribute the spatiotemporal orientations we are given?

Similarly with psychological and ideological evidence, whether explicit or only implicit:

> To whom do we attribute these traces or revelations of psychological or ideological orientation? Who is their immediate source?

## 3.6  Narrators and narration

In section 3.4 I introduced a distinction between

1   The orientation we infer to be that from which what gets told is told; and
2   The individual or 'position' we judge to be the immediate source and authority for whatever words are used in the telling.

The former we distinguish as focalization, the latter as narration, and it is to this latter domain that I now turn.

The business of specifying just how many optional or obligatory roles are involved in the process of narration can soon get remarkably complex. The scheme most widely-adopted by narratologists is the following (see, e.g. Chatman, 1978: 151):

$$\text{real author} \rightarrow \text{implied author} \rightarrow (\text{narrator}) \rightarrow (\text{narratee}) \rightarrow \text{implied reader} \rightarrow \text{real reader}$$

In Chatman's discussion, the real author and reader are left out, on the grounds that their 'implied' counterparts are the functioning substitutes in the business of narrative transmission. Furthermore, Chatman claims that the narrator–narratee pair are optional positions. I will propose an alternative simplification which, I hope, will not ignore the potential complexities involved; I will argue that, notwithstanding the potential relevance of the 'implied author', 'narratee' and 'implied reader' constructs, the three core roles in literary narrative transmission are author, narrator and reader:

$$\text{author} \rightarrow \text{narrator} \rightarrow \text{reader}$$

It is no accident that of the six roles usually discussed in narratological studies, these three are the ones that are robustly present on the surface of narrative texts, and the most deeply recalled when we ordinarily think about narratives. We (the reader) open *Great Expectations* and somebody tells us how he stumbled over his own name, of Philip: whoever he is, this Philip, the narrator, is distinct from the author, Charles Dickens. Or we (as readers) read the opening paragraphs of 'That Evening Sun', and are told 'about half the time we'd have to go down the lane to Nancy's cabin and tell her to come on and cook breakfast' and, a page later, that 'father' tells Quentin to go and see if Nancy has finished in the kitchen, whereupon 'I went to the kitchen'. So Faulkner, the author, has established Quentin as narrator. And so on. By contrast, the implied author, the narratee, and the implied reader are rather more notional: potentially analytically important, but in more oblique ways.

### 3.6.1 *Implied author: a construct but not a primary role*

The implied author is the mental picture of the author that a reader constructs on the basis of the text in its entirety. It is easiest to see that we do (or at least can) perform such a (re)construction in the course of reading if we imagine an anonymous text. Perhaps the text is a crime novel, with a grizzled Metropolitan Police detective as protagonist, and the action is set in the pulsing streets and edgy deals of contemporary Soho, involving drugs, prostitution, protection-rackets and electronic fraud. However we visualize and pigeonhole the implied author, we probably do not expect that they are a retired nun who has never left Sri Lanka, or an overworked junior doctor, or an eco-warrior, or a ten-year-old, or James Joyce. But more important than the vague provenance a narrative might project as belonging to the implied author (such as male, in his thirties, streetwise, has knocked about a bit in London or somewhere very similar, knows police-work 'from the inside', etc.) are the *values* that, rightly or wrongly, the reader imputes to the implied author (perhaps, that he has a sordid fascination with commercial sex, narcotics, transgression, violence, that he seems to derive a certain pleasure from outsmarting the reader with his inside knowledge of electronic financial dealings, that deep down he mainly believes in private property, protecting your own, carrying a big stick, and coming out ahead when you can ...). If he didn't tacitly subscribe to those values – so the reader reasons, in explaining the picture of the implied author they have drawn – why would he construct the kind of narrator he has, and write about the kinds of things he does, in the ways that he does?

An implied author can be retrospectively projected on any text, narrative or otherwise. In the case of literary narratives, the account of an implied author that a reader develops tends in practice to have much to do with authorial intention and meaning. It amounts to an answer to the reader's own question: 'What sort of person, with what sort of interests and values, must the author be, to have produced this text with the preoccupations and meanings that I take it to have?'. Thus one can imagine a reader of 'That Evening Sun', perhaps one with no previous knowledge of Faulkner or his other works, reading that story and being struck by the tacit and not-so-tacit racism; the domesticity of the focus (little sense of a larger world, beyond the semi-lawless town); the fractiousness and dysfunctionality of the Compson family; the cross-generational 'gender alliances' that link Caddy with Nancy, and the narrator Quentin with his father; the tangled dialogue on the page in which, repeatedly, A's remark to B is followed, before the latter's reply is given, by C's request to D; Jason's insufferable whininess; Nancy's desperate, ruined circumstances; and the way a story that includes cocaine-addiction, an attempted suicide, and fear of murder unravels to a wretched close, with Nancy declaring she's 'just a nigger' and Caddy telling Jason he's worse than one. In the light of all that, and all that it means – the characterization, the way and tone of narration, the topics and treatment – whatever picture we infer of the mind of the author is our 'implied author'.

The notion of the 'implied author' was first proposed by Wayne Booth:

> As [the author] writes, he creates not simply an ideal, impersonal 'man in general' but an implied version of 'himself' that is different from the implied authors we meet in other men's works ... the picture the reader gets of this presence is one of the author's most important effects. However impersonal he may try to be, his reader will inevitably construct a picture of the official scribe who writes in this manner.
>
> (Booth, 1961: 70–1)

In subsequent discussions of the implied author, the emphasis has tended to be on the word 'implied': in Booth the emphasis seems to me to be far more on the word 'author'. There the claim is that we project or reconstruct back, from the text, some sort of version or picture of the author. Clearly that version of the author is not the author herself; it may be a version that the actual author vigorously rejects, or that is unduly flattering or derogatory of her.

It is not clear, however, that the implied author is a distinct level of narrative structuring. We can retain the term 'implied author' to refer to the picture of Faulkner we conjure up from *The Sound and the Fury* (a very different picture, surely, from that which we conjure up from *The Reivers*), but we might as happily simply distinguish the Faulkner of *The Sound and the Fury* and the Faulkner of *The Reivers*, or the Joyce of *Dubliners* and the Joyce of *Finnegan's Wake*. As far as these novels and narratives are concerned, these are the only versions of the author we know, and there is no 'real author', unitary, unchanging, standing behind these narrative-derived versions. If we've read Blotner's biography of Faulkner, or Ellmann on Joyce, we have read another narrative presenting (much more fully and directly) another version of the author. Even if we also know an author personally, we still perform the same process of forming a mental picture or representation (itself a kind of narrative) of that author to ourselves, as an integral part of the activity of knowing a person. In short, the pictures we have of authors are always constructions, so that all authors are, if you like, 'inferred authors'. But we can and should separate such pictures from the actuality of authorial narrative production: those pictures may be important in narrative reception and critical theory, but they are irrelevant to narrative production. The implied author is a real position in narrative processing, a receptor's construct, but it is not a core or necessary role in narrative transmission. It is a projection back from the decoding side, not a real projecting stage on the encoding side.

### 3.6.2 Narratees and implied readers

While the production side of narrative transmission can focus on author and narrator, the reception side, similarly, should recognize the reader as core participant, and narratee and implied reader as secondary. The narratee is an individual, involved in or quite detached from the events of the story, directly addressed by the narrator. Very occasionally a narrator addresses her discourse to herself, but much more typically the specific narrative addressee is a character–receiver within the story, if rather marginal to the action (the psychiatrist Dr Spielvogel who is told all the young man's hangups in *Portnoy's Complaint*, the seafarers who are told Marlow's story in *Heart of Darkness* and so on). Sometimes, as in Sterne's *Tristram Shandy*, a narratee is playfully conjured up and has her ears boxed for inattentiveness:

> How could you, Madam, be so inattentive in reading the last chapter? I told you in it, that my father was not a papist! You told me no such thing, Sir. Madam, I beg leave to repeat it over again, That I told you as plain, at least, as words, by direct inference, could tell you such a thing ...
>
> (1967: 82, quoted in Rimmon-Kenan, 1983: 105)

We readers enjoy the joke in which a fictional entity, as if in our position, gets ticked off in a way that we know we sometimes deserve. But we do also see that this is an 'as if' relation, that this is a strategy or device (if the narrator were really scolding us we would probably resent and resist that impertinence). Any residual nervousness on the part of any Madam-reader that she is being directly addressed is dispelled, of course, by the direct speech attributed to this other, fictional Madam.

In all these cases and others besides, the narratee position is not a foundational part of the framework of the telling, but an integral device in narrational strategy. In all the cases cited above – and almost always, in fact – the narratee is addressed by an intradiegetic narrator, i.e. not the narrator of the narrative in our foundational sense (the source or agent for everything that gets told). As Bal says of this 'foundational' narrator:

> We ... do not mean a story-teller, a visible, fictive 'I' who interferes in his/her account as much as s/he likes, or even participates as a character in the action. Such a 'visible' narrator is a specific version of the narrator, one of the several different possibilities of manifestation. ... We shall rigorously stick to the definition of 'that agent which utters the linguistic signs that constitute the text'.
>
> (Bal, 1985: 120)

Typically, a narratee is a visible fictional character whom we witness being addressed by an even more visible second-order narrator, and behind their fake dialogue is some storyteller (the first order or foundational narrator) whom we take to be the agent of all their words (both the visible narrator's and the narratee's), and any other material besides (e.g. the insertion of chapter breaks in the telling, chapter numbers, headings, etc.). Narratees, then, are real but secondary and infrequent textual entities.

By contrast the 'implied reader' is another reader-based construct, like the implied author: it is a picture, based on the text in its totality, of the kind of reader or archetypal reader that real readers assume that the text has or had in mind as its audience. Inferencing and stereotyping is involved in positing any text's implied reader. We usually feel most secure sketching the implied reader for narratives which are themselves rather generic and which, though we may enjoy them, we do not hold in the highest esteem. Thus it is easier to sketch the identity and values of the assumed, targeted reader of novels by Barbara Bradford Taylor, Dick Francis, Sue Grafton, and so on; it is harder to say who is, or is not, the implied reader of *Middlemarch* or *White Noise* or *Pnin*. The notion of implied reader, and its implication that *certain* readers are directly addressed or interpellated while others are not, is always likely to provoke contention and controversy. But the ascription of a particular kind of implied reader to particular kinds of texts certainly happens, and to that extent this secondary role or notion is valuable. Rightly or wrongly, in the face of certain kinds of writing (which is, for example, noticeably sexist, or class-conscious, or soft-pornographic, or religious, or technically-detailed about some activity) we assume that the author had a particular kind of reader in mind. But then again perhaps they did not, or perhaps – as reader – I don't care even if they did, and refuse to comply with that oblique effort to include or exclude me. As Walter Ong (1975) pointed out, the writer's audience is always a fiction, a convenient provisional target. Real readers, real audiences, can apprehend stories in quite unpredicted ways, seeing a different point to them, and picturing quite dissimilar authors of them.

## 3.7 Simpson's typology of narratorial modes

Literary criticism operates with an array of well-established terms for distinguishing kinds of narrator and, by extension, kinds of narration. Many of these terms constitute binary alternatives: *third-person* versus *first-person* narration; within third-person narration, *omniscient* versus *limited* narration; and, within omniscient narration, *intrusive* versus *impersonal/objective* narration. Although invaluable, these terms are far from uncontroversial in application. But most importantly they immediately direct attention to the narrator, whereas the schemes to be introduced below direct our attention to the narration (and derive tentative characterizations of narrators therefrom). These latter schemes are thus more text-linguistic and less psychological in orientation, and thus more suited to a linguistic study of narrative.

As a preliminary step, we can follow Rimmon-Kenan (1983: 96–8), based on Genette, in setting up different categories of narrator depending on whether that narrator is extradiegetic or intradiegetic, and whether she is a story participant or not (homodiegetic versus heterodiegetic). In addition to such a categorization, we can assess the visibility of a narrator by looking for the following kinds of textual material, which are indicative – in increasing order of intrusiveness – of narratorial presence:

1   descriptions of settings;
2   identification of characters;
3   temporal summaries;
4   *definition* of characters;
5   reports of what characters did not think or say;
6   commentary – interpretation, judgment, generalization.

The above six types of material reflect – in order – greater and greater narratorial knowledge and understanding of whatever story is articulated. Narration embracing only types 1–3, for example, would not be unlike the kind of official and minimally-interpretive account of an incident that might be found in a police report or a description of an accident for insurance purposes. In addition, within each of the six types of report there can be greater or lesser degrees of specificity, insight, and understanding. (See Rimmon-Kenan and Bal for demonstrations of incrementally intrusive narration, and also the notes and exercises for this chapter.)

But there are other very useful typologies of narrational mode that are worth consulting, including that of Uspensky (1973), and, a simplification of this, Fowler (1986). More recently yet, Simpson (1993) has proposed a revision and expansion of the Uspensky/Fowler scheme which is particularly worthy of attention, not least since it is concerned with the kinds of engagement that different narrators have with the material they narrate. It is with a brief outline of and commentary upon Simpson's scheme that I will end this chapter.

To begin with, it is worth emphasizing that all these proposals are attempting to look in an orderly and systematic way at the different kinds of narration that a careful reader is almost inevitably going to notice, at some level of consciousness. That is, the reader who reads this:

> It is vain to say human beings ought to be satisfied with tranquility: they must have action, and they will make it if they cannot find it. Millions are condemned to a stiller doom than mine, and millions are in silent revolt against their lot. . . . Women are supposed to be very calm generally: but women feel just as men feel. . . .
>     (Bronte, *Jane Eyre*, Penguin, p. 141; quoted in Simpson, 1993: 57)

knows that they are being addressed differently, or being addressed by a different kind of narrator, than when they read this:

But suddenly a woman rose up before me, a big fat woman dressed in black, or rather in mauve. I still wonder today if it wasn't the social worker. She was holding out to me, on an odd saucer, a mug full of greyish concoction which must have been green tea with saccharine and powdered milk.

(Beckett, *Molloy*, Picador, p. 23; quoted in Simpson, 1993: 52)

Both are first-person narrations, but neither fits more traditional categorizations well (the former passage is both character-based *and* 'omniscient'; the latter is both character-based *and* 'estranged'), and clearly both run through all six degrees of informativity on the Genette/Rimmon-Kenan scale. What we need is a classification that will begin to recognize and distinguish the fact that, whatever the narratorial intent, a reader may find the former to be serious, even dogmatic, while the latter may appear sometimes absurd or ludicrous. The former is full of sweeping generalizations and prone to the melodramatic (*a stiller doom than mine*); the latter seems unsure even about the particular (*dressed in black, or rather in mauve*) never mind moving to the general, or it combines vagueness with uncanny detail, in ways which in this short extract feel closer to the low-comedic than the sinister. Simpson's model helps us to discuss these differences systematically. His approach entails looking at narration through grammatical eyes, and thinking about the degree to which different narratorial stances are expressed through demonstrable aspects of the grammar of their construction. So there is a continuity here with the interest in the grammaticization of plot with which the previous chapter concluded (2.6): the Simpson model probes the extent to which we can say that key narratorial modes are grammaticized. In what follows I rehearse Simpson's system, but add one or two glosses which may make the system easier to memorize.

Simpson's scheme distinguishes nine types or modes of narration. First we can make a three-way distinction of narratives on the basis of relatively explicit and well-recognized contrasts: is the narration first-person or third-person, and if third-person, is the narration focalized through one character's consciousness (as happens in Henry James's novels and many since) or is the third-person narration 'non-aligned', emanating from some detached point outside the consciousness of a particular I or a particular she or he? In Simpson's terms these three category alternatives are A, B (R) and B (N), respectively, where A denotes first-person narration, B denotes third-person, of which R denotes the Reflector or character-mediated variety and N denotes the impersonal Narratorial option. This tripartite distinction might also be annotated using personal pronouns, labelling the three types *I-*, *s/he-*, and *they*-narration respectively. Calling Simpson's category A, or first-person, *I*-narration needs no explanation. In a passage of *she-* or *he*-narration – Simpson's B (R) – the third-person is used, but the orientation is from the point of view of a particular *she* or *he*: just what that *he* or *she* sees is what gets narrated. In a passage of *they-*

narration – Simpson's B (N) – again the third-person is used, but there is no adoption of the viewpoint of any particular *she* or *he*, rather we are more detachedly told what *they,* one or more individuals viewed externally, do and say. The contrast between *she/he-* and *they*-narration is not on the basis of singular versus plural, but on the basis of point of view alignment (*she/he-*) or detachment (*they-*). *They*-narration need not report the acts of two or more detachedly-viewed characters; it may report just one person's acts, but from a detached perspective, in which, I am suggesting, that person is treated as a 'they'.

The second axis upon which Simpson distinguishes types of narration, again proposing three prominent types, is bound up with modality and evaluation, a topic which is too complex for me to go into in any detail here (the reader is directed to a number of useful summary accounts, starting with Simpson's own). In essence, in grammatical and textual studies, modality refers to some of the crucial means by which a speaker qualifies what would otherwise be absolute statements (like *It's wet and cloudy in Lima*; *Tony borrowed my bike*; and *Tanya ate the pasta*). So modality introduces a kind of colouring of the discourse, investing utterances with some of the commitments and reservations of its speaker or author (*It seems that it's wet and cloudy in Lima*; *I didn't mind Tony borrowing my bike*; *Tanya must have eaten the pasta*). Modality is a powerful indicator of point of view, of the speaker's or writer's subjectivity; it is one of the means by which an addressee feels they are hailed by a person with a voice and human feelings, needs, burdens, and uncertainties. So it often supports or fosters *interactivity* or connection between addresser and addressee. In dialogue and conversation, it gives rise to a sense of negotiation in which, implicitly at least, the addressee feels that they have possibilities of taking up the modalized claims of the speaker, rather than simply receiving and submitting to them. In narrative – particularly completed written narrative – the reader cannot practically 'negotiate' with the author, but the sense of a modalized written telling as one that contrives to draw you into a writer–reader conversation remains as a textual effect.

Simpson groups the various kinds of modality that one might identify into two large tendencies: positive modality and negative modality. And both of these must be contrasted with the third alternative, which is near-total absence of modalization: flat, categorical, non-subjective statements (of the *Tanya ate the pasta* variety). Within positive modality are all the linguistic means of expressing the deontic (what must or ought to be done, including duties and obligations and impositions in all their forms, from strongest – *I order you to* – to weakest – *I beg you to*) or the boulomaic (what is desired, wanted, wished for, or pleasing, again across the range from strong to weak). To this 'positive' modality, we can add generalizing and opinion-expressive sentences of the kind found in the *Jane Eyre* passage above (there are many, the last of them being *Women feel just as men feel*). And we should mention evaluative adjectives and adverbs generally, along with verbs reporting a character's thoughts, perceptions, and reactions (*she noticed ... it annoyed her that ...*) collectively known as *verba sentiendi*. A passage of narration which uses some of these resources is, like the *Jane Eyre* passage, noticeably positive in modality, which here means that the narrator appears to be engaged with and 'upbeat' about the story they are telling, confident and in control of their material – also with a sense that the material *is* 'their' material, that is, that they are in possession of it. Relatedly, such a passage will tend to be marked by a backgrounding or total absence of epistemic modality and words of estrangement (these two will be explained below, under 'negative modality'). The tone or tenor is emphatic, confident, assured and addressee-reassuring.

By contrast, within negative modality fall the linguistic means of expressing certainty and uncertainty about whatever is being reported – again, using a range of means that include modal verbs such as *might (have)* and *must*: *She must have eaten the pasta (it was in the fridge this morning)*, modal adverbs such as *conceivably* and *undoubtedly*, clausal constructions like *It is highly unlikely/probable that*, and more idiomatic means: *No question, Tony was the one who took the bike*. There may also be various verbs of 'speculative cognition': *she supposed that*; *I imagine that*, etc. In addition to these, narrative passages with negative modality include a number of constructions that appear to refer to human perception (*It's obvious that ... Obviously ...* and similarly with other adjective/adverb partners: *clear(ly)*, *evident(ly)*, *seems/seemingly*, *looks/sounds like*, and many more). Equally predictably, the narrative will have few or no generic sentences, and verbs reporting characters' thoughts and reactions will be qualified: not *she strode along, intent on confronting the whole village* but *she strode along seemingly intent on confronting the whole village*. Or, most indicatively, using *as if*. Many of these features can be grouped together and called 'words of estrangement', in that they add to the reporting the impression that an outsider's account is being given, rather than that of someone with 'insider knowledge'. A tone of doubt or guardedness, even of lostness or alienation, may predominate: narration with negative-mode modality is often the product of a narrator who is not in confident proprietorial control of the story they are telling, but is tentative, confused, somewhat overwhelmed by it or alienated from it (they are 'self-questioning', Simpson suggests). The contrast between positive and negative narration, at the extreme, is all the difference between:

1    the narrator who buttonholes you with their story because, themselves knowing it completely, they wish to share it with you in the belief that it is amusing, or instructive, or similar – at any rate, that it has a clear point and effect.

and

2    the narrator who shares a story with you because its shape, point and effect are, perhaps, unclear to them, as narrator, and they narrate as if

in the hope that sharing the story may help clarify the message, like the messenger who conveys a message that they themselves do not fully understand or associate with.

Clearly, type 2 narratives are much the more paradoxical and intriguing.

If positive narration implies, 'Here's a story and I, partly revealing myself, know exactly what it means' while negative narration implies, 'Here's a story but I, partly revealing myself, don't know quite what it means', then neutral narration falls outside these two and implies simply, 'Here's a story (and I am neither revealing myself nor saying what it means)'. In the neutral modes – which like positive and negative modes can apply to first- or third-person (narratorial or reflectorial) narrations – there is a nearly complete absence of narratorial modality. The teller tells things categorically and 'non-subjectively', so that the tone is cool and detached. Neutral modes are suited to physical description rather than psychological development. Camus's *The Outsider* is famed for its non-modal reporting of topics (grief, desire, murderous hostility) where one ordinarily expects modalization; other authors who draw heavily – but by no means constantly – on the powerful effects of neutral narration include Hemingway, Chandler, Carver, and a host of 'hard-boiled' crime-fiction writers.

It is illuminating, in principle, to be able to create and compare versions of a particular passage in several of the modes or styles listed above. Some such transpositions are relatively easy to achieve, others are virtually impossible, and those differences are themselves instructive. Thus, as Simpson shows, transpositions between A, B(N) and B(R) versions of a narrative passage, keeping the modality or lack of it the same, is straight-forward. Thus transposing between what I have called *I*-narration, *they*-narration, and *s/he*-narration, preserving the positiveness (for example) of the original but modulating from an involved first-person narrator to an external narrator to a reflector–narrator (or vice versa), is easily done and can help to highlight the particular effects that an author's chosen mode permits. But 'intracategory' transpositions are significantly more problem-atic. Transforming a neutral (unmodalized) account into a modalized one (positive or negative) can be done, but not the reverse. For doing the reverse, for example, converting a positive account to a neutral one, remov-ing subjective and modalized language, usually renders the passage so full of gaps as to render it incoherent. This is because many of the features we have itemized as reflective of positive or negative narratorial shading are not merely reflective of but constitutive of the passages in which they appear. Consider, for example, the *Jane Eyre* passage cited earlier, which is first person (note the *mine* in line 3) and positive:

> It is *vain* to say human beings *ought to* be satisfied with tranquility: they *must have* action, and they *will* make it if they cannot find it. *Mil-lions are condemned to a stiller doom* than mine, and millions are in

silent revolt against their lot. . . . Women *are supposed to be* very calm generally: but *women feel just as men feel*; they *need* exercise for their faculties, and a field for their efforts as much as their brothers do;

Converting this to third person is straightforward, but dispensing with the evaluative lexis, the generic sentences, the deontic and boulomaic modality, and replacing these with epistemic and perception modality, and estranging comparatives (*looked/seemed as if . . .*) yields an entirely different passage:

It seems that not all human beings are satisfied with tranquility: some search out action, or they create their own. There may be many who endure a more passive condition than that woman's, and perhaps they are in silent revolt against their lot. . . . Women appear very calm generally: but some of them feel as some men do, and like them they seem to need exercise for their faculties, and a field for their efforts.

Contriving such a 're-write' is quite a dubious and controversial exercise, so that what one is inclined to conclude is that the nine modes are like horses for courses, and each has to be appreciated for its own qualities rather than viewed in too much of a comparative perspective: there is no way of writing A positive passages of *Jane Eyre*, in B(N) negative style, that preserves the text as a *Jane Eyre* passage at all. The 'conversion' possibilities are summarized in the following diagram:

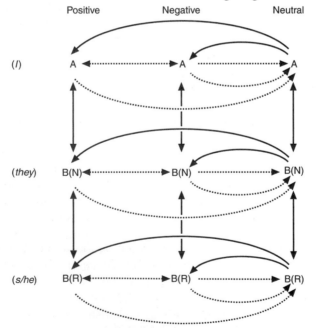

Arrows with solid lines denote permissible transpositions (and their direction).
Arrows with dotted lines denote impermissible transpositions.

In analytical practice, it is often more appropriate to assess passages holistically, for an overall impression of the positive, neutral or negative stance of the narration. That is, it is unwise to approach a text hunting for epistemic or obligation modals, or generic sentences, or evaluative vocabulary, or verbs of feeling and reaction and so on – very often one is bemused to find few of these, or equally confusingly, a mixture which the positive/negative contrast does not seem to predict. Rather it is best to assess the passage as a whole, for its tone, before proceeding to look for confirmation, in specific linguistic features, of its predominantly positive, negative or neutral stance. So while this approach emphasizes the possibility of pinpointing tonal colouring and stance in the particularities of textual choice (modals, *verba sentiendi*, generics, evaluatives, and so on), it does not and cannot reduce to 'item-spotting'. We have noted, for example, that descriptions introduced by *as if/as though*, and *like* can project estrangement and uncertainty (*as if he were angry* [<u>was</u> he angry?]; *like a doctor* [<u>is</u> she a doctor?]). But what of the following lines, from the highly-descriptive opening of D. H. Lawrence's story 'Odour of Chrysanthemums', where both *as if* and *like* figure:

> A large bony vine clutched at the house, *as if* to claw down the tiled roof.... Beside the path hung dishevelled pink chrysanthemums, *like* pink cloths hung on bushes. (emphases added)

Here we cannot simply note these forms and 'read off' narratorial estrangement, removedness, or uncertainty. Here, both forms introduce metaphors, and a narrator who adds metaphorizing elaboration (whether of setting, character, or action) is usually asserting and enacting epistemic engagement or confidence, rather than neutral or negative modality. Indeed all the words of estrangement lack their negative-mode associations when they are used in figurative elaboration rather than literal or factual report. This example is offered to show ways in which the nine-mode model and its textual indices need to be applied alongside increasingly detailed description.

With that said, it may be appropriate to close the chapter by looking at a passage from one of this book's 'favoured' literary narratives, and assessing its choices among the narrational modes. What follows is the close of 'Barn Burning', where young Sartoris has run away from the entire patchwork of misery and wretchedness engendered by his father:

> The slow constellations wheeled on. It would be dawn and then sun-up after a while and he would be hungry. But that would be tomorrow and now he was only cold, and walking would cure that. His breathing was easier now and he decided to get up and go on, and then he found that he had been asleep because he knew it was almost dawn, the night almost over. He could tell that from the whippoorwills. They were everywhere now among the dark trees below him, constant and

inflectioned and ceaseless, so that, as the instant for giving over to the day birds drew nearer and nearer, there was no interval at all between them. He got up. He was a little stiff, but walking would cure that too as it would the cold, and soon there would be the sun. He went on down the hill, toward the dark woods within which the liquid silver voices of the birds called unceasing – the rapid and urgent beating of the urgent and quiring heart of the late spring night. He did not look back.

This seems to fluctuate between B(R) and B(N) positive, depending on the extent to which we feel that, despite being in language well beyond that which we would associate with young Sartoris Snopes (but as we know, 'who speaks?' is a different question from 'who sees?'), nevertheless much of this passage is told from Sarty's perspective, judging that it is he and not the narrator who reflects that walking will cure his cold and stiffness. On balance it seems more appropriate to attribute these to Sartoris, making him the focalizer of most of the passage – but they can also be attributed to an external narrator, and there are no decisive indicators either way. There are *verba sentiendi* here, abundant evaluative vocabulary, and most strikingly a recurrent use of predictive *would*, postulating a future that has not yet happened but which someone foresees will come to pass: it would be dawn, he would be hungry, walking would cure his feeling cold, and so on. Some of these latter are plausibly interpreted as past tense reports of what Sartoris thought to himself, exploiting a style known as Free Indirect Thought which will be fully explained in Chapter 5. Thus,

> He got up. He was a little stiff, but walking would cure that too as it would the cold, and soon there would be the sun.

can be annotated, to highlight Sartoris's thoughts:

> He got up. He was a little stiff [he realized], but walking would cure that too [he thought to himself] as it would the cold, and soon there would be the sun.

Too mechanical a search for modal markers might treat these *would*'s as expressive of epistemic tentativeness, and the negative mode; but in context there is clearly nothing tentative about them. In fact they are an important element in a passage where, for the first time, the reader glimpses young Sartoris *not* oppressed, tentative, or out of his depth: no longer reacting in panic and despair to circumstances created by others.

# Further reading

As in the previous chapter, the best places to begin further reading on the topics discussed are Rimmon-Kenan (1983) Chapters 4, 6 and 7, and Bal (1985; revised second edition: 1997). Rimmon-Kenan's discussions of time and focalization, in particular, include numerous useful examples from the literary canon, while Bal's long chapters on text and narration explain her distinctions painstakingly, with much careful comparative analysis of simple constructed examples. Familiarity with either of these should be adequate preparation for an analeptic move back to their chief source, the work of Genette (1980; 1988). Genette (1980) includes a lucid forward by Culler; it is essential to have some familiarity with Proust's *À la recherche du temps perdu*, on and around which the theory is elaborated, in order to appreciate Genette's analysis properly. Chatman's books (1978 and 1990) contain extensive stimulating discussion of these and related issues, with copious exemplification from well known films and literary texts. Verdonk and Weber (1995) contains many useful stylistic studies of narrative fiction. For the most direct antecedent of the Simpson scheme of narrational modes, see Chapter 9 of Fowler (1986), which concludes with a brief analysis of perspective switches – and their functions – in a crucial scene in Mervyn Peake's novel, *Titus Groan*. Among the more advanced and technical discussions of narration and focalization, the following are important contributions: Prince (1982); Lanser (1981); Jahn (1999); van Peer and Chatman (2001); and Lodge (1977) and (1981) – Chapters 2 and 4 of the latter are attractive applications by a critic and novelist interested in but not uncritical of narrative theorizing. Also to be recommended are, especially, Fludernik (1993) and (1996), magisterial syntheses and proposals touching on many fundamental issues in narratology; Berendson (1981; 1984); Ryan (1981); Fowler (1981); Uspensky (1973); Rifelj (1979); Nelles (1984); Warhol (1986); and Herman (1997). Simpson's nine-cell typology of narrators is set out thoroughly in Simpson (1993). This chapter has entirely neglected the always intriguing business of second-person narrative; a special issue of *Style* (28: 3), devoted to that topic, edited by Fludernik, can be recommended.

# Notes and exercises

1 Re-read William Faulkner's story 'That Evening Sun', and then work through the story's opening paragraphs in sequence, making notes on what is going on in each of them in terms of temporal order, duration and frequency; focalization; and narration, and considering the following issues:

   i   Is paragraph 2 analeptic or is paragraph 1 proleptic?
   ii  What are the temporal boundaries of the basic story?
   iii At what point(s) do we move from iterative-frequency narration to singulative narration, and how is this shift achieved?
   iv  The description of Nancy in paragraph 3 invokes the image of her carrying a balloon, and in paragraph 6 she refers to the children as 'little devils': in relation to the story that unfolds, what unexpected significances may these two allusions have, in terms of proleptic force, character elucidation, or insight into the narrator–focalizer?
   v   What insights, however slight and inconclusive, into the psychological and ideological partialities of the narrator–focalizer might be felt to be revealed in paragraphs 1 and 2? Is the 'we' of paragraph 3 and onwards ('we would go a part of the way down the lane') the same group as the 'we' of paragraph 1 ('we have a city laundry')?
   vi  Most of this story seems focalized by the boy Quentin, aged nine. What is the evidence to support this view? But paragraph 1 cannot have Quentin as a child as focalizer: it is a view of a scene that only comes into existence

when that child is an adult of twenty-four. And who speaks, in the sense of 'narrates', in this story? Is it an adult narrator who writes (p. 292)

> Dilsey was still sick in her cabin. Father told Jesus to stay off our place. Dilsey was still sick. It was a long time. We were in the library after supper.

vii  Among the focalizeds, can we point to any differences (e.g. in detail of description) between the way the other children, Caddy and Jason, are focalized by Quentin, and the way Nancy is? Why might such differences arise?

viii  Which of the Simpson narrational modes does this story use?

ix  In terms of the six degrees of narratorial intrusion and interpretation listed early in 3.7, there seems scarcely any intrusive commentary here beyond rank 4, i.e. few claims to special knowledge of characters' motives and impulses. What kinds of extra interpretive burdens does this place on the reader? By contrast with the story's 'non-interpretive' norm, consider and discuss the following two cases of intrusive commentary. Are these departures from the general trend defensible, or are they blunders of 'inconsistency in telling'?:

> A  'What is it?' I said. 'What is it?'
> 'I aint nothing but a nigger,' Nancy said. 'It aint none of my fault.'
> She looked at me, sitting in the chair before the cold stove, the sailor hat on her head. I went back to the library. It was the cold stove and all, when you think of a kitchen being warm and busy and cheerful. And with a cold stove and the dishes all put away, and nobody wanting to eat at that hour.
> B  'Jason!' mother said. She was speaking to father.
> You could tell that by the way she said the name. Like she believed that all day father had been trying to think of doing the thing she wouldn't like the most, and that she knew all the time that after a while he would think of it. I stayed quiet, because father and I both knew that mother would want him to make me stay with her if she just thought of it in time. So father didn't look at me.

2  Guided by the kind of questions raised above in the discussion of 'That Evening Sun', attempt a similar analysis of time, focalization, and narration in one of the following short stories: Joyce's 'Counterparts', Flannery O'Connor's 'Revelation', Saul Bellow's 'Looking for Mr Green', or John Updike's 'A & P'; or in the opening paragraphs of Virginia Woolf's *Mrs Dalloway*.

3  In the case of 'Eveline', it was argued, a Genettian relational assessment of duration might conclude that there was no clearly determinable change of pace, since we cannot conclusively determine the real-time duration of events in either of the story's two sections. And yet many readers do feel a great shift in mood, an extraordinary tension between Eveline's frozen attitude and the urgency of departure in the quayside scene. What are the grounds for that impression? The answer may simply be that in the second and concluding section of the story, a *number* of events are actually happening, and Eveline's developing reflections respond to those developing events. In the first section of the story, by contrast, only one thing is happening at basic story level (she is reviewing her past and her plans), even though that one 'action' involves recalling, as embedded particulars, many events and incidents. In terms of perception of narrative pace, as in many other respects, it seems that there is all the difference in the world between (a report of) living a thing and simply recalling it. The second section may be short in time, but is packed with sequenced events. The crucial thing seems not to be a ratio of story time to textual extent but of story time to story events.

4 Much of the discussion in the later stages of this chapter leads towards a consideration of what happens when a narrator wilfully or unwittingly distorts, misleads, or suppresses. The topic of narrational unreliability is an extremely rich theme, and has been probed by critics and theorists extensively for a very long time (cf. Lawrence's warning: 'Never trust the teller, trust the tale'), especially vigorously in the last forty years, since Booth's *Rhetoric of Fiction* appeared. Of particular concern is the (un)reliability of intradiegetic narrators, i.e. narrators visible – if only by way of the first-person pronoun – within the narrative. That is to say, the detection of 'corrupt' narration is especially commonly a challenge set for readers by intrusive/evaluative narrators (Simpson's A and B(R) positives). Narratorial unreliability in modern fiction is very widespread, but often discussed examples include Bellow's *Dangling Man*, Golding's *Free Fall*, Flannery O'Connor's 'Everything that Rises Must Converge', J. M. Coetzee's *Waiting for the Barbarians*, Nadine Gordimer's *The Conservationist*, Ishiguro's *The Remains of the Day*.

   We attribute unreliability to any narrator the veracity of whose account we come to suspect. Some narrators are liars, or consciously flatter themselves and are clearly intended to be seen as attempting to deceive; other narrators mislead for less culpable reasons: e.g. they may have the limited knowledge of a young narrator, or be learning disabled like Benjy in *The Sound and the Fury*. Personal involvement with events – especially when the narrator is a direct or indirect victim of those events – may often give rise to narratorial suppression, distortion, prevarication, and so on (as one example, consider Rosa's account of events in *Absalom! Absalom!*). In a more general way, abnormal values may give rise to a type of unreliability that makes it difficult to decide whether we have a normal narrator telling terrible things with much covert irony, or simply an awful narrator. In assessing veracity and reliability, we have to act rather like a juror, weighing the evidence, looking for internal contradictions in what a narrator says (especially when they serve that narrator's purposes) or a clash between a narrator's representations of things and those of (other) characters whom we have independent grounds for trusting and respecting. The great attraction and danger of unreliable narration is, as Booth (1961) rather regrets, that no clear moral or ideological stance is spelt out and held to, and we as readers are not *told* what to think. But a fully articulated theory of what unreliability consists in, and of the grounds for attributing it to one narrator but not another, remains elusive and contentious. For important recent discussions of the topic, which also usefully challenges us to rethink what we mean by *reliable* narration, see Yacobi (1981), Wall (1994), Nünning (1999), and Fludernik (1999a).

5 In 3.2 I proposed that 'time is perceived repetition within perceived irreversible change'. What warrants that *within*? Why not say, on the contrary, 'time is perceived irreversible change within perceived repetition'? The former formulation assumes change, variation, dynamism, chaos, out of which we pluck or impose the orderly measuring that is the naming of times and dates; the latter formulation assumes an underlying order, structure, and design, from within which erupt changes, departures, and developments (whose location in time is, as it were, already determined). These contrasting foundational assumptions about time, repetition and change can be associated with two sharply counterposed worldviews, which might be called the Nietzschean and the Platonic (see discussion in Lothe, 2000: 65–6, and references there to Deleuze and Hillis Miller).

# 4    The articulation of narrative text II
## Character, setting, suspense, film

## 4.1 Character

Character, and everything it entails in the way of deep insight into the minds of imagined others, their uniqueness of motive and difference of worldview, is often what most powerfully attracts readers to novels and stories. Yet it is the element in narratives that seems least amenable to systematic analysis. As a result it remains relatively neglected within narratological studies. To begin with, many narratologists were unconvinced that here was a genuine topic to explore: what is called the ontological status of character, individuals, and the self, was widely questioned (the ontological status of a thing means its status as a part of existence: in what sense does it 'really' exist, relative to other 'really existing' things?). This was probably part of a widespread reaction, in mid-twentieth-century literary studies, to criticism and analyses which tended to assimilate characters in literature to real people. Thus A. C. Bradley's treatment of Shakespeare's tragedies as if they were the case-histories of real people, which formerly had a profound influence on the study and performance of Shakespeare, was increasingly seen as partial and distorting. There was also something of a reaction against the heavy emphasis on character, the 'bourgeois self-determining Subject', found in both nineteenth-century British novels and traditional literary criticism about them. Nouveaux romanciers such as Robbe-Grillet and Sarraute wrote their novels in a manner defiant of the cult of the individual and any over-valuing of the allegedly unique experience and response of particular personages whose psychologies were to be dramatized. On the contrary, in such experimental fiction at least, similarity of experience and personal behaviour, rather than difference, was asserted. And in tune with this, the structuralist preference was to treat character 'as a myth', as Culler succinctly put it (Culler, 1975a: 230).

Character entails an illusion in which the reader is a creative accomplice. Out of words we make a person. A variety of descriptions of some posited individual, together with descriptions – implicit or explicit – of that individual's actions and reactions, suffice to lead most readers to conceive of a person of whom these references and insights are just glimpses. An iceberg principle is at work in the way most people read characters: we operate on the assumption that the evidence we are shown is a necessarily limited selection of material, that much more lies beneath the surface of the novel, in the rest of that 'person's' life.

But in the textualist–structuralist spirit alluded to above, many have sought to revalue a new literalism which reminds us that novel characters are really 'just words', are radically non-representational, and should not be unthinkingly 'recuperated' by means of any direct and unguarded application of amateur (or professional) psychological analysis. One of the complaints about such responses – common enough in literature classes – is that they ignore the art and textuality of novels, the degree to which character, event, and everything else is a literary production, a construction. The mere verbal surface of novels having been ignored, there is no clear limit to the arabesques of psychologizing: they can spiral on with precious little need for grounding in the text. Surface text can be dismissed as censored testimony, heavily repressed, requiring startlingly unexpected symbolic readings. By contrast, the 'purist' approach to character asserts the non-referential or non-mimetic dimension in narrative art. In Weinsheimer's memorable words (1979: 187):

Emma Woodhouse is not a woman nor need be described as if it were.

There are real differences of foundational assumptions separating the psychologist student of character and the structuralist analyst of the actant. But once we have acknowledged these contrasting viewpoints, it is often sufficient to say that they are adopting quite different criteria for reading narrative, and for identifying great narrative. A dual perspective can find room for both:

In the text characters are nodes in the verbal design; in the story they are – by definition – non (or pre-) verbal abstractions, constructs. Although these constructs are by no means human beings in the literal sense of the word, they are partly modelled on the reader's conception of people and in this they are person-like.

(Rimmon-Kenan, 1983: 33)

The latter part of this quotation tellingly emphasizes 'the reader's conception' (strikingly rare in some of the earlier narrative theory), and recognizes that characters are 'partly modelled' on real people. No matter what some theories assert, readers continue to apprehend most novel characters as individuals (whether seen dimly or sharply, whether recognizable, comprehensible, lisible or impenetrable, alien, and unfathomable). And as those apprehensions are built up, revised, and articulated, all sorts of extra-textual knowledge, including our knowledge of characters in the real world, is brought to bear. Thus while it is a mistake to assume that mimesis or faithful 'capture' of the essential elements of real people is the truest and highest goal of fictional characterization, it would also be mistaken to assume a more radical gulf between the 'fiction' of novels and the 'fact' of the real world than there really is. It is not that literature in all its motile fabricatedness cannot 'map onto' solid stable reality because of the former's instabilities and artifice; rather it is because our sense of reality itself is a fluid construction, prone to shapechanging, that an enduring mapping of it in literature or by other means is impossible. If, instead, we think of the semiotic constructedness of people, things, and non-fictional texts as of the same order as the semiotic constructedness of novels, then we may come to see a middle way. From this perspective, art is not a supplement to life, and hence cannot be simple-mindedly mimetic of it: both art and life generally are understood to be representational.

## 4.2  Greimas' actant model

One way in which character analysis has proceeded, both informally and by more formal and systematic means, involves working with some notion of 'trait', and that is the approach I will chiefly discuss in this chapter. It amounts to a 'bottom-up' approach, a noticing of the accumulating evidence to justify calling a particular character 'athletic' or 'musical' or 'morbid' or whatever the proposed trait might be. But here first, and briefly, I will mention an explicitly 'top-down' approach, the actant model of Greimas (1966). For all its reliance on intuitive schematization, it remains workable and a stimulus to further reflection on character types.

Greimas worked along similar lines to Propp who, we have seen, had earlier identified seven broad narrative roles filled by the main characters in his Russian folktales, but he insisted that these roles were subordinate to the 31 core functions or event-types, which he saw as the backbone or main driving force of all the tales. Now Greimas proposed an inversion, with events subordinated to character. As general categories underlying all narratives, he suggested that there were just six roles, or actants as he termed them, comprising three interrelated pairs:

$$Giver \ + \ Receiver$$
$$Subject \ + \ Object$$
$$Helper \ + \ Opponent$$

The six roles are usually diagrammatized as follows:

sender (superhelper) → object → receiver (beneficiary)

↑

helper → subject ← opponent

Such a model fits many traditional folk and fairytales remarkably well: the subject or hero, perhaps a young man of lowly origin, seeks marriage to a beautiful princess (object), in which case the man will also be the beneficiary (possibly the princess and the country will too). In his quest he is helped generously but with limited success by a friend or relative (helper), but their combined efforts count for little in the struggle against specified opponents (e.g. a wicked uncle of the princess, or some other eligible but ignoble suitor), until a sender (often, in effect, a superhelper), such as the king, or God, or some individual with magical powers for good, intervenes. Here is the actant diagram again, but with possible exponent characters filling the six core roles:

beneficent witch in  → marriage to →   young man, common
    the woods        princess         weal, etc.
↑
friend of young man → young man ← wicked uncle of princess

Despite the model's simplicity, and despite the need to annotate it variously so as to fit different genres better, the scheme can be usefully applied to a range of texts. It is worth noting that two of the roles, sender and object, are frequently not strictly characters at all in modern stories. The sorts of things that count as object in our narratives, and the sorts of special help we may get in our quest of those objects, are more often abstract than concrete. Modern literary narratives are likely to have conditions summarizable as fulfilment, liberation, happiness, self-knowledge, or mental peace, as their object. At the same time there remain plenty of spy stories, Westerns, romances and detective stories where a particular tangible object clearly is the target: a particular criminal or lover, a secret agent or document, or a coveted artefact of some sort. In many genres of modern narrative, the role of giver/sender/superhelper has become quite attenuated; but, again, there is an abundance of science fiction stories, TV series, and Hollywood blockbusters where the intervention of a supporting agent with higher powers remains *de rigeur*. One is tempted to think that this persevering investment or faith in the idea of an intervening superpower is part and parcel of a belief in a transcendent power, authority, and standard. This is often much on display in American popular culture, perhaps related to America's being at present the sole superpower, but versions of it can be found in every culture's narratives. American popular culture often restates a belief in America itself as a superpower, with a special right and mission to intervene, rescue, and restore (the implicit identification of the Rocky/Rambo personae with an imagined America, in those films of the 1980s, particularly suggests this). As long as people embrace myths of American can-do knowhow – or of plucky sangfroid British resourcefulness, for that matter – or of a divine plan ensuring that the virtuous and the oppressed will be finally rewarded – then the superhelper role will surely survive in some of our narratives.

One among many applications of Greimas' six-role schema is offered by Vestergaard and Schroder (1985) in their book on the language of advertising. They demonstrate how well the roles fit the *dramatis personae* in an advertisement for Sanatogen multivitamin tablets. The addressee ('you') is both subject and receiver, continued good health is the object, and your pursuit of this goal is ordinarily assisted by vitamins and minerals from meals (the helper), but made more difficult by some undesirable consequences of your assumed busy life: snack lunches, dieting, reheated food and skipped meals (the opponent). In steps Sanatogen as superhelper: 'Sanatogen multivitamins give you essential vitamins and minerals.' As Vestergaard and Schroder observe:

> Of particular interest are the facts that the role of object is not filled by the product but by some quality or state associated with it, and that the consumer is both subject and receiver. Advertising, in other words, does not try to tell us that we need its products as such, but rather that the products can help us obtain something else which we do feel we need.
>
> (1985: 29)

And the pattern revealed by the Sanatogen ad does seem to apply to a variety of other utilitarian products too: face creams, tampons, beer, radial tyres, breakfast cereals, washing powder, one-coat paint, toothpaste, shampoo, after-shave lotion, and so on. In all advertisements in which, then, there is a narrative-style emphasis on change of state, with a before ('How *can* I get rid of this dandruff?'/'Why *does* my family need so many fillings at the dentist's?') and an after ('I've said goodbye to dandruff, thanks to *Glam*'/'Now we've switched to *Gleaminfangs* the dentist has nothing to do!'), the product fulfils the role of important aid or accessory in reaching or maintaining a certain quality of life whose inherent desirability is – for some targeted audience – unquestionable. I add that caveat about targeted audience because over the last few years there has been an enormous growth of commercial advertising, in narrative format or otherwise, which uses mass-audience media (TV, radio, billboards) while implicitly singling out a particular group of addressees and calculatedly opting to exclude and even alienate a significant proportion of the potential audience.

In some contrast to the advertising of everyday items like lotions and breakfast cereals, it is noticeable that an explicitly narrative format tends to fall away when it comes to promotion of truly luxury items such as perfumes, watches and jewellery, fur coats, very expensive cars, holidays, and so on. In these, a more synecdochic or metonymic relation seems to operate, where the product is presented as an intrinsic part (however small) of the chic and elegant lifestyle that the advertisement typically portrays. (Synecdoche/metonymy is the rhetorical use of a phrase referring to a part of or association with a larger whole, when reference to that larger whole is to be understood; thus two common ways of synecdochically referring to your car are by using the phrases 'my wheels' or 'my motor'.) Instead of representing the sender/superhelper, the product is part of the object. As a consequence, the roles of superhelper, helper and opponent (at least), and any marked sense of a before and an after, are usually absent. Such luxury product advertisements are much more a description than a narrative.

If we turn to application of the Greimas model to a literary narrative, such as Joyce's 'Eveline', we can use it to highlight the degree to which the story is enriched by ambiguity and the paralysing effect of uncertainty, to the point that these become part of the story's theme. Eveline herself is fairly clearly the subject and receiver, and her object would appear to be freedom (especially freedom from verbal and physical abuse) and happiness (at one point she reflects that 'she wanted to live. . . . She had a right to happiness'). In pursuit of this object it first appears that Frank is her helper, while her potentially violent father is chief opponent. But at the close of this very short story it is fairly clear that Eveline does not join Frank on the steamer that would take her away to Buenos Aires. Why is this? Is it due to the failure of a superhelper to appear? For the text reports Eveline invoking such a superhelper:

> Out of a maze of distress, she prayed to God to direct her, to show her what was her duty.

But Eveline's not going is more complex than this. Her prayer is not for assistance with her escape, but with identifying 'what was her duty', i.e. with deciding what *should* be her object, her first consideration. The neat, five-role scenario sketched above is suddenly revealed as susceptible to a rewriting, in which her current hard-working life ('now that she was about to leave it she did not find it a wholly undesirable life'), looking after her father ('Sometimes he could be very nice'), fulfilling her promise to her mother 'to keep the home together as long as she could', collectively undermine previous assumptions as to which (staying or going) is the better object. In pursuit of this reinstated object of familial care and duty, there seem to be two helpers: her father (on some occasions at least), and her brother Harry, who 'always sent up what he could'. The opponent is now Frank, of course, and whether his intentions are honourable or not becomes newly suspect.

But again, we seem to lack a powerful superhelper who might intervene to arbitrate and resolve the choice between going and staying, choosing Frank or the family. No doubt some will see Eveline's 'set[ting] her white face to [Frank]' as a clear choice, where the subject – as in so many modern stories – has looked to resources within herself for the required extra help. But the text does go on to describe her as 'passive, like a helpless animal', which hardly fits an interpretation of Eveline as decisive arbiter, come into her own powers. Ironically, a couple of textual clues may prompt us to consider a physiological dysfunction, a weakness of the heart in the face of acute anxiety, as a covert influence. In the course of Eveline's anguished uncertainty at the quayside, a distress which 'awoke nausea in her body', we are told that 'All the seas of the world tumbled about her heart'. This may be sufficient textual warrant, perhaps, to recall an earlier cryptic allusion to heart trouble:

> Even now ... she sometimes felt herself in danger of her father's violence. She knew it was that that had given her the palpitations.

In their notes on revisions to 'Eveline' between its first magazine appearance and its subsequent publication in the *Dubliners* collection, Scholes and Litz remark on 'the interesting addition of the palpitations' (Scholes and Litz, 1969: 239). As we read those earlier sentences we are entitled to question this analeptic allusion: *What* palpitations? At the close of the story, with Eveline paralysed physiologically as well as imaginatively, we possibly see their effect.

## 4.3  Character traits and attributes

In many modern narratives of the more complex kind, the basic role or function of a character as explored in the previous section – what the character *does*, in the plot – turns out to be far less interesting to the reader than what the character is like. This is something of a paradox: what a character does in a story may be essential for the text to count as a well-formed narrative ('He gets the girl in the end'/'She detects and traps the killer', etc.), but what interests us is what kind of super-helper Sherlock Holmes is shown to be, and just how he conducts himself in the course of particular scenes and episodes. Details of characterization, the kind of material that we have seen Barthes label as Indices or (mere) Informants, often irrelevant to story, are equally often just what the reader finds engrossing in a text. In deciding these judgments of type and manner of character conduct we are inevitably very much guided – as Bal (1985: 80) notes – by data from reality or extratextual situations. We carry to our reading of a Sherlock Holmes tale plentiful knowledge gleaned from various sources about doctors, detectives, crimes and human entanglements. We may have ideas about more marginal aspects too, that are relevant to a Holmes story, such as the nature of housekeepers, of pedestrian traditional policework, and of Victorian beggars and urchins (and social stratification in general). We may have even stood in London's Baker Street, looking – at least metaphorically – for 221b, Holmes's fabled residence.

What this amounts to saying is that, in our making sense of any particular text, we have extensive resources of knowledge (sometimes called extratextual knowledge, or knowledge of the world), which we can bring to bear on our intepretation of the text under scrutiny. That 'bringing to bear' will vary from reader to reader in at least two broad ways, to do with the quality (depth, accuracy) of a reader's knowledge, and the interpretive evaluation the reader makes of that knowledge. We might summarize these two components of adducible background knowledge as facts and ideology.

To take a simple example, suppose I am reading a text which runs:

> It is August 1880, and the prosperous streets of London's West End are busy with the carriages of ladies on leisurely shopping expeditions. The afternoon is warm and sunny, but in the shaded doorway of a house off Regent Street can be discerned the crouching form of a beggar.

In the final words here an individual has been specified and, potentially at least, we have encountered the first introduction of an important character. But even without reading on, a certain fleshing out of that single descriptive phrase, 'a beggar', takes place. I have some ideas about what 'a beggar' is or means, but I additionally have ideas about what a London beggar *circa* 1880 would be like, based on my own knowledge of late Victorian social history, from whatever sources.

That knowledge is partial – in two senses, the factual and the ideological. The partial factual knowledge means that I cannot bring to mind a depth of knowledge, and perhaps understanding, of the beggar that is available to someone familiar with the details of the economic, social, spiritual, etc. life of Victorian beggars. The ideological partiality means that I may have a certain view of Victorian beggars in general; I may regard them as the victims of callous and inhuman neglect, a living index of a moral degeneracy in the larger society. Ideologically of course that is just one way of looking at Victorian beggars, and other readers may alternatively assume that the dysfunction lies principally within the beggars themselves. Notice, too, that in these ideological glossings of the simple textual denomination 'a beggar', I have been treating the beggar as some sort of problem to be solved. That kind of emphasis seems triggered by the very term 'beggar'; it seems to be part of the interpretive semantic field the term invokes, of a kind that is more extensive and subjective than anything covered by a traditional dictionary entry. By comparison, consider what may happen interpretively if the text instead ends in this way:

> in the shaded doorway ... can be discerned the crouching form of a Buddhist monk.

Now a rather different body of extratextual knowledge is brought to bear in a reader's probabilistic characterization. Among other things, they might note greater incongruity here, on the assumption that Buddhist monks were rare in the London of 1880. But, despite the fact that Buddhist monks rely on begged donations of food to live, the text has not called this individual a beggar nor is the reader likely, ideologically, to take the monk's begging as the primary issue to have a view on.

Before proceeding it is perhaps worth stressing that limitations of knowledge and partiality of view are not inherently disqualificatory. Some readers will have fuller extratextual knowledge than others, or ideologies more congruent with the narrator's than other readers have, but we cannot predetermine the relevance of those facts and views. The knowledgeable reader may read too much into a marginal reference or character. Background facts and views are to do with actual Victorian beggars in general: this particular beggar may be a very special one – Sherlock Holmes in disguise, or one with mystical powers – so that the general type is of limited help in our grasp of this particular character. The essential fact, despite the need for revision and amendment of our probabilistic assessments as our reading of a text proceeds, is that we do undertake this inference-based fleshing-out of seemingly slight textual data, in character-comprehension as in other matters. (The role of inference in relation to children's narratives will be examined in Chapter 7.)

## 4.4  Distinctive feature characterology

The interactive matching of textual facts and ideology with extratextual facts and ideology that I have outlined above is, like the method of event identification sketched at the close of Chapter 2, a 'bottom-up' type of processing: it is, I would submit, an important feature of the experiential real-time activity of reading, something we do as we read a text, not something postponed, or really postponable, until the entire text has been read, when a holistic overview can be attempted. In principle, the 'semantic feature' approach to character that I am about to discuss could be undertaken either developmentally and incrementally or holistically, although it tends to be presented in the latter way and may therefore appear overly static. But if applied non-statically this resolutely structural approach can be of value too.

A semantic feature analysis of the characters of a text involves specifying a limited list of what the analyst takes to be the crucial features or attributes which distinguish particular characters. Assuming that no two characters are identical, a rather limited set of attributes needs to be drawn up, attributes that (in a simple system) a character can either have or not have, such that no two characters are assigned an identical set of attributes. This method asks: What are the most important ways in which any two characters differ? What are the narratively significant differences between characters? In this way, it is intended, a simple but useable schematic picture can be drawn up of all the crucial ways in which particular characters are the same as others and different from others. The approach is based on distinctive feature phonology and componential semantic analysis: influential methods of analyzing the fundamental dimensions of sounds and meanings, respectively, in a language. For introductory discussion of these methods see, e.g. Finegan (1994), Fromkin and Rodman (1978), or Bolinger (1981). An interesting demonstration of distinctive feature (or semic) analysis of characters is to be found in Fowler (1977: 36–8).

Although Bal suggests we might extend the modelling to note variations in degree (how weak or strong?) and modality (how probably?) of attribute manifestation, this would be departing some way from the analytical simplicity of the basic technique. That technique, within its own limits, is interesting in its highlighting of essential distinctions between characters as the analyst sees them. There need be no requirement in distinctive-feature 'characterology' (as there would be in standard distinctive feature analysis conducted by different analysts on the same dialect), that all reader–analysts see the same set of features as significant, and agree over their presence or absence, in a text's characters. Such variant emphases in analyses are in themselves, and in their reflection of analysts' assumptions, an indication of interpretive and even ideological divergences.

Among the fundamental elements in character analysis, a particular delimitable topic that often attracts attention is simply the way a character is designated in a text: in making reference to the character, in what ways and in what proportions does the narrative make use of a proper name or names, of definite descriptions, and of pronouns? The diverse and potentially nuanced ways of naming a character, in the course of the narrative, can create effects of irony or of sympathy, of narratorial approval or distaste. And these can be quite complex, given that there is usually an ongoing designating of several characters in any stretch of text by these varied means. In the opening paragraph of Henry James's story 'The Pupil' (discussed in Leech and Short, 1981), for example, the young man applying for the position of resident tutor is referred to, in order, in the following varied ways:

> The poor young man ... him ... he ... (his) ... he ... he ... he ... (his) ... he ... the candidate for the honour of taking his [the boy's] education in hand ... this personage ... he ... (his)

None of the phrasal descriptions here (*the poor young man, this personage*), we may surmise, would be adopted by the man to describe himself or his position (we learn his surname, Pemberton, only in the second paragraph). Embedded in the given text, the definite descriptions in particular are a simple means of characterization which is also subtly evaluative, covertly creating a tone of distanced sympathy for Pemberton, distanced enough to permit ironical treatment of his situation. The picture is further complicated in that, for example, in:

> [the little boy] looked straight and hard at the candidate for the honour of taking his education in hand

the description of Pemberton is as if it were the boy's view of the situation. And that example is a small indication of the complexity that emerges once we consider the varied sources from which our information about characters may come (from the character him- or herself, from another character, from an external narrator, and so on).

Another heavily exploited means of characterization, often with the assumption that outer surfaces reflect inner essence, is description of characters' outward appearance – especially their clothes and facial features. Given the rarity (still) of surgical adjustments, we tend to think of the latter as attributes a character is simply blessed with or stuck with, and we may tend to reject any claimed causal link between appearance and personality (such theories of physiognomy and phrenology, popular in the nineteenth century, influenced writers such as Balzac and Dickens). On the other hand powerful cultural and biological traditions associate appearance with identity and character, the immediately 'readable' former being taken as to some degree indicative, expressive and even constitutive of the latter – as you can confirm if you frown at the next person you make eye-contact with. Among countless literary examples we can mention Cyrano de Bergerac's protruding nose as one of his more significant attributes, thwarting his romantic quest, while Falstaff's vast belly or 'womb' is similarly non-incidental to character and story: his great waist reflects his culpable great waste(fulness) as well as his verbal or situational fecundity, as the play's puns insist. And the smallpox that (mercifully, only temporarily) disfigures Esther Summerson (in *Bleak House*) does threaten her likelihood of marrying and so threatens to alter the course of the story. Then again, some features of physical appearance such as body shape, hair style, facial expression (propensity to frown, with head lowered, as opposed to a smiling disposition with an enquiring tilt of the head) are judged to be partly under a character's control, something for which they can be held accountable.

The source of character apperception that I have neglected most severely is the business of implicit characterization, based on how a character *acts*. We can always be judged by our deeds, of course, and in some narratives oriented to events, descriptions and evaluations of characters are so scarce that such indirect characterization is a reader's only recourse. Sometimes this points to the narrator's rather limited interest in 'telling character': instead, what happened is the overriding interest. But sometimes an indirectness of presentation is adopted for other reasons, where an interest in characters and individuals remains strong. As Rimmon-Kenan has noted (1983: 60–1), a good proportion of twentieth-century fiction has tended to opt for indirectness of presentation, a 'showing' of character; often this is done out of respect for the ability of the reader to infer, evaluate, and draw conclusions on the basis of presented behaviour, rather than of direct (and directive) presentation, an authoritative 'telling' of how a character is.

## 4.5 Setting

I have space only to touch on a few key aspects of the role of setting in narrative text. Perhaps the first thing to say is that, although an elaboration of setting is less essential to written narrative than event and character are (we require a narrative to contain a sequence of events involving change, and prefer those changes to involve or affect individuals with whom we can sympathize or identify), the establishment of an identifiable setting is a strong psychological preference in most readers. We like, in our reading of narratives, to know where we are, and look for clear spatiotemporal indications of just where and when a thing happened. And it must be emphasized that all of this discussion relates to setting in verbal narratives; in film narratives, by contrast, setting is in a sense immediately and overwhelmingly available, and plays a prominent role in the process of narration.

Just how specific a written narrative setting is expected to be seems relative to genre, type, and so on. Thus a story about a hen that outsmarts a fox, a fable-like text whether for adults or children, does not need precise anchorage to some particular farm of specified layout, with its fields, machinery, and livestock described. Such particularity would even strike us as bizarre, where the story's power rests in its generic truth, its 'pansituational' universality. We can even cope quite happily with stories about hens and foxes where the word 'farm' never appears: unless we learn to the contrary, we simply assume a stereotypical rural background. Relatedly, in Fielding and Austen novels that revolve around big houses and their estates, parsonages, inns, and so on, the particularities of those backcloths are rarely important. Settings in broad terms are of course important here, for example, the fact that Fanny Price's parents live in a poky little house in Portsmouth while her uncle and aunt live in a grand house at Mansfield Park. And, in the same novel, it is important that the library in which the younger people present their entertainment is not quite a suitable setting, just as the whole enterprise of the play is not quite suitable. But the details of these settings are rarely crucial, since they are rarely instrumental in plot development or a refraction of character.

In many modern novels, however, in which the oppressions of the built environment (industrialized, technologized, homogenized) may be a prominent theme, setting may be much more than backcloth. It may be instrumental – like another character – in leading a character to act in a certain way. This fuller role for setting – quasi-animate, menacing or soothing, chorus-like or emblematic – goes back in the classical English novel at least as far as Dickens, and continued to develop and modulate in the work of George Eliot, Hardy, and Lawrence. But one genre of novels where setting operates like a participant long antedates Dickens: the Gothic novel tradition. Interestingly, for most modern readers, there is 'too much setting' in the Gothic novel, or it is cast in an implausibly prominent role – with its dark, mysterious mansions bristling with medieval towers, secret chapels, and concealed hallways and tunnels. In American fiction setting seems to have been more prominent in the early literature than more recently: in Cooper's Leatherstocking novels, in Poe copiously (most memorably, perhaps, in 'The Fall of the House of Usher'), in the American Gothic tradition that descended through Hawthorne to Faulkner, and in Twain (what would *Huckleberry Finn* be without the raft and the river?). Setting is probably to the fore in that literature for good reason. Post-Independence American culture was sharply aware that it constituted a new nation emerging on new terms in what was (for the settlers) a new land: 'received' European settings would not do. But for all its memorable depiction in more recent American fiction – in Ellison, Bellow, Pynchon, Updike, Morrison, Silko and DeLillo – it is doubtful whether setting routinely has quite the same instrumental role in postmodern fiction that it perhaps had in modernist fiction. Increasingly – it may be argued – our post- or late-modernist globalized condition makes particularity of setting unimportant.

In simple terms, the relations between setting on the one hand, and character and events on the other, may be causal or analogical: features of the setting may be (in part at least) either cause or effect of how characters are and behave; or, more by way of reinforcement and symbolic congruence, a setting may be *like* a character or characters in some respects. As an example of character:setting causal relations might be cited in Miss Emily's decaying house in Faulkner's 'A Rose for Miss Emily', which in turn is reminiscent of Miss Havisham's wedding breakfast room in *Great Expectations*. In most Dickens novels, it is easy to find causally-determinative or -determined settings, from the fog-choked Chancery of *Bleak House* to the debtor's prison of *Little Dorrit*. In Faulkner, similarly, setting counts: in 'Barn Burning', the wretched temporary hovel which the Snopes family move into matches their miserable and oppressed temperaments just as surely as the shining white mansion of their new landlord, Major De Spain, suits the grandeur and refinement of the major and, especially, his Eastern-travelled wife. But contrary to Sartoris's hope or assumption, there will unavoidably be some dirty intercourse between these impossibly different worlds – here in the form of the soiled, unrestorable rug.

Examples of analogical relation, where setting is like character in some respect, are too much the norm to merit extensive comment. This is the case particularly in relation to habitation where, in normal circumstances, a character is likely to have some control over the kind of rooms or house that they are shown to live in: in such cases, it should be unsurprising that the house 'fits' or reflects its occupier. On the other hand in many narratives a character does not have such control over their own living conditions, so that an 'unlikeness' is equally possible. Toni Morrison's Sethe in *Beloved* and Dickens's Oliver Twist are two examples of this, but we might also mention Eveline, seemingly looking for the last time around the dusty room which is not *her* room. But where it does obtain, analogical relation of setting to character is more interesting when it involves a matching of character with the larger natural environment, rather than merely with residence. For this can hardly be by character design: Heathcliff and Catherine (in *Wuthering Heights*) have not *made* the wild, stormy, elemental moorlands match their temperaments, so that if this is by design it is that of a higher invisible power. And similarly Captain Ahab (in *Moby Dick*) and Kurtz (in *Heart of Darkness*) are mesmerizingly congruent with their extremity of setting. But perhaps more common than clear instances of causality or analogy are texts which are indeterminate between these two types of relation. Hardy's 'characterizations' of Egdon Heath in *The Return of the Native*, for example, are so distracting and compelling partly because we sense, but cannot fathom, the influences that the heath has on specific characters.

While many of these examples tend towards the broadly Gothic or personifactory, it is also true that far more conventional, 'undramatized', settings play an important part in promoting verisimilitude and indirect characterization. Senior civil servants have to live in a 'civil servant' style of housing (unless there is good reason for the unexpected in domiciliary setting): that is the unmarked option. Here the broad details of the house (detached; with several bedrooms, a large kitchen and a detached brick garage; in Surrey or Berkshire), and the garden (half-acre; well-kept; lawn, roses, and fruit trees), in their emphases on the comfortable, rational and unostentatious, will be assumed to be characterizing. So too will the specifics of the internal furnishing (the living room has an original Victorian landscape over the genuine and occasionally-used fireplace, the comfortable armchairs are from Heal's, no television can be seen, but the hi-fi – with CD and DVD player – is well-stocked with Deutsche Gramophon recordings, etc.). All such details of setting articulate their owner's intelligence, conservative good taste, moderate wealth, cultured values – and utter remoteness from, say, refugees or eco-warriors.

The above stereotyping need not be very close to the facts about real senior civil servants' homes and interests, some of whom may be so abnormal as to vote for the Green Party and guzzle Diet Coke while playing their Abba favourites. The point is that, in simplifying and standardizing the world around us, we construct stereotyped portraits of civil servants – and doctors, spies, politicians, travel agents, farmers, shopkeepers, garage mechanics – and of how they live. In particular texts – again, unless there is good reason for things to be to the contrary – we expect particular spies and farmers broadly to match our stereotypes.

A false impression could easily be drawn from the foregoing concentration on stereotyping, extratextual, knowledge-based inferencing, and on familiarity and predictability of characters and their behaviour. It could be inferred that characters are mere assemblages of devices, artificial constructs whose seemingly natural properties are themselves convention-bound, being the kinds of attributes particularly valued or 'privileged' by the societies from which those narratives have emerged. But the view of character as convention-based and convention-bound, common in structuralist treatments, can easily be overstated. It will seem most plausible if the analyst focusses on similarities in characterizations within and between texts to the neglect of those differences not amenable to structuralist explanation. In the case of literary narratives at least, I would want finally to emphasize their richness of narratorial and characterological texture. This permits the construction or projection of characters who are not 'natural' of course, but are still sufficiently distinctive and unique to transcend dismissal as merely conventional; they are what Forster called 'rounded' characters. What would Dorothea Brooke have done if she had met Ladislaw before Casaubon? How would Lambert Strether have lived if he had stayed on in Paris? Did Cash spend the rest of his life with Anse Bundren and his new wife? Will Sethe and Paul D marry? We may speculate (and it does not immediately seem absurd to do so), but we can hardly project mechanically, for these characters are neither so static nor so predictable.

If these points are plausible, a revaluation of Bradley's analyses of Shakespeare's characters seems in order. His approach cannot claim to furnish adequate accounts of the tragedies as aesthetic wholes, but, as Chatman shows in a spirited and persuasive defence (1978: 107–38), analyses invoking relevant categories from the general vocabulary of psychology can lead to original and plausible interpretative conclusions.

## 4.6  Character and setting in 'The Dead'

In order to demonstrate in more detail the textual means by which character and setting are articulated, I will concentrate on the final story in Joyce's *Dubliners*, 'The Dead'. The story's opening is as follows:

> Lily, the caretaker's daughter, was literally run off her feet. Hardly had she brought one gentleman into the little pantry behind the office on the ground floor and helped him off with his overcoat then the wheezy hall-door bell clanged again and she had to scamper along the bare hallway to let in another guest. It was well for her she had not to attend to the ladies also. But Miss Kate and Miss Julia had thought of that and had converted the bathroom upstairs into a ladies' dressing-room. Miss Kate and Miss Julia were there, gossiping and laughing and fussing, walking after each other to the head of the stairs, peering down over the banisters and calling down to Lily to ask her who had come.
>
> It was always a great affair, the Misses Morkan's annual dance. Everybody who knew them came to it . . .
>
> (175)

This opening is focalized from Lily's orientation, and bears many traces of her speech which we may remark on later in this chapter. But here the chief things to note are that three named individuals are introduced, the first an employee of the other two. We do not yet know whether any of these will play a major role in the story, but in the given situation at least, it being 'the Misses Morkans' annual dance', the two sisters will be prominent since they are the hosts. And the setting is evidently a modest private house, one which is both a residence and a place of work, if the reference to the ground-floor office is rightly interpreted. For this special occasion – an annual dance – *pro tem* conversions of a ground-floor pantry and an upstairs bathroom, into dressing-rooms, have been contrived.

Already the indices of genteel standards upheld despite straitened financial circumstances are numerous. We note again, in the setting description, the 'wheezy hall-door bell', the 'bare hallway', and the evidently short distance separating Kate and Julia at the head of the stairs from Lily down below. This is no grand house, nor one that is opulently furnished. Modest means, and a sense of things worn but still functioning (the bell is wheezy, but works) seem to be the tenor. Perhaps, analogously, the Misses Morkan are 'worn but still functioning', but we cannot yet be certain of their age. They're old enough to throw – annually – a party for ladies and gentlemen, and we may associate their 'fussing', in particular, with stereotypical spinsterly behaviour. But equally important are the indications that they go together, behave alike, and have a shared life: they are named together in a coordinate phrase, we are told (analeptically) that they had resolved the dressing-room problem together, and they respond identically to their sense of excitement, 'walking after each other to the head of the stairs', and so on.

On the basis of the above evidence, we are already entertaining quite elaborate ideas about the women introduced and their manner of living. All this is under way even before the second paragraph, a mixture of analepsis and descriptive pause, which reports that the residence is a dark gaunt house on Usher's Island, the upper part of which they had rented from Mr Fulham, the corn-factor on the ground floor (176) and that the Misses Morkan's only niece, Mary Jane, lives with them and is now 'the main prop of the household'. Typical of the revisions we may often have to make in our constructions of character and setting, we now – in the light of the reference to the corn-factor on the ground floor – have to cancel any supposition that the ground-floor office is the Morkans' place of work. Other inferences are confirmed, however: the sisters are old – Julia is quite grey, Kate is too feeble to move from the house. Yet these women are resilient, independent, committed to certain standards: from Lily's focalizing perspective, they consume 'the best of everything: diamond-bone sirloins, three-shilling tea and the best bottled stout', and 'would not stand ... back answers'.

To begin on a distinctive feature or trait analysis we need simply to draw up a list of characters, set out across the page, and a list of attributes set out down the page, and note the occurrence or otherwise of each attribute in each character. But an ambiguity arises where the absence of a trait is noted: absence may mean 'no indicators of the presence of' or 'evident lack of'. For example, if a character is marked as

'+ strongminded', does the negative counterpart denote average strength of mind or downright pusillanimity? Here lies a problematic difference from distinctive feature phonology; there, anything not [+labial] is inescapably [−labial], but we cannot similarly say that anyone not strongminded is automatically weakminded. I proceed below on the assumption that, in the case of gradable attributes such as youthfulness (by contrast with absolute attributes, such as male/female, single/married), I am marking only presence or absence of the specified trait, with no further assumption that absence of a trait implies the presence of its opposite. Thus, in terms of the example above, we will need to note positively weakminded characters on a separate trait dimension from that of +/−strongminded.

Table 4.1 is merely a first approximation. On rereading the story several of these may be dropped from the reckoning as not being particularly salient, while yet others may merit inclusion. A close look at the table will show, for example, that 'self-conscious', 'narcissistic' and 'superior' have identical profiles and thus do nothing to distinguish the characters: two of these classifiers can be discarded, or the three categories can be merged. And some of these attributes are greatly in need of annotation. Thus the important adjective 'generous' I attribute to Kate and Julia (the party puts them to real expense they can ill afford, their concern for their guests seems utterly genuine), to Gretta in the generosity of her memory of Michael Furey, but not to Gabriel, despite the numerous textual allusions to his generosity. For all those allusions are suspect or qualified in some respect, whether it is his self-restoring tipping of Lily; or his wife asserting,

*Table 4.1* Character-trait inventory for 'The Dead'

|                | Kate/Julia | Miss Ivors | Gretta | M. Furey | Gabriel | D'Arcy |
|----------------|:----------:|:----------:|:------:|:--------:|:-------:|:------:|
| Female         | +          | +          | +      | −        | −       | −      |
| Young          | −          | +          | +      | +        | +       | +      |
| Old            | +          | −          | −      | −        | −       | −      |
| Married        | −          | −          | +      | −        | +       | −      |
| Vulnerable     | +          | ?          | +      | +        | −/+     | −      |
| Vigorous       | −          | +          | −      | −        | +       | ?      |
| Passionate     | −          | ?          | ?      | +        | −       | −      |
| Emotional      | +          | −          | +      | +        | ?       | −      |
| 'Generous'     | +          | ?          | +      | +        | ?       | −      |
| 'Mortal'       | +          | +          | −      | +        | −/+     | −      |
| Frank          | +          | +          | +      | +        | −       | +      |
| Covert         | −          | −          | −      | −        | +       | −      |
| Fussy          | +          | −          | −      | −        | ?       | +      |
| Narcissistic   | −          | −          | −      | −        | +       | +      |
| Superior       | −          | −          | −      | −        | +       | +      |
| Humble         | +          | −          | −      | +        | −/+     | −      |
| Self-conscious | −          | −          | −      | −        | +       | +      |
| Erotic         | −          | +          | +      | +        | ?       | −      |
| Prosperous     | −          | ?          | +      | −        | +       | +      |

'You are a very generous person, Gabriel' (217) even as Gabriel, fired by covert physical desire for her, strives 'to restrain himself from breaking out into brutal language about the sottish Malins and his pound'; or the 'generous tears' that fill his eyes later (223), which are not so much tears for Michael Furey but a self-pitying sorrow that he, Gabriel, has never felt so selfless a passion for a woman. Similar qualificatory annotation should accompany the trait 'mortal' – by which I mean whether or not a character seems to have a sense of his or her own mortality. At the opening of the story, *mortal* seems no more than a playful meiosis to Gabriel, complaining of the 'three mortal hours' it takes Gretta to prepare for the party (thereafter the story duration itself extends to little more than three mortal hours); by the story's close, all his thoughts are on death and fading away. In this respect, and perhaps in others (from −[sense of] vulnerability to +vulnerability?), it seems clear that Gabriel changes in the course of the story. In the table I have separated earlier and later attributions with a slash mark. Some such marking of characterological development – where that occurs significantly – does require representation. So −/+ in the table does not mean 'simultaneously having and not having the attribute' but, developmentally, 'initially not having and later having the attribute'.

I shall leave the reader to explore in detail what the table implies about individual characters and 'overlapping' characters. I will simply note that it does draw our attention to the extent to which Gabriel is more like D'Arcy than he is like Michael Furey, and the extent to which Gretta is more like Michael Furey than she is like Gabriel. If we set aside the first four attributes (none of which are conditions on the basis of which we could reasonably pass a moral judgment on a character), it is quite striking that, at least at the outset of the story, Gabriel and Michael Furey contrast on practically every trait. We might also note that the table implies that Gabriel is the only character that displays 'trait-change': might it be that those characters showing trait changes, or question-marks against trait-attributions, are those that readers find most interesting?

If we turn to setting in the story, we find subtle exploitations of the ambience of setting, of change of ambience with change of setting, and of noticeable inappropriateness of behaviour to setting. There is first the public setting of the drawing room, where the music and dancing goes on, and the more private back room, where the drinks are dispensed. In very broad terms, there seem to be styles of interaction appropriate to those domains, but it may be that the major determinant of these styles is the fact that one room has the music and more women than men while the other has the alcohol and more men than women. The public discourse of the drawing-room setting can degenerate into the inconsequentiality of Mrs Malins's ramblings (rendered in free indirect discourse),

> Her son-in-law was a splendid fisher. One day he caught a fish, a beautiful big big fish, and the man in the hotel boiled it for their dinner.
>
> (191)

while in the drinks room a discordant note may be struck when the prevailing tenor, of masculine familiarity, is over-extended, as when Mr
Browne speaks 'a little too confidentially' to the young ladies. This
refreshments room undergoes a change of status, however, when it
becomes the supper-room dominated by a table laden with Christmas
delights, the stage for Gabriel's speech of thanks extolling 'genuine warm-
hearted courteous Irish hospitality' (203), 'good fellowship' and celebrating 'the Three Graces of the Dublin musical world' (204). But
particularly telling are the arhythmic awkwardnesses of atmosphere in the
transitional scene that takes place in the hall as various guests prepare to
leave. This is the occasion both of D'Arcy's needless but revealing rude-
ness and of his rendition (distantly) of 'The Lass of Aughrim', a song that
stirs such strong memories in Gretta (whose outward reactions stir such
strong but unrelated feelings in Gabriel).

Because the main dialogue takes place in the hall itself, but the characters and their words also relate both to the pantomime with the cabman
out on the street and to D'Arcy singing upstairs, complex spatial relations
between the near and the far develop. If the antics with the cabman are a
farce which the audience impatiently waits to depart, the song, expressing
tragedy, is a performance the audience yearns to draw near. Like Pnin's
memories of Mira Belochkin, the song retells (brings near again) an old
grief, but only works properly when heard at a distance: D'Arcy's voice is
'made plaintive by distance' (210). (Here, in fact, is a spatial articulation of
grief that we can set beside the temporal one sketched earlier in 3.2.1.)
And it is just the special configuration of perspectives and focalizations
that Gabriel experiences – 'a woman standing on the stairs in the shadow,
listening to distant music' – that makes him think of this as a picture, as
symbolic. The reader, relatedly, is prompted to interpret this 'audio-
spatial' scene symbolically – but with the enrichment that for us Gabriel,
too, is within the symbolic scene.

But nowhere in 'The Dead' is setting more powerfully used than in the
closing paragraphs, as Gabriel lies down beside his sleeping wife, and
reflects on the evening's events, which have concluded in such an unforeseen way with his wife's revelations. Critics continue to dispute whether
Gabriel here 'transcends' his earlier limitations and inversions of vision
and sympathy. But what seems beyond dispute is that setting here takes
on the role of companion and herald, then catalyst, and finally, in the
ubiquitously falling snow, of essence. Certainly, as he and Gretta
approach their hotel bedroom, and seeing things from Gabriel's viewpoint as we do, the setting they are approaching promises to determine
events: always usually surrounded by family and responsibilities, for this
one night Gabriel imagines they can be young lovers again, filling the
room with their passion and lust. But we see how his projection of setting
and events modulates into a different version as Gabriel comes to see the
room as a cold, dark, rented box to lie down in. There is a challenge here
to the stylistic analyst to chart the linguistic means by which, quite

rapidly, the categories of character and setting begin to dissolve, the text announcing at one point, 'His own identity was fading out into a grey impalpable world' (223).

## 4.7 Creating surprise and suspense in narratives

A crucial means of enriching character and event presentation, closely tied to matters of plot progression, is the topic of this section: the ways in which narratives are made more experientially engaging of the reader by effects of either suspense or surprise. How exactly are these quite different effects narratively created? My interest is specifically in *plot*-based suspense and surprise and not, for example, the arguably less-powerful suspense created by delayed identification of the true perpetrator in crime and detection stories.

Consider Katherine Mansfield's short story, 'Bliss'. The story thematizes Bertha's 'bliss', her sense of charged gladness at being who she is and where she is, and now, at the dinner party that is the story's backcloth, seemingly alive with sexual desire for her husband Harry for perhaps the first time, blissfully in love with him and their life together. And then, to our and Bertha's devastating surprise, at the very close of the evening, she finds that Harry is evidently embroiled in a passionate affair with Pearl Fulton, the cool enigmatic beauty with whom she, Bertha, had thought – when jointly admiring a pear tree in the garden – that she had achieved a special communion. Turning towards the glittering pear tree, Bertha ends the story on a note of painful suspense: 'Oh what is going to happen now?'. Two further examples will be given: from Jane Smiley's novella, *The Age of Grief* and Hemingway's story, 'Indian Camp'.

*The Age of Grief* tells the story of a marital break-up interspersed with the story of a virulent influenza, which in turn hits every member of this affluent professional-class Canadian family who, one might imagine, could not be damaged by something so banal, so nineteenth century, as the 'flu'. Both parents, and each daughter in turn is laid low by the sickness, only to gradually recover; and then Stephanie, the toughest child, succumbs, her fever rising to a steady 105 degrees, and eventually falls unconscious. Smiley brilliantly builds the suspense over whether Stephanie will actually die from the 'flu' – all focalized from the viewpoint of the father, a successful dentist like his estranged wife. And it is partly because the focalized narrative has shown us, in detail, other family members falling sick but then recovering, that we all the more fear that the outcome with Stephanie may be different, and bad.

'Indian Camp' appears to be the story of how Nick Adams and his doctor father and his uncle George, on a fishing trip, come to the aid of a pregnant Indian woman who goes into labour prematurely. Her life and that of the baby can only be saved – if they can be saved – if Dr Adams performs a Caesarian section using whatever tools are to hand, and, of course, without anaesthetic. Suspense is created as the reader hastens to learn the fate of woman and baby. Despite the woman's terrible pain (it causes her to bite George, who is helping to hold her down), she and the baby come through, and all appears to be ending well, with Dr Adams particularly proud of his efforts: we are told he feels 'exalted . . . as football players are in the dressing room after a game'. But with the suspense past, the reader is in for a powerful surprise. With his patients settled, the doctor turns to the Indian woman's husband.

> 'Ought to have a look at the proud father. They're usually the worst sufferers in these little affairs,' the doctor said. 'I must say he took it all pretty quietly.'

The reader is unlikely to have remembered the text's earlier brief references to the man, who is lying under a blanket on the bunk bed above his wife's bed: the wound in his foot, his smelly pipe smoking, or his subsequent rolling over against the wall. Now the doctor draws back the blanket to see the man, and the reporting is quite straightforward, matter-of-fact, and unconcealing: 'His throat had been cut from ear to ear', and this by his own hand – an open razor is found in the blankets – evidently having found his wife's suffering unbearable.

Stories such as *The Age of Grief* and 'Indian Camp' would suggest that plot-based suspense is created where two broad conditions obtain:

1   the narrative 'forks' in a Barthesian sense of reaching a point of development where very few (often just two) alternative continuations or outcomes is highly predictable, so that one or two (just a few) narrrative completions are clearly 'foreseen' by the reader.
2   at this point of narrative forking between broadly predictable completions, both or all such completions are 'withheld': the disclosure of just which completion obtains in the present narrative is noticeably delayed, beyond its earliest reasonable report.

A simple example of condition 1 would be where a character in a story decides to smuggle an illegal item through customs. Several pages of narrative might then report the character's journey to their point of departure from the first country. None of those pages would be suspenseful in the sense specified here, though they could be 'gripping', interesting, anxiety-inducing, etc. But once the character reaches customs, so that imminent reporting can be expected as to whether or not they are stopped and caught, then any delay or elaboration of those next steps creates and constitutes suspense.

Where it occurs, suspenseful text is likely to be marked by quasi-Labovian (see Chapter 6) evaluative text: descriptions of states, moods, settings, ongoing circumstances without clear temporal limits (with intensifying effects); reports of flashbacks, flashforwards, hypothetical and imagined outcomes, and contemporary events other than those of the presently-focussed-upon narrative line (comparator and correlative effects); and reports of background causes, motivations (explication). Sometimes, suspense can be achieved by 'cutting' to seemingly entirely unrelated events, such as a wholly separate narrative line (as Dickens does in cutting between two narratives in *Bleak House*).

Conditions 1 and 2 above do not include any requirement to the effect that a resolution or outcome must be disclosed, so as to bring an end to the prolonged uncertainty created during condition 2. In Raymond Carver's story 'The Bath', a little boy called Scotty is knocked down by a car on his birthday, the day on which his mother was to have collected a birthday cake ordered from a local baker. Scotty then lies in a coma for several days at the hospital, attended by his desperately anxious parents. From soon after Scotty's removal to hospital, then, the story is suspenseful as we, like the parents, wait for a completive resolution. But the story ends with the beginning, only, of a phone call: 'This has to do with Scotty, yes ...' – so that no end to the suspense is reached. (In Carver's later re-working of the story, 'A Small, Good Thing', suspense is released since we witness Scotty's death; thereafter a minor secondary suspense is created when the wife goes down to the baker's premises intent on assaulting him for his harassing phone-calls.)

Narrative surprise of the kind that is of interest here seems to occur where, somewhat in contrast to suspense, a different initial condition obtains:

1   the narrative has approached and may be presumed to be passing an unproblematic 'milestone', where there is little or no sense of potential forking into different sequels and where, rather, a stereotypical or schematic next event or scene is strongly predicted. Hence, in 'Indian Camp', the stereotypical story schema is that of the worried husband attending his wife's difficult labour, but since this turns out alright and mother and child emerge safe and sound, one expects that if the narrative turns back thereafter to the father, it will be to describe and record his relief, outpouring of joy, humble gratitude, and so on.

Thereafter:

2   the expected 'non-forking' schematic or automatic progression does not go through as predicted, and something relevant and related, 'imaginable in the circumstances if we had operated with full foresight or imagination', happens. And this foreseeable but unforeseen development pulls us up short, causes us to re-assess much of the narrative whose shape we *thought* we already understood.

To summarize, the essence of narrative surprise is that a reader experiences a new development as unforeseen but, upon reflection, foreseeable. Thus not every kind of arguably 'surprising event' amounts to a narrative surprise in this sense; when Scotty is knocked down by a car in both 'The Bath' and 'A Small, Good Thing', this calamity is something of a surprise, but it is not foreseeable on a long view, reaching back to the beginning of the narrative. To say that an event is, on analytical reflection, foreseeable is also to say that it 'fits' the larger structure of narrative conditions and developments in the entire story: it is not a detached addendum, but a fact or outcome that can be fully integrated (often belatedly) with everything else, filling a gap we had not even noticed was there. Surprises, when they come, are most effective when they are felt to be in no way absurd or inexplicable, but reasonable and possible. To experience a really effective narrative surprise is to be caught up in an activity of self-teaching, of reflexive critique, and this is part of what makes them so valuable. They do not entail simply a revision, by the reader, of their grasp of the narrative; with a little jolt of correction, they also compel the reader to examine and find lacking their own understanding: 'I should have seen/realized that this had happened or was going to happen or was the case. Why *didn't* I?' And these surprises are finally about understanding, and not about information-failure on the part of the narrator. Obviously, no shame or chastening accrues to the reader who, before being so informed, fails to foresee that a particular character has brown eyes, or was born in Buenos Aires, or checked out of the Savoy hotel at 10 a.m. on the Monday morning; it is entirely reasonable not to have foreseen such narrative facts and events and not having foreseen them reflects no fallibilities of understanding. By contrast, genuine narrative surprises present us not merely with unforeseen information; they display to us a moment or a space where our understanding (of facts and events integrated with motives, psychology, and latent forces) has failed.

In Jane Smiley's 'The Age of Grief', suspense is brilliantly created. The influenza at first seems incidental to events, the 'grief of the last weeks' (187), in which the parents have teetered on the edge of the absolute break-up of their relationship. Members of the family succumb to the flu (and begin to recover) in series: the father, then Lizzie, the oldest, most independent child; then Leah, the youngest and incredibly clingy one, then the mother (Dana), and finally Stephanie (p. 195), at which point the narrator-father comments: 'I was nearly jovial. I thought I knew what I was doing.' He says to Stephanie: 'but I have a feeling it will go away fast for you and Mommy.' Soon, however, the narrator is telling us 'in myself I felt panic, a little void, needle-thin but opening' (p. 196), a typical proleptic pointer to a negative outcome; as are the immediately following remarks on 'the permanent threat of death'. Even more ominous and suspense-creating is the long ensuing reflection on commitment, especially 'the commitment of risk, ... of heart' that comes with being 'an involved father'. All such reflections, like the essence of Labovian evaluation (see Chapter 6), serve to convey that the events the teller went through are momentous experiences, and that, whatever the outcome not yet disclosed to us, the entire process was of great importance to the teller/

participant. What is conveyed to us, by all such extended event-suspending observations, is that the events and their conclusion were not routine or inconsequential. Similarly, even a relatively inconsequential event can be invested with significance because of its placement – as here where the steady charting of Stephanie's temperature, in the 104.6 range, is interrupted by a long description of the father carrying his sick wife back to her room, and reflecting on his wife's build, strength, dress preferences, and other suspense-generating 'distractors' (p. 204). Similarly there is a dramatizing or heightening effect achieved by the long paragraph situating Stephanie in her room on pp. 205–6, culminating with the father's attempt to wake her up. Her unresponsiveness, floppiness, is, via presupposition – 'I was glad she seemed to be getting sounder sleep' – coded as relaxed sleep; but the reader is probably already inclined to interpret her behaviour as comatose unconsciousness, which is confirmed by the thermometer reading of 105.2.

Again, rather than immediately reporting the panicked reaction we assume is somewhere submerged within the father's reaction, we are given thoughts about his 'vision' of the stars as seen once before, before the text circles back to focus on the child-as-tiny-star-in-the-universe. Given this extensive build-up, culminating with the father's tearful breakdown on the phone to the hospital, followed by his preparations for taking Stephanie in, the resolution of this mini-episode is powerfully swift, casual, and embedded (208.3):

> and I knew that the next morning, when Stephanie's fever would have broken, I would be extremely divorced from and a little ashamed of my reactions, and it was true that I was. They sent us home from the hospital about noon. Dana was making toast at the kitchen table, Leah was running around in her pajama top without a diaper, and Lizzie had escaped to school.

## 4.8  From prose to film: radical translation

After the following chapter's study of characters' discourse in fiction, this book turns from narratological issues to approach narrative from a sociolinguistic orientation. But before leaving the narratological phase, mention – however necessarily brief – should be made of that contemporary narrative genre with possibly the greatest cultural significance: film narrative. The following observations are presented as postulates for discussion and critique, and are chiefly confined to one particular issue among the very many that might be addressed: What is involved – linguistically especially – in making the film of a novel (or the book of the movie)? Comparing the written and film narratives of *The Dead* or *Sense and Sensibility*, where are the differences or changes, and what is added, lost, or cut?

a　Consumption/processing time: with respect to the novel, the reader has considerable control of this; with respect to film (especially in the cinema), the director in large degree has control (a 110-minute 'default') and 'one pace fits all'.

b   The narrative film is multiple-authored, a joint telling, with director, producer, camera and sound crews, location and set designers, scriptwriters, all kinds of editors, and actors all having a direct 'intentional' hand in how and what gets told. At the same time the film typically lacks a single 'brooding' or perceptible narrator. Novels by contrast are almost invariably single-authored.

c   Bakhtin did not write much about film; he would surely have embraced its heterogeneity and hybridity (not merely of content – as in the novel – but of production and authorship). Popular culture in the last 100 years has seen the development of powerful new forms of hybrid/heterogeneous narrative – now including pop songs with videos attached, and hypertext fiction.

d   Everything in the novel is achieved through *written* language (including its representations of speech and thought, its showing or reporting of emotion, etc.). But in film there is a blend of several modalities: visual representation (depictions of settings, of characters, of actions …); non-verbal aural representation (music, sound effects, indices of setting); non-verbal human noises (of fingers typing on a keyboard, of someone brushing their teeth, etc.); speech; and even writing (as a distinct subtype of non-iconic visual representation). The choices concerning 'how to tell it' in the novel are between contrasting written formulations. But the choices in telling, in film, are far more varied. They are less constrained particularly concerning how, via which modality, to tell the individual events of the story. For example, a single event, such as 'Jenny receiving bad news in a letter' can be told in (at least) any one, or any combination, of the following four modalities:

| 1 | and/or | 2 | and/or | 3 | and/or | 4 |
|---|---|---|---|---|---|---|
| *visual* | | *aural* | | *speech* | | *writing* |
| *representation* | | *representation* | | | | |

And then within each of these broad modalities the director has a rich variety of options. If they choose to tell of 'Jenny receiving bad news in a letter' via visual representation, they may further choose to have Jenny's face and/or the letter in shot or not, close-up or at a distance, darkly or brightly lit, centred in the frame or not, in one continuous shot (with zooming or other movement or not) or several shots edited to highlight discontinuity. Because the film is so much less formally constrained than the novel, comparing the formal restriction or framework of the novel with the open-ness of the film is analogous to comparing the delimitation of the sonnet form with the technical freedoms of the novel.

e   With respect to showing versus telling, in film narrative showing is overwhelmingly the preferred option, and the chief dilemma is to decide *what* to show (and in what detail, at what length, from what or whose point of view).

f Language – and arguably written language in particular – is the best modality for analysis (particularly of characters, their desires, aspirations, fears, etc.). Such analytical presentation of character ('inward' portrayal) is largely denied to film, where we instead get outward or external presentation, from which we must *infer* the significant details of character. We have to judge characters by appearances, witnessed reactions, displayed emotions, and interpretive visual representations of mental processes – all on offer to us in abundance and (or but) seemingly without teller-interpretation.

g It is useful to identify written narratives that would seem to be *impossible* to render in film, and films that would seem to be impossible to conceive of as novels. And to explain why, in both cases. Presumably in the former impossible 'conversion', crucial telling inheres in the texture of the narration (which abstracts away from character, dialogue, setting, and events), as in a Beckett novel or a John Barth story. In the latter impossible 'conversion', crucial telling must inhere in those visual and non-verbal aural modes that resist representation in words (e.g. narrated experience of an overwhelming battle or disaster).

h The *verbal* record of setting and characters at the opening of a novel must be replaced (or cut) in any film treatment. If replaced, replaced by other, holistic, non-linear representations (e.g. a visual one).

i At the heart of film narration lies editing, the selection and combining of one shot with the next, invariably paying attention to the kinds of graphic, rhythmic, spatial and temporal relations that are thereby created between the sequenced shots. There are no full equivalents of shots and editing in written narrative, but there are arguably counterparts. Thus the sentence is a kind of shot, and the full stop is the point of splicing or cutting. The author can contrive to make the reader, proceeding from one sentence to the next, experience rhythmic, spatial and temporal continuities or disjunctions just as the film director can cause the viewer to, via editing choices. (But in the novel there are arguably 'higher level' shots and cuts too: the coordination of one paragraph with the next, and, optionally, the coordination of one chapter or section with the next.)

j A major topic in novel versus film comparative study must concern the *sequentiality of the telling* in one *vis à vis* the other. Written text draws on all kinds of conjunctions and temporal and locative phrases: *then, right after that, six weeks later, but out at the back the house*, and so on. A judicious combination of these, together with reliance upon the reader's powers of inferencing in seeing the connections between reported events or scenes, will be instrumental in creating narrative coherence. In film, a great deal of reliance, typically, must be placed upon visual processing to achieve similar ends. We are not literally *told*, by verbal means, that 'what happened next was *this* and then right after that *this* happened'; typically, we are simply *shown* B happening after A, and C after B. We need to perform a 'mental processing' in order to make sense of what we have seen, in order to store it at least in short-term memory for the duration of the film, and in order to be able to talk about the film afterwards, and form general interpretive opinions. Just how we do these things is rather less clear, and less stable, than in the case of the novel, where we typically have the text in front of us to refer back to. The 'reading' of a written text is very different from the 'reading' of a film, to a considerable degree because, being in words and sentences, the written text is already 'propositional'. A certain kind of interpretive work has thus already been done for the novel-reader, by comparison with the film-viewer (but in a sense 'too much' work has been done, creating a propositional 'overload'). The comparative propositional scarcity of film is what Chatman means by its verbal impoverishment: 'Film gives us plenitude without specificity. Its descriptive offerings are at once rich and verbally impoverished' (Chatman, 1990: 39).

k  This last idea relates particularly to the intepreting of character. Take the proposition 'Emma Woodhouse is, for much of the story, selfish'. In the novel, all sorts of verbal clues guide the reader to an observation of this kind (along with many other observations). How does a viewer of the film *Emma* get to a similar point in interpretation? This is a substantially different task because the attentive viewer will see a range of depictions (not read descriptions) of Emma doing, saying, perhaps thinking (e.g. via voice-over). And from those depictions the viewer has to derive interpretive conclusions. But outside the film's representations of characters' speech and thought, the film-viewer's evidence is to a considerable degree non-verbal. From that fusion of characters' speech and non-verbal depictions, the viewer must deduce interpretive conclusions.

l  To what extent *must* film and written renderings of e.g. *Trainspotting*, or *Like Water for Chocolate* have different goals and in fact not be the same narrative? Is the rendering of a book into a film or vice versa comparable to literary translation? The French language has two verbs for 'changing': *changer* (where mere alteration or adjustment is involved) and *échanger* (where substitutionary displacement, is involved, as when you change shoes or jobs). Perhaps the change from a film to a written narrative, like interlingual literary translation, is an *échanger*.

m  Raymond Carver's bleak short story, 'Little Things', about a couple fighting over a baby begins with a naturalistic apartment setting, and it getting dark outside. Then the text adds: 'but it was getting dark on the inside too'. How could you film this? (How would you film the *too*?) The story ends without clear indication of who keeps the baby (or whether it dies in the struggle). But the text reads: 'in this manner, the issue was decided'. Again, how would you film that?

n   The contrast between novel and film is not simply words versus images, but the processing of serially displaced words as opposed to that of serially displaced images.

o   If we conclude that between film and written narrative it's a matter of radical translation, of *échanger* and not merely *changer*, it may be because finally the essence of a verbal narrative like Joyce's 'The Dead' or Carver's 'Little Things' is *in* the (dispersed but accumulating and mutually displacing) written words more than anywhere else. And by the same token, the essence of a filmic narrative like *Citizen Kane* is *in* the (dispersed but accumulating and mutually displacing) projected images – again, more than in anything else (spoken words, music, sound).

p   Because a prose narrative and subsequent film narrative (or vice versa) are such incommensurably different discourses, brought together by some commonality of underlying story, one relates to the other on the basis of translation or transformation or *échanger*. Certainly 'adaptation' seems inadequate to describe the process (and is only used to describe prose-to-film conversions, admittedly much the commoner progression). These prose-to-film radical translations are also perhaps exceptional in their very frequency of occurrence: how rare, by comparison, are musical 'versions' of paintings or poems, or sculptures of ballets, or short-story versions of Beethoven string quartets.

## 4.9   The grammaticization of character and situation

In the final section of Chapter 2, I suggested a number of ways in which the special status of certain clauses in a narrative, as main carriers of the plot, may be typically reflected in the grammar of those clauses; and at the close of Chapter 3 came a discussion of the role of modality in narrational modes. Similar claims can be made about the grammar used in portraying characters and settings: the grammar, examined closely, is found to match the nature or conditions of characters. In making such a claim it is necessary to stress that I am using the term 'grammar' in a relatively enlarged sense, to denote not so much a formal syntactic description but a meaning-oriented functional description of the language in question. By grammar, then, I mean a systematic account of the principles governing choices of words and sequences of words within a language, with the additional requirement that the account is attentive to the meanings that speakers associate with those choices. One of the most useful and usable contemporary meaning-oriented grammars of English is that of Halliday (1994). The newcomer to linguistics will find this to be a sometimes difficult read, but they are well-served by a number of invaluable introductions to Halliday's systemic grammar: Bloor and Bloor (1995); Butt, Fahey *et al.* (1995); Eggins (1994); and Thompson (1996). Below I sketch that part of Hallidayan grammar, namely choices in the transitivity of clauses, which seems most relevant to the analysis of character and setting.

In Halliday's systemic grammar, transitivity concerns rather more than purely syntactic questions such as whether or not a particular verb takes a direct object (cf. *smile* versus *embrace*). The theory assumes that the semantic processes and participants expressed by particular noun phrases and verb phrases in a clause are a representation of what we take to be going on in the world. By means of choices from among a delimited set of process types and participant roles, these being expressed in the grammar of the clause and, in particular, its verb, we characterize our view of reality. When we say *John hates chocolate*, we represent a particular situation as one in which an individual, John, interacts (negatively) with chocolate by means of a mental process; and this is a standard English-language way of talking about people not liking chocolate (cf. also the colloquial *Chocolate doesn't agree with me*). In a different linguo-cultural world, one might by contrast standardly say things equivalent to: *Chocolate fights John's stomach*, or *John is square but chocolate is circular*. But we find these to be strange grammaticized representations by comparison with our own, taken-for-granted, patterns.

A process consists, potentially, of three components:

1   the process itself (typically realized by a verb phrase); there are just five core types of process;
2   the participants in the process (typically realized by noun phrases and, in the case of attributes, adjectival phrases); this grammar recognizes about twenty such participant types, four or five distinct ones associated with each process type;
3   circumstances associated with the process (realized by prepositional phrases, adverbial phrases, and adverbial subordinate clauses); these can be classified along fairly traditional adverbial distinctions (place, time, manner, reason, and so on).

Transitivity (or process) analysis is a fundamental semantic parsing. The analyst identifies the process or action that a clause expresses, and the participants that are recognized. So in the sentence *Bear drew Cat a big plate of food with his magic pencil*, the following parsing (and labelling) would be applied:

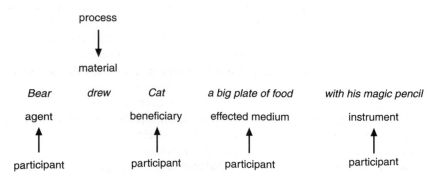

In the given example, then, a particular occurrence (a mini-narrative, in fact) is represented as one involving a material process of drawing and four participants: an effected medium that is brought into existence, an agent responsible for the process, and two further participants, the beneficiary and instrument, which did not have to be mentioned grammatically (cf., *Bear drew a big plate of food*) but were. Those, according to this transitivity analysis, are the essential semantic components of the given sentence, and by proceeding in the same way to analyse all the sentences in a text, the essential semantic components of an entire text can be identified. I will introduce and explain these labels (agent, material process, etc.) very shortly. But straight away I should state that the transitivity-parsing system is interesting in narrative analysis since it systematically highlights, for any text, just what kinds of process tend to go on, which individuals are (and are not) frequently agents, who or what tends to serve as medium, and so on. The entire business of representing the processes and participants of reality is what Halliday has termed the ideational function of language. In relation to this ideational function, the clause is the basic vehicle for representing patterns of experience. Below I offer a few more explanatory notes on the major types of process and participant in the English clause (these notes are heavily indebted to the lucid lecture hand-outs of my former colleague, Anneliese Kramer-Dahl).

### 4.9.1 *Material processes: processes of perceptible action*

Material processes are those processes that might answer the questions, 'What happened?' or 'What did (someone) do?' By way of accompanying participants, they always involve what is called a *medium* (the affected entity, called the theme in some grammars) and this medium usually pre-exists the process, but is further specified as the *effected medium* if it only comes into existence by dint of the process (as when someone bakes bread, paints a portrait, or builds a patio). Further participants that may be involved are *agent* (a human or quasi-human entity, acting intentionally), *force* (any inanimate agent), *instrument* (always under implicit control of an agent), *beneficiary* and *recipient*. Given limitations of space, I will do no more here than give a few explained examples:

> *John lit the bonfire with paraffin*
> (where John is agent, the bonfire is medium, and paraffin is instrument),
> *The lightning hit the tree*
> (the tree is medium; the lightning is not an agent, nor a controlled instrument, but simply a force),
> *It is raining*
> (where there is really only a process, and no participant),

*Emma painted a large watercolour*
(where the watercolour is effected medium, Emma is agent),
*Oliver collapsed*
(where Oliver's experience is hardly intentional: he is medium, not agent, like the orchids below),
*The orchids grew quickly*
*John wrecked his car*
(where, assuming he acted unintentionally, John is both perpetrator and victim, hence may be best labelled agent/medium).

And a final example where one embedded process serves to specify the medium of another:

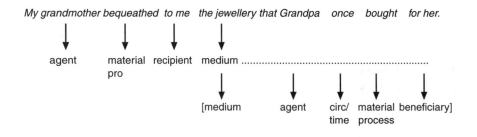

### 4.9.2  *Mental processes: processes of sensing*

Mental processes entail verbs of feeling or mental reaction (*like*, *fear*), perception (*see*, *hear*), and cognition (*think*, *believe*). These involve a human or human-like participant, the *senser*, and a thing or fact that is perceived, felt or thought, known as the *phenomenon*. Note that some mental process verbs take an active, engaged agent rather than a mere senser: the processor who listens, watches, learns, etc., is more agentive than the one who merely hears, sees, or understands. The former processes are more developmental, and can take a progressive aspect. Grammatically, mental processes are distinguished by being able to introduce, as the process's phenomenon, an entire clause (which will have its own transitivity analysis into process and participants). In this they differ from all the other processes, particularly the behavioural ones with which they seem to overlap. Mental processes are accordingly said to 'project':

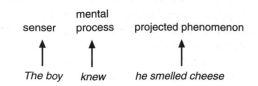

### 4.9.3  Verbal processes

Verbal processes are processes of saying or telling in a broad sense, with participants known as the *sayer*, the *said*, and the *addressee*:

> *He told me he was sorry.*

### 4.9.4  Behavioural processes

Behavioural processes are processes of relatively spontaneous or uncontrolled human activity, internal or external. They lie at the physicalist or materialist end of two other core processes (verbal or mental), so can be thought of as instances of these represented in rather a materialist light: looking, watching, staring, listening, breathing, coughing, grimacing, frowning, smiling, dreaming, screaming, choking, blinking, and crying out. They are semantically and grammatically halfway between material and mental processes, with, typically, just one participant, a human *behaver*. Like material processes they freely progressivize. Like typical verbal and mental processes they involve a human do-er, but unlike both they do not 'project' (or they are such processes used in a non-projecting way: not *I worry that we'll have no money left*, but *He worried about money*).

### 4.9.5  Relational processes: processes of being

Relational processes are ones of characterization or identification, and entail intensive verbs, or verbs expressing circumstantial or possessive relations, the 'default' verb being *be*:

1  intensive: '*x* is *y*'
2  circumstantial: '*x* is at/about/like *y*'
3  possessive: '*x* has *y*'

> *George was victorious.*
> *George was the winner.*
> *It took place at 3 o'clock.*
> *He has a great job.*

To repeat, what can be gained from careful transitivity analysis of scenes and characters is a preliminary picture of who is agentive and who is acted-upon medium (for whatever reason: they may be passive, or powerless, or just lazy), whether characters are doers or thinkers, whether instruments and forces dominate in the world represented, and so on. Invaluable applications of the transitivity analysis apparatus in the description of characters – their dispositions, ability to control things and infer causal connections, or their powerlessness – include Halliday (1971), Burton (1982), and Kennedy (1982). Hallidayan transitivity will be applied extensively in the course of analyses in Chapter 8.

## Further reading

Good places to begin further reading on character and setting are Rimmon-Kenan (1983), and Bal (1985: 25–36, 79–99). Fowler (1977: 33–41), cited in 4.4, demonstrates the application of a distinctive feature approach to character and setting in *The Great Gatsby*. Chatman (1978: 96–145) is invaluable on, *inter alia*, character 'traits', A. C. Bradley, and the role of setting in 'Eveline'. Interesting literary critical discussions of character include Price (1968), Harvey (1965), Bayley (1963), and, with a more theoretical orientation, Culler (1975a), Frow (1986), Iser (1978), Docherty (1983), Margolin (1989; 1996); Emmott (1997); and Culpeper (2000 and forthcoming).

Lodge (1977: 73–124) contains an extended thesis to the effect that there are two most fundamental and contrasting means of discourse-development: the metaphoric (where inherently disparate things are somehow linked and some illuminating context-specific similarity is posited), and the metonymic (where inherent associations between things are drawn upon, and consequently a richer, more textured picture of a single area of reality is achieved). A metaphoric dynamic involves an adjoining of a second topic to a first on the basis of its local and specific relevance (despite its logical and intrinsic irrelevance) – e.g. associating fog in the city of London with the Chancery law courts. The metonymic dynamic advances the text by passing from one topic to another, logically or traditionally associated topic. Lodge's theoretical account, inspired by work by Jakobson, leads to original and insightful analyses of just how the depiction of setting proceeds in many literary texts, including the openings of *Bleak House* and *A Passage to India*.

On thrillers, surprise and suspense, see, e.g. Rubin (1999), Palmer (1978), Sauerberg (1984), and Luelsdorff (1995). On Hallidayan transitivity applied to literature, Simpson (1993), Chapter 4, is very clear. Toolan (1998), Chapter 4, could also be consulted, and also Short (1996). See also Halliday's own influential paper on the changing styles in Golding's *The Inheritors*, Halliday (1971), together with a recent reexamination of it, Hoover (1998).

## Notes and exercises

1  Bedient (1969: 84) has declared this, of the characters in *Middlemarch*:

> When we read the problems of Lydgate's marriage, or about Casaubon's 'inward trouble' or about Bulstrode's public fall, it doesn't occur to us that these are imagined realities.

Do you agree?

2  One cluster of claims in Chatman (1978: 120) raises issues concerning real-world representation and the interpretibility of character and setting in fiction by reference to real-world counterparts:

> A trip to Dublin cannot but help us understand the special quality of paralysis attributed to its denizens by Joyce, and meeting a Dublin working-class girl, even in 1978, will give us deeper insight into Eveline's predicament and personality ... I have never been to Ireland, but I know that the peculiar sort of 'strutting' that Eveline's father does would be clearer if I had.

On what grounds might one agree or disagree? The quotation appears to assume that understanding Eveline, who represents a 'Dublin working-class girl' *c.* 1910, can be facilitated by encountering an actual Dublin working-class girl *c.* 1980 (or, now, *c.* 2000). Arguably all three descriptors (which might also be called traits), that is, the meaning of 'Dublin' and 'working-class' and 'girl', have changed profoundly in the years since 'Eveline' was written. But equally arguably, most stable of these three, despite its material transformation, is 'Dublin', the sign that denotes a setting. There was a Dublin in 1910, and there still is (while in fact the story's protagonist, Eveline, never was). Does all this reflect the fact that setting, rather than character or event or discourse, is the narrative element that most forcefully asserts a 'referential connection' with conditions in the real world?

It is tempting to say that Dublin and working-classness and being a girl (young woman) are so fundamentally changed today, by contrast with 1910, that inspection of contemporary exemplars will be of no help in interpreting the working girl in 'Eveline'. But in practice readers must get their background pictures, which help them to interpret Eveline's predicament and personality, from somewhere (these background pictures are the mental schemas and world knowledge discussed in 4.3). And those background pictures, although they may be of spatially or temporally remote categories (such as working-classness *c.* 1910) and may be informed by a variety of historically and sociologically reliable sources, will nevertheless carry an inescapable contemporaneity: they are *present-day* pictures of what that projected world, back in 1910, was like. Are they, then, fundamentally different from what is entailed in visiting present-day Dublin to derive a picture of Dublin, 1910?

3 A common entry point for discussion of characters is the paying of particular attention to their names. Dickens is commonly cited, with his roll-call of evocatively- and characterizingly-named individuals: Podsnap, Pecksniff, Ebeneezer Scrooge, Fagin, Gradgrind, Bounderby, Jupe, Wackford Squeers, and so on. But one can take the names of characters in very many modern fictions and analyze them for their expressivity, for their semiotic quality (see Doherty, 1985, for discussion). There seems almost a compulsion, in both authors and readers, to make character names be message-bearing. And from the authorial point of view, since a character's name so often serves, when used, to trigger recall of the multifaceted notional substantiality of that character, it must be hard and unnatural for an author to resist ordaining a name which is in some senses encapsulating. How *intentional* that encapsulating or trait-evoking effect is will often remain uncertain. At issue is a kind of enlarged onomatopoeia, encompassing all kinds of semantic and evaluative association: did Faulkner's prior selection of the name Flem Snopes 'guide' the author to the qualities of curmudgeonly and calculated meanness that the character has because these were already 'in' the name, or has the character's behaviour caused a kind of pejoration of a perfectly neutral and arbitrarily-signifying word, in effect 'giving the word *Snopes* a bad name'? And what, to you, does the name *Pnin* signify? Conversely, try to find novels where the names are 'transparent', semiotically null: are such novels from particular authors only, or in one genre only? The naming/meaning conundrum is not confined to fiction: most of us who become parents will find ourselves confronting it when trying to decide (agree . . .) on a name for a new baby.

4 Perhaps the commonest and most important element in fictional settings is the house. Everywhere in English fiction, from *Mansfield Park* to *Bleak House*, *The House of the Seven Gables*, *The Little House on the Prairie*, *Howards End*, *Brideshead Revisited*, *The Mansion*, *The Hotel New Hampshire*, and endlessly on, there are novels whose titles themselves are names of houses that are an essential, mood-determining, story-shaping, arena for characters and events. Take a novel by any author of your choice (even at random), and examine the extent to which allusions to the house(s) therein go beyond the basic required notation of place. Can you find particular local narratological motivations – or a more general generic one – for such 'excesses' of attention? Why are some fictions – e.g. Gothic

novels – apparently saturated with annotations of setting, while others – e.g. Beckett's later prose – have almost none?

'The house' is of course only one of many recurrent, emblematic or association-rich 'basic settings', invoked and varied in countless fictions, and used as a kind of hub for the entire narrative (often being mentioned in the work's title). Some others that immediately come to mind include the beach, the sea, the college, and the hospital. But yet other commonly-experienced settings, I would suggest, are rarely invoked in this way, as the hub or foundation of, say, an entire novel. Thus we do not find novels 'rooted' in the park, in quite the way we find them based on and around the beach. *Mansfield Park* is not an exception. Without intending any disrespect to Mansfield (any town might be mentioned here), it is fair to say that Mansfield Park is effective as Austen's title so long as we know – being able to decode the exclusivist metonymy – that Mansfield denotes a big house and country estate and that the novel is not, heaven forbid, a story set in a park in Mansfield. It may be interesting to attempt to explain why house, beach and college earn the higher status while other settings do not. Why is it that the park, the recreation ground, the airport, the shopping mall, to name just a few, lack this 'foundational setting' status that seems accorded to houses and beaches?

5 Compare and contrast the two basic settings in 'That Evening Sun' – Nancy's cabin and the Compsons' house (actually there are clearly sub-domains within the latter: the kitchen is a somewhat different setting from the library). Setting plays a prominent role in this story. It could be argued that 'change of setting' appears to amount to a solution to Nancy's problems: if she can stay with the Compsons and sleep on their kitchen floor she will be all right, she says. But this is a solution that the Compson parents are evidently quite reluctant to accept.

6 Chatman notes the very effective use in 'Eveline' of climactic metaphors precisely at the moment of the heroine's greatest anguish (Chatman, 1978: 142): the bell clanging upon her heart, all the seas of the world tumbling about her heart, Frank drowning her in those seas, and so on. These metaphors are especially apt since, at the quayside, clanging bell and tumbling seas are part of the actual setting. Eveline is subjected to 'the onslaught of setting'. Could it be argued that at the close of 'The Dead', similarly, Gabriel's consciousness is subjected to the onslaught of setting? We might look further in *Dubliners* to see whether this gradual promotion of setting into a character, a shaping influence, applies to other stories in the collection. Note that the title *Dubliners* itself is an act of defining characters by their setting.

As one means of probing the degree to which setting may seem to become agent-like, the Hallidayan categorization of transitivity processes (4.9) could be put to use. By contrast with earlier in the story, are there more occasions at the close of 'Eveline' where some element of the setting is agentive or quasi-agentive in the clause – typically, in subject position (in active sentences) with a transitive verb and an affected object? My initial impressions are that the early domestic setting – tame, unthreatening – comprises objects that are also syntactic objects, things affected by a human agent (Eveline 'had dusted' the familiar objects once a week for so many years). But at the quayside, setting includes elements that are quite agent-like, at least to the extent of taking up subject position in either transitive or intransitive sentences, with no mention of a human causer: 'A bell clanged upon her heart', 'All the seas of the world tumbled about her heart'. Does a more detailed analysis support those initial impressions of a growing dynamism of setting?

7 Each of J. K. Rowling's *Harry Potter* books is peppered with suspense and surprises. Examine, for instance, the final pages of Chapter 16 and the opening of Chapter 17 of *Harry Potter and the Philosopher's Stone* (Bloomsbury): comment

in detail on how the suspense of Harry's quest of the stone in its guarded hiding-place is supplanted by the surprise, at the opening of Chapter 17, of finding that Quirrell is *not* a p-poor s-stutterer.

8 Put any two or three of the alphabetized points in 4.8 to the test, using in evidence any well-known fiction-to-film pairing.

# 5 The articulation of narrative text III
## Representing character discourse

## 5.1 Achieving immediacy in the narration of thought

> Although Bertha Young was thirty she still had moments like this
> when she wanted to run instead of walk, to take dancing steps on and
> off the pavement, to bowl a hoop, to throw something up in the air
> and catch it again, or to stand still and laugh at – nothing – at nothing,
> simply.
>
> What can you do if you are thirty and, turning the corner of your
> own street, you are overcome, suddenly, by a feeling of bliss –
> absolute bliss! – as though you'd suddenly swallowed a bright piece of
> that late afternoon sun and it burned in your bosom, sending out
> a little shower of sparks into every particle, into every finger and
> toe? ...
>
> Oh, is there no way you can express it without being 'drunk and dis-
> orderly'? How idiotic civilisation is! Why be given a body if you have
> to keep it shut up in a case like a rare, rare fiddle?
>
> 'No, that about the fiddle is not quite what I mean,' she thought,
> running up the steps and feeling in her bag for the key – she'd forgot-
> ten it, as usual – and rattling the letter box. 'It's not what I mean,
> because – Thank you, Mary' – she went into the hall. 'Is nurse back?'
>
> (Katharine Mansfield, 'Bliss')

As we advance through these remarkable opening paragraphs of 'Bliss',
we can hardly fail to notice that a masterfully controlled storytelling is at
work. It is a storytelling in which external facts about a character on the
one hand, and a version of her intimate thoughts on the other, share the
same sentential envelope without strain. The routine information that
there is a woman called Bertha Young who is aged thirty gives way to disclosures of her sudden impulses – *like this* – to run, dance, laugh at
nothing, and so on. Such disclosures appear without either noisy signalling
or discoursal effort, and this is partly due to the avoidance of cumbersome
clauses of self-perception (She realized that, she felt that ... etc.) or any
sudden appearance of confessional first-person pronouns ('I want to ...', 'I
feel ...'). That much of this – from around line 3 onwards – is a subtle ren-

dering of Bertha's thoughts and emotions is supported by the belated appearance of a 'she thought' in paragraph 4; but we do not need that 'she thought' to know this.

The first intimation of a veiled immediacy of telling comes with the unexpected phrase, 'like this' in the opening line. The expression swiftly aligns us with the character Bertha's own immediate orientation to her world, 'like this' being not so much cohesive, tied to some co-textually specified moment, but rather expressive and deictic, alluding to the current moment, one we would have no difficulty identifying were we Bertha herself. From that phrase onwards, for the entirety of the story, we can argue that Bertha is the internal character-focalizer (and often the focalized too).

In that first paragraph, too, the reader is cleverly led to assume that Bertha is, at this point in the narrative, walking along a street, on a pavement, in the open air – though none of this is directly reported. All that is directly reported are her blissful impulses – and these might have arisen even if in actuality she were lying in bed, or eating lunch, or kneeling in church. Yet no such situation comes to mind as we read the paragraph: we assume that reported impulses to frolic in the street indicate that the woman is actually in the street, although perhaps only the exophoric definite article used in the reference to 'the pavement' is an explicit formal cue. With an art that conceals art, the narrative has modulated from the distanced description of the character, 'Bertha Young was thirty'; to the immediacy of the relaying of Bertha's thoughts in, especially, paragraph 3; and back to the externality of the direct speech in paragraph 4. Those modulations have also involved switches in tense, from past to present to past – but we are too distracted on a first reading by the larger textual effect, its representation of bliss, to notice such mechanics. Abstracted from its carefully crafted context, a sentence like this one in paragraph 4 might strike us as absurd, a clumsy mistake:

'It's not what I mean, because – Thank you, Mary'

But in context it is brilliantly effective.

Now consider another passage:

Isabel noted afresh that life was certainly hard for some people, and she felt a delicate glow of shame as she thought how easy it now promised to become for herself.(1) She was prepared to learn that Ralph was not pleased with her engagement; but she was not prepared, in spite of her affection for him, to let this fact spoil the situation.(2) She was not even prepared, or so she thought, to resent his want of sympathy; for it would be his privilege – it would be indeed his natural line – to find fault with any step she might take towards marriage.(3) One's cousin always pretended to hate one's husband; that was traditional, classical; it was a part of one's cousin's always pretending to adore one.(4) ... You could criticize any marriage; it was the essence of a marriage to be open to criticism.(5) How well she herself, should she only give her mind to it, might criticize this union of her own!(6) She had other employment, however, and Ralph was welcome to relieve her of the care.(7) Isabel was prepared to be most patient and most indulgent.(8) He must have seen that, and this made it the more odd he should say nothing.(9) After three days had elapsed without his speaking our young woman wearied of waiting; dislike it as he would, he might at least go through the form.(10) We, who know more about poor Ralph than his cousin, may easily believe that during the hours that followed his arrival at Palazzo Crescentini he had privately gone through many forms.(11) His mother had literally greeted him with the great news, which had been even more sensibly chilling than Mrs Touchett's maternal kiss.(12) Ralph was shocked and humiliated; his calculations had been false and the person in the world in whom he was most interested was lost.(13) He drifted about the house like a rudderless vessel in a rocky stream, or sat in the garden of the palace on a great cane chair, his long legs extended, his head thrown back and his hat pulled over his eyes.(14) He felt cold about the heart; he had never liked anything less.(15) What could he do, what could he say?(16) If the girl were irreclaimable could he pretend to like it?(17) To attempt to reclaim her was permissible only if the attempt should succeed.(18)

(Henry James, *Portrait of a Lady*: 338–9)

In this passage, as in that from 'Bliss', we see the subtle narrative presentation of characters' thoughts, again with an attenuation of the sense that any narratorial figure is relaying those thoughts. No matter how audacious Isabel's views become, no narratorial voice of 'true judgment' intrudes to censure the character, dissociate itself from Isabel, and alert the reader to the errors being broadcast. That is not James's way. It is enough that we see Isabel's shallow petulance immediately juxtaposed to Ralph's actual views, again, relayed without noticeable narratorial editorializing.

And yet that this passage is still narrated seems clear. In particular, Isabel continues to be designated by the third-person pronoun, *she*, as someone different from the teller (who is always an *I*), and the tense continues to be the past tense of narration, rather than the present tense of direct experience. Furthermore, the passage begins by telling us what 'Isabel noted' and by reporting as the text of an intrusive omniscient narrator (Simpson's type B(R) positive) what she thought and what she felt as she thought. But by sentence 4 that narrator has almost completely withdrawn (and remains so until sentence 10), their omniscience giving place to Isabel's own limited wisdom – a wisdom that confidently and blindly assumes that Ralph 'classically, traditionally' always pretended to adore her. *Pretended*, the reader who has reached page 338 asks? The mismatch between Isabel's distorted picture of things and the reader's own fuller one is too striking to ignore. The narrative mode adopted so as to narrate

Isabel's thoughts in an uncensored form engages the reader in the computing or construing of many such ironies. The irony just noted may be chiefly poignant. But when, in sentences 5 and 6, this newly-engaged young woman announces to herself that the essence of a marriage is its openness to criticism, and that she could – if she thought about it – criticize her own impending union, but that she had other things to do (impliedly more important), then a serious and extensive waywardness of judgment is laid bare.

The narrative mode at work here, in sentences 3 to 7, 9 and the latter half of 10, is Free Indirect Discourse, which will be explained and discussed at length in the following sections. The phenomenon is often referred to by other names; perhaps commonest, from a very long list, are: free indirect style, *style indirect libre*, represented speech and thought, quasi-direct discourse, *erlebte Rede*, and combined discourse. Among the many narrative tasks Free Indirect Discourse can help perform are ironies and mismatches of the kind found in the commentary on Isabel above; equally, it can be used in the service of empathetic disclosure as in the depiction of Ralph or, in the earlier passage, Bertha. Wherever it is employed, it seems to involve subtlety and complexity and demands a commensurate care from the reader. Note, for example, how despite Isabel's insistence on her own patience towards Ralph, her indulgence, her refusal 'to resent his want of sympathy', she *does* resent his unspoken reservations and wearies of waiting. Or, somewhat differently, consider the narrator's clever collusion with the reader – 'We, who know more about poor Ralph than his cousin' – when he picks up Isabel's complaint that 'he might at least go through the form' (i.e. wishing her joy and happiness, etc.), and uses the same phrase in the next sentence in a tellingly different sense.

## 5.2 Modes of speech and thought presentation

We should begin with fundamental principles. When a narrator sets about telling some individual's story, there will be various actions and events involving the character, which they will wish to narrate. Where these actions are physically overt and observable by any careful witness – *She sat at the window watching the evening invade the avenue* – I call these Pure Narrative sentences. Very often, exercising their option to be as revealing of a character's inward feelings as they wish (the narratorial option to disclose 'up to omniscience'), information that goes beyond external witnessing will be related: *in her nostrils was the odour of dusty cretonne*. As long as those inward details remain matters of which the character is not consciously aware, I would still call them part of the Pure Narrative (PN). Similarly, reports of mental or verbal activity which do not purport to be a character's articulated speech or thought – *His mind went blank*; *he couldn't get his thoughts straight* – are here grouped within PN, however intrusive into a character's psyche they may be. These tend to be metadiscoursal commentaries on *how* the character was thinking or speaking, rather than reports on *what* they thought or said (but see Short *et al.*'s proposal, as an alternative approach, discussed in Notes and exercise 3, pp. 141–2). In simplest contrast to Pure Narrative sentences are those that relay what are vouched to be a character's actual speech – direct speech (DS), here set in italics:

> Lily called out: – *Miss Kate, here's Mrs Conroy.*

And by extension, where a narrator reports what is offered as a reliable version of the sense, but not the precise words, tense, and pronouns of a character, we encounter (here in italics) Indirect Speech (IS) :

> Both of them kissed Gabriel's wife, said *she must be perished alive ...*

To a greater and lesser degree, respectively, direct and indirect speech 'give voice' to the character whose utterances are reported, making for a more vivid and dramatized story. But very often characters may not outwardly *say* things in response to their circumstances, they simply *think* them, and by a further extension beyond Direct and Indirect Speech, narrators have come to make extensive use of two standard options for reporting thoughts. The first of these purports to convey the exact words a character has formulated in thought, their precise mental utterance as it were (Direct Thought); the second, parallel to Indirect Speech, offers the sense but not the precise grammar or wording of a character's thought (Indirect Thought). The two direct forms *show* a character's words – spoken or thought – without internal amendment; and the narrator doing the showing in effect moves away from the quoted utterance, which expresses purely the character's viewpoint. The two indirect forms *tell* a character's words, suitably cast to make sense from the point of view of the telling narrator, who remains invisibly present and responsible for the wording.

At this point we should mention what I call the 'framing clause', also known as the clause of communication or the *inquit* clause (*inquit* being the Latin for 'he said' or 'she said'). Normally when speech or thought is included in narration, the particular character who is the source of that speech or thought is also identified, in a framing clause, as in the following examples, which are examples of DS, IS, DT, and IT, in italics, preceded by framing clauses, from 'The Dead':

DS  After a pause she [Aunt Julia] asked: – *And what are galoshes, Gabriel?* (189)
IS   As they [the young ladies] said *they never took anything strong* he opened three bottles of lemonade for them. Then he asked one of the young men to move aside ... and filled out for himself a goodly measure of whiskey. (191)
DT  He thought: *'I have never felt like that myself towards any woman.'* (based on 235)

IT   He realized that *the time had come for him to set out on his journey westward*. (based on 236)

By convention the standard version of all four modes mentioned so far, DS, IS, DT and IT, is one in which a framing clause of the kind exemplified occurs in the text, unambiguously anchoring or attributing it to a particular character. But all four modes are equally possible *without* a framing clause, hence without unambiguous anchorage:

'And what are galoshes, Gabriel?'
They never took anything strong.
I have never felt like that myself towards any woman.
The time had come for him to set out on his journey westward.

When the four modes occur without a narrator's framing clause, they are said to be Free. Thus the four immediately preceding example sentences are Free Direct Speech, Free Indirect Speech, Free Direct Thought, and Free Indirect Thought, respectively. Of these, Free Indirect Speech and Free Indirect Thought are immediately the more interesting, because in actuality a *range* of formulations of a character's speech or thought, indirectly but freely rendered, is always available: an author can opt for a more distant and narratorial variant, or a more character-proximate variant one. Take, for example, the third utterance above (FDT), but recast in Free Indirect Thought mode:

He had never felt like that himself towards any woman.

While that is a fairly soberly narratorial version, an author could alternatively compose a more informal and character-expressive version:

He had never ever felt so … so *lost* in passion, he supposed it was, for any woman.

Or even:

He had never – how did Swinburne put it? – 'hold in the music of the Almighty' Gretta or anyone else, not Mother, not even the children, the way that fellow Furey did …

Any of these, and innumerable others, which would count as Gabriel's Thought, but Indirectly relayed, and lacking a framing clause, would on those grounds be classed as Free Indirect Thought. It is the most versatile hybrid form which can carry all of the idiosyncrasy of phrasing, lexical choice, dialect, epithets and exclamations of the character, *as if* this were a direct rendering, with the sole proviso that the grammatical orientation devices of deixis, the tenses and pronouns, are those of the narrator and narrative.

Having elaborated matters to the point that we can distinguish a total of eight distinct modes which a narrator can draw upon in the presentation of characters' speech or thought, mention should be made of the fact that very often in analyses and commentaries, one subsuming category, of discourse, is referred to rather than the two subtypes, speech and thought, of which it is composed. Thus eight modes are reduced to four: Direct Discourse (i.e. DS and DT), Free Direct Discourse, Indirect Discourse, and Free Indirect Discourse. On the other hand, it is often quite useful to discuss and evaluate the full set of eight modes, keeping speech and thought distinct, for reasons that will become clear later.

In addition to the eight modes introduced so far, just three more need to be noted at this point. Most important of these is Stream of Consciousness (SOC), also known as Direct Interior Monologue. This can be thought of as lying beyond Free Direct Thought on the thought–representation continuum: like FDT, it presents the source character's thoughts in present tense and first person, but it is usually more inward-looking, less orderly or 'public in grammar', more reliant on unstated inferential connections and associations, less censored as it were, than FDT. Quite often it is implied that in SOC passages we are scrutinizing the impulse-driven flow of a character's mental activity, put into words that are only partially ordered and marshalled: it is as if the character him- or herself has not really experienced these words as an articulated sequence 'in the head'. A final pair of modes to mention are those where the narrator reports a character's speaking or thinking, but in a way that is sufficiently recast and summarized that they need to be seen as different from the Indirect Forms, being even closer to entirely narratorial text; following Leech and Short (1981) I will call these Narrative Report of Speech Acts and Narrative Report of Thought Acts respectively (NRSA and NRTA).

By way of practice at identifying some of the eleven categories that have been introduced, two short extracts from 'The Dead' follow, with annotations of portions of the text that appear here in italics (the remainder of the text is what I term Pure Narrative, which can be thought of as a twelfth category):

> Gabriel asked [Mrs Malins] *whether she had had a good crossing.* She lived with her married daughter in Glasgow and came to Dublin on a visit once a year. She answered placidly *that she had had a beautiful crossing and that the captain had been most attentive to her.* She spoke also *of the beautiful house her daughter kept in Glasgow, and of all the nice friends they had there.* While her tongue rambled on Gabriel *tried to banish* from his mind *all memory of the unpleasant incident with Miss Ivors. Of course the girl or woman, or whatever she was, was an enthusiast but there was a time for all things. Perhaps he ought not to have answered her like that. But she had no right to call him a West*

*Briton before people, even in joke. She had tried to make him ridiculous before people, heckling him and staring at him with her rabbit's eyes.*

Gabriel's anodyne conversation with Mrs Malins is initially reported via Indirect Speech (his *whether she had had a good crossing* is anwered by her *she had had a beautiful crossing and that the captain had been most attentive to her.* But the narrative rapidly modulates to one even more removed from the character, that of NRSA, lightly summarizing her numbing banalities. An elegantly crafted middle sentence narratorially reports that Mrs Malins is still talking but, like Gabriel, it does not bother to note her words, turning instead to Gabriel's internal reflections. These begin in NRTA format (it is unlikely that the words *banish all memory of the unpleasant incident* are precisely the words that run through Gabriel's mind: these are a narrative summary of his first thoughts here). But the narratorial presence drops away, and Gabriel's inner voice takes charge with *Of course the girl or woman*, and so on, until the close, in full-dress FIT, eloquently disclosing both Gabriel's sexist pomposity and his hypersensitive vulnerability, which seem to foster a mean and petty reaction.

> Gabriel asked himself *was he the cause of her abrupt departure. But she did not seem to be in ill humour: she had gone away laughing.* He stared blankly down the staircase.
>
> At that moment Aunt Kate came toddling out of the supper-room, almost wringing her hands in despair.
>
> – *Where is Gabriel?* she cried. *Where on earth is Gabriel? There's everyone waiting in there, stage to let, and nobody to carve the goose!*
>
> – *Here I am, Aunt Kate!* cried Gabriel, with sudden animation, *ready to carve a flock of geese, if necessary.*

For systematicity's sake, I would classify *was he the cause of her abrupt departure* as IT and not FIT, even though it has the question inversion which is characteristic of the latter (canonical IT would be *Gabriel asked himself if he was the cause of her abrupt departure*), because it remains explicitly introduced by a framing clause. But as indicated, it is a quite 'free' variety of IT (alternatively, some analysts might say that here a sentence which begins as IT modulates to FIT at some point as it unfolds). The following sentence, although it could be purely narratorial, in the context seems more likely to be a further report of Gabriel's impressions, now without disambiguating frame, hence FIT. But the third sentence (*He stared blankly ...*) cannot plausibly be Gabriel's thought: the narratorial camera has 'pulled back' to a medium-distance shot, now outside Gabriel's consciousness, to give us a quick observer's glimpse of what Gabriel might have looked like from the viewpoint of another guest. Equally interesting is the final sentence quoted: *Here I am, Aunt Kate!* is of course Gabriel's direct speech, immediately framed by *cried Gabriel, with sudden animation*, which is the narrator's evalua-tive report. But *ready to carve a flock of geese, if necessary* could be either the narrator's meiotic interpretation of Gabriel's animation, or it could be a resumption of Gabriel's direct speech, a playful exaggerating reply to Aunt Kate's request that he carve the goose. On balance I assume the final phrase is Gabriel's direct speech, and not narrative report, but the implied modulation from narratorial *with sudden anima-tion* to the semantically congruent *ready to carve a flock of geese* from Gabriel is so seamless as to be experientially imperceptible in the ordin-ary process of reading. Such examples justify claiming that in some uses of the discourse-representing modes (especially FDD and FID) we find the subtlest local or temporary alignments of narrator and character, in wording as well as viewpoint.

Just one of the attractive features of Free Indirect Discourse is that most readers are not consciously aware of it being at work. It is a hybrid and a marked or exceptional form, neither pure narrative nor pure charac-ter-expression, and in many situations it manages to blend into the narra-torial background. As we have seen, it comprises two sub-types, not always easily distinguished, Free Indirect Speech and Free Indirect Thought (henceforth, FIS and FIT respectively). The former of these is often easier to perceive (and was particularly drawn upon in nineteenth-century novels), but ultimately more attention needs to be directed to FIT, which is more common and more important in modern fiction.

But to end this section with the modes with which it began, Direct Speech and Indirect Speech, let us note how widespread these are in tradi-tional novels, as well as in other discourses in which the speech of indi-viduals is reported. Both hard news and human interest stories in newspapers, for example, are heavily dependent on direct and indirect speech reporting of the actual words of those involved. Direct speech pre-tends to be a faithful verbatim report of a person's actual words (although we accept, in literature and in non-literary contexts, that all sorts of likely pauses, reformulations, repairs, and dialectal features are partially if not completely removed). If direct speech reporting of, e.g., a sports celebrity in a newspaper story purports or pretends to be a faithful record of the actual words spoken, then direct speech in fiction is a simulation of a pre-tence; and sometimes the author may choose not to pretend or simulate very hard – just as Shaw or Beckett did not feel bound in their plays to give their characters dialogue that sounded undetectably similar to every-day natural conversation.

In indirect speech, the narrator or reporter purports to provide an accurate version of what the speaker said, but not by simply reproducing that speaker's own words: instead, the narrator's words and deictic orien-tation are retained. Accordingly, indirect speech versions can be fairly remote from their hypothesized direct speech source. Thus Leech and Short (1981: 323) note the use of quite summarized and remote versions of indirect speech. And while the privileges of occurrence of all eleven speech and thought presenting modes are notionally equal, the actual use and distribution of the modes may vary in striking ways. Indirect Speech, for example, is extremely sparingly used in the exemplary short stories ('Eveline', 'That Evening Sun', etc.) of this study. On the other hand it is extensively used in certain kinds of oral narratives and in newspaper stories.

## 5.3 Differences between Direct and Indirect Discourse

We can list some of the formal ways in which Indirect Discourse (IS or IT) *normally* differs from Direct Discourse (DS or DT). To make this commentary more tangible, cumulative alterations (highlighted in italics on first occurrence), in line with the list presented, are made to a simple sentence which starts out as a narrative framing clause followed by Direct Thought:

> Gabriel thought: – The time has come for me to set out on my journey westward.

1  Indirect Discourse will be in the same tense as that used in the encompassing pure narrative text (in traditional fiction, this is past tense; in some contemporary literature, this may be present tense). Direct Discourse remains in the present tense which is the normal choice for our expression of current actions and reactions.

> Gabriel thought: – The time *had* come for me to set out on my journey westward.

2  First and second person pronouns in the Direct version, denoting the speaking character and his or her addressees, are matched by gender-appropriate third person pronouns in the Indirect version, being the narratorial designations of these characters (to themselves, every character is an *I*; but to an external heterodiegetic narrator [unlike, e.g. Pip in *Great Expectations*] every character will be a *he* or a *she*). This makes indirect speech more explicit than the direct with respect to the gender of the addresser and addressee (an issue relevant to gender-ambiguous or gender-concealing narratives).

> Gabriel thought: – The time had come for *him* to set out on *his* journey westward.

3  IS is not set off by inverted commas (speech marks) or other graphological flagging-up of directness, such as indentation and dashes and capitalising the first direct word. While inverted commas used to be a standard marker of direct speech, many twentieth century fiction writers, including Joyce, dispense with speech marks for DS, instead

marking the onset of a character's turn of talk by a new line, an indent, and a long dash. (As a result the beginning of a character's direct speech at least – though not the end – is unmistakeable).

> Gabriel thought the time had come for him to set out on his journey westward

4    The reporting and reported clauses relate to each other differently: in ID they are syntactically related hypotactically, rather than paratactically as in DD. That is to say, the clauses are linked together in a superordinate:subordinate relation (the reporting clause being the head or superordinate); by contrast the relation between reporting and reported clauses in DD is one of coordination of 'equals', hence paratactic. One consequence of this is that certain 'robustly paratactic' DD constructions, such as imperatives and exclamatives, resist incorporation into ID format. Thus when Mr Brown tries his whiskey:

> – God help me, he said, smiling, it's the doctor's orders.

It is hard to devise a truly plausible ID counterpart of this: *?He smilingly cried that God should help him but it was the doctor's orders.* The main clause-subordinate clause relation in ID can be made explicit by, typically, the presence of the subordinator *that* (but use of *that* to introduce ID is optional, unlike obligatory *que* in comparable French constructions). But other introducers besides *that* preface ID utterances: a character's polar (yes/no) question, indirectly reported, will be introduced by *if* or *whether* (like *that*, impossible in Direct Discourse); but content questions will be introduced by the same *Wh*-forms that would appear in the DD equivalent. Another consequence of DD's paratactic status is that the framing clause can freely occur either before or after the DD:

> He said: – It's the doctor's orders. ⟷ – It's the doctor's orders, he said.

But such reversibility of projecting clause and projected clause in ID is much rarer, and sometimes impossible (e.g. with the *that* and *if* subordinators):

> He said that it was the doctor's orders. ⟷ *That it was the doctor's orders, he said.

> Gabriel thought *that* the time had come for him to set out on his journey westward.

5    Points 1 and 2 above noted that in ID, tenses and pronouns are

aligned with the narrator's perspective. This can be stated more generally: the grammar of ID entails a wholesale adoption of the deictic orientation of the narrator. This means that all deictic indicators that might appear in a character's direct utterance, keyed to the character's assumed point in space and time (besides tense and personal pronouns, words like *here*, *today*, *this*, and *now*), will be displaced by deictic indicators which make sense from the narrator's perspective (typically, the 'non-proximate' deictic forms: *there*, *on that (same) day*, *that*, *then*). Among the deictic indicators must be included the use in DD of a few verbs of specific directional movement, implying movement towards or away from the speaking character (*Come here!*; *Go away!*); by contrast in ID the movement verbs will be directionally non-specific, or, like other deictic elements, oriented to the narrator. It is because *come* and *go* are as orientational as *here* and *there* that some combinations of them sound unnatural or absurd: *?They will come there tomorrow*; *?Go here this minute!*. In the example sentence, in addition to *now* being displaced by *then*, there is arguably some residual 'Gabriel-orientedness' in the verbs *come* and *set out*, which can be expunged with a little effort:

> Gabriel thought that the time had *arrived* for him to *begin* his journey westward.

And if there had been a *now* in the original DD version – *the time has now come* – then this would be substituted by *then*. But at this point there is a danger of saturating the example with indirectness features, to the point that it looks implausible.

6 Signally lacking so far from the list of differences between DD and ID is the way that the 'colourful' idiosyncratic and dialectal qualities of the speech or thought of a character who is reported directly fail to transfer to the ID version. Being rooted in the specific subjectivity and evaluations of that character, they cannot be retained in any standard ID version, which purports to convey – and this usually quite sparingly – the subjectivity of the narrator. There are difficulties, too, in representing DD commands, interjections and rhetorical questions, in ID. But those are, like the items listed in the previous section, grammatical or grammaticized features; here we are focussing on matters of lexis, vocabulary, with their seemingly more direct expression of specific world-view and personality. It is the 'loss', as it seems, of the character's vivid, colloquial, partisan and engaged lexis that is one of the most striking characteristics of ID, by comparison with DD. Still, it is worth emphasizing that what is certainly lost, in ID reporting, is not 'colourful language', necessarily, but 'the *character's* (possibly colourful) language'. That is to say, typically and conventionally, especially in literary fiction, narrators are more 'neutral' and formal than the characters of whom they tell. But this is only a convention or

pronounced tendency, and will be overridden in many particular cases. One is the novel *The Adventures of Huckleberry Finn*, where Huck himself, as first-person narrator, reports nonstandardly the presumably standard speech of some of the protagonists in his story. Or consider a 'lovable Cockney criminal', about to go into court to face a charge, who uses IS to report the advice of his lawyer to him: 'The brief said it didn't make no difference to the jury that I'd been nicked twice before because they couldn't be told that till after they'd given their verdict'. The verb-choice *nicked*, and the nonstandard multiple negation are assumed to be the speaker's, not the lawyer's. Finally, returning to the Gabriel sentence we have been reworking, out of an original DD mould and into an ID one, it has to be conceded that the DD original shows no glaring lexical or phonological idiosyncrasy of the kind that ID routinely removes. At the same time, however, the DD original does use a construction which is rather metaphorical and characteristic of Gabriel's tendency to think in tropes and poetic figures. It is quite possible that, if Joyce had been compelled to render the sentence in ID, he would have replaced Gabriel's figurative formulation with something more literal and narratorial:

> Gabriel thought that the time had arrived when he should begin confronting his own limited lifespan.

But we cannot be sure: in Joyce's actual text, it is a FIT version that appears:
> The time had come for him to set out on his journey westward.

The preceding six-point listing of differences refers to particular features being contrasted, in DD by comparison with ID, by their absence or presence. This was to avoid talking in terms of 'removal' (of, e.g. speech marks) or 'insertion' (of, e.g. the subordinator *that*), which might have fostered the false assumption that the Indirect Discourse was a transformed version of the Direct Discourse, and that the latter 'must have come first', before the former was derived from it. Although there is a conventional logical priority of real-world direct speech over real-world indirect speech, this does not compel a treatment of all IS and IT as necessarily traceable to DD antecedents. People are quite capable of 'reporting' things that their reportees never said. Besides, as noted earlier, the notional priority of DD brings few restrictions concerning the actual form that any indirect discourse report may take.

In light of the six contrasts between DD and ID listed above, and in particular in view of the last of these, we can begin to reflect on why and where an author elects to use one and not the other. For example, where a speaker's use of highly interactive language features such as interjections, and dialectalisms and exceptionalities of language *is* narratively significant, then this may be sufficient justification for narratorial recourse to Direct Speech. To opt for Direct Speech reporting is also to accept a scenic slowing of pace, enhanced focus on the specificity and detail of an interaction, and a greater pressure on the author to make such text redeemingly interesting (to offset the inevitable fact that the narrated action will proceed – if it does at all during the DS dialogue – far more slowly).

This can be confirmed if we review some of the episodes of dialogue in 'The Dead'. Gabriel's conversation with Mrs Malins is mercifully briefly recorded, and mostly in indirect speech: any more extended airing of her dullness would merely have laboured a joke and irritated the reader. By contrast, Gabriel's grilling from Miss Ivors is rendered in Direct Speech, and at considerable length (the reader gets a far fuller version of it than Gabriel is subsequently prepared to share with Gretta). And it earns its place in the narrative: it is far better for Miss Ivors to be seen putting Gabriel on the spot in her own words – '*I have a crow to pluck with you*' – than via some stilted, distancing phrasing, which would simply fail to dramatize the scene: *She abruptly announced that she had a complaint to make to him.* Equally vivid, and engaging (it makes Gabriel colour) is her rhetorical question, '*Who is G. C.?*'. And when she then declares:

O, innocent Amy! I have found out that you write for the *Daily Express*! Now aren't you ashamed of yourself?

it is more or less impossible to render this in Indirect Speech (or Narrative Report of a Speech Act) in ways that are not grossly unsatisfactory:

She declared he *was* an innocent Amy, to have been found out writing for the *Daily Express*, and asked him whether he wasn't ashamed of himself.

She told him she was shocked to find he was writing for the *Daily Express*. She thought he should be ashamed of himself.

These are unsatisfactory because these Indirect versions make the reporting too prominent: it intervenes and distracts our attention from the reported. The 'she declared' and the 'she told him' keep reminding us that a narratorial third party is present, seemingly taking notes on this lively spat. But we don't need such reminders or such third parties (even if at the back of our minds we know they must be on hand): we prefer the sensation of being as close to this quarrelling couple as if we were dancing next to them in the Lancers, catching Miss Ivors's every ego-chafing word directly and unedited.

In broad terms, then, DD and ID may be said to differ in their effect on the reader. Usually the reader feels a greater distance and detachment from characters and their words when these are mediated via Indirect

Discourse. DD is an environment where characters appear to be in control and speak for themselves, while in ID the narrator is more overtly still in control, and reports on behalf of the characters. But the appearance or illusion of character control should not be overstated: behind all the fictional individuals, however reported, stands the controlling teller, as is made newly vivid when, for example, stretches of direct speech are set in sharply evaluative framing contexts (see Fludernik (1993) and Sternberg (1982) for discussion).

But if character vividness and seeming autonomy are potential corollaries of DD reporting, then equally ID becomes positively desirable when a narrator judges that projecting such vividness is not appropriate. This might be because the topic of speech or thought is mundane, or has already been recorded earlier in the narrative. Or it may be that projecting character depth, authenticity and autonomy is inappropriate because the particular character is quite minor in the larger story, and it would be misleading to endow them with so much individuality. On other occasions, including a second reporting of thought or talk more fully presented previously, something even more abridged than ID is desirable: an entire phase of a relatively unimportant conversation or meeting or telephone call or mental assessment needs to be condensed into a sentence or two, on the grounds that a fuller telling would be aesthetically ill-advised. Those are the occasions on which NRTA or NRSA will be most suitable.

## 5.4  Different again: free Indirect Discourse

The narratorially most fascinating styles of discourse reporting, however, are those that appear to lie between orthodox Direct and Indirect Discourse, revealing some of the formal features of each of those two formats. If we list again the six major contrasts between DD and ID, in abbreviated form:

1   DD has character's tense; ID has narrator's tense.
2   DD has character's pronouns; ID has narrator's pronouns.
3   DD is graphologically set apart; ID is not.
4   DD is paratactic and complementizer-free; ID is hypotactic and complementizer-prone.
5   DD has character's deixis; ID has narrator's deixis.
6   DD has character's lexis/colouring; ID has narrator's lexis/colouring.

then FID is a remarkable selecting and blending of the ID or narratorial option for 1, 2, and 3 (tense, pronouns, and graphological non-removedness), but the DD or characterological option for 4, 5 and 6 (main clause syntax – especially noticeable in interrogatives and imperatives and exclamations; no complementizers; and character's space/time deixis and lexis/colouring). But FID is not *simply* a judicious combination of DD and ID features, nor simply some *middle way* between these two. Both DD and ID are accompanied by a framing or matrix clause: FID eschews one altogether.

FID styles of thought and speech representation, then, are neither direct nor indirect according to orthodox prescriptions, but mixings or mergings of narratorial indirectness with characterological directness. As noted, and despite first appearances, it really is not a blend, however subtle, of DD and ID. This is because the mode it most crucially complements or contrasts with is neither DD nor ID, but PN, the narrator's direct interpellation or address of the reader. Accordingly I have elsewhere proposed a schematic spatial distribution of DD, ID, FID and PN (where the latter is taken to include NRTA and NRSA) along these lines:

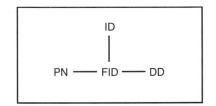

This is intended to suggest, for example, that PN and DD are most sharply distinct, with ID and FID as intermediate, but with the further condition that FID is closer to both PN and DD than ID is to either of these (see Toolan, 1998: 113 for fuller discussion). Despite formally appearing to be a mixture of DD and ID, it is rarely confused with either of these, but rather with PN. And this is rather more interesting precisely because between DD, ID and FID we finally have only variations in the fullness or editedness of rendering of the same individual's 'voice'; but where we cope with the risk of confusing FID and PN we are in danger of misattributing or misidentifying two entirely different voices and two different individuals, the character and the narrator.

If there is one linguistic feature that seems noticeably more prominent in FID than in alternative modes of discourse representation, it is modality. FID is marked by frequent use of modal verbs (*must, should, had to, could, might, would*) and sentence adverbials (*certainly, perhaps, maybe, surely, of course*, etc.) expressing judgments about the likelihood or necessity or desirability of some action or state transpiring. All such modality discloses the character's needs and wants. All such modals are woven into contestable judgments. They prompt an FID reading of the text they accompany in just those cases where we find it implausible to imagine that it is the teller who, perhaps rather abruptly, intrudes into the story to tell us what some character ought to do, or what possibly had happened or would happen.

Whenever a reader wishes to try to confirm for themselves that a particular portion of text is FID essentially sourced in the character, and not Narrative report sourced in that usually abstract narrator, a simple framing or commutation test is sometimes useful. The test helps sharpen vague or uncertain impressions, and uncertain judgments about the intonation of a passage. All the reader needs to do is to assess the plausibility, or conversely the jarring effect, when either of two frames is added to the target stretch of text. Those frames are:

> *I, the narrator, tell you, the reader* [insert text to be probed, unmodified]

and, alternatively,

> [insert text to be probed, with any pronouns referring to the putatively discoursing character converted to first person, and with tenses converted to the present tense of thinking/speaking], *the character remarks, to themselves or other characters*

The former probe explicitly casts the utterance as a narrator-to-reader communicative act, or Pure Narrative; the latter casts the utterance as a character-to-self-or-other-character communicative act. Any sentence, or sentence-part, can be put to these framing tests to help clarify their FID or PN status. Consider these snippets from an early point in Gabriel's final revery:

> Perhaps she had not told him all the story.(1) His eyes moved to the chair over which she had thrown some of her clothes.... (2) Poor Aunt Julia! She, too, would soon be a shade ...(3)

Taking these slightly out of order, the second of these sentences is clearly narratorial: while it fits the narratorial frame quite unexceptionally, it is clearly ludicrous if explicitly cast as characterological, via the second frame:

> ?My eyes move to the chair over which she has thrown some of her clothes, the character remarks (to himself).

People (characters) simply do not think things like that. Conversely, sentence (3) is almost as incontestably characterological, FIT. This could be an intrusive omniscient judging narrator's disclosure to the reader, but this would be an inexplicable and unmotivated departure from the norm established throughout the book so far, and it would not sit well with adjacent text. The adjacent text tells us that Gabriel is looking at things and thinking about things, and it is far more fitting to assume that this is one more thing Gabriel thinks, and indeed that it is a thought he takes further in subsequent sentences of this paragraph. And it fits the second probe test perfectly:

Poor Aunt Julia! She, too, will soon be a shade, the character remarks (to himself).

Finally, the first sentence *Perhaps she had not told him all the story*, taken alone would seem to pass both the narratorial and characterological probe test: good evidence that, in theory, the sentence could be either narrator's suggestion or character's speculation. Again, context and co-text (and content: despite his rather protracted interrogation of her, it would be in Gabriel's character to fear or suspect that not even Gretta had been entirely honest with him) make it overwhelmingly more appropriate to read this potentially ambiguous observation as Gabriel's, in FIT.

As much as anything else, it is the modality in this last example – *Perhaps she had not told* etc. – and the expressive evaluation in the previous example – *Poor Aunt Julia! She, too*, etc. – that encourage us to assign FID interpretations. In seemingly narrative text, FID has the capacity to 'put back' all the immediacy and subjectivity and expressivity that otherwise, in standard ID, gets edited out. And this 'restored' subjective expressivity can extend to eccentricities of spelling and writing in general, reflecting the non-standardness of the character: such features are comfortably accommodated in some kinds of FID. All of this amounts to a restoration of the colourful individuality of characters' direct expression. We feel FID to be more vivid and colourful than PN and ID report because both the latter tend to be more detached, sober, restrained, and standard-English-speaking than the words of the character *in situ*, undergoing the experience, and talking and thinking their way through that experience in frank and uninhibited ways. Of course the latter is an *effect* of direct experiential reaction, but no less significant for that.

But these contrasts of PN sobriety and FID expressivity are reversible patterns rather than rules. As suggested earlier, we could easily encounter vivid and earthy narration of the life of a dull bureaucrat (himself stilted in word and thought), a style that then gave way, where the character's own discourse was conveyed by either direct or free indirect means, to plodding banality, arid and colourless. As elsewhere in narrative study, it is the perception of difference (here between character speech and narrator speech), which is the true criterion. And in some narratives, as in the novels and stories of Henry James, where narrator and characters seem to share a single lect so that contrasts scarcely arise at lexicogrammatical levels at all, the differences can only be painstakingly derived from the *content* of protagonists' discourse (e.g. its varying degrees of reasonableness), and the content of their character.

## 5.5 Who speaks, who thinks?

If the crucial question in focalization was 'From whose spatiotemporal orientation is this conveyed?', here in FID it is 'To whom do we attribute these spoken words or articulated thoughts?' The 'Who is saying/thinking this?' question is useful to keep in mind, since FID is a very open category. Despite the foregoing list of usual indicators of FID, there is no single *necessary* feature of FID, which you have to have in order for a phrase or clause to qualify as FID. Narratives in the present tense (where there will be no tense-difference between direct and indirect discourses) or with first-person narrators can just as easily contain FID as other types. As Leech and Short (1981: 328–33) show in the following two examples, a single character-attributed expletive, or even a single character-expressive punctuation mark, can signal the presence of FID rather than narratorial indirect discourse:

> He said that the bloody train had been late.
> He told her to leave him alone!

We assume that the *bloody* is the character's (*He*), and not the narrator's, and similarly that the exclamation mark (and presumably at least the word immediately preceding it) is the character's. We thus have marks of what must surely be FID, but we do not have clear indications of its extent – of 'how much', before and after the word *bloody*, is also essentially attributable to the character. This amounts to another interestingly undecidable dimension of FID. In the second example, do we decide that the entire clause 'leave him alone!' is FID, or only 'alone!', or merely '!'?

FID is a long-established technique that can be usefully related to such fundamental literary distinctions of narrative method as those between showing and telling, or mimesis and diegesis. While the former places the emphasis on a direct characterological representation or impersonation, the latter implies a more indirect, detached teller-oriented conspectual presentation. In the narration of events mimesis is associated with a scenic presentation, while diegesis is linked to a condensed or 'edited' and summarized account – with, consequently, a larger role played by the teller who condenses or edits. Mimesis presents 'everything that happened' in one sense, but really only everything as it would be revealed to a witness within the scene; in these latter respects it is quite partial and far from comprehensive. And as Stanzel (1981) notes, it typically comes with internal character-focalization. Diegesis presents 'everything that happened' in another sense, but only everything that a detached external reporter decides is worth telling – a reporter who is able to reflect, reorganize, and decide upon the point or teleology of the story prior to narrating it. We can accordingly predict that diegetic narration will have more manipulations of temporal order, duration and frequency, and more evident ranking or hierarchical ordering of event-presentation.

## 5.6  FID: functions and effects

In the neo-Platonist terms mentioned earlier (mimesis and diegesis), FID amounts to a mimetic diegesis (a telling that shows or presents aspects of the character's 'own' words or thoughts). But there are numerous ways of characterizing FID, in fact: as substitutionary narration; as combined discourse; as a contamination, tainting or colouring of the narrative; as a dual voicing. My own preference is for viewing it as a strategy of (usually temporary or discontinuous) alignment, in words, values and perspective, of the narrator with a character. I favour the word 'alignment' because it doesn't prescribe whether that closeness of narrator to character is going to be used for purposes of irony, empathy, as a vehicle for stream-of-consciousness or the clashing of two voices, or whatever: the alignment is perceived, then the function (or 'naturalization') is worked out by the reader. The term 'alignment' also helps us keep in mind that, in terms of lexicogrammatical markers and aesthetic or narrative effect, there is a continuum from pure narrative words to pure character words, with any number of points on that continuum.

Like McHale and others (Ginsberg, 1982; Pascal, 1977), Jefferson recognizes that a key source of the impact of the FID sentence is its ambiguous mixture of proper narrative and proper speech or thought:

> The dual voice of FID which is responsible for the superficially realist effect of immediacy is also an ambiguity which is highly unrealistic. From a realist point of view, FID is a doubly disconcerting use of language: its ambiguities cut it adrift from the two points at which we commonly imagine language to be anchored to reality, the speaker and the referent. It is neither fully expressive nor fully referential, and this *invraisemblance* differentiates it most profoundly from other forms of reported discourse.
>
> (Jefferson, 1981: 42)

By *invraisemblance* Jefferson alludes in part to FID's lack of *vraisemblance*: the effect or convention of faithful and 'realistic' representation of the real world that many novels foster and many readers demand. The *invraisemblance* of FID stems from the fact that it gives rise to sentences, like *Perhaps she had not told him all the story*, and *She too would soon be a shade* and *Yes, the newspapers were right* which, in just those forms and with just those referential commitments, none of us in the discoursing of our everyday lives, including our storytellings embedded in conversations, could ever actually say. FID sentences are in this sense unsayable or unspeakable, impossible to anchor to one speaker at one place and time, since they are impossibly divided between two distinct speakers (narrator and character) and anchorages. We can no more ordinarily speak (that is, use) an FID sentence than we can 'do both voices' when we greet someone else and are replied to by them: *How are _fine, and you?_

At this point mention should be made of Banfield's challenging and wide-ranging theory of narration and discourse (Banfield, 1982). Banfield's theory of unspeakable sentences argues that not merely FID but all narrative sentences are marked off from ordinary communicative discourse by their unspeakability. Narration is unspeakable because, unlike discourse (which is both communicative and expressive), it is a text with neither a genuine addressee (nor any textual traces of one) nor a genuine expressivity-disclosing speaker. FID, in partial contrast, carries abundant expressivity (that of the character), but still no genuine I–you communicativity, and as a result remains unspeakable. The theory is fascinating, wide-ranging, and presented in great technical and critical detail, and for those among other reasons it merits scrutiny; but its declared adherents are few. In the first edition of this book, I presented and critiqued Banfield's argument at length, and will not do so here; interested readers may wish to read that earlier assessment, together with those of McHale (1983) and Simpson (1993: 35–8), both of whom, like me, dissent from Banfield's conclusions (which, *inter alia*, include a rejection of the 'dual voice' approach to FID outlined above).

As a final point of orientation we should note some of the influential work of Short and his colleagues (e.g. Leech and Short, 1981; Semino, Short and Wynne, 1999; Short, Semino and Culpeper, 1996) which surveys and analyses trends in literary and non-literary discourse representation, increasingly using corpus materials and methods. It is they who have drawn attention to the fact that, in newspapers particularly, a newsworthy item of *written* discourse (e.g. an open letter of resignation from the CEO of some major public body) may be slightly – or even significantly – differently reported on separate occasions, even where both purport to be the *verbatim* record. For example, the letter of resignation may be quoted, in the front page story, as

> 'I now feel, in the light of this shabby persecution by the press, in which I have been subjected to cruel and unreasonable harassment, that I must relinquish my post to defend my reputation.'

But on an inside page, one might find the following fuller version, equally purporting to be the *verbatim* record:

> 'I now feel, in the light of this shabby persecution by the press, in which I and my family have been subjected to cruel and unreasonable harassment, without the possibility of setting the record straight in a timely fashion, that I must relinquish my post in order to defend my reputation.'

In this example, an original letter has been reproduced in slightly different versions, on the inside and front pages of the newspaper. To situate this practice alongside other kinds of discourse representation, Short *et al.* propose that both versions be called Direct Writing (DW). But of course where you can get Direct Writing report you can also get report via Indirect Writing:

In his letter Sir Nigel said that his whole family had been subjected to harassment by the press.

Indeed, the entire menu of Writing report options, parallel to those for Speech and Thought, is available: FDW (Free Direct Writing), DW (Direct Writing), FIW (Free Indirect Writing), IW (Indirect Writing), NRWA (Narrator's Representation of Writing Act), and NW (Narrator's Report of Writing). One application of these terms could be to plagiarism: Free Direct Writing passed off as (genuine) writing. Another is to literature: near the opening of Jane Austen's *Mansfield Park*, for example, the narrative reports a letter written to Lady Bertram by her impoverished sister Frances. The letter is particularly concerned with the future prospects of Frances' many children:

> Her eldest son was a boy of ten years old, a fine spirited fellow who longed to be out in the world; but what could she do? Was there any chance of his being hereafter useful to Sir Thomas in the concerns of his West Indian property?

This is Free Indirect Writing, a deictically indirect or narratorially-framed version of the written discourse which, we understand, Frances Price has sent to Lady Bertram.

But perhaps the most influential of the observations made by Short and his colleagues are some that appeared in Leech and Short (1981) concerning the contrasting 'norms' of speech-reporting and thought-reporting, and, as a consequence of these different norms, the customary and different reception that readers accord to FIS and FIT. Here, then, the two modes are *not* collapsed into a superordinate FID category, and rather the distinctive effect of each type – FIS and FIT – is assessed comparatively, but separately. Leech and Short's starting-point has the force of common sense. Under normal conditions, we expect that any ordinary close witness (W) to an incident, a series of events involving speech and action, should be able to report both the actions of the observed individuals and, in Direct Speech, their actual words. (A court of law would prefer it: 'Can you tell the court the exact words that the defendant used?', the barrister will ask.) This remains the case even though numerous studies show that *verbatim* recall is rarely achieved.

By contrast we do not accept that an ordinary witness (W) to an incident can reliably report the sententially-composed thoughts – or even the chaotically-jumbled ones – that ran through A's head, or B's, at any point during the incident. At best, if W were a close friend of A or B, and interviewed them afterwards, they might glean from them an account of what they had been thinking – but in W's subsequent narrative report of the incident, any indications of what A or B had been thinking, however presented (across the range of options from FDT to NRTA), would in fact be only a report of a report. W has no direct access to A's thoughts, common sense tells us; only A has. In light of this, and again other things being equal, a witness/narrator does surprise us, and is regarded as in some respects *imposing* on us, the addressees, and on the thinking character reported, when they offer a heterodiegetic report of direct thought. (And the rules of evidence in criminal law would completely exclude a witness from anything so outrageous as 'telling the court what thoughts ran through the defendant's mind'.)

The upshot of these common sense predispositions in readers and addressees, Leech and Short suggest, is that while Direct Speech is 'normal' as the means for reporting speech – a character's speech is expectably reported directly unless there are contingent reasons for opting for some other mode – Indirect Thought is 'normal' as the means for reporting anyone else's thoughts besides your own, including a character's in a heterodiegetic narrative. And again, if IT is the norm, departures from that norm become 'accountable': we will tend to expect there must be a (good) reason why the default option of IT has not been adopted. If one visualizes the Speech-mode continuum on a horizontal line, with FDS at the far left, then most departures from this putative DS norm will be 'to the right', which is also to say, by recourse to modes which adjust the character–narrator weighting increasingly in favour of the narrator: as one moves towards NRSA, one adopts modes that carry less and less of the character's expressivity and subjectivity in their own words, and more and more of the narrator's controlling and editorialized version of those words. Even FIS, most crucially, gives the narrator 'more of a say', and more opportunity to insinuate narratorial intonation and covert comment, than the DS norm does. Accordingly, Leech and Short argue, FIS is often read or heard as a narratorial 'stepping back' from allowing the character full and uncritiqued rein, as DS would tend to do; FIS often discloses character's words laced with narratorial *irony*.

On the other hand, again if the Thought-mode continuum runs horizontally, with SOC and FDT leftmost and NRTA rightmost, then a move away from the IT norm 'to the left', to FIT, is a contrasting move to that entailed in adopting FIS. FIT, by comparison with IT, gives the character's expressivity and subjectivity fuller disclosure, pushing down the narrator into a less prominent role, carrying less scope for implicit editorial critique. And the assumption is that this option is taken typically where the narrator has no inclination to critique or ironize the represented thinking character; rather, there is implicit narratorial *empathy* with the character.

If these trends are as robust as is here suggested, they would be reminiscent of what are called scalar implicatures in linguistic pragmatics (Levinson, 1983: 132ff.). Consider the set of quantifying terms:

*all*, *most*, *many*, *some*, and *few*

We ordinarily expect a speaker to use the 'leftmost' appropriate term, so as to be cooperatively informative, in any situation, even though any terms to the right of a particular item must be true if that particular item is true. Thus if all my ten siblings live in Belgium, I should normally say, 'They all live in Belgium' and not that *many* or *some* of them live there, even though these are true: they are true but would be insufficient and misleading. Anyone who knows or discovers that all my siblings live in Belgium will assume I am signifying or implicating something if I use a lesser quantifier like *most*. In a roughly comparable way, possibly, recourse to less direct speech-presentation than DS may prompt the reader to infer some narratorial implicature involving comment or criticism; while recourse to more direct thought-presentation than IT may similarly invite the inference of narratorial respect, empathy, an 'entering' of the character's intimate mental space that is licensed on the grounds that the narrative does so without any intent of controlling or managing that thought-world, but simply of being its platform.

All this is schematically summarized in the following figure, based on Leech and Short (1981: 344):

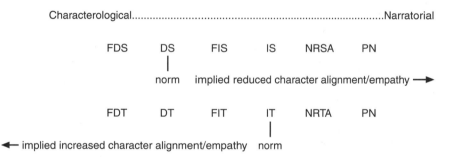

Finally, whether the theorist dwells on the undecidability of FID, or its 'unspeakability', or its dialogism, all commentators recognize that no ordinary speaker, speaking to us face-to-face (rather than, for example, narrating) would produce the kind of discourse that FID inhabits. That is because in such FID-coloured narrative two radically distinct situations of utterance are simultaneously implied: situations with quite different participants (character-to-character versus narrator-to-reader) and quite different spatiotemporal settings (the 'then' of the story versus the 'now' of the telling/reading), and with convergence only in the area of subject matter (a character's represented thoughts or speech are experiential subject matter for that character, but also the subject matter of the narrative for its reader). The oddity of encountering two amalgamated situations of utterance should be evident if we reflect upon Lyons's much-quoted characterization of 'the canonical situation of utterance':

This involves one-one, or one-many, signalling in the phonic medium along the vocal-auditory channel, with all the participants present in the same actual situation able to see one another and to perceive the associated non-vocal paralinguistic features of their utterances, and each assuming the roles of sender and receiver in turn.... There is much in the structure of languages that can only be explained on the assumption that they have developed for communication in face-to-face interaction. This is clearly so as far as deixis is concerned.

(Lyons, 1977: 637–8)

FID, we can see, is at a fascinating distance from this 'canonical situation of utterance'. By contrast the main subject-matter of the next chapter, oral narratives of personal experience, are typically to be found wholly embedded in precisely that canonical situation.

## Further reading

The literature on both the theory of free indirect discourse and literary exploitations of it is voluminous. A good starting place is Chapter 10 of Leech and Short (1981). Pascal (1977) is a clear and detailed account of FID's role in, especially, nineteenth-century European fiction; McHale (1978) is an authoritative survey, making connections to fundamental issues in the theory of poetics. Also to be recommended in this vein are Hernadi (1972) and Ginsberg (1982), while longer innovative studies include Cohn (1978), Stanzel (1984) and Fludernik (1993). Sternberg (1982), is excellent on 'the indirections' of direct speech. More linguistic discussions of FID begin with Bally (1912), and include Voloshinov (1973), Bickerton (1967), Jones (1968), Bronzwaer (1970), Fillmore (1974), Dillon and Kirchhoff (1976), McKay (1978; 1982), Banfield (1982) and, for various languages other than English: Hagenaar (1996), Redeker (1996), Kullmann (1995), Vuillaume (1998), Hummel (1999), and Hirose (2000). Discussions of Banfield's work in McHale (1983) and Simpson (1993) are also very useful. Other work to be consulted includes Duchan *et al.* (1995), Ehrlich (1990), Dry (1995), Oltean (1993), Mezei (1996), Baron (1998) and Ferguson (2000). On reporting speech in non-literary contexts, see, e.g. Slembrouck (1992), Waugh (1995), Vincent and Perrin (1999) and Myers (1999). On the thorny issue of 'faithfulness' in discourse reporting, a recent paper is Short, Semino and Wynne (2001). Advanced studies of FID and related topics continue to appear in such journals as *Poetics Today*; *Journal of Narrative Technique*; *Narrative*; *Language and Literature*; *Journal of Literary Semantics*; and *Style*.

## Notes and exercises

1 Much of the narrative of 'Eveline' is not plausibly FID, and close attention to the text reveals a highly fluid, even volatile, style of narration that moves from intrusive narration, summarizing her thoughts, in sentence 1 below, to the almost entirely impersonal report – except for the word 'mournful' – in sentence 2, to the probable FID of sentence 3:

> She felt her cheek pale and cold and, out of a maze of distress, she prayed to God to direct her, to show her what was her duty.(1) The boat blew a long mournful whistle into the mist.(2) If she went, tomorrow she would be on the sea with Frank, steaming towards Buenos Ayres.(3)

(40)

Similarly, it is implausible to suggest that such sentences as the following, the work of an intrusive omniscient narrator, represent Eveline in her own thoughts and words:

> As she mused the pitiful vision of her mother's life laid its spell on the very quick of her being – that life of commonplace sacrifice closing in final craziness.
>
> (40)

This sentence provoked an interesting difference of interpretation between two noted Joycean scholars, Chatman and Hart. Of it Hart wrote that its 'strong note of falsity' reflects Eveline's inability to love, or think of her situation except in 'tawdry clichés' (Hart, 1969: 51). In rebuttal, Chatman protests that Hart has confused character viewpoint and narrator's voice, misreading the scene as a result:

> Surely the objectionable words are not Eveline's but the narrator's. It is he who is parodying pulp-literature sentimentality in tawdry clichés ... [using language that is] not in her vocabulary.
>
> (Chatman, 1978: 153, fn. 9)

Chatman may be right, but the issue is not at all easy to decide; and if he is right, it leaves in need of explanation *why* it is that Joyce creates, for a story so much told from Eveline's point of view, a narrator who adopts parodying clichéd language which inevitably tends to mock and belittle Eveline and 'fictionalize' her situation. A careful charting of the strategic changes in narrative orientation in 'Eveline' will uncover many such complexities – and authorial risks.

2  It has already been implied, in references in the chapter to 'coloured' ID, that some types of ID are a good deal closer to FID, having dual-voice qualities, than other types of ID. Indeed some of the former would simply be called FID by some analysts, despite the presence of a framing clause. It may be quite instructive, using a corpus of literary examples or plausible composed examples, to attempt to specify what character-oriented or FID-like grammatical features do seem allowable in ID, and which such features seem positively disallowed. That is, among the inventory of FID features, which are possible in ID and which are impossible, and why? Among FID features worth testing for are:

> Subject–auxiliary verb inversion in reported questions
> Topicalization (stating the clause Subject or Object initially, and then a second time pronominally: *He said these pistachio nuts, I can't stop eating **them***)
> Language-mixing (narrator's dialect with character's dialect)
> Attitudinal disjuncts attributable to the character not the narrator (i.e. not *He turned to her and said bluntly that was her problem*, but *He turned to her and said **frankly** he couldn't give a fig.*)
> Incomplete sentences
> Subjectless Imperatives
> Direct address (*She went to the bottom of the stairs and yelled that Claud, Charlotte and Lau-raaaah!, DINNERtiiime!*).

Good commentaries on this topic appear in Banfield (1982) and Fludernik (1993).

3  As mentioned in 5.2, over the years since Leech and Short (1981), Short and his co-researchers have proposed a slight revision to the categorization of the kinds

of indirect reporting of a character's speech or mental processing, to capture kinds of representation that are somewhat distinct from all the extant types (see Short *et al.* 1996). These are Narrator's report of Voice (NV) and Narration of Internal States (NI), the latter being similar to what Cohn (1978) has called 'psychonarration'. These comprise allusions to or annotations of characters' speaking and thinking which differ from all the other modes for reporting character's discourse in that they carry no mention of the content of the speaking or thinking, but chiefly report its manner or style. They arguably therefore fall outside the domain of discourse-report altogether, and into that of Narration. Unlike all the other discourse-representing modes, for example, it is hard to see how one might convincingly re-cast an instance of NV as IS or DS (and similarly with respect to NI), which is always to a degree possible, across all the other modes, even if one begins with something as abridged as an NRSA occurrence. On the other hand it is true that sometimes only a fine line distinguishes NV from NRSA, or NI from NRTA. Thus one of Short *et al.*'s examples of NV, taken from J. G. Ballard's *The Empire of the Sun*, is

Voices fretted along the murmuring wire.

Presumably if this had run *Their voices quarrelled back and forth along the telephone line*, this might be classified instead as NRSA.

# 6 Narrative as socially situated
## The sociolinguistic approach

## 6.1 Labov and narrative structure

A great deal of important work on naturally-occurring narrative – particularly the narratives of ordinary people in their extraordinary everyday lives – stems from just two seminal essays by the American sociolinguist William Labov. The first, written jointly with Joshua Waletzky, appeared in Helms (1967), under the title 'Narrative analysis: oral versions of personal experience'. The second appeared as Chapter 9 of Labov's *Language in the Inner City* (1972), and is titled 'The transformation of experience in narrative syntax'. Much more recently, Labov has published 'Some Further Steps in Narrative Analysis' (1997), in a special issue of the *Journal of Narrative and Life History* devoted to Labov-influenced commentaries from a host of scholars celebrating the thirtieth anniversary of the 1967 paper. That recent paper makes only slight adjustments to the widely-adopted Labovian account.

Labov and Waletzky's hypothesis is that fundamental narrative structures are to be found in oral versions of personal experience – the ordinary narratives of ordinary speakers. They wish, by looking at many narratives, to identify and relate formal linguistic properties of narrative to their functions. And like all structuralists, their analysis is based on the perception of a delimited set of recurrent patterns and the setting aside of what they take to be local differences in the pursuit of the deeper structural similarities: 'We will be relying upon the basic techniques of linguistic analysis, isolating the invariant structural units which are represented by a variety of superficial forms.' (Labov and Waletzky, 1967: 12).

They relate those identified linguistic-structural properties to functions, nominating two broad functions in particular as core. The first of these is the referential function: narrative's functioning as a means of recapitulating experience in an ordered set of clauses that matches the temporal sequence of the original experience. Versions of this 'sequential recapitulation' function have arisen before in this book, in the definitions of story or bare narrative. The second function has been less universally emphasized, partly because narrative has not always been properly related to its contexts of occurrence, its role as an instrument or resource for its human 'users'. The second function then, which Labov and Waletzky term 'evaluative', attends to the users of narratives, and the requirement that a narrative has a point, is worth telling, as far as the teller (and preferably the addressee also) is concerned.

Unlike Propp, whom they suggest focussed on 'large semantic units' (13), Labov and Waletzky concentrate first on

> the smallest unit of linguistic expression which defines the functions of narrative [i.e. the smallest unit which can ordinarily realize those functions] – primarily the clause . . .
>
> (13)

And their first task becomes that of attempting to relate

> the sequence of clauses in the narrative to the sequence of events inferred from the narrative.
>
> (20)

This task is more manageable than it might appear (if we think back to Genette and Nabokov's *Pnin*, discussed in earlier chapters), because, as Labov has reiterated in his 1997 paper, among the kinds of 'crisis' narratives of personal experience that were studied (usually someone's account of a situation where they genuinely feared for their life), without exception clauses reporting events were told in the same order as the putative original events would have happened. So Labov is prepared to assert that oral narratives of life-threatening personal experience are invariably recounted chronologically.

This, in turn, points to the quite sharp difference between the kind of oral and 'real time' production that sociolinguists such as Labov tend to study, and the kind of crafted written literary production that narratologists like Genette study. A review of the enduring connections and commonalities between these seemingly different narratives and analyses will be included in this chapter. Techniques of temporal reordering and Proustian complexity, however, have no place in the Labovian studies:

> The basic narrative units that we wish to isolate are defined by the fact that they recapitulate experience in the same order as the original events.
>
> (1967: 20–1)

Accordingly, and in just these terms, the following sample constitutes a narrative:

> Well, this person had a little too much to drink and he attacked me and the friend came in and she stopped it.

while the following version, where there is presentational reordering through subordination, is simply not a narrative in Labov and Waletzky's terms, even though it is an acceptable recapitulation of experience:

> A friend of mine came in just in time to stop this person who had had a little too much to drink from attacking me.

It displays the kind of temporal/clausal manipulation that they simply did not find actually produced by their informants, as an exemplar of the particular text-type that interested them. This preference might be summed up by saying that, in telling narratives of personal life-threatening experience, a 'blow by blow' account is obligatory. In passing, Labov and Waletzky acknowledge that narratives in their restricted sense are just one distinct kind of storytelling.

The foregoing remarks should serve as a warning that their assumptions and procedures differ in some respects from those we have previously looked at. The attraction of their principles lies in their clarity, replicability, and their search for a basic pattern from which more complex narratives might be derived. And their differences from the narration analysts should not be overstated: after all, Genette no less than they develops his taxonomy of diegetic variations on a foundational 'natural' order of event recapitulation.

## 6.2  Fixed narrative clauses, free evaluative clauses

The Labovian thesis, then, is that true narrative clauses, the backbone of narrative as they narrowly define it, are temporally ordered independent clauses (along with their dependent subordinate clauses) that must occur in a fixed presentational sequence. There is a 'shiftability' of subordinate clauses, around the main clause on which they depend, that excludes them from consideration as fully narrative clauses; in Labov (1997) the independent clause that is the 'head' of a narrative clause is termed a sequential clause. The fixity of sequence of properly narrative clauses is quite crucial: any reordering of narrative clauses would create a different story. Compare

1   John fell in the river, got very cold, and had two large whiskies.

with

2   John had two large whiskies, fell in the river, and got very cold.

Clearly, despite many similarities of form, the differently-ordered clauses here represent two radically different stories, with different cause-and-effect relations between events, and different probable evaluations by teller and hearer (the listener might comment 'serves him right' about the second John but could hardly do so about the first).

Labov and Waletzky present a rather more formal account of the non-shiftability of narrative clauses (relative to each other) by specifying the displacement potential of clauses in narratives. Setting a narrative out on the page with just one main or independent clause per line of text, and labelling the clauses alphabetically, they annotate the letter-label of each clause by noting, either side of it, the number of previous and subsequent clauses that any particular clause could displace. Accordingly narrative 2 above might be annotated as follows:

0a0   John had two large whiskies,
0b0   fell in the river,
0c0   and got very cold.

which postulates that none of the three clauses can be moved earlier or later without 'changing the inferred sequence of events' (Labov and Waletzky, 1967: 21) in the original experience. But if the following observation is added at the story's close:

This happened when he was still at school.

it seems that this is freely shiftable to any position earlier in the story without interference with the inferred sequence of events:

John had two large whiskies – this happened when he was still at school – fell in the river, and got very cold.

If this additional comment were to come at the end of the sequence, the annotation would be:

0a0   John had two large whiskies,
0b0   fell in the river,
0c0   and got very cold.
3d0   This happened when he was still at school.

The annotation 3d0 states that clause 'd' may occur as many as three clauses earlier, but no later, in this narrative, without alteration to the inferred sequence of actual events, the essence of the narrative. The previous three clauses, on the other hand, continue to be locked into their given interrelated positions. A clause like 'd', describing the circumstances surrounding the fixed sequence of events of a narrative and with the potential of being moved anywhere in the text, is known in Labovian terminology as a free clause.

Narrative clauses (reporting the ordered experience of the interrelated events) and free clauses (reporting the context of the events, and participants' perspectives) are the most sharply contrasted pair of clause types that Labov identifies. Each is the basic means for enacting the two functions of narrative cited earlier: the 'referentially' ordered recall of temporally ordered experience, and the 'evaluative' staging of the story so as to convey its point and tellability. But there are two further types of clause, intermediate between narrative and free ones; they are types of clause which are movable within limits, and with intermediate functions. The first intermediate type are those linked narrative clauses, usually only pairs or triads, that can be mutually reordered 'freely'. These are called coordinate clauses – the coordination here being not so much in terms of grammar as in terms of narrative sense. Many grammatically coordinated clauses are not coordinated in this special sense of permissible narrative reorderability (*She took arsenic and died*, for example, is grammatically but not narrationally coordinate; the clauses in *She drank coffee and alcohol. She smoked cigars. She ate red meat all the time*, are narrationally but not grammatically coordinate). Revising the 'drunken drenching' story, Labovian coordination can be demonstrated:

0a0   John had two large whiskies,
0b0   fell in the river,
0c1   got very cold
1d0   and ruined his suit.
4e0   This happened when he was still at school.

Clauses c and d are coordinate: the order in which John's getting cold and ruining his suit are reported is freely reversible without alteration to the basic narrative.

Conversely, there are some free clauses that are not entirely freely shiftable to just any other place in the sequence. They have a limited domain of occurrence or reach, and are termed restricted clauses. In the following version:

0a2   John got this urge to be the star of the party.
0b0   He had two large whiskies,
0c0   performed a standing somersault on the embankment wall,
0d0   fell in the river,
0e1   got very cold
1f0   and ruined his suit.
6g0   This happened when he was still at school.

clause 'a' here is a kind of comment in parallel to the main action, and – arguably, at least – could come a little later in the sequence. It could occur after 'b' or 'c', but no later than this, if we interpret the contents of 'd' as an unintentional lapse from 'star of the party' behaviour (he fell, he did not simply jump). The event that 'd' reports, we imagine, must have considerably dampened the urge that 'a' discloses. But a greater degree of arguability of the analysis enters with the notion of restricted clauses: some readers may contest the analysis offered above, and might want to reclassify 'a' as a wholly free clause. We may expect, then, that in more complex narratives these restricted clauses will be a source of much satisfying analytical-interpretive trouble as they generate uncertainties and larger debates about the 'what happened when, and why' of particular texts.

What then, for Labov, is a narrative? Minimally, and similar to my own definition in Chapter 1,

> a minimal narrative [is] a sequence of two clauses which are temporally ordered ... a minimal narrative is defined as one containing a single temporal juncture.
>
> (Labov, 1972: 361)

And by temporal juncture, as we have seen, is meant the non-reversibility of two narrative clauses without change of the original semantic interpretation of the story. Having characterized narrative clauses, Labov and Waletzky go on to specify the heads of those clauses: these are, as we might expect, the main clause finite verbs, and usually occur in the simple past or present. Progressive aspect (*he was performing somersaults*) and perfective aspect (*he had performed two somersaults*) are rare though not impossible in narrative clauses: such aspectual elaborations are much commoner in restricted and, especially, free clauses. Procedures are also outlined for isolating the primary sequence of any narrative, a postulated simplest unmarked order of clauses, but such refinements need not occupy us here.

We should instead consider now Labov's essay of 1972, which, as noted, expands the earlier one, applying the model to actually-occurring narratives from New York Black English vernacular culture. In this later paper a six-part structure is posited of a fully-formed oral narrative:

1    *Abstract*: What, in a nutshell, is this story about?
2    *Orientation*: Who, when, where?
3    *Complicating action*: What happened and then what happened?
4    *Evaluation*: So what? How or why is this interesting?
5    *Result or resolution*: What finally happened?
6    *Coda*: That's it, I've finished and am 'bridging' back to our present situation.

These are related in Labov's famous 'diamond' picture of the progression of an oral narrative, which I reproduce below. Notice how evaluation, while associable with a 'most expected' place in the progression of a narrative, namely at the 'high point' before the crisis is resolved, is shown – by the spreading waves – to be something that can permeate the telling. Evaluation can and does occur anywhere in narratives; in linguistic terms it is often better to think of it as a prosody rather than a section.

What follows are more detailed commentaries on the six structural

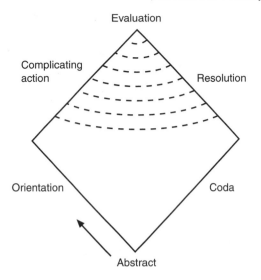

parts or phases of this model. Besides reproducing some of Labov's own examples, I will refer extensively to a literary 'oral narrative of personal experience', Mr Casey's story of the 'famous spit', which he tells at the Christmas dinner table, early in Joyce's *Portrait of the Artist as a Young Man*. Besides being a magnificently crafted story, set with a richness of highlighted contextualization that seems particularly available in literary narratives, the story exemplifies the similarities between ordinary narratives and literary ones. Since it is presented as spoken by Mr Casey and yet known by us to have been written by Joyce, we could argue that as a type the story lies somewhere between the purely oral narrative and the purely written one.

## 6.3 Abstracts and orientations

Together with the coda, the abstract can be thought of as one of the optional margins of a narrative. They fall not so much at the beginning and the end of a narrative, as *before* the beginning and *after* the end, respectively. In sharpest contrast with them, the Complicating Action is the phase in which most of a story's positionally fixed narrative (=sequential) clauses occur; it is, as it were, the obligatory nucleus. The term 'nucleus' is here taken over from its use in describing the structure of the English syllable: the syllable is standardly said to contain a vowel as obligatory nucleus, this being optionally flanked by an onset and coda, each of which comprises one or more consonants. Interestingly, the alternative British terms for the margins of a syllable, arrest and release, seem applicable to narratives too: an oral narrative arrests the flow of multi-party talk, buttonholing the addressees; with the story's completion there is a freeing-up of the suspended turn-taking possibilities and a release, too, from the state of being absorbed and 'caught up', as teller or listener, in an experience of the narrative.

A typical abstract outlines or advertises the story that a teller intends will follow. (I choose that form of words, rather than 'intends to tell', because, as will be discussed later, one person can produce an abstract intending that someone else goes on to tell the fuller story.) An abstract may then sketch a narrative in a severely abridged form, but it is never a proper telling of it, as the following examples should indicate:

1   An' then, three weeks ago I had a fight with this other dude outside. He got mad 'cause I wouldn't give him a cigarette. Aint that a bitch?
(Labov, 1972: 356)

2   – Tell me, did I tell you that story about a very famous spit?
   – You did not, John, said Mr Dedalus.
   – Why then, said Mr Casey, it is a most instructive story.
(Joyce, *Portrait of the Artist*, 34)

But abstracts also do something else (at least in the view of many socio-linguists), as example 2 indicates. They often contain requests for the extended turn at talk necessary to tell a story. The teller's addressees are thus politely given the opportunity to indicate their preference not to hear the story, for whatever reason (they may be pressed for time, or they may have something very important they want to say first, or they may have heard the story before). But where an abstract is a bid for the floor among friends, interacting casually or competitively, it may have few marks of a polite request and rather more marks of a friendly battle for attention. This is reflected in a third common characteristic of abstracts, besides those of story summarizing and requesting telling rights: abstracts are often advertisements or trailers for stories, making exaggerated claims for what will follow, promising more than gets delivered. This third character-istic is noticeably absent both from Labov's data and from his description of the element. But that abstracts performing requesting, advertising or floor-wresting functions are absent from Labov's corpus is hardly surpris-ing: typically his informants are supplying stories after they have been invited to do so, so that for any of them to then request-to-narrate would be rather odd, indicative of some misunderstanding, or an extreme of timidity or politeness. In sum, then, abstracts in one respect mark an exiting of direct interaction in their summary heralding of the monologue text that is intended to follow, but in another respect they remain interac-tive in their functions of checking or announcing – or insisting upon – the tellability in principle of a narrative.

A variant of the normal pattern in which a single teller provides both abstract and following story is that where a co-conversationalist supplies an abstract of a story considered worth the telling, so as to prompt or invite another participant to tell it. This technique may appear in any setting where at least two of the participants know each other well, e.g. from a couple at a social gathering. One interesting consequence of the technique is that worries about tellability are no longer, as usually, directed at one's addressees: the prompter has effectively gone on record as asserting the tellability of a story, and the prompted teller has the luxury of proceeding or not, depending on whether he or she thinks the story is tellable.

The collaborative story introduction is, however, fraught with uncertainties when compared with the solo story introduction. We might compare it to the difference, in soccer, between shooting at goal yourself or passing to a team-mate for them to shoot at goal. Some prompted tellers dislike being 'forced' into telling a story, but are also aware – as is everyone else – of the awkward 'misfire' feel if they decline to proceed. Such an action puts either the prompter or the prompted in a bad light, and may be adjudged uncooperative if it is viewed as a refusal to make a contribution that has been explicitly requested (see Grice, 1975, on the cooperative principles that may be said to underwrite our construction and reception of utterances in conversations). Even with cooperative goodwill, however, a prompted teller may fail to tell a story, or fail to tell it adequately, due to poor recall of the detail of the story events. In such cases the initiating prompter has made a mistaken judgment as to just how well their partner remembers the story – a clear case of poor teamwork.

The orientation specifies the participants and circumstances, especially of place and time, of the narrative, and is equivalent to what was called setting (not to focalization) in the narratological chapters. Labov notes that while orientation material can be embedded within opening narrative clauses, it more commonly comes in a block of free clauses prior to the development of the narrative action. Or at least we might think of the position between abstract and complicating action as the unmarked and logical position for orientation. In the orientation we can expect verb forms other than extensive verbs (i.e. transitive or intransitive verbs involving action) in the simple past tense. Thus here we may find past perfectives and past progressive verb phrases, and intensive verbs (*be*, *become*, *seem*, etc.) in relational process clauses specifying attributes and identities (as described in 4.9).

But the most interesting use of orientation is where components of it are strategically delayed, and we are told salient facts about the setting late in a narrative. This, like analepsis, may create effects of considerable surprise, even of shock. It may be particularly used where the teller himself, as a participant in a sequence of events, only belatedly learned some salient facts of a situation and wants to put his audience in a similar experiential position.

## 6.4 Evaluation

Evaluation consists of all the means used to establish and sustain the point, the contextual significance and tellability, or reportability, of a story. It may take many forms and appear at almost any point in the telling, although it is often particularly clustered around the 'hinge' or climactic point of the action, just before – and in effect delaying – the resolving action or event. It is the pre-eminent constituent by means of which the narrator's personal involvement in a story is conveyed. In Labov's words, it is

> the means used by the narrator to indicate the point of the narrative, its *raison d'etre*: why it was told, and what the narrator is getting at.
>
> (Labov, 1972: 366)

The Labovian sub-types of evaluation are first distinguished according to whether they appear inside or outside the fixed-position clauses of narrative. Evaluations appearing outside the narrative clause are of five sub-types.

1    Wholly external evaluations – as external as you can get; here the narrator breaks the frame of the story-telling itself to address the listener directly, interrupting the narrative to express a speaker's current or still valid general evaluation of the distant events:

> It is a most instructive story ... the story is very short and sweet
> ...                                                      (Joyce: 35, 36)
> It was the strangest feeling.
> It was quite an experience.

2    Evaluation embedded as a comment reported as made by the teller-as-participant at the time of the events themselves:

> And I said to myself: 'This is it!'

3    Or embedded as a comment made by the teller-as-participant to another participant:

> And I said to Mary: 'This is it!'

4    Or embedded as an evaluation coming from another participant:

> And Mary said to us: 'This is it!'

5    Evaluative action: how some participant responded in physical rather than merely verbal terms to the ongoing events:

> I never prayed to God so fast.
> I was shakin' like a leaf.

The first of these last two examples, it may be noted in passing, reflects one set of cultural assumptions, in which prayer is implicitly classified as a kind of evaluating rather than a kind of doing. Prayer here is not conceived of as narrative action, occurring at a fixed point in a sequence of causally-linked events. Devout believers might see things differently, interpreting any happy outcome that followed the prayers as caused by (the deity supplicated in) those prayers.

All these modes of evaluation involve a temporary suspension of the action, a brief 'time out' from the telling of the story proper. When well placed, such manoeuvres do indeed create suspense, set apart whatever narrative follows (often the concluding resolution), and heighten the listener's interest. But all such external suspensions can be contrasted with the narrative-clause-internal modes of evaluation to which I will turn in Section 6.6. Before doing so, a few observations on a central assumption of Labovian method are necessary.

## 6.5 Doing and saying

Labov and Waletzky studied 'danger of death' narratives. There they found, and thereafter adopted as a working assumption, that what is *said* (by teller or others) will not be the core of the story; rather, the narrative core is occupied by what is *done*. The 'what is done' then becomes the core narrative text of clauses – actions – while the 'what is said' becomes evaluative commentary on those actions. Now this pattern is common enough to be a reasonable assumption in many cases, and one can immediately see why 'danger of death' stories of the sort Labov elicited would promote identification of a sharp division between salient actions such as physical assaults and accidents on the one hand, and verbal reactions on the other. But more complicated integrations of words and actions are also possible, where the sayings are the most important doings – are the 'action' of the narrative – revealing a fixity of sequence of those sayings, temporal juncture, and so on. From the work of the philosopher J. L. Austin has developed a renewed recognition that our use of words in interaction is typically a performing of actions and not merely an asserting of true or false (hence evaluative) statements. Labov's own informants demonstrate this vividly in other interactions that he analyzes (1972): as their enhanced skills of duelling, rapping and sounding make very clear, there can be verbal contests (where participants are in 'danger of loss of social prestige') as well as physical ones.

But no narrative of sayings, you might complain, can break your bones or put you in danger of death. Again, however, we might question this assumption. There are too many recorded cases of individuals placed in a position of great danger by their own or others' verbal acts, which some violent party finds provocative or threatening. Or someone comes to the brink of suicide or murder, incited by acts of speech, and then is carefully 'talked down' by individuals who are themselves at risk. Sayings may indeed put someone in danger of death. As they can, also, in a murder trial where the oral testimony of a key witness might be decisive. And in our increasingly textual worlds, where growing numbers of us make our living through our verbal work rather than our non-verbal actions, we may predict that 'what is said/written/promised/denied/argued, etc.' will more commonly constitute the essential complicating material in narratives.

Not least in literature: in the 'famous spit' story of Mr Casey, for example, the 'doing' that makes up the complicating action to be evaluated is a verbal 'doing': the old woman's series of increasingly offensive insults. And the terminate or resolutory action of spitting itself is reported less as a doing (Casey does not announce 'I spat at her') than as a saying:

> – And what did you do, John?
> – Do! said Mr Casey. She stuck her ugly old face up at me when she said it and I had my mouth full of tobacco juice. I bent down to her and *Phth!* says I to her like that.
> He turned aside and made the act of spitting.
> – *Phth!* says I to her like that, right into her eye.

Casey's *Phth!* has some of the marks of external-evaluation of type 3, but we know it is also a crucial sequentially-fixed action: an inextricable merging of evaluation and narrative action, of saying and doing. Similarly we can ponder the old woman's reaction to this verbal-cum-non-verbal action:

> He clapped his hand to his eye and gave a hoarse scream of pain.
> – *O Jesus, Mary and Joseph!* says she. *I'm blinded! I'm blinded and drownded!*

We infer, from Mr Casey's accompanying gesture of clapping his hand to his eye, that the old woman reacted in other ways than simply saying these things. But again, the woman's verbal response is itself very important to the story: the unpleasant physical consequences of the spit are far less to the point, but in any event do not include literal blinding or drowning. The tellable reaction is the verbal one, directly mimicked, with its non-standardism, its ludicrous hyperbole, and the irony of its probably profane invocation coming from the lips of this self-declared defender of the faith and guardian of morality.

The above unravelling of the narrative/evaluative dichotomy is broaching a very important topic, for in Labov as in other *fabula/sjuzhet* theorists the separability of the plot from surrounding or interpolated discoursal elaborations and recastings is an operational necessity. And in working with that dichotomy, all our language reflects an assumption that plot is core, that the clauses of narrative action are the heart of the matter, the inner narrative, and that evaluation is to a degree external, and always intrusive. Now that assumption is one I am prepared to accept, with the caveat voiced above (that core narrative clauses may be ones of speech rather than action, and look very like evaluations) and a further caveat I will now introduce. This is that adopting the categories of fixed narrative clause and freer evaluative clause is not in itself a claim about the 'status in reality' of the actions and sayings these report. In particular, it is not an assumption that material presented as main-clause narration 'really did' happen the way the narrator claims. Put thus the warning seems obvious, that narrators 'aestheticize' their experiences, assert cause-and-effect chains where no chains are there, and so on; but the point is well made by Culler (1981: 184–5); see also the related point in Hoey (2000: 105), that happenings do not exist as structured forms, prior to their telling. If we imagine that first we have the sequence of actions (narrative) and then we work on the reporting of them to enhance their point or tellability (evaluation), we are ignoring the possibility of a reverse order of impulses, namely that, guided by the prior awareness of the tellability-requirement, our evaluations shape our plots.

## 6.6 Internal evaluation

Internal evaluations, as noted, are those evaluations woven into the structure and composition of the core Narrative clauses – those clauses, with their dependents, that carry the core sequential 'spine' of the narrative, filling the Complicating Action and Resolution sections. Such evaluations are grouped by Labov into four sub-types:

1   *Intensifiers*: here are included:
    gestures (often accompanied by deictic *that*),

> He turned aside and made the act of spitting.... He clapped his hand to his eye.

expressive phonology, onomatopoeic sounds, and intonational emphases:

> *Phth!*; 'I'm drownded!'

exaggerating quantifiers such as *all*,

> such booing and baaing; paid all her attention to me; right into her eye

repetitions,

> I let her bawl away [reported twice]; Phth! says I to her like that [reported twice];

and ritual utterances.

Unlike the following three types, Intensifiers do not significantly complicate the syntax of the narrative clause. They are clearly a kind of embellishment, as their name would suggest, akin to the use of underlining and bold face in writing.

2    *Comparators.* Why, in the telling of what happened, would you mention various things which did *not* happen? That is the question that Comparators invite. For while Intensifiers evaluate directly, telling what happened in an exaggerated or elaborated way, Comparators evaluate indirectly, by drawing attention away from what actually happened by alluding to what might have but didn't happen. The main types of comparators include:

expressions of negation,

> You never heard such booing and baaing; I couldn't say a word;

modality and modulation,

> We had to make our way to the railway station;

and futurity:

> I won't sully this Christmas board.

All of these are concentrated in, but not confined to, the auxiliary verbal elements; also included are questions, hypothetical claims, imperatives, and, most overtly, comparative or superlative constructions. They involve an indirect evaluative departure, in the lexicogrammar, from the simple direct telling of the narrative actions. A more complex departure is the use of simile or metaphor, when these occur in narrative clauses (we may surmise that they would be more common in free clauses). And they all have the effect of introducing a branch or fork, into an otherwise simple or un-branched point in the telling; every comparator evokes an alternative narrative development which becomes background or relief or illuminating contrast to the actual narrative development that proceeds.

3    *Correlatives*: these bring together events in a single independent clause, and require complex syntax (and are hence often beyond the control of young narrators):
progressives (*be* + V-*ing*), and appended participles (adjacent verbs in non-finite V-*ing* form), both of these emphasizing simultaneity of distinct actions,

> She kept dancing along beside me in the mud bawling and screaming.

double appositives,

> there was one old lady, and a drunken old harridan she was surely

double attributes,

> a drunken old harridan

and 'left-hand' participles or 'deverbal' adjectives,

> an unsavoury-looking character.

4   *Explicatives*: These are appended subordinate clauses which qualify, or give reasons for, the main events reported: for example, clauses introduced by *while*, *although*, *since*, *because*, and so on:

> sure I couldn't say a word in any case because my mouth was full of tobacco juice.

Such clauses enhance tellability by more fully specifying the extent or motivation for a particular action. In a structural sense they are strictly inessential to the telling of a narrative's fundamental sequenced events; but in the reality of interaction, they are virtually indispensable: rarely are they completely absent from oral narratives of personal experience, in western cultures at least.

## 6.7 Coda

As indicated earlier, codas and abstracts can be seen as related. A coda signals the sealing off of a narrative, just as an abstract announces the opening up of one. There seem to be two most common devices within codas. One is the explicit declaring that the narrative proper is over, so that for an addressee now to ask, 'And then what happened?' should be absurd (or demoralizing: it indicates they did not 'get the point'). The element is often realized by a near-redundant narrative-external comment, using pro-forms that are both textually anaphoric (pointing backwards to earlier co-text for interpretation) and distancing in their deixis:

1   And that is the end of the story.
2   And that was that.
3   And that – that was it, you know.

In versions 1 and 3 the item *that*, it can be assumed, is cohesively tied to some previous text in which a state or resolution has been reported; but it is also deictically pointing to that resolution, and now locating it at a distance from the speaker and her current position (*that*, not *this* or *here*), no matter how vivid and immediate parts of the telling of the narrative might have been.

This brings us to the second device common in codas. As the above indicates, codas are commonly the site of a deictic shift, especially in the more involving narratives of personal experience. In telling such narratives, the teller who is also a principal participant often switches the deictic anchorage to the spatiotemporal orientation of himself-as-participant, selecting items such as *this*, *here* and *now* relative to that individual, rather than relative to the currently present one telling the story to an addressee. But it would make no sense, once the story was finished and the interaction was in the process of returning to conversational mode, in 'real' present time, to persist in using present-time deictics with reference to the past story. Putting this another way, the teller seems best advised to signal, before the close of his long narrative turn, that he has exited from the marked past narrative to present deictics mode, and that all can resume normal use of present deictics to designate relatedness to the present context of situation. Accordingly, tellers often do signal such a switch in their codas:

4    And ever since then I haven't seen the guy 'cause I quit, I quit, you know. No more problems.
5    And you know that man . . . is a detective in Union City and I see him every now and again.

These use distal deixis (*the* or *that*) now to denote elements of the story, and present tense (with or without perfective, 'current relevance', aspect) to denote the shared current time of the speaker-as-conversation-participant, no longer speaker-as-narrative-participant. Labov talks of codas as having

> the property of bridging the gap between the moment of time at the end of the narrative proper and the present. They bring the narrator and the listener back to the point at which they entered the narrative.
>
> (Labov, 1972: 365)

Codas bridge a constructed gap, mutually agreed upon in the abstract, which creates a distinctive space for the narrative to occupy. Relatedly, we may look for a counterpart in reverse, near the outset of narratives, of the coda's deictic switch or bridging. This does seem to occur fairly often, although it is centred more in the orientation than the abstract. Thus abstract 1 in Section 6.3 alerts the addressee to orientational switch by alluding to 'this other dude' (cf. 'another dude' or 'some other dude'), and by marking the temporal gap from the present ('three weeks ago'). While abstract 2 does not perform an orientational switch, Mr Casey's very next turn, which is both orientational and externally evaluative, does:

– Why then, said Mr Casey, it is a most instructive story. It happened
not long ago in the county Wicklow where we are now.

(Joyce, *Portrait of the Artist*: 34)

The seeming redundancies of the second sentence here should give us
pause. Why, we might ask, doesn't Casey simply say:

It happened here not long ago.

or at the most,

It happened not long ago here in the county Wicklow?

Is the loosely-appended adverbial, *where we are now*, tellable material at
all? Ordinarily not, but here perhaps the sentence as a whole is a nicely-
judged establishment of both the story's detachment from the present and
its heightened current relevance (the time was 'not long ago', the place
was hereabouts). Casey is a cunning storyteller, and this story's underlying
purpose is to suggest that the foul-mouthed old woman who denigrated
Parnell within the story, and Dante, who is one of its present addressees
and has similarly condemned Mr Casey's political hero, are analogues,
meriting analogous treatment (to be spat upon). The seeming redundancies of Casey's introductory turn highlight the situational contiguities just
as, later, the old woman's heaping of abuse will be reported as if parallel to
Dante's censure.

But having dwelt at length on the form and function of codas, it should
now be stressed that in an oral personal narrative a coda may not appear.
This is especially so in narratives told in the course of a single conversation
where sequences of stories may get told 'back to back' by one teller or
several. In such sequences it may happen that some aspect of the resolution of one story serves, in some direct or remote way, as the trigger of the
next. The associative links that particular tellers construct, so as to
enhance a story's sense of being 'locally occasioned' and 'sequentially
implicative' (Jefferson, 1978) are immensely varied.

## 6.8 Stories in societies

Another approach to evaluation in stories, less directly attentive to linguistic form than Labov and more interested in community-wide motivations,
comes in the work of Polanyi (1978; 1981). She has argued that the kinds
of things that we seem to agree make stories tellable reflect and disclose
our cultural presuppositions and values. Similarly, Tannen (1979) demonstrates in some detail how our 'structures of expectation' based on past
experience influence the particular ways we construct our stories, and
interpret those of others. This in turn would predict that the kinds of
stories that get told, and are valued, in one cultural milieu may differ quite

considerably from those that get told in another. And more recent studies by Tannen, on both ethnic-based and gender-based differences in 'horizon of expectation' – concerning narrative construction and other verbal behaviours besides – confirm this (Tannen, 1991; 1994).

One very influential study of this kind was reported in Heath (1983), a comparative study of language use in two small-town working-class communities in the rural south-east of the United States, one black (Trackton), the other white (Roadville). These two communities reveal quite different views of stories and storytelling, as Romaine summarizes:

> In Roadville stories stick to the truth and are factual. They maintain strict chronicity, end with a summary statement or moral, and serve the function of maintaining values and reaffirming group membership. Any fictionalized account is a lie. Trackton stories, on the other hand, are hardly ever serious. The best stories are 'junk', and the best story-tellers are those who can 'talk the best junk', i.e. make the most wildly exaggerated comparisons and tell outlandish fictional narratives.
>
> (Romaine, 1985: 102–3)

And as Heath (1983: 189) concluded, of these radically diverging norms of behaviour:

> For Roadville, Trackton's stories would be lies; for Trackton, Road-ville's stories would not even count as stories.

In the face of Heath's findings, which are supported by extensive data, it should be evident that reading off cultural values or ideology from the points that a community's stories have will not be easy, precisely because a community's cultural presuppositions and values are often, being presuppositions, *not* explicitly stated or rehearsed in everyday cultural activity. The 'said' of a culture is deeply embedded in its 'unsaid' (Tyler, 1978). As the Trackton–Roadville study confirmed, it is not the case that everything else besides a story's main evaluated point is kept constant across communities. It may well be that communities have different kinds of story points because they have different perspectives on the proper functions and nature of storytelling. If that is so, we are driven back from the easier task of correlating delimited story points with possible cultural values, to the harder task of holistically assessing all of a community's tendencies in narrative use in relation to inferred cultural values.

## 6.9 Narrative performance

Over the past few years a number of sociolinguistic studies have appeared using the folkloristic term *performance* to describe a certain type of particularly involved and dramatized oral narrative. The term has been adopted and espoused despite resistance from some traditional folklorists, for whom the term standardly denotes the retelling of stories that are part of a tradition, are collectively known, and are non-innovative.

The idea that narratives are often performances seems to have first emerged in the work of Hymes and Goffman, and received fuller sociolinguistic exposition in Wolfson (1982). Wolfson's work is most directly relatable to Labov's; but she makes reference to a larger corpus of stories, told in a greater variety of contexts (of situation, formality, and of familiarity, age, sex and status of the tellers and addressees, and so on). Working with this set of possible variables, Wolfson probes the varying formal reflexes of individuals' experiential involvement in their storytellings as dramatized re-enactments:

> When a speaker acts out a story, as if to give his audience the opportunity to experience the event and his evaluation of it, he may be said to be giving a performance.
>
> (Wolfson, 1982: 24)

To perform a story is to furnish one's addressees with a more vivid and involving experience of that story, while exploiting special performance features as resources for highlighting the story's main point. The performance features Wolfson particularly singled out for their instrumentality were the following:

1   direct speech
2   asides
3   repetition
4   expressive sounds
5   sound effects
6   motions and gestures
7   conversational historic present (CHP), alternating with narrative past tense.

Roughly, the more your story has of all of these, the more 'performed' it is. Most of these items are already implicit in some part of Labov's typology of evaluation devices; only items 2 and 7 are noticeably new. I will comment briefly on both. In an aside a teller exits briefly from the time reference of the story dialogue he is recounting in order to add some comment about the content which has continued relevance in the present time of the teller and listeners. Such comments highlight, for the listeners, the teller's own viewpoint and sympathies with regard to the interrupted dialogue. Thus asides are an interruption of direct speech, and are therefore somewhat related to that mode of evaluation; they are also somewhat like external evaluation, with time reference to the present time of the teller-as-conversationalist; while in their explanatory function they are rather like Labov's explicatives.

The most innovative section of Wolfson (1982) is the account of the use of historic present tense in storytelling. Wolfson contests the traditional grammarian's view that historic present, in conversation-embedded narratives, is there simply to make a story more vivid and immediate. Rather, the historic present when used in conversation-embedded narration has a distinct function – hence the emphasis on *conversational* historic present – and that function relates not directly to the occurrence of CHP itself, but to the patterns of switching between historic past and present tense that it permits. The switches or alternations are said to facilitate three main effects: (a) an intervention by the teller; (b) a focussing of attention on certain portions of the narrative; and (c) a dividing-up of the flow of action into distinct events. Relatedly, Schiffrin (1981), found historic present tense almost wholly confined to the complicating action section of personal narratives (significant because this is precisely the section of stories where tense does not have to do any special task of temporal orientation, since temporal and presentational order can be assumed to be congruent). So CHP is emphatically an internal evaluation device (Schiffrin, 1981: 58).

Perhaps unsurprisingly, Wolfson (1982) also found that stories were more likely to be performed (not merely told) when conversationalists were of the same sex, of similar age and status, similar in attitudes and background, and so on. In principle, at least, what Wolfson did for performedness – probing what kind of conversationalists in what kind of relation opted to perform their narratives – could be done for the whole range of Labovian evaluation devices. But a major difference would then emerge, for evaluation undertakes a larger, more crucial task, than that of performance: the task of articulating the point of a story and persuading the audience of its tellability. Thus while performed stories give the impression that they contain a number of extra evaluative features added to stories told between intimates but not between people remote from each other in various ways, a reverse trend may apply when we compare the amount of evaluation in the stories of mature tellers. In other words, it may be the case that the fewer the dimensions of similarity between conversationalists, the greater the role that evaluation devices may have to play, in spelling out the significance of a tale for a teller to a listener who does not share unspoken understanding.

## 6.10  Dispersed, embedded, and group oral narratives

There are other types of personal narrative, more subtly interleaved with the ongoing conversation, than those Labov extracted. Polanyi, for example, draws attention to the 'diffuse story' (1978: 109ff.), in which a chunk of story is followed by a chunk of multi-party conversation glossing, clarifying and amplifying aspects of the story chunk just told. In such a format, story evaluation can become a collaborative exercise. Diffuse story format shades into practices of embedding where, for example, several short stories are spread out and interrupted by conversational interludes, but can also be treated as the several sections of a single, overarching story.

Uppal (1984) has just such an example, a story comprising four conversationally embedded stories (I am most grateful to Ms Uppal for permission to reproduce data from her study). The stories emerged in the casual conversation of a mixed-sex group of Singaporean university students, good friends, reminiscing about their schooldays, sitting around a table in a college canteen. The numbers (1) to (4) in the lefthand margin mark, in my analysis, the onset of each of the four embedded stories within the ongoing conversation. Text in square brackets is my glossing of utterances or explanation of the ongoing interaction; I have provided only minimal 'translation' of the many features of colloquial Singaporean English in the teller's speech. At the opening of the transcript, S is referring to his time in Sixth Form, the final two years of high or secondary school (here the classes or grades are called 6A and 6B), where less academically successful students are sometimes required to repeat a year of schooling once or even, here, twice.

(1) *S:*  My one ah- my one ah- I was saved by my intelligence y'know. Because ah- I was in 6A, y'know. Eight of us were caught gambling, y'know. Seven 6-repeat-2. That time they got 6-repeat-once, repeat-2 y'know. Repeating the second time repeating the first time. Seven 6-repeat-2. Then 6A. All public caning. Because the teacher caught us gambling y'know. So all public caning. Some more [= what is more] I prefect y'know. Kena [*got (+ Verb)en, caused to happen*] lost badge, all. Everything gone nah, koyak [*spoilt, broken*]. So kena, er, public caning. Some more I gabrah [*make/made a mess of things*], boy. Some more public is like, principal office no sweat, y'know, but public is like they call your parents round.

*V:*  Huh?

*S:*  Ya, so parents will stand by the side, know.

*G:*  Ayooo!

[some dialogue ellipted]

(2) *S:*  Because, because it seems that you know is so- the son something goes wrong, parents have to be notified y'see. So they give public caning. Then- some more standard y'know. Okay next, come ah. Fellow'll squeeze your bums all, know. Because beginning stages I think someone put book all. /katabah/ Got sound, y'know.

*G:*  [uninterpretable]

*S:*  So the fellow he squeeze squeeze your bum all. He make sure soft, know # Cushion # You see funny funny things ah. The fellow is, ah, the senior assistant is the one who canes nah, not the principal. Principal was a woman nah, so senior assistant. He feel feel. Then he smile at the school, y'know. Then he take out wallet. Beautiful wallet # *Three* handkerchiefs [i.e. wallet and handkerchiefs were intended to protect the boy's backside]. Take out all. One by – ((*S* makes lashing sound)) Wahh Lan [*Damn!*]. I tell you cry, dah. 6-repeat boys crying, dah. 6-repeat that time you respect. Wah, that time the terrors of the school.

B:    This one your grandfather stories, ah?

S:    Public caning terok [*severe*], y'know. I tell you.

V:    Is it really that painful or because of the ( ).

H:    *Pain* boy.

S:    Damn pain na, I tell you. Damn pain. I never kena but I know damn pain. See boys cry, I know damn pain. The canes also got different ones, know. You know Kim Seng.

(3)    I escaped because I was in 6A. The principal came. He saw- he saw all 6-repeat. Then he called down my teacher. 'Explain why your 6A boy is doing with the 6-repeat student.' The teacher got no explanation. So he said, 'I want you to account for his behaviour.'

N:    Like real, ah?

S:    Then I excused y'know, I excuse. Go back. My teacher to account for my behaviour for the rest of the year lah. So I kena [*got to, had to*] sit sit in front. Smile smile everyday.

N:    So unfair, know. How come you never kena [sc. *got caned*]?

S:    Exactly. I kena- after the six boys moody already.

N:    Ya boy.

H:    No members [= friends] na, alamak.

N:    Some more, never mind. They are the terrors of the school, y'know you go home nah.

(4) S:    But they- they're okay nah. The reason I got to know them was badminton. You see, I played badminton for school, y'know. Then the whole school team formed by 6-repeat students, except I. Only 6A feller playing badminton for school. So slowly lah. Slowly got into the ideas of life lah. Then ah you know school, afternoon school. Twelve o'clock come. What do you do?=

G:    =True=

S:    All first started with the Saturday, know, play Saturday. Carry on. Then slowly switched to five cents nah.

G:    ((/)) [backchannel acknowledgement noises]

S:    Then slowly slowly switched to ten cents, twenty cents. Then after that ting-tong already.

G:    Mm.

S:    Move lah, advance. Ting-tong, kena sway sway [*had some bad luck, a catastrophe*]. *Cards* only kena caught. Moody. Advance through what.

G:    ((/)) [backchannel acknowledgement noises]

S:    Actually we tell them, know. We say, 'Sir, this one second time only.' Tell them, 'Gambling playing for fun.'

G:    Mm.

S:   Actually six months ago we started already.

Story 1:   How the teller, with others, once contemplated a public caning for gambling.
Story 2:   How public caning at school was an ordeal, involving removal of padding/protection, and painful.
Story 3:   How the teller escaped caning on the condition that his teacher could thereafter account for his behaviour to the principal.
Story 4:   How the teller, a 6A boy, got in with the 6-repeat boys, and their gambling.

There are ways in which these are four largely free-standing narratives, as the summaries immediately above suggest. But there are respects too in which these are four episodes or components within a single elaborated narrative: story 1 supplies an abstract, orientation, and some complicating action, story 2 adds further orientation and evaluative description, story 3 contains the resolution, while story 4 is a flashback explaining how the situation at the beginning of the complicating action was arrived at. But each of these stories is itself adequately formed, with temporally-ordered action and resolution, and all four come from a single speaker.

To strengthen the claim that they are not merely a ribbon of loosely-related stories but rather also constitute a single 'macro-story', we should at least require some degree of temporal juncture between these stories, and further evidence that these four parts all cohere around a specific topic and resolution. Here the main story we might call a 'danger of caning' one: the teller recalls how, when he, a model student, was caught at school gambling for money with boys from a 'repeat' class, he alone escaped the pain and humiliation of a public caning. The main story resolution is as follows:

> Then I excused y'know, I excuse. Go back. My teacher to account for my behaviour for the rest of the year lah. So I kena sit sit in front. Smile smile everyday.

This appears towards the close of subordinate story 3. Prior to it, story 1 perfunctorily reports the fact that the boys were caught gambling, and the minor actual resolution (the teller is stripped of his prefect's badge) plus the possibility of a more major resolution (public caning). But most prominent in story 1 is emphasis on the crucial orientational facts that the other boys are in a repeat stream, distrusted hard cases, while the teller was in the prestige fast stream. Story 2 tells the embedded story of public canings in general, and the caning of his co-gamblers in particular, all the more vivid and hilarious in colloquial Singaporean English.

It is clear that the public caning reported in 2 must have been preceded by the conditional letting-off of the teller-as-participant reported in 3, and that orderliness of event recapitulation has not been maintained (the order of actual occurrence of events reported in the stories being 4^1^3^2; that is, Gambling^Detection^Reprieve^Caning). On the other hand we may still maintain that here is a well-formed macro-story if we classify story 2 as evaluative within the larger context, an extended comparator exploring the path of punishment that, to the teller's relief, was *not* taken in his case. As noted earlier, the main point of this macro-story is then not what happened to the other boys, but how *this* boy got away lightly – which indeed is how *S* announces his narrative at the outset. Story 2 effectively heightens our interest in just what treatment the teller will receive, artfully suspending the action before that resolution.

We may notice, too, even from the sparse transcript above, the different roles taken up by different addressees of *S*'s extended telling. *G* is a supportive backchanneller, as less prominently are *H* and *N*. *B* on the other hand is briefly sceptical, but doesn't pursue the doubt about the veracity/credibility of the story; but not insignificantly, *B*'s challenge is immediately followed by *V*'s, a serious challenge to the story's tellability (is public caning truly painful?). That challenge is comprehensively crushed, with *S* telling four times over that (though he himself never got caned) the pain is 'damn pain'.

If the above is accepted as a type of dispersed story, the more common phenomenon is for stories to relate more directly to surrounding conversational discourse and prior stories in noticeably relevant ways. Usually the onus is on conversationalists as individuals to insert their stories appropriately, showing attentiveness to what others have said, and so on. But sometimes group stories are told, by all or several conversationalist–participants working together: a narrating that does not involve suspension of the turn-taking mechanisms. At first glance the group story appears to be an admirably egalitarian and collaborative storytelling mode, built on a heightened degree of interdependence. The division between tellers and listeners falls away as does anxiety over tellability, and a spirit of benevolent mutual indulgence may prevail: all are contributing to a story that each already knows. But, in some ways, and with more scope than usual, a competitive rivalry can also shape the several contributions to the telling: there may not be full agreement on the point, on whom among the teller-participants comes out of the story well, and so on. And since there will be general familiarity with the broad outline of the story in question, the exercise may become more oral-literary, with great attention paid to the most effective and entertaining methods of verbal expression.

As Polanyi notes (1978: 143) the group story is an area where greater fictionality may be tolerated; credibility or vraisemblance is not a prime concern, since focus is less on any particular teller than on the tale for the tale's own sake. Or, as Bennett (1983) notes of her related story type, the group saga, the retelling is for purposes of reminiscence and social binding, with the emphasis less on the incidents themselves than on painting a rich picture of the situation. Alternatively, as Uppal (1984) notes, a group story may become more a series of hypotheses or conjectures about what might have been the case (the true resolution, the proper evaluation) concerning some set of events, particularly where all the group-tellers were detached witnesses of those events, with limited inside knowledge. And the more that a group's talk becomes an unordered set of overlapping conjectures, the more the talk returns from narrative mode to that of ordinary conversation or gossip. Putting things the other way around, it may be that a collective style of telling is more frequently adopted where there is individual and collective uncertainty about just what happened and just how things ended up: each in the group helps to piece the story together.

Along these lines, we may see crime and detective fiction as a literary genre partly built upon the group story principle. When P. D. James's Superintendent Dalglish or Sue Grafton's Kinsey Milhone piece together the testimony of a range of individuals connected in some way to a crime, sleuth and reader must process a radically dispersed and potentially defective group story. The dispersal stems not merely from the fact that there is usually no Aristotelian unity of time or place as far as the characters' contributions (within the story) are concerned, but more directly from the fact that in crime stories the guilty party, often along with other investigated individuals who have information they wish to remain hidden, will contribute misleadingly rather than sincerely cooperatively: any implicit declarations, by all parties, that they are collaboratively intent on helping the investigator to 'get the true and full story' told have to be treated as unreliable. Defectiveness and contradiction are probabilities since one or more of the group may construct their contributions so as to conceal their own guilt: fictionality with a vengeance, for self-protective and not merely aesthetic purposes.

## 6.11 From Labov to literature

The extent to which the Labovian six-part formalist analysis of the oral narrative of personal experience applies or is relevant to literary narratives has also become a matter of some contention. This section will review some of those matters of contention, and conclude with the suggestion that relevance, rather than direct application, is the more helpful final emphasis.

In Pratt (1977), a substantial chapter is devoted to exploring some of the ways in which Labovian analysis could be extended and applied to literary fiction – 'written narratives of invented others' experiences'. Numerous examples are given of novels and short stories revealing various forms of abstracts, orientations, and so on. Of course the sheer scale of a novel makes for huge differences of magnitude of these narrative components by comparison with a brief oral narrative. Thus Pratt notes that Hardy's *The Return of the Native* opens with an entire chapter of orientation, and really only a small part of orientation at that: a description of the Egdon Heath landscape on a particular November afternoon. Pratt adds:

The human characters and complicating action do not arrive until the second chapter, aptly titled 'Humanity Appears Upon the Scene, Hand in Hand with Trouble.'

(Pratt, 1977: 53)

Furthermore, as Pratt notes, all sorts of departures from the 'underlying' unmarked or canonical narrative format, with adequate abstract, orientation, and so on, are to be found in literary narratives. Nor, in the face of such creative departures from the standard format, are we inclined immediately to reject the text as a defective narrative: we are used to paying more attention, working harder, being more challenged by literary texts than non-literary ones. Thus many novel- and story-openings project us *in medias res*, into the middle of ongoing events, with deliberately insufficient orientational briefing, as if we were already familiar with the world and actors depicted. Cast into this position, we sometimes feel we indeed become familiar with the world presented very rapidly; on other occasions, however, we remain somewhat disoriented throughout, and effects of mystery, disorder, obscurity, and lostness, are achieved (intentionally or otherwise). Texts by Kafka, Beckett and Pinter are among those that immediately come to mind.

The broad point Pratt makes, by further copious exemplification of forms of resolution, abstract and coda in literary narratives, is that no radical gulf separates literary from 'everyday' narrative: the same devices, used for the same purposes, emerge in both.

What is important about the fact that literary narratives can be analyzed in the same way as the short anecdotes scattered throughout our conversation? To begin with, it casts grave doubt on the Formalist and structuralist claims that the language of literature is formally and functionally distinctive.... Unless we are foolish enough to claim that people organize their oral anecdotes around patterns they learn from reading literature, we are obliged to draw the more obvious conclusion that the formal similarities between natural narrative and literary narrative derive from the fact that at some level of analysis they are utterances of the same type.

(Pratt, 1977: 67, 69)

At this distance those last claims seem overstated, a hinting at some 'deep structural' human rules for storytelling (applied in superficially different ways in conversation and in novel-writing) that subsequent studies have not endorsed. The implied picture is vertically or hierarchically-oriented: deep structural formats 'surface' in oral or literary narratives. Currently theorists tend more to subscribe to a horizontally-oriented picture, in which nineteenth-century novels, modern short stories and contemporary personal oral narratives are generically separated, like languages or cultures across a continent, with no 'governing' or derivational relations between them, and plenty of scope for borrowing, appropriation, and other hybridities. Within this more Bakhtinian picture of intertextual and cross-genre clashings and mergings, it is not at all implausible to suggest that people sometimes introduce into other parts of their everyday lives, including their oral storytelling, forms and patterns they have learnt from reading literature. As we have seen, Hart has suggested that this is how Eveline comes to use pulp-romance-fiction language in the *Dubliners* story (see Notes and exercises 1, in the previous chapter).

Since Pratt's study, narratologists have differed over the usefulness to narrative poetics of the Labovian approach. Chatman (1990), for example, is sceptical about the 'contextualism' that he sees Labov's and similar studies harbouring. He suggests for instance that evaluation in literary narrative is rather different from that in personal storytelling:

> The insistence that every narrative include an evaluation of the experience narrated seems to fly in the face of the efforts by novelists since James and Flaubert to eliminate judgement and other commentary from the narrator's pronouncements.
>
> (1990: 317–18, fn. 9)

And as noted in this chapter, everyone agrees that oral personal narrative's iconic chronology is radically different from the repertoire of anachronies to be found in contemporary artistic fiction and film where, arguably, they are so common a feature as to have become the unmarked norm. And what of Free Indirect Discourse: where the teller is also protagonist, narrating *in praesentia*, as in Labovian narratives, what need or scope is there for this complex device? Character and setting, too, are radically minimized in oral personal narratives when compared with typical fictional stories, although here we should not overlook the way some writers on occasion supply even less in the way of setting or characterization than an oral teller. Nor should we overlook the extent to which all these differences may be artefacts of the profoundly different contexts of production and consumption in which the novel and the conversationally-embedded personal narrative are situated.

In view of these manifold differences, many students of narrative have questioned whether any meaningful *rapprochement* between Labovian analyses and narratology remains possible. But on the other hand a number of relations and continuities remain. Fleischman, for example, argues that literary-narrative anachrony remains grounded in cultural and common sense chronology:

> If our cultural and literary competence did not include a narrative norm, one component of which is iconic sequence, then the anachronies of literary and cinematic narrative could not produce the effects they do on readers and spectators.
>
> (1997: 164)

For Fleischman, too, the palpable differences between robust Labovian Resolution and the kind of unresolved or open-ended terminations of modern novels, which may even introduce further complicating action and orientation, is not beyond explanation. It is not so much that modern narrative art has 'abandoned narrativity' as that, under various cultural pressures, it has developed or changed quite substantially. Besides, it is a mistake to neglect the extent to which tellers and addressees continue to crave or orient to *The Sense of an Ending*, to quote the title of an important book on this topic (Kermode, 1967). Of most modern artistic films and novels it is still appropriate to ask someone who has seen or read them, 'So what finally happens?'. More generally, sequentiality remains a defining property of narrative fictions, ancient and modern, even when these choose not to affirm that sequentiality in the simplest chronology-iconic narration.

Equally comparatively complex, and thus different from Labovian narratives in degree rather than in kind, are the Evaluation resources of literary narrative. Let us begin with Chatman's observation, quoted above, to the effect that Jamesian fiction with its impersonal non-arbitrating narration, is designed to produce evaluation-free narrative. In a sense this is surely true, but a number of factors might be added to the account:

1   Almost no-one comes away from a James (or Flaubert, etc.) novel or story complaining that the narrative had no point, or that it wasn't worth telling; some readers may react with a, 'so complex!', but few if any ask, 'So what?'. Jamesian fiction fulfils the Evaluation function or rationale somehow, even if not in ways immediately akin to those identified in oral personal narratives.

2   In terms of Simpson's nine-mode schema, while James and Flaubert both adopt B(R) narration, only Flaubert is characterized as typically neutral, while James is said to standardly adopt B(R) Positive mode. It seems reasonable to suppose that all six of Simpson's modalized modes (all the positive and negative ones) are by definition Evaluative. If this presumption is correct, we should note the overlaps and differences between Simpson's formal markers and Labov's: the way Labov emphasizes negation while Simpson alludes to it only indirectly (although with further analysis and specification it might be possible to relate negation to negative mode narration), or the way generic sentences figure in Simpson's profile of positive narration but are not directly invoked by Labov (although, again with careful qualification, generic sentences might be recognized as 'absolutely' free clauses in narratives – so narratively unbounded or free from punctual particularity as to be a kind of 'anti-narrative' device – see Toolan, 1998: 64). Among overlaps one would have to note the ways that both Labov and Simpson highlight modal constructions as evaluative. Finally one might reflect further on repetition, recognized as prominently evaluative in Labov but not mentioned by Simpson: while repetition may be

found in all kinds of narration, it is arguably most noticeable in the third-person narratorial styles which Simpson has called neutral B(N) and B(R) – Hemingway and Flaubert are his best exemplars, respectively. Like hard news reporting with which they are sometimes compared, these deploy extensive repetition, as a brief glance at the opening of almost any Hemingway story will confirm. Such repetitions may be neither positive nor negative in Simpson's terms, but they are surely evaluative in Labov's.

3   Even the Jamesian or Flaubertian narrator who may eschew Labovian external evaluation, and many forms of internal evaluation (most Intensifiers, Comparators, and Explicatives), can hardly be held to shun Labov's fourth category of internal evaluation, Correlatives. On the contrary, these are used in abundance.

4   Finally there is a sense in which all the above factors miss the main point, or at least, have to be re-situated once the main point is made. And this main point is that a Jamesian novel is not merely more complex than an oral personal narrative in the sense that it contains a multitude of inter-connected narratives, each of which is locally tellable and evaluated by its teller who is potentially different from all other tellers within the novel; it is also more complex in that entire narratives may constitute part or all of the Evaluation of a different or larger narrative with which it connects – and connects in ways which do not reduce to the grammatical choice between chaining (parataxis) and embedding. Consider Gretta's narrative of her loving and losing Michael Furey; this is abundantly evaluated by Gretta of course, its teller, and indirectly by Gabriel, its reactive recipient. But how does it 'fit' into the encompassing narrative called 'The Dead'? In a sense it is Complicating Action ('what happens next is that Gretta explains . . .); but it is also Orientation (it tells us more about the 'who' that Gretta is than we – and even Gabriel – had imagined); and it contributes to the Evaluation of the encompassing story in a number of ways: just one of the ways is the way that Michael's reported selfless unconditional love for Gretta becomes a comparator in the evaluation of Gabriel's love for Gretta and other women: it is an order of love that, Gabriel recognizes, he himself has never felt. So Gretta's story contributes to the evaluation of Gabriel and the narrative about him. But you could hardly specify these relations in advance, on the basis of form or expression held up for inspection, segregated and detached from its embedded use. Nor could one assert with any confidence that *all* readers, at all times and in all places, will agree with the attributions of value and significance that I have made of these situated elements. And were any theorist to propose, as one of the 'rules' of evaluative narration, that a late-disclosed love affair and tragic death, revealed in just these circumstances, will always be Orientational and Evaluative, this would be clearly a mistake: it would be an attempt to subject phenomena that can only be assessed in their integrated situatedness as if

they were decontextualizable and segregatable elements (on integrationism, see Harris, 1998). This is why Chatman is ultimately wrong to call the Labovian approach 'contextualist': by the standards of thoroughgoing integrationist commentary, Labov is not nearly contextualist enough. In short, literary narratives are not merely more complex than oral personal ones, they are exponentially more complex, exploiting resources for evaluation (narrative ellipsis and pause are two more that come to mind) which are virtually non-existent in the simpler form.

## Further reading

Labov and Waletzky (1967) and Labov (1972) are obviously the place to begin further reading, and then Labov (1981) on speech actions and physical reactions (relevant to 6.5). Thereafter, Chapter 2 of Pratt (1977) applies the Labovian model to literary examples; see also Watts (1984), and Toolan (1988), while Culler (1981: 169–87) contains useful critique. Among the sociolinguistically-oriented studies that have applied Labov's model are: Carter and Simpson (1982), Bennett (1983) and Polanyi (1982). Narrative performance and CHP are discussed in Wolfson (1978; 1979; 1981; 1982), Schiffrin (1981) and Silva-Corvalan (1983). On cultural presuppositions and their shaping of the stories we tell, see Polanyi (1978), Tannen (1979) and Linde (1993).

If there is one theme that predominates in the sociolinguistic study of narratives, stories, and performed tellings, it is that diversity of situation generates diversity of stories, structures, features, and expectations. From one situation to the next, it seems, 'the same person' can tell the same story so differently that it is *as if* they were *not* the same person. See, among others, Johnstone (1990; 1996), Johnstone and Bean (1997), Harré (1998), McConnell-Ginet and Eckert (1995), Neisser and Fivush (1994), Linde (1999) and Norrick (2000). And on narrative analysis applied to healthcare and psychology, see e.g. Crawford, Brown, and Nolan (1998), Crossley (2000) and Payne (2000).

As a result narrative as a genre or kind has been problematized anew, and viewed through the lens of social theory (using Bourdieu and Foucault among others). Recently, the work of Gee (particularly on the diversity of narrative styles that children and adults disclose, defying easy class- or ethnicity-categorization), who has developed something of an alternative to the Labovian model, a verse-stanzaic approach, has been very influential: see Gee (1991; 1996) and Hymes (1982).

A great deal of attention has been directed to the question of the ways in which spoken and written discourse differ. For a revision of the prevailing assumptions about the greater syntactic complexity of written narratives, see Beaman (1984). Tannen (1982) sees written narrative as combining the syntactic complexity of writing along with spoken discourse features used to enhance interpersonal involvement – hence a merging of oral and literate strategies; see also Tannen (1988). Ultimately we may need to pay more conscious attention not simply to the sociolinguistic environment but also to the wider cultural setting from which a story emerges. For recent anthropologically-minded study of narratives, see Bruner, who has been widely admired (1984; 1986; 1990; 1992) and Bauman (1986).

But one publication stands out as a 'snapshot' of the range of applications (and partial rebuttals or reformulations, it should be noted) of the Labovian structuralist approach to narratives, a snapshot that captures the range of ways, towards the end of the 1990s, in which those seminal papers inspired researchers and practitioners in education, first and second language acquisition, psychology, psychotherapy, law, social constructionism, cultural and media studies, anthropology, and so on – an array of disciplines ranging far beyond sociolinguistics. This is the 1997 special issue of *Journal of Narrative and Life History*, edited by Bamberg (1997a), an absolutely essential resource. It opens with a reprint of the 1967 Labov and Waletzky paper and closes, as noted earlier, with Labov's more recent thoughts on narrative analysis. In between, some fifty distinguished scholars contribute to this compendium of concise and focussed papers, showing how their work has adopted, modified or otherwise profited from the Labovian proposals, whether in harmony with them or by means of the more clearly-articulated dissent or critique that they helped make possible.

## Notes and exercises

1 There is no better place to start, in seeing how effective the Labovian scheme of narrative analysis is, than with data that you yourself have elicited. Record a story from someone you know well. The story could be prompted by, for example, asking them if they have been in a car crash, if they've ever had an operation, or whatever, or the choice of story topic could be left up to the informant. The recording could be open or surreptitious. Just whom you record, obviously, will make a very great difference to the type and structure of story told: five-year-olds produce stories somewhat unlike those of teenagers, who produce ones somewhat unlike those of octogenarians. And the teller's closeness to you, the recorder, will also cause considerable differences. That 'closeness/distance' can be measured in all the ways listed in Section 6.9, but also in countless other variable ways as well. With all the 6.9 factors held constant: is the teller 'in a good mood' at the time of the recording? Have they always openly or secretly felt competitive with you? Is there a lot of distracting background noise, or activity? What time of day is it (how tired are you both)? And so on, potentially endlessly. But at this stage the chief thing is to 'get' a story.

   Once that is done, you will need to transcribe it. Or so runs conventional sociolinguistic wisdom and practice. It is important however to reflect on how in so doing one level of abstractive artificiality – setting about recording oral stories by overt or covert mechanical means – is being compounded by another – the reinterpretation of embedded speech-involving activity as displayed in inspectable written text. Proceeding from taped record to written transcript is full of paradoxes: most analysts would agree that an audiovisual record of a conversation was fuller and in some sense better than a merely audio record, and yet most might also agree that, as a readable transcript, one of an audio-only recording is far more manageable than one of an audiovisual one. The latter are often regarded as unworkable. But the reality is that good-quality transmissable audiovisual recording is becoming increasingly easy to achieve (as easy as good quality sound-recording in the mid-1960s), and that this is often preferable to pure audio in involving less exclusion of potentially relevant signifying material. The real challenge is to develop annotative systems that can be applied selectively in commentary and analysis of played and displayed sequences: for interesting proposed descriptive categories, see Kress and van Leeuwen (1996) and Baldry *et al.* (2000). But already, with present capabilities for computer handling of digitized sound and image records, there should arguably be a good deal less reliance on transcription of such records which, as noted, tends to displace analytical attention from the recorded activity to the transcript.

   Notwithstanding those remarks, it is reasonable to *begin* the gathering and analysis of oral narratives by working with audio recordings initially, together with written transcripts of these. There is no great mystery about transcriptions, because there is no possibility of getting them perfectly 'correct'. It is best to start by trusting your own judgment, simply setting out as full a written record of the taped material as you can. You will soon encounter difficult questions of specific practice and general theory. Should one measure pauses: are they sometimes an evaluative device? Are there different kinds of pauses? Should one annotate stress and intonation, and changes of pace of delivery? What about eye contact – or lack of it – between teller and listeners; and both the teller's and listeners' body movements? Can we legitimately ignore these dimensions of the speech event? Where the answer is no, this highlights those respects in which an audio-tape may mislead us more than it assists. But all empirical study must resolve such questions: for useful discussions of sociolinguistic methodology see Labov (1972) who famously drew attention to the Observer's Paradox, as it has been called: that the sociolinguist needs to observe how interactants behave when they are unobserved. See also Wolfson (1976), Stubbs (1983: 218–46), Ochs (1979) and more recently Wolf (1996), who proposes an integrational linguistic dissolving of the Labovian paradox, at least in his study of New Orleans residents with French-origin names, and those name-bearers' reactions to variant pronunciations of those names: "the facts are constituted in and by the process of observation, and by virtue of the interaction between interviewer and [name-] bearer, as between bearer and interlocutor generally."

Now at last you can test out the Labovian model outlined in this chapter on your sample narrative. Identify the orientation, complicating action, resolution, and abstract and coda (if any) of the narrative. Is there any significantly delayed orientation, and if so, are such delays motivated or accidental? Tellers may well display something other than 'perfect competence': they may forget to include important background, and may even neglect to relate important narrative events. What store can be set by such errors or infelicities? Focussing now on evaluation, is there a distinct section of this, as Labov's diamond diagram suggests, prior to the resolution, and/or is evaluation dispersed throughout the text? Are certain types of evaluation device more prominent than others (e.g. many intensifiers, few explicatives or comparators); is this a performed narrative, in Wolfson's sense? (Many of these questions only become really interesting once a comparative analysis of a number of narratives is attempted.) Finally, in what ways do you feel – or suspect – that the Labovian model is inadequate relative to your target narrative? Is there temporal reordering of the kind disallowed by Labov? Are there dimensions of evaluation that his categories seem not to cover?

2  Attempt a six-part (abstract, etc.) analysis of Joyce's 'The Dead'. How satisfactory does this seem to be? Does it help if we treat the text as two narratives – the story of the Christmas party and the story of Gabriel and Gretta's night at the hotel – each with its own trajectory from orientation to resolution? Argue the case for or against this proposal, taking into consideration the kinds of sequential cause-and-effect relatedness that each approach might highlight. Think also of the possible evaluative function of the text's recurring references to, for example, warmth, generosity, mortality, darkness, and coverings. These may operate at a level of narrative texture, mentioned at the opening of Chapter 4, which I have entirely neglected. Thus, in the copious references to darkness and covering and gauntness, from the 'three mortal hours' it allegedly takes Gretta to dress, to the lugubrious conversation about the monks who sleep in their coffins – a macabre topic which is 'buried in the silence of the table' (201) – there are numerous allusions to the fact of dying. These, too, the reader incorporates into their sense of why the story is being told.

To say so much is not, however, to claim that the 'point' of 'The Dead', or any moral or message, can be easily extracted and summarized in a sentence or two. That this is so first begins to be apparent when we try to decide where (if at all) resolution leaves off and coda (if any) begins. Is Gabriel's dreamlike sense of dissolving, at the close of the story, a coda appended to the already-past events of the party and of Michael Furey's life and death? Or, more integrated into the narrative, are these concluding thoughts a kind of resolution to all the preceding events: selfconscious as codas often are, but inescapably a result as a resolution is? Is our choice between seeing this as coda or resolution affected by whether we feel the revery is genuinely revelatory insight, or maudlin self-indulgence?

3 But at least as interesting as applying Labov to such large narrative units as whole novels or stories is applying the model to the stories within stories. Here in 'The Dead', analyze Gretta's direct speech account of her involvement with Michael Furey, and comment on any oddities in the structuring of her story that emerge. How important to the telling is its addressee, Gabriel?

4 If the question is asked, 'Where or what are the evaluation elements in Faulkner's "That Evening Sun"?' – to say nothing of a more extended narrative – how might one go about developing an answer? Ultimately I think it has to be concluded that in anything as notional as evaluation, answers and modes of proceeding analytically will be contentious. But two potentially useful procedures may be starting-points.

One of these begins by assuming that it is worth attending to what a reader *takes away*, after the event, from a narrative, and combines this with a focus on point and tellability. With both these in mind, it seems reasonable to ask one or more informants (individually or jointly), who have recently read 'That Evening Sun', what they *recall* being the point of the story, and what they recall being some of the most striking means by which Faulkner or the narrator conveyed that point.

A second procedure (bottom-up rather than, as in the previous suggestion, top-down) would entail asking first-time readers of the story, as they proceed through their first reading of one or more passages, to mark all those stretches of text which they sense are *not* strictly telling what happened (next), nor supplying orientation. By either means, it may be that readers agree that some parts of the story are saturated with evaluation, while other passages seem to be largely sequences of action (although not necessarily actions with a clearly reached resolution, hence liable to attract interpretive evaluation, by the reader, as scenes of ineffectuality or routineness or even disorder – depending on whether the reader assumes that the protagonists would *like* to reach particular goals).

In the course of 'That Evening Sun' Nancy attempts to tell a story to the children, who are overtly resistant addressees (one challenges her: 'You don't know any stories.'). She of course, throughout the larger story, is convinced she is in 'danger of death', and that Jesus (hiding in the ditch) will come in the night and kill her: it is to detain the children, to keep them with her that bit longer, that she attempts to tell the story. Comment in detail on whether Nancy's story – only fragments of which are directly related to us – is one of vicarious or personal experience; comment, too, on how young Quentin, the narrator, who is here one of the addressees of Nancy's story, conveys evaluations of *Nancy's* efforts at evaluated narrating; and also comment on Caddy's and Jason's reported remarks, during and just after Nancy's storytelling, and how they get to the nub of the evaluation and credibility issues that sociolinguists emphasize are crucial to stories told in the course of talk, as this one is.

5 In this chapter I have emphasized that in order to justify the telling of a story, what gets told must be to some degree special, and that non-trivialness must be adequately communicated. On the other hand, from the ethnomethodologist Harvey Sacks has come an emphasis on another aspect of people's stories, an aspect potentially at variance with the non-trivialness condition mentioned above. This is that, to protect our stories from dismissal as outrageous fabrication, immediately suspect, we render our stories as ordinary as possible. Sacks

suggests that the stories we typically encounter in everday interaction are 'over-whelmingly banal', and that people strive to establish the 'nothing happened' sense of truly catastrophic events. Thus ordinary people have to work their way between the Scylla of the 'so what?' question (by making their stories not unin-teresting) and the Charybdis of the 'I don't believe you!' reaction (by making their stories not incredible).

It would be interesting to explore the repertoire of linguistic means that we might identify as, in part at least, performing this task of 'ordinariness construc-tion'. Again, we need recordings or transcripts of narratives of incidents that we know (from personal involvement or further questioning of the teller) to be extraordinarily ghastly, fortuitous or whatever. Some of the means we might predict will contribute to 'ordinariness construction' might include downtoning modifiers (*rather*, *a bit*, *somewhat*, etc.); hedges (*sort of*, *kind of*, etc.); vague lan-guage; epistemic modals and qualifying verbs (*I suppose*, *I guess*, *seemingly*); less emotive predicates (*hit* instead of *smash*); plentiful description of the ambient routine events, settings and background; a flattening off of pitch and volume variations; and restricted changes in pace of delivery. Sacks's ordinariness hypothesis would be to some extent confirmed if we could find a teller telling the same story twice over, once to close friends, once to more distant acquaintances, and found more downtoning in the latter case than in the former. It may also be the case that the expression of ordinariness varies with different tellers: more prominent in the stories of introverts, relatively neglected in the stories of extro-verts.

6 Compare and contrast a spoken and written telling of the same story. If you are lucky, the informant you used for exercise 1 might be persuaded to write down the story she has told you. It's probably best not to mention you'd like a written version of the story until you have extracted the oral version, even if that infor-mant declines to continue. And perhaps the most crucial thing to do is to keep the data manageably short: many informants just won't do a good job of writing up a story that, in the oral telling, took ten minutes or more. The best way to grasp what, as a data-gatherer, you are up against is to do the exercise yourself: produce oral and written versions of some brief narrative from your own life before inflict-ing this chore on others!

Now compare the two versions of the 'same' story in any ways you think appropriate, but focussing especially on the formal differences. Are abstracts, codas, evaluations, etc., 'done' the same way in the different media? Despite dif-ferences of form, are there pairings or counterparts: for example, are there ele-ments of the written form that do the job done by stress and intonation and pace of delivery in the spoken version?

7 The single most delimiting aspect of Labovian description seems to be the requirement that only independent clauses can carry the fundamental, fixed-order clauses of narrative. In practice, Labov found sufficient apparent obser-vance of a main-clause/main-event chronological pairing to suggest that this was a requirement – a requirement, at least, in the kind of narratives, from the kind of speakers, in the kind of settings, and so on, that he studied. But, as suggested, in other kinds of narratives different clause/event pairings may arise.

Look for instances of main-event reordering in any spoken or written narra-tives of personal experience that you have access to. Do these appear in particu-lar types of subordinate clauses (e.g. of time and reason)? Do they relate to particular types of happening (e.g. hidden motivations)? Are they more common in the written narratives than the spoken? Does the temporal distance of the narrated events from the teller's present time seem to affect any tendency to reorder? And – widening the net now – are they more frequent in narratives of vicarious experience than of personal experience?

Finally, a deeper difficulty, which links this exercise up with some of the remarks appended to exercise 1 above. This exercise (as at various points in the chapter) has talked about the independent clauses and subordinate clauses *in* the oral narrative a speaker delivers. But just how conclusively instances of these categories are *in* a teller's narrative, as distinct from being found by an analyst to be in the narrative, is a contentious matter. Bear in mind, first of all, that analysts almost invariably 'find' their independent and subordinate clauses in the transcript (often their own transcript) of the discourse rather than the discourse itself or its oral/audio recording. Analysts almost never (I suggest), *in situ*, as the story is being told, make a mental note to themselves that 'Ah, there's an independent clause, and there's a subordinate clause which goes with the preceding clause, no, the following clause ... ' and so on. Nor do they do this with the audio tape. Instead they put the thing in writing, at which point a host of resources or categories are almost unthinkingly brought to bear on the transformed discourse, in ways which make the analyst's task considerably more manageable. To begin with, a helpful and consistent spacing appears between what are now usually and recognizably words (and where an analyst has found words, they can – and do – the more easily find sentences (or 'sentoids'), full stops and initial capitals, and clauses). This despite the well-attested fact that there is no regular audible gap between words in speech. No analyst in practice would record the Singaporean story presented earlier and transcribe the opening as follows:

myoneahmyoneahIwassavedbymyintelligenceyknowbecauseahIwasinsix-ayyknoweightofuswerecaughtgamblingyknowsevensixrepeattwothat time

The only people whom I recall presenting 'transcripts' of this kind are poets. To summarize, when the analyst makes a transcript of oral interaction this is nothing like a mere 'copying out', but rather entails a range of spoken and unspoken interpretive assumptions and decisions, a kind of 'marking up' of the text in ways which will ensure that such basic elements of written language as words, sentences, and clauses will be easily found. And that marking up into writing is guided by resources which fall entirely outside the system of writing itself, most notably intonation. It is the speaker's heard intonation, *in situ* and recorded on the audio tape, that is most determinative of an analyst's placing a period and sentence boundary at the end of the following chunk of talk:

MyoneahmyoneahIwassavedbymyintelligenceyknow

So categories of writing (the sentence, the clause) are being found on the basis of criteria (intonation, etc.) which are no integral part of writing at all.

# 7   Children's narratives

## 7.1  Stories for, by, and with children

Even within stories *for* children (as within those *by* and *with*) we can observe and contrast many sub-types: spoken or written; face-to-face or 'removed' (e.g. radio or cassette); one-to-one or one-to-many; spontaneously constructed or text-dependent or scripted; and many more, in numerous distinct combinations. Even with everything else held constant except the prompt or priming, significant differences can emerge: Stein and Albro (1997) have found that children 'primed' with a story opening about a big grey fox produced considerably more complex narratives than when given a story 'stem' to elaborate about a little boy or girl. So the potential dimensions of situational variation are numberless. But a very useful preliminary categorization of situations can be achieved by considering Halliday's three macro-dimensions of discourse, which he calls the field, mode, and tenor of the discourse.

*Field* designates, broadly, the nature of the social activity that is going on and that the participants are engaged in (e.g. children sharing a personal-experience story with their teacher and peers). The discourse topic will be important, but field concerns larger behavioural questions: understanding what type of social activity is in progress, what the activity is or is about, and not merely what the discourse is about. In a segment of courtroom interaction, the discourse topic might be a particular incident involving particular stolen goods, but the field remains the administration of criminal justice. Like other Hallidayan categorizations, field assumes some degree of motivated 'fit' between language practice and cultural practice, where a society's language patterns articulate or 'construe' its view of the world.

*Tenor* concerns participant relations as shaped by the statuses and roles that are being observed (e.g. friend to friend, father to son, doctor to patient, sales assistant to customer); this is a fascinatingly rich area since most of the roles we occupy, and consequent relations with others, are more temporary and contingent than we imagine. Focussing on tenor chimes with new approaches, broadly social-constructionist (for a variety of appproaches, see among others, Muhlhausler and Harré, 1990;

Bamberg, 1997b; Edwards, 1997) which emphasize and explore how we 'take on' particular roles or statuses in particular circumstances – the kind of thing that conversation analysts vividly characterize as 'doing being X'. Thus no-one is spontaneously, a-socially and at birth, Catholic or female or a professor or a general practitioner or a single parent or British or Maori; rather all these categorizations (cf. the character attributes discussed at 4.4) must or will to a large extent be *performed* in the course of communicative interaction, including verbal discourse. As indeed we know from the possibilities of 'passing' and impersonation. Nor are these categories stable or permanent, with a fixed value: the categories 'housewife' or 'divorced person' or 'atheist' have nothing like the social force (and consequences for tenor, for the ways in which people so categorized tend to be discoursally addressed, and talked or written about) that they once had. And new categories arise, such as 'single parent'.

*Mode* encompasses variations in the medium of the text and the expectations that the addresser and addressee have of the language they are using (e.g. whether the text is written or spoken, planned or unplanned, integral to some ongoing activity or a detached reconstruction; and whether the language aims to instruct, persuade, emote, and so on). For much fuller discussion of field, tenor and mode see Halliday (1978), Halliday and Hasan (1985), Martin (1992), and Matthiessen (1995).

The above reminders of situation-dependent variation are also relevant to two caveats that should be entered concerning analysts' assessments of tellers and tales. The first concerns the use of data from children's performance with stories (skills at constructing, comprehending, summarizing, and so on) as evidence of their cognitive skills or linguistic competence more broadly defined. If situation-dependency makes major differences to the stories that tellers produce, we must be circumspect about moving from an assessment of a particular performance in a particular (perhaps highly problematic) situation, to any general assessment of narrative (let alone cognitive) ability. The second concerns the actual analysis of a child's tales: if our judgments are dominated by unexamined preconceptions as to what a 'good' story should be like, and neglect the likelihood that what is good in one set of circumstances may be quite inappropriate in a different set, then any conclusions drawn may be valueless, if not positively harmful. We should never end up with the young wag dogged by his tale.

On the other hand, while ackowledging differences, we can and should also look for patterns of similarity and relationship across a range of cases. Otherwise we fail to identify connections within what we can intuitively accept as a coherent area of study. Ultimately analyses of children's narratives lead to some fairly sharp issues of relation and causation. Can specific linguistic evidence be identified that supports the frequent claim that children's oral storytelling is a preparation for written narrative composition? Similarly, if written narrative is a distinct kind of writing and a competence-base from which older primary-school children build their developing control of other varieties of language such as argumentation and description, which particular linguistic features of the known variety are a help, and which are a hindrance, in progress towards those 'target' varieties? Are children's narratives evaluatively and structurally simplified versions of adult ones, modelled on the narratives they hear from adults, or are they constructed according to other principles; what linguistic evidence is there on either side? Can we nurture production of more complex stories (written or spoken) in children – and if so, how? What role do recall exercises, probe questions, and shared retellings play in the development of narrative skills? How does reading narrative relate to the writing of narrative, should the former be graded for optimal effectiveness, and how do we determine grades of narrative complexity or difficulty?

## 7.2 Storytelling and emergent literacy

An increasingly well-explored area of children's language development is that of the child's nurtured receptiveness to writing and reading, and familiarity with some of the disciplines and constraints of writing and reading, somewhat before they are formally taught to read or write. The fundamental recognition here is that, as the introduction to one recent collection of studies of children's emergent literacy puts it,

> Practically all children in a highly literate society such as ours do bring knowledge about literacy to school with them.
>
> (Farr, 1985: vii)

A number of related theses, which I have space only to list in summary fashion here, accompany this basic insight. Literacy begins at home, these studies show, where that home is characterized by valued relationships with parents, siblings and friends. Recurringly, close ethnographic studies such as those reported in Farr (1985) and Bissex (1981) show that where the interactant is highly attuned to the child's current stage of writing competence, is supportive and enthusiastic and not overly corrective of 'errors', then that interactant can be instrumental in developing the child's literacy skills in a greater variety of ways and more rapidly than if the child were left to their own resources. It also seems that the effectiveness of the support an interactant offers cannot be separated from the value the child puts on that interactant as a person. This is a sharp reminder of the non-autonomous nature of narrative productions and receptions: what you give and what you get may vary sharply depending on the relations – of respect, affection, or otherwise – between addresser and addressee. Halliday's notion of tenor, introduced earlier, attempts to address at least the lexicalized and grammaticized aspects of these complex and changing ties.

The idea of the interactant as an essential ally in the assault on 'forward positions' of language development, otherwise beyond the individual child's current powers, is based solidly on the psychologist Vygotsky's notion of the zone of proximal development. Indeed Vygotsky's theories of cognitive development in the individual are the dominant theoretical underpinning of much current research in the field. While Piaget's theories have the attraction of indicating quite explicit stages in cognitive development which, at differing pace, all children must go through in the specified order, following a 'biological timetable', those theories have been felt to concentrate on development driven by interaction between the learner and the object-of-knowledge (e.g. a language) to the neglect of development driven by growing and changing cultural and personal interaction. In a sense Vygotsky is more comprehensive than Piaget, allowing biology a role but arguing that cultural development, fostered by interaction with significant others in one's immediate environment, dominates. And from that interaction, as Vygotsky famously asserted, internalization proceeds: 'An interpersonal process is transformed into an intrapersonal one' (Vygotsky, 1978: 57). That which was learned through social interaction becomes knowledge in the individual. And Vygotsky's emphasis on the social environment makes it all the easier for researchers to expect and allow for variation in different children's orders and manner of narrative development, given different social environments and different interests and purposes in the child. These brief remarks on Vygotsky may serve to give some indication of the theoretical background of current orientations in child development research.

The specific strategies adopted by kindergarten teachers in the nurturing of children's skills of writing and storytelling are of many kinds. But most commonly discussed are the activities of 'sharing time' (reviewed in the next section), dictation and dramatization. In dictation, a child dictates a new story, or retells a familiar one to a teacher-scribe. The teacher-scribe is thus in a position to monitor the telling as it is in progress: suggesting improvements, pointing to information gaps, etc., while the child retains responsibility for the production. Dictation is in effect 'doing writing without doing the writing', and gives the child a particularly immediate sense of how marvellous a knack it is to be able to record one's own story productions with fixed graphic symbols (reproducible, increasingly unmysterious). Dictation entails a degree of detachment from the events of a story that we noted earlier was essential for consistency of orientation in any telling, and it also nurtures reflexive self-awareness. The dictated story is usually read back to the child, with the teacher checking with the child that she is happy with the story as it stands. The larger world of 'second thoughts', self-correction and assisted improvement, of verbal production as externalizable and separable from its originator but something that the originator may retain responsibility for and ownership of, begins to take shape. All this goes a step further when such dictated stories are then dramatized, with the teacher declaiming the story, in chunks, as its original teller and other children act out its events: the teller learns the need for a story to be coherent and tellable to its addressees in the most direct way possible. In acting out a story the children reconstruct the world of events which the teller's words represent, and in the process, awkwardnesses of match, between words and world, can become newly apparent.

## 7.3  Differing styles, differing orientations

In 6.8 I mentioned Shirley Brice Heath's findings that what counted as narratives in two small-town North Carolina working-class communities (one black, one white) were drastically different. How easy is it, one might wonder, for anyone from Trackton to tell a good, appreciated story in Roadville, or vice versa? And not just in Trackton and Roadville. Much recent research from psycholinguistic, sociolinguistic and social psychological perspectives has uncovered just how much cultural specificity and relativism attends narrative practice. Let a hundred ways of telling flourish, the observer might suggest, but the consequences may be undesirable where contrasting 'ways' meet. Sometimes the exponents of the preferred style get more rewarded, even without the rewarders being aware that it is chiefly to differences of style that they are responding. Heath (1982) vividly presents the moral and educational dilemmas that emerge when orientation to narrative and literacy is recognized as plural.

Another persuasive elucidation of the problems broached here is charted in the work of Michaels (1981; 1985; Michaels and Collins, 1984), who shows that

> [First-grade] children from different backgrounds come to school with different narrative strategies and prosodic conventions for giving narrative accounts.
>
> (1981: 423)

This matters because 'sharing time' activities in which, prompted and supported by the teacher, individual children describe things or narrate past experiences to the whole class, are an important and widely-used educational resource; they are a potentially rich practice ground for using (and learning) *literate* discourse strategies. In an empirical study Michaels found that children whose already-established discourse style matched the teacher's own literate style and expectations did well at 'sharing time' activities and benefited from this 'oral preparation for literacy' (1981: 423). But where the child's style and the teacher's expectations diverged, teacher–child collaboration was often unsuccessful and longer-term adverse effects on school performance and evaluation were a danger.

Among the discourse expectations that Michaels found a particular teacher disclosing, in her regulatory reactions to her children's stories, were the following:

1   explicit spatiotemporal grounding of the talk;
2   full description and naming of objects involved in a story, even of those in plain sight;

3   minimal assumptions of shared background knowledge between the
    teller and his or her addressees; and
4   lexicalization of topic shifts, marking any thematic relatedness that
    persisted despite change of topic.

In sum, the teacher – 'Mrs Jones' – 'seemed to expect a literate-style, decontextualized account centering on a single topic' (Michaels and Collins, 1984: 223).

The problem that Michaels identifies related to the sharing style of the African–American children in Mrs Jones's class, a style which turned out to have its own 'systematicness' but was at variance with the teacher's preferred style. While the white children brought to sharing time a discourse style that was already at least embryonically 'topic centered' in the ways outlined above, the black children brought to the task an established 'topic associating' style. In topic associating discourse, the teller presents 'a series of implicitly associated personal anecdotes' (1981: 429), which are actually built around an unstated thematic focus. Information is broken into chunks prosodically, by means of a high sustained pitch on *and*, followed by a pause; no other lexical connectives besides *and* were used to link anecdotes.

> This kind of rhythmically chunked, topic associating discourse is evidently difficult to follow for those who, like the teacher and student teacher, expect the discourse to focus on a single topic and to be prosodically marked with sharp rising contours (signalling 'more to come') or falling contours (signalling full closure).
>
> (Michaels, 1981: 430)

Children who used this 'topic associating' style had acute problems with meeting the teacher's requirement, for their sharing time stories, that they tell of just one thing of importance: the style itself made it seem (to the teacher) as if there was no particular topic whatsoever. Telling about just one thing made sense 'only if one had a topic centered schema to begin with' (Michaels, 1981: 434).

In order to get a fuller lexicogrammatical description of the differences in the discourse styles (topic-centred versus topic-associating) of such children, Michaels and Collins analyzed the oral retellings, by four first-graders (two white, two black), of a short film. To enlarge the comparative exercise, they also looked at two fourth-graders' narratives, both oral and written, of the same film. They found that

> Of the four first-grade narratives, two use a wide variety of lexical and syntactic devices to signal agent focus, causal connections, old *v.* new distinctions, and coreference relations. We call this a literate discourse style.... The other first grade narratives rely more on prosodic cues such as duration and special contouring to signal agent focus, causal

connections, and so forth. We call this an oral discourse style because prosodic cues such as duration and contouring, although essential for oral communication, are precisely what is not available in written language.

(Michaels and Collins, 1984: 232)

Repeatedly, necessary textual connections are marked lexically in the literate discourse style, but prosodically in the oral discourse style. For example one of the literate-style speakers first introduces one of the main protagonists thus:

> there was a man/. . . that was . . . picking some pears/

Twenty-four lines later she can recycle the relative clause to confirm that here is second mention of the same man:

> they walked by the man who gave/. . . wh-who was picking the pears//

By contrast one of the oral-style speakers introduces the same character thus:

> it was about/ . . . this man/ he was um/. . . um . . . takes some . . . peach-
> /. . . some . . . pea:rs off the tree/

using two independent clauses. Twenty-five lines later, on second mention of this character, the speaker relies almost entirely on prosody (vowel elongation and high rise-fall contour on man) to signal old information, subsequent mention:

> and when that . . . when he 'pa:ssed/ by that ma:n/ the man . . . the ma:n
> came out of the tree/

In fact there is some lexical signalling of coreference here: the speaker's use of the deictic word *that* in the phrase *that ma:n*. But it is reasonable to argue that this is an insufficient lexical marker of the coreference intended.

Another lexis/prosody contrast concerns the marking of an important resultative connection between two narrative events in the story. This is marked in the literate-style speaker's account by the standard written connective, *so*, while in the oral-style speaker's account it is signalled prosodically by a stressed high fall on *then*. In other words when *then* is prosodically marked in this particular way it is intended to convey causal relation and not merely temporal relation; whether addressees derive that meaning-difference or not is precisely the problem at issue.

Similar oral style versus literate style disparities, with attendant difficulties, were found in the oral narratives of the fourth-graders (both of whom were fluent readers and writers 'at the top of their class'). And the potential problems in the oral-discourse speaker's spoken narrative become actual defects when that person constructs his written narrative. For Paul, the literate-discourse speaker, 'learning to write involves enriching a system he already knows and uses effectively in oral discourse'.

> Geoffrey, on the other hand, tends to rely heavily on prosodic cues in speaking; these cues are often the sole indicators of highlighted information, coreference relations, and perspective shifts in his oral narrative. His written narrative is characterized by weakly signalled transitions and ambiguous identity relations. For him, with prosodic options lost, learning to write means learning a new system for signalling thematic cohesion.
>
> (Michaels and Collins, 1984: 241)

## 7.4  Children's narrative development

The previous two sections have chiefly considered some of the ways that emergent narrativity in the social setting of the school seems to be best supported – together with some of the ways in which, despite the best intentions of child and teacher, frustrations may arise. But we also need to know more about just what development does occur typically in children's narrative ability. For these purposes several large-scale studies of children's stories can be referred to, and I will turn to these shortly.

One classic study of children's linguistic development is Piaget's pioneering work (1926). Focussing on story-recall ability in 6- to 8-year-olds, Piaget identified a number of failings in the recall productions of his younger subjects, failings which are far less frequent in the older children. Those major failings concerned order, causality and orientation: the actual order of events in a story was not reproduced in recall, cause-and-effect relations were not properly marked, and egocentric use of pronouns (tending to orient narrative events to the child herself) led to misdirections, in the recall texts, over who was doing what to whom in the narrative. Despite many decades of critical review, Piaget's basic findings are still widely accepted (with the qualification that children can produce non-egocentric text at a rather earlier age – four years – than he claimed). But just what conclusions we should draw from such findings remains a matter of debate.

More recently, children's developing grasp of temporal order and causality in stories, as well as of complex qualities such as that narratives should appear adequately 'completed' and evaluated have been probed in invaluable studies by Peterson and McCabe (1983) and others (McCabe and Peterson (eds), 1991; McCabe and Peterson, 1996). The 1983 study was important because, despite the authors' broadly psycholinguistic interests, they eschewed highly artificial recall and comprehension tests in favour of analysis of the ordinary stories that particular children chose to tell them – not quite spontaneously, but certainly in relaxed and informal situations. Peterson and McCabe conducted an analysis of 288 stories, elicited during casual conversation, from a controlled sample of ninety-six children ranging in age from 4 to 9 years (eight children for each of the twelve age/sex combinations). Each story was subjected to analysis according to three methodologies: the Labovian, the psycholinguistic 'story-grammar' approach (see the 'Further reading' of the present chapter), and a third, more syntax-focussed method; only the first two of these are discussed here.

First applying Labovian methods (or what they call 'High Point analysis', referring to the top of the diamond in Labov's famous diagram), they found some interesting shifts in the type of narrative that children tend to produce at different ages. 'Leap-frog' narratives were the commonest single type of story produced by the 4-year-olds, narratives 'where the child jumps from event to event unsystematically, leaving out important events' (1983: 48), which put a heavy processing burden on the listener. At age 4, the classic pattern (i.e. the full Labovian diamond, with a clear climax and resolution) was still relatively rare. Within a year, however, the leap-frog pattern itself seemed to become rare and then disappeared completely, while the classic pattern became increasingly common, dominating in the productions of the 7-year-olds and above. But in addition they found that 'chronological' stories persist, albeit with some decrease in frequency, at all ages. Stories classified as chronological are those where there is temporal sequence of events without adequate point or integratedness to the material, i.e. stories that fulfil the referential function of narrative but not the evaluative one. Narratives that Peterson and McCabe labelled impoverished (too few events, too often repeated) or disoriented (confused, contradictory) also become rare.

When Peterson and McCabe subjected the same corpus of stories to a story-grammatical analysis they uncovered an equally developmental picture. There was a steady increase with age in both the length of narratives produced, and their structural complexity. A broad and cumulative shift emerges, from production of mere *sequences* (such as clusters of statements that report descriptions or actions without any protagonist's motivations linking them up) to production of *episodes* (where some sort of purposeful planned behaviour is explicitly asserted, or can be inferred, from the actions of a protagonist). Sequences outnumber episodes in the 4-year-olds' narrative structures by more than two to one; episodes outnumber sequences in those of 9-year-olds by four to one.

> But one type of sequence persists (often alongside episodes) in narratives at every age examined: this is the reactive sequence, in which a set of changes ... automatically cause other changes with no planning involved.... Something happens that causes something else to happen, although there is no evidence of goals.
>
> (Peterson and McCabe, 1983: 71)

An example is the following, from a 6-year-old boy:

*E:*   What happened in the accident that you saw?
*L:*   Car got burned up.
*E:*   A car got burned up? Tell me about what happened when the car got burned up.
*L:*   There was three kids in there. Everybody got out in, just in time, and, and, and then, my Dad didn't keep his eyes on the road and we were almost wrecked.
*E:*   You were almost wrecked?
*L:*   Yeahhhhh. I wouldn't want that to happen. I'd be out of school about a week.

(Peterson and McCabe, 1983: 73)

Peterson and McCabe noted both the increasing tendency for older children to focus on planning and the unexpected persistence of reactive sequences:

> Several investigators ... have suggested that the goal-directed, problem-solving episode may have psychological reality. It may be an important underlying pattern that is used by people in processing and producing both fictional stories and narratives about actual life experiences. However, the present research suggests that it may not be the only one, since reactive sequences are common at all ages and cannot be described as goal-directed behaviour. It is inevitable that important things occur in the lives of children that are not planned, although they elicit reactions. Reactive sequences seem to be the best way of capturing the sense of these important externally imposed events.
>
> (1983: 99)

If we acknowledge that 'plan-less' reactive sequences are sometimes a perfectly appropriate narrative to share – there being plenty of tellability, for example, in a car that burns up, nearly killing three kids and nearly causing Dad to crash the car – we can equally recognize the common ground of such sequences with many 'hard news' stories (briefly discussed in Chapter 8). Another broad trend is the increased elaboration and embedding (roughly akin to coordination and subordination) within older children's narratives: multi-structure narratives, and structures within structures, yielding 'a more fine-grained analysis of their experience' (1983: 100). In specific response to Piaget's claim that young children have a deficient grasp of causality (a claim which itself is based on findings of children's deficient mastery of causal connectives), Peterson and McCabe argue the need to probe for children's incipient understanding of causality by means other than how they use particular linguistic expressions (such as causal connectives).

If Peterson and McCabe supply abundant evidence of the structural development in the narratives of children from age 4 to 9, Umiker-Sebeok (1979) gives us a vivid insight into the younger child's coming-into-awareness of just what narratives are and can do as a distinct type of social activity, a distinct field of discourse. She reports a study of the intra-conversational narratives of infants (3- to 5-year-olds) in their nursery schools. One striking finding was the tendency of the youngest children to produce narratives about situationally proximate matters, i.e. about events that had just occurred in their immediate environment (not just within the school but even within the same play period). The 3-year-olds did this in 89 per cent of their intraconversational narratives. The 5-year-olds, however, described events that occurred outside the preschool environment in 53 per cent of the total narratives, i.e. narratives about 'remote' matters. This looks like a striking example of learning to walk before attempting to run. Umiker-Sebeok also found that older children's narratives were far more interactive with their listeners, eliciting relevant responses from their child listeners (e.g. questions about orientation, evaluation or result).

It is interesting to compare all the above findings with those of Kernan (1977), who undertook a Labovian analysis of a much smaller corpus of narratives from somewhat older children – girls in three age bands: 7- to 8-year-olds, 10- to 11-year-olds, and 13- to 14-year-olds. Kernan's findings are interestingly complex or mixed. Thus the older girls tended to supply an abstract or introducer for their stories (such as 'Well see, this what happen') far more regularly than the youngest group; but why they did so is open to speculation. In line with others' findings, the older children also did more elaborate identification of their stories' main characters and locations (i.e. supplying more than a bald name). But Kernan also adds that the teens' provision of richer background information was done less for reasons of structural or factual completeness, but rather to help ensure proper 'uptake' of the story.

Also of interest in Kernan's study is evidence of a change in relative frequency of use of two simple sets of clausal connectives: *and*, *then*, and *and then*, on the one hand (where the clauses so linked are said to be either quite independent of each other, or have only a temporal-sequential interrelation); and *so*, *so then*, and *and so then*, on the other hand (where the following clause is said to depend on the preceding one in order to be understood properly). Frequency of use of connectives from the two sets, combined, declines steadily from the youngest to the oldest girls; and the distribution between the two sets, heavily skewed towards the '*and*' set in the youngest girls' narratives, is much more balanced in the oldest girls' narratives.

But perhaps most significantly of all, Kernan finds a steady growth with age of occurrence of clauses that serve what he calls an expressive function:

> clauses that indicate in some way the feelings of the narrator toward the events he is relating and that are used to attempt to convey that feeling to the audience.

(Kernan, 1977: 101)

In Labovian terms, these are the means of evaluation that are external to the narrative clause: expressions of the teller's attitude to the events she is recounting. It can be argued that they involve the self-as-teller maintaining a kind of distance from the self-as-protagonist – sufficient distance for that teller to be able to 'take up a position' on the events and protagonist. Viewing these expressivities in this light, it is highly significant that the most orientationally detached of these external devices, framed direct speech – e.g. *I said, I'm getting out of here* – is never used by Kernan's youngest age group, but becomes frequent later.

Confirmation of this development of perspectival control, this ability to frame one's own narration, is found in Hickmann's study (1985) of children's ability to transform dialogues into cohesive texts. Hickmann's youngest children (4-year-olds) never used direct or indirect quotation frames to separate the act of reporting from the speech that was reported, but used pitch and intonation signals to distinguish different speakers. Older children (7- to 10-year-olds), however, did use direct quotation frames. (It is a curious mirror symmetry that has children learning to disambiguate attribution by adopting framing clauses in their spoken narratives, while sophisticated writers in turn have learned to dispense with disambiguating framing clauses, in free discourse – direct or indirect.) Thus the progression is similar to that noted by Kernan, though Hickmann's tellers are using framed quotations earlier. In other situations, reported speech in narratives may in effect combine the Labovian referential and evaluative functions. In a number of studies (e.g. Ely *et al.*, 1996), Ely has found a positive correlation between parents' focus on talk in their interactions with their children and the children's subsequent resort to quotation in their narratives. Ely also found a consistent gender difference, with females using reported speech more frequently than males.

## 7.5 Children's narratives and the development of registers and genres: the systemic-linguistic approach

If narrative is only one use of language, how does it compare and contrast with others, and what are those others? And with regard to the development of language skills in children, is there perhaps too much attention to narrative style, and insufficient attention to other styles (argumentative, expository, etc.)? The work of Martin and Rothery, two linguists who adopt Halliday's systemic-linguistic approach, tackled just these questions. They sought 'to identify some of the distinctive features of different genres and some features of development in [children's] writing' (Rothery and Martin, 1980: preface); their work is presented in this section. And in the following section, a summary is given of recent systemic-linguistic proposals for revisions to our categorizations of (adults') conversational stories: something of an enlargement and a corrective to the Labovian

model that was presented in the previous chapter. (This summary of systemicists' work could have appeared in that chapter, and is not exclusively
relevant to children's storytelling; on the other hand it is only in the
present chapter that the systemic approach to register and genre has been
introduced, so on balance this seems the best place to report these developments.)

On the basis of their analysis of the kinds of writing children actually
produce from kindergarten to high school, Rothery and Martin argue that
there is a standard order in which registers and genres are mastered. The
first genre to appear is what they call observation/comment, as in the
following production from a 6-year-old:

> My surprise
> Oun day my mum bought me
> o some books. and I falte
> glad.
>                     (from Christie *et al.*, 1984: 69)

This most basic type of written text, in which some personal experience is
recorded together with an evaluative comment, is the foundation from
which, it is claimed, two major styles of writing develop: a narrative style
and an expository style. The narrative style entails temporality and an
affective trajectory; the expository style is a-temporal, has no affective trajectory, and is basically a process of describing by means of increasing
depth and detail of analytical observation.

Accordingly, two genres appear a year or two after observation/
comment in children's writing. Recount represents the first narrative-style
genre to be grasped, while report is the first expository-style genre to be
mastered. Recounts are akin to a chronological sequence in Peterson and
McCabe's terms: a series of events temporally sequenced, often with 'and
then' as conjunctive link, optionally framed by an orientation and, at the
close, a reorientation. Reports are a more factual and objective description
than observation/comments, and are relatively depersonalized. Below I
reproduce the developmental genre typology that Rothery and Martin
propose. The two strands of the typology develop from left to right across
the page, with the year of school in which a typical child begins to control
a particular genre indicated underneath.

As the diagram shows, in fourth grade children begin to write personal
narratives, a genre distinct from recounts: in a narrative, awkward or
unforeseen events arise (complications requiring resolution). Fleshing out
the picture of genre-development we can again draw on the notions of
field, mode and tenor. As far as story subject-matter is concerned (one
aspect of field), children progress from writing stories about personal
experiences to writing ones about vicarious experience. In mode we see a
shift to relative context-independence (far less reliance on accompanying
pictures, less assumption of addressee's shared knowledge, and a growing

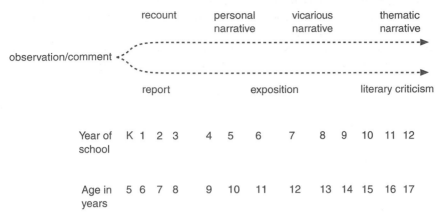

grasp of the fact that texts may address a remote hypothetical audience, and not just the teacher and classmates). In tenor there are transitions from stories disclosing an inflexible spirit of solidarity with, for example, friends of the teller, to stories where there is far greater neutrality of tenor, where evaluations are no longer the stock counters such as 'yuck', 'great' and 'lovely'. Growing flexibility in control of tenor is, of course, part of a developing non-egocentric sense of point of view, of the possibility of writing a story from another's viewpoint.

Martin (1983) provides an insight into the enlarging linguistic repertoire that indicates developing mastery of the register of narrative. He reports the performance of ninety British schoolchildren (in three age groups: 6 to 7, 8 to 9, and 10 to 11 years old), of both sexes, of average ability and predominantly working-class, on several storytelling and re-telling tasks. In particular, he tested their skills at suitably introducing and referring to story participants. But first it is worth outlining what a teller's linguistic options for referencing are. In the chart of reference options below (taken from Martin, 1983: 11), the most basic choice between introducing an entity as new or alluding to an entity as given, is labelled as a choice between presenting and presuming.

TYPES OF REFERENCE

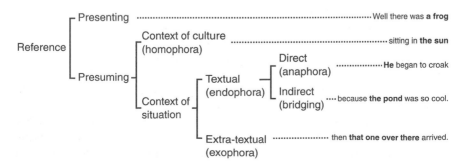

Within the types of referring that presume the listener can retrieve the information, each terminal label indicates just where the listener has to go to identify the entity referred to. Thus homophoric reference obtains when, even on first mention of the entity, definite reference is used, as if there were only one entity of this kind in the ambient culture. Hence references to the moon and the sun will normally be homophoric; and by the same token, indefinite reference would be distinctly odd for the targets of homophoric reference: *?Make sure you keep out of a sun in the middle of the day.* Presuming reference that involves a disambiguating co-textual verbal tie may be direct (e.g. by way of pronouns) or indirect, via the bridging links that are discussed in 7.7 (where there are frogs we can expect ponds). Most significant in analysis of children's text production is the reliance, on both first and subsequent mention, on exophoric reference to immediate context, standardly by means of a definite noun phrase (*the cat*) where more mature storytellers might be expected to follow the convention of *presenting* the entity as new on first mention, and drawing on anaphoric means of reference in subsequent mentions. Compare these two retellings of the same previously-presented story, from a 6- to 7-year-old boy and a 10- to 11-year-old girl respectively (exophoric nominal groups are underlined, noun phrases involving bridging inferences are in italics):

1    Well there was a frog in the jar. The boy was looking it in the jar with the frog. then the boy was in bed and the frog jumped out then it was morning. the frog then the boy looked in the jar and he saw the frog was gone. then he got dressed no then he looked in the boots his boots. Then it wasn't there. Then he looked out *the window*. The dog got the jar on and then the dog fell out. Then the jar broke. then he called for the frog. Then the then a deer came. He got then he climbed on the uh rock and then a deer came and got the boy on *the antlers*. Then he ran and then the deer stopped. Then the boy fell in the river. Then they sat down and then the dog was on the boy's head. Then they looked over the log. Then they saw the family. Then *the little babies* came out. Then the boy walked in the river.

2    Tommy was laying at the bottom of his bed looking at his pet frog with his dog. While he was asleep with the dog on his bed the frog tried to get out of the glass jar. *The next morning* they saw the frog had gone. So they looked out the window and the dog had a glass on his head. The dog fell out the window and smashed the glass and Tommy came out and held the dog and the dog licked his face and they called for him. They went down to *the woods* and there was a swarm of bees coming out of a bee-hive. He went to the top of a rock and *the next minute* he was on top of a reindeer. The dog went behind the rock and the next thing they knew the reindeer was running after the dog with Tommy on his head. They fell into the water off a cliff top and Tommy saw a hollow tree so they both went over the tree and

Tommy told his dog to be quiet and they saw his pet frog and another frog and lots of baby frogs. Tommy took one of the baby frogs home with him.

(Martin, 1983: 19–20)

By contrast with the seven exophoric nominals introducing participants in text 1, Martin finds only two in text 2 (arguably the first mention of Tommy is a third). The generally appropriate management of entity-introduction (appropriate in relation to mainstream storytelling conventions) in text 2 clearly contrasts with inappropriate means in text 1. (And the 'definite reference' introduction of 'Tommy' in text 2 can be defended as conforming to story introduction conventions: we often dispense with the near-redundant 'There was a boy called Tommy'). Again, when we consider the bridging references in the two texts, it is the mainstream norms of appropriateness that highlight 'the little babies' in text 1 as rather awkward. The three noun phrases classified in text 2 as bridging references can be interpreted differently: two simply as temporal connectives, not entities in the story, and the third – *the woods* – as exophoric, but easy to interpret given the preceding text with its dog and frog. These alternative interpretations highlight the way that whenever a lexico-grammatical descriptive system attempts to capture differences to do with meaning, then different analysts are unlikely to produce absolutely identical analyses.

What is more interesting to realize is that, for example, frequency of noun phrases involving bridging is not in itself an index of maturity: rather it is increasingly appropriate *recourse* to bridging that we should look for. Nor do the above remarks even broach the question of intention, though that issue is surely important. For example, did the speaker of text 1 *intend* us to bridge between 'the family' and 'the little babies'? One final point to consider would be the ways in which entity introductions that are identical in terms of the system of choices set out above are yet substantially different as regards effective storytelling. Thus first mention of the frog in both texts is by means of presenting, but notice how much more appropriate is the fuller description in text 2, *his pet frog*, than the bald *a frog* in text 1. The special relationship between boy and frog conveyed in text 2 fails to be explicitly recorded in text 1. Similarly contrast the narrative adequacy of *his pet frog and another frog and lots of baby frogs* in text 2 with the multitudinous possible referents of *the family*, the description that is its counterpart in text 1.

## 7.6 The systemic-linguistic account of story genres

A little more will now be said about recent developments in systemic-linguistic studies of narrative structure. If there is one tendency that most palpably unites most of this recent work it is a focus on the situatedness and cultural embeddednes of language patterns, seeking to specify what is typical in the lexicogrammatical, register, and genre choices in, say, a medical case conference as distinct from a disciplinary meeting, as distinct from a child's bathtime interaction as distinct from local council guidelines on keeping a dog; and so on. As well as describing these diverse cultural typicalities, systemicists wish also to understand and explain them, without neglecting the ideological issues of power and positioning, affiliation and exclusion, that may be motivating factors.

The more that systemic linguists (and other socially-oriented linguists) have focussed on how context shapes the typical grammar of types of interaction, the more the notion of genre has been invoked and elaborated. And because of this 'generic' turn in socially-oriented linguistics, Bakhtin's long essay on 'The problem of speech genres' has been accorded a place of theoretical priority and prominence – not as 'the final word' on these matters but rather since it contains the complex reflections of this most innovative and inspiring of proto-sociolinguists (other influences on recent systemic studies include: Mitchell, 1957; Sinclair and Coulthard, 1975; Hasan, 1984). The core of Bakhtin's argument is summarized by Jaworski and Coupland:

> Bakhtin presents a highly dynamic view of speech genres, inter-penetrating and 're-accentuating' each other and being continually renewed as they are used. These claims are the basis for an intertextual perspective on discourse, seeing discourse as the recontextualizing of already existing forms and meanings, one text echoing and partially replaying the forms, meanings and values of another.
>
> (Jaworski and Coupland, 1999: 53)

And, it may be added, in *partially* replaying the forms and meanings of other texts, each new text partially does *not* replay prior forms and meanings. In short, nothing semiotic is fixed, or determined in advance, even if everywhere there are would-be fixers. If these things are true of language activity generally, they are true also of narrative and narratives.

By 'genres' systemic linguists mean, following Bakhtin in this, 'relatively stable types' of interaction, extending beyond the traditional literary genres to all the interactional types:

> Thus, a transactional encounter such as buying meat at the butcher's is a genre, as is a recipe in a magazine or a staff meeting in the workplace. [And] systemic linguists define genres functionally in terms of their social purpose. Thus, different genres are different ways of using language to achieve different culturally established tasks, and texts of different genres are texts which are achieving different purposes in the culture.
>
> (Eggins and Martin, 1997: 236)

In systemic-linguistic accounts, a community's lexicogrammar and the arrays of options this fosters are tightly woven into the community's social and cultural worlds: the language reflects and construes the social order that sponsors it. There are three crucial strata or phases of organization: the lexicogrammar itself; the level of register (where combinations of options from among the field, tenor and mode possibilities alluded to at the opening of this chapter arise); and the most culturally-embedded level of genre (where 'staged, goal-oriented social processes' [Eggins and Martin, 1997: 243] are modelled).

At the same time it is probably as well to guard against assuming that, armed with grammar, register and genres, the analyst can show that everything we do with language 'fits' without gaps or overlaps. The basic idea of a genre, if as indicated it can include such things as buying meat at the butcher's, is perhaps not so far away from Barthes' idea of the narrative sequence alluded to in 2.3: a 'marking off' of a normative and conventional goal-directed sequence of moves, treated as a unified instance. But just as we would be hard put to state just how many events had happened to us in the last week (or in the last hour) – that is, event-hood is either culturally or subjectively relative and arbitrary – so we would be hard put to show that our interactional lives involve a steady progression through one genre-instantiation to the next, without residues, blends, or awkward hybrids. Perhaps the well-recognized genres are like mountain peaks, the easiest parts of the landscape to see and to orient by; but there seems to be plenty of 'travelling' between these established activity types, where any sense or evidence of being genre-embedded is attenuated.

All of this is relevant to narrative, since systemicists argue that *several* genres of story need to be recognized as occurring in the course of everyday conversation. This account stems particularly from the work of Plum (1988), but is advanced also by Martin, Eggins and Slade, and others. They contend that the Labovian crisis or 'high point' narrative (often involving a 'triumph over adversity'), is only one type in a set of alternatives, and should not be promoted as the normal or unmarked format. For a range of reasons, people often tell 'well-formed' stories in conversation that are other than the six-part Narrative with all the trimmings (just as the English breakfast is no less a meal for lacking a dessert or cheeses). Four chief story genres, in partial contrast with each other, are identified: **Narrative**, **Recount**, **Anecdote** and **Exemplum**. All may have stages that approximate an Abstract, Orientation, and Coda, but then the differences emerge (see table below). The **Narrative**, as in Labov's model, has all three 'internal' constituents: Complication, Evaluation and Resolution. The **Recount** is structurally nearest to the Narrative, perhaps, but it signally lacks Evaluation and Resolution (cf. the reactive sequences noted by McCabe and Peterson, discussed in 7.4): without a high point or crisis, what is there to resolve? The kinds of story contribution that is easiest to recognize as Recounts, I would suggest, are those produced at someone else's initiation, often shaped by politeness factors. Take yesterday evening: in a sense, very probably, nothing much happened to you, nothing that is easily fashioned into a Narrative that you currently *spontaneously* feel like contributing to the conversation. But if your friend says to you 'What did you do last night?', you might well reply with a brief sequence of unexceptional, non-problematic events or activities: 'Oh I got home, made pasta, watched *ER*, phoned my mum, and then went to bed . . .'. No high-point, no Resolution.

The **Anecdote** has just one remarkable or problematic event rather than several actions, this being followed by a quasi-evaluative Reaction and, certainly, no Resolution: telling of being disturbed by a cockroach running over your foot when you were taking an exam, or of suffering a 'whiteout' as a novice skier on a steep slope (both examples from Eggins and Slade, 1997: 245–51). So the major emphasis is on plentiful ongoing Evaluation, including listener-contributed Evaluation. And Eggins and Slade suggest that there may be some socially-driven, gender-based preferences at work here, with men often preferring to tell their lives as Narratives and women preferring to tell Anecdotes.

The **Exemplum** is arguably more minimalist than the Anecdote: it also has just one event, but not a particularly remarkable or exceptional one, reported *in order to* be interpreted. So the core structure is Incident + Interpretation (it is debatable whether Exemplums really have a distinct coda section in addition, or whether the Interpretation section *is* a required coda). Plum describes the Exemplum as 'an anecodote designed to point a moral' (1988: 233) and there is certainly a message of 'which just goes to show that x (where x encapsulates a moral)' made reasonably explicit at the story's close, having been at least implicit throughout. It is this characteristic, and the sense that the teller has planned the telling of the incident so as to further some ulterior purpose, to instruct the addressee rather than to entertain, which distinguishes the Exemplum from the Anecdote. Where the incident in the Exemplum is a means to an end, a warrant for a claim, namely the conversationalist's 'offloading' of a *generic* judgment, the entire structure can be said to be marked by attenuated narrativity: sometimes the Exemplum administers the pill of strong opinion sweetened by a rich narrative instance. To summarize the structures of these conversational story genres (with optional elements in parentheses):

| Genre | | | Generic structure | | |
|---|---|---|---|---|---|
| *Narrative* | (Coda) | (Orientation) | Complication | Evaluation Resolution | (Coda) |
| *Recount* | (Coda) | (Orientation) | Record of events | | (Coda) |
| *Anecdote* | (Coda) | (Orientation) | Remarkable event | Reaction | (Coda) |
| *Exemplum* | (Coda) | (Orientation) | Incident | Interpretation | (Coda) |

(adapted from Eggins and Slade, 1997: 268)

Having identified these four relatively distinct types, the implications of those different types can be explored: why they develop and are sustained culturally and socially, who uses which type in which situation, what types are 'barred' from what contexts, and so on. Generic analyses of texts, in this Hallidayan tradition, are always also gravitating towards producing social and even ideological analyses.

## 7.7 Stories for and with children

Much of the research reported above, on the kinds of stories children produce, would suggest that even at a very early age, even under 2, children have a well-developed sense of what normally happens in stories and what can be expected, in structure and content. But when we turn to popular, commercially-published stories for children, it is clear that children want and appreciate *some* creative departures from and exploitations of the mainstream norms. This blend of the standard and the unexpected, the given and the new, very probably answers to a child's need for both the reassurance provided by the familiar and the mental stimulation provoked by the unexpected.

Now it might be argued that the requirements of reassurance and mental disturbance apply to narratives for all ages, but there seems not to be as strong an emphasis on the instructional function of stories for older readers. Accordingly, both traditional and original stories for the young are often marked by their structural similarity to fables, and their 'happy outcome' codas often carry an implicit moral that could be cast as a generic sentence or proverb. Relatedly, fiction for adults permits all sorts of unreliability of narration, and immoralities of thought and action that go uncondemned and unpunished within the narrative. In stories for young children, by contrast, narration is almost invariably – and marvellously – reliable, reliably reporting good conquering evil.

In what follows I want to discuss the text of one or two stories for young children, noting both those elements that confirm and conform to the canonical format and those aspects that are absorbing and entertaining breaches of the norm. I will begin with the text of a very simple story that combines – as do all those I will discuss – text and pictures. What follows is the entire text of one episode about Mooty and Grandma; this comprises six captions, as listed here, and each in turn accompanies a distinct, double-page picture:

*Mooty and Grandma*

1   Mooty was a lovely little mouse. He had twinkling eyes and a long curly tail.
2   One day, Mooty fell asleep under Grandma's favourite chair. His long curly tail lay in a coil on the floor. He dreamt of cheese and bread crumbs. He dreamt of sweets and juicy plums.
3   His tail twitched as he dreamt. It curled and it straightened. It straightened and it curled till his dreams stopped. Then it lay quietly in a little gentle curve on the floor.
4   Grandma came into the room. 'Oh, how careless I am,' she thought.

Grandma came into the room.
"Oh, how careless I am," she thought.
"I've dropped my sewing thread again."
She bent to pick the long strand of thread
from the floor.

'I've dropped my sewing thread again.' She bent to pick the long strand of thread from the floor.

5    Poor Mooty! Poor Grandma! 'Help!' screamed Mooty as he tried to wiggle free. 'Help!' screamed Grandma as she dropped him on the floor.

6    Mooty ran into his hole as fast as his legs could carry him. Grandma ran into the kitchen as fast as her legs could carry her. They both quivered and shook. Poor Mooty! Poor Grandma!

(Jessie Wee and Kwan Shan Mei, *Mooty and Grandma*, Singapore:
Federal Publications, 1980)

The role played by the illustrations accompanying this text is of great interest. The pictures perform many functions: tautologically, we can say they depict, but we should clarify what that in turn involves. First, to depict is to supply visual validation or confirmation of what the text asserts. Thus the first frame depicts a green Mooty, in lovable pose, with huge ears, large bright eyes, and long curling tail, dressed in a red lungi and red slippers. The text's asserted *verbal* descriptions (*He had twinkling eyes and a long curly tail*, etc.) are thus confirmed, and young listeners in need of reminders of what 'mouse', 'twinkling' and 'curly tail' mean can profit from the kind of ostensive definition the picture provides. In addition, for viewers alert to such things, the lungi and slippers, together with his name, identify Mooty as an Asian mouse.

Pictures thus regularly confirm, clarify, explain and elaborate; they carry on the work of narration by other than verbal means. For example, the picture of Mooty's dream shows more types of edible goodies than the text lists. At a more abstract level, pictures stimulate the child to grasp that words can represent pictorial scenes even when no scenes are provided in advance. The business of experiencing and understanding the implications of text/scene matching, which all illustrated stories nurture, is a crucial step to the more decontextualized children's story, the one with text alone, where the child is required to produce in her own mind, using her imaginative resources, satisfying mental pictures of what is going on.

This important progression is surely one of the clearest cases of Vygot-skyan interpersonal capability becoming transformed or enlarged so as to become an intrapersonal one, particularly where the storytelling is shared between adult and child. The adult can engage the child with reflexive tasks and questions, such as 'Show me Mooty's red slippers' and 'Do you see what Mooty's dreaming of?'. At the later, fully intrapersonal stage, the child in effect sees and shows *themselves* the things represented in the nar-rative text, and those representations will be in words alone.

Grammatically, we have here several of the characteristic means of supplying an orientation and of reporting complicating action. The main character is introduced by means of stative verbs of relation, in which his name, his species and his most crucial plot-determining attribute (his long tail) are recorded. From these permanent states, caption 2 focusses on a singular occasion of Mooty's sleeping and dreaming, with imaginative depiction of what Warren *et al.* (1979) would call the internal psychologi-cal cause for his tail's enthusiastic twitching. Accordingly, the text's elab-orate focussing of the reader's attention to the moving tail in caption 3 seems well motivated, even though the tail really needs to be still when Grandma sees it. In reporting the preparatory steps to that encounter, the tail's actions are reported in the expected format: dynamic verbs in past tense and active voice, with the tail as subject, and repetition of the salient feature of setting – 'on the floor' in captions 2 and 3. The most important narrative development prior to Grandma's intervention is reported at the close of caption 3, where the verb *lay*, open to both stative and dynamic interpretations, is used. We readers–listeners know that here the stative description is also terminative, a point of rest after all the excitement (of the dream) is spent. For Grandma, however, there is not even a residual impression that what she sees as inert could ever be mobile.

We should also take account of the significant role played by inference and implicit messages, even in such a simple text as this Mooty episode. Notice, for example, that there is no explicit *verbal* confirmation, in caption 4, that what Grandma interprets to be a thread is in fact Mooty's tail. (The accompanying picture manages to avoid disambiguation, too: it shows Grandma's reaching hand, and the thread/tail, but not the rest of Mooty's body: see p. 198).

Similarly, although caption 4 ends by reporting that Grandma 'bent to pick the long strand of thread from the floor', there is no direct reporting of Grandma's act of picking it up, nor of her immediate shock of realiza-tion. Both of these have to be inferred in the light of the caption and picture that follow. Even in simple stories for the very young, then, it seems that important plot-developing judgments and events may some-times be left implicit, to be inferred, rather than spelt out. Whether this is a good thing deserves more detailed review. My own impressions of my children's reactions to the Mooty story are that they do make the neces-sary inferences, and are aware of the logic of cause and effect involved.

But we should not dismiss out of hand a very different view, which might argue that in stories for very young children who may not yet have properly grasped the orthodoxies of sequence and consequence we require in narratives, it is ill-judged to have stories that fail to reinforce those orthodoxies as explicitly as they might.

The text above comprises the first of the two episodes that make up the story. In the second episode a flour-blanched Mooty, and Grandma in her white nightclothes again manage to terrify each other, with the same parallel reporting of their ludicrous and reciprocal misapprehensions:

> 'I've seen a ghost,' they both cried as they pulled their blankets over their heads.

The outcome of these episodes, then, is an interesting variant of the 'happy outcome' norm, heavily mitigated, however, since the child knows that the characters' misery is unjustified, laughable. And behind the laughter lies a clear fable-like message, of how unfortunate inter-species misapprehensions may stem from fear, ignorance and prejudiced first impressions. The clear analogy here with inter-racial relations arguably should not be spelt out to the child (cf. the systemic linguistic category of Exemplum). It is more important that they get the general point that appearances and impressions can be deceptive.

Another story that can be seen creatively blending departures from and conformities to mainstream cultural and textual norms for children's stories is *Burglar Bill* by Janet and Allan Ahlberg. Bill is a decent, hard-working thief who in the course of his work acquires a 'nice big brown box with little holes in it'. Upon returning home he discovers that it contains a baby, and is introduced to the responsibilities of care-giving (as distinct from those of property-taking). That same night Bill himself is burgled, but he catches the intruder – Burglar Betty – redhanded. When these two professionals get into conversation it transpires, in the fine traditions of the eighteenth-century novel, that Betty is the widowed mother of the baby, Bill has acquired. This well-matched pair repent their wrongdoings, make literal restitution by putting back everything they've stolen, and begin a new life together (a church wedding, in white). Burglar Bill becomes Baker Bill.

That story summary should indicate fairly clearly how the unorthodoxy of having a burglar as hero becomes only transitional to the final state of rampant nuclear family orthodoxy. But there are textual unorthodoxies here too: there is a jaunty sense of the unusual in the way Bill's life as a burglar is described, very much at odds with the high moral assumptions of the orthodox children's story. Much of the rhythmic poise of the opening lies simply in the brazen recurrence of the adjective *stolen*, even in cases where we suspect the narrator of dishonest exaggeration:

> Burglar Bill lives by himself in a tall house full of stolen property.

Every night he has stolen fish and chips and a cup of stolen tea for supper. Then he swings a big stolen sack over his shoulder and goes off to work, stealing things. Every morning Burglar Bill comes home from work and has stolen toast and marmalade and a cup of stolen coffee for breakfast. Then he goes upstairs and sleeps all day in a comfortable stolen bed.

But the non-standardness extends to speech as well as behaviour: Bill and Betty speak vivid working-class Cockney English. Together they produce dialogue such as the following, a long way from the 'correct' mainstream speech that dominates children's stories:

> 'Who are you?' says Burglar Bill.
> 'I'm Burglar Betty,' says the lady. 'Who are you?'
> Burglar Bill puts on his own mask.
> 'Oh,' says Burglar Betty, 'I know you – it's Burglar Bill! I seen your picture in the Police Gazette.' Then she says, 'Look here, I'm ever so sorry – breaking in like this. If I'd have known ... '
> 'Don't mention it,' says Burglar Bill. He holds out his hand. 'Pleased to meet you.'
> 'Likewise, I'm sure,' Burglar Betty says.

And with this tenor of discourse established between the pair, there is more than a hint of tolerant mockery of our standard expressions when Bill, repenting his thieving, declares:

> I can see the error of my ways ... I've been a bad man.

The final children's story I will consider is the magnificent *Bear Goes to Town* by Anthony Browne. Bear has a magic pencil, so that whatever he draws comes into existence – itself a subtle exploitation of the requirement of text-to-pictures match discussed earlier. Bear thus has the power to 'narrate' everything but events. Although his good friend Cat is seized and imprisoned by menacing guards, Bear uses his pencil to free Cat and other animals, and remove them to a created pastoral haven, far from the threats of the town. The core of the plot, then, is slight. What is absorbing, however, is the extent to which the details over and above the basic plot create a richness of thematic texture. This texturing is achieved more by the messages in the pictures than the words, and it is quite striking just how dependent the story is on the pictures to articulate developments and connections that the text does not spell out. Consequently a rather high degree of inference-making is required in the reader/listener. And it is only when higher levels of theme and analogy are considered that several scenes can be understood as properly motivated parts of the narrative rather than somewhat incidental occurrences in a mere report or sequence. Thus the second frame of the story book depicts Bear, in town, being knocked over by the human traffic that dwarfs him, and the accompanying text reads, in part,

> It was rush hour. Bear was small and people could not see him. They knocked him down.

Strictly irrelevant to the main plot, and evidently an accidental mishap, this incident can nevertheless be treated as thematic prolepsis, presaging the threat to the animals that humans can be and, soon enough in this story, will be. The next frame has a cat's face looking down into Bear's, the latter still lying flat on his back from the fall. The caption simply reads 'Bear saw big yellow eyes looking down at him.' Without any further introduction, Cat becomes a full participant in the story – the text continues:

> 'What is that?' asked Cat, looking at Bear's pencil.
> 'It's my magic pencil,' said Bear.
> 'Then draw me something to eat,' said Cat.

And on the spot Bear draws, and thus creates, a rich variety of foods for Cat to eat. Somehow Cat has immediately understood just what Bear's magic pencil does – and the child reader has to accept that Cat understands. This seems to have less to do with standard inference-making and more to do with this particular story's chosen dynamics of informativeness. In other words, the interpretive leap assumed in Cat, expected in the reader, is just one of many sense-making bridges that the child has to supply when reading this story. And, what is equally important to report, if the experience of my own child and her peers is representative, it seems that these sense-making demands are neither baffling nor beyond them, but rather make *Bear Goes to Town* a favourite, preferred to stories with plodding explicitness of informational links between actions and reactions.

In the course of this chapter I have attempted to show that, behind their seeming simplicity and playfulness, stories for and by children are, on closer consideration, remarkably complex, and an aid to and index of the interactional and cognitive development of the child. Relative to respective ages and quantities of experience, the fact that many adults do cope with Joyce's 'Eveline' (and *Ulysses*) seems a far less impressive achievement than that 3-year-olds manage to cope with *Bear Goes to Town*. When one makes allowances for the age of the child and her limited acquaintance with story processing and story production, one is almost drawn to end on a gloomy note, and remark on how scant is the enlargement of reading and writing skills from childhood into adulthood. Be that as it may, what should be clear is that all the key elements of sophisticated narratives, as discussed in the foregoing chapters of this book, are present in simpler form in children's narratives: causal connectivity of events, temporal order and reordering, scenic and summarized presentation, focalization, inferred linkage, and so on.

One curious effect in *Bear Goes to Town* seems striking confirmation that 3- and 4-year-olds are already aware of the way narrative voice can shift. In the middle of the story, there is a scene where Bear is absorbed by a shop's window display and Cat walks on along the street, unaware that a menacing black-coated figure is lurking in a doorway. In a sudden departure from the narrative's neutral reportage stance, the text suddenly cries out (without the quotation marks used elsewhere to frame the words or thoughts of participants):

Look out, Cat!

It is fascinating to see just how regularly children comment on this as they hear the story – especially if they are hearing it for the first time. 'Who says that?', they ask, or 'Where did that come from?'. Who indeed? Whether this modulation of voice is best described as one from the impersonal to the personal, or from the extradiegetic to the intradiegetic, the important thing is to have recognized – as these infant story-recipients, astonishingly, clearly do – that a shift in narratorial voice has occurred.

## Further reading

On children's narrative development: Peterson and McCabe (1983), Cazden (1981), Applebee (1978), Piaget (1926), Vygotsky (1962); and, from a systemic-linguistic perspective, Rothery and Martin (1980), Christie *et al.* (1984), Hasan (1984), Ventola (1987), Eggins and Slade (1997), White (1997) and Christie and Martin (1997). On emergent literacy and children's storytelling, see Heath (1983), Romaine (1985), Bennett-Kastor (1983; 1986; 1999), Farr (1985), Cook-Gumperz and Green (1984), Eaton, Collis and Lewis (1999). On children's narratives in health and clinical contexts, see Perez and Tager-Flusberg (1998) and Reilly, Bates and Marchman (1998). Relevant journals include *Journal of Education, Journal of Child Language, Applied Psycholinguistics,* and *Language and Education.*

As indicated at 7.4, a large body of psycholinguistic research has been undertaken into the question of whether humans develop mental models of story structure, which they use as an aid in the comprehension, storage and recall of actual stories. These mental frameworks are termed story schemas, and their probable configuration can be represented on the page as a grammar; hence researchers in this area are often described as story-grammarians. The psychological status and the implications of such modellings remain controversial, but have been extensively explored. Among key texts adopting a broadly psycholinguistic approach, see: Rumelhart (1975; 1977), Mandler and Johnson (1977), Stein and Glenn (1979), Warren, Nicholas and Trabasso (1979), Clark (1977), Brown and Yule (1983); Schank and Abelson (1977) and Johnson-Laird (1981).

In recent years, seemingly part of the same movement away or beyond the delimited formalism of Labovian analysis (as noted in the 'Further reading' of the previous chapter), child language theorists and researchers have urged a renewed attention to the symbolic uses to which children's narratives are put. In a broader sociocultural or social-constructionist framework, it is argued, the functions of narratives as vehicles of children's meaning-creation and identity-construction, and of self-projection, can and must be addressed (see, e.g. Bruner, 1986; Bamberg, 1997b; Muhlhausler and Harré, 1990; Nicolopoulou, 1996; 1997; Ely, Bleason, and McCabe, 1996). One simple but powerful point to note is that in much formalist-structuralist analysis of children's stories, there has been a remarkable disregarding of content, of what children actually choose to talk about. Only in very recent years, for example, have researchers begun systematically to study the ways children talk in their stories about being sad, or angry, or feeling they have failed – all, unquestionably, developmentally important affective responses. In a very useful survey Nicolopoulou (1997) speaks for many in arguing that a sociocultural approach that may reveal children's narrativized development of counterposed realities (differences of gender, ethnicity, class, and so on), must perforce be a comparative and contrastive analysis.

## Notes and exercises

1  The story-grammars mentioned in the 'Further reading' section above often adjudge that the simplest stories are about a situation in which some want arises and prompts an action which helps children's narratives fulfil the want, or prompts proceeding to some different action. An 'if ... then ...' logic is particularly visible in such schemes.

It may be that such simple schemes are themselves most apparent in stories for young children, who are only just beginning to encounter stories in books. Consider the following text, for example, which is taken from a words-and-pictures storybook entitled *Dear Zoo*, by Rod Campbell.

> I wrote to the zoo to send me a pet. They sent me an ... [flapped picture of an elephant]. He was too big! I sent him back.
> So they sent me a ... [flapped picture of a giraffe]. He was too tall! I sent him back.
> So they sent me a ... [flapped picture of a lion]. He was too fierce! I sent him back.
> So they sent me a ... [flapped picture of a camel]. He was too grumpy! I sent him back.
> So they sent me a ... [flapped picture of a snake]. He was too scary! I sent him back.
> So they sent me a ... [flapped picture of a monkey]. He was too naughty! I sent him back.
> So they sent me a ... [flapped picture of a frog]. He was too jumpy! I sent him back.
> So they thought very hard, and sent me a ... [flapped picture of a puppy]. He was perfect! I kept him.
>
> (comments in square brackets are my additions)

The storybook is aimed at children still some way from actual reading, but old enough, and familiar enough with books, to participate while an older person reads the text. At every point in the text where there is ellipsis indicated above, the child has to lift a flap representing one side of a crate or container. And behind the flap is a picture of the animal to be identified and named by the child.

Comment on the sorts of skills and understanding that such a book may nurture in the child. Think especially about the idea of storytelling collaboration mentioned both in 5.10 and 6.2; about appropriate timing of the flap-lifting; about the skills of recognition, recall and naming that are involved; of how the text performs the two fundamental Labovian functions, of reference and evaluation, in a particularly overt way; and of the association of attributes with individuals in the course of characterization, which was discussed in relation to literature in 4.3 and 4.4.

2  There is a fundamental assumption within Michaels' and others' treatment of

the dichotomy between oral-style and literate-style storytelling by infants that needs fuller review. This is the assumption that the two styles, the two ways of narrativizing experience, are 'equal but different'. Similarly, Wolf (1984: 71) argues that 'children from different language backgrounds all have systematic repertoires of narrative genres and registers' and that the challenge is for educators to recognize those skills, and use them as a link to literacy. This seems incontestable. Whatever the repertoires a child is identified using (and however 'literacy-removed' these are deemed to be), somehow these systems have to be built on, rather than simply ignored or overriden, in the fostering of literate language use, i.e. written language with its reduced integration with immediate situational context but its complex cotextual articulation.

But the question remains: *are* the oral and literate styles equally effective ways of making sense of human experience? Can we demonstrate that both styles can satisfactorily present logical and cognitive grasp of the events or situations? The secondary issue, of whether those two styles are equal in the real world, is one we can address subsequently; but we should first consider whether these two styles are equal as effectively sense-making, suitably interpretive, and successfully message-conveying formats. If they are, then we might wonder whether promoting a rather sharp change of style, as when oral-style users are encouraged to develop a literate 'code', is justified. Why shouldn't such oral-style users continue with their 'equal but different' style in their written language? The self-evident answer to this, that oral-style prosody-based signalling just won't work in written language, should prompt us to ask further why the oral-style will not work.

3

> Once there was a dog named Whiskers. He got run over, because he ran in front of a car. He was very sick after. He had to be rushed to hospital by Ambulance and fast. At the end he ended up dieing isn't that 'Sad'.
>
> (quoted in Christie *et al.*, 1984: 78)

Analyze the text above, or others gathered from children, in relation to the linguistic features of narrative genre that systemic linguists have drawn attention to:

a  the types of processes the verbs express (on process-types, see 4.9);
b  the types and variety of lexical items;
c  the consistency or variation of sentential theme (see 2.6);
d  the manner of introducing protagonists and making subsequent reference to them;
e  the types of conjunctive relations that there are between clauses, and whether these are given explicitly or only implicitly. Under the umbrella term 'conjunction' consider here two independent bases of subclassification:

   i  semantic or logical type – the four basic logical types of connective are additive, temporal, consequential (including purpose, cause, condition and concession), and comparative (contrast and similarity);
   ii implicit or explicit – is the conjunctive relation explicitly expressed or simply to be logically inferred?

# 8 Narrative as political action

## 8.1 The contexts of narratives

In the previous chapter we explored children's growing control of narrative texts as decontextualized texts. 'Decontextualized' here does not mean 'entirely removed from context' (an impossibility and theoretical incoherence) but 'freed from immediate reliance upon and disambiguation by a co-present teller and addressee'. As the previous chapter suggested this involves learning to use language and genres and conventions. But while narrative text can be decontextualized as far as immediate situation is concerned, it can hardly be so as far as the broader cultural framework is concerned. A narrative is never without contexts which both shape and come to be shaped by the story that is told and heard. Contexts may be put in the plural for the too-often-neglected reason that the teller and addressees of a narrative may assume quite different grounds for a particular tale being told, and may separately deduce rather different morals or consequences. It is because any narrative inevitably has some effect on its addressees and consequences in the real world that we have to recognize that narratives are, among other things, a kind of political action. This is true of all narratives, even the most escapist, or those turned to 'just for a bit of fun'. Narratives, in short, invariably carry political and ideological freight.

In the following sections there is space to present only brief glimpses of the political contexts and contents of narratives. But by looking particularly at the language of stories in the press, in the legal courtroom, and at the narrative aspect of certain types of cultural commentary, I hope to show that the worlds our narratives represent and make sense of may be politically distinct worlds, with differing and even clashing assumptions.

## 8.2 Hard news stories in the newspaper

A newspaper is a hybrid compendium of discourse colonies (see Notes and exercises 2, in Chapter 1), with each colony somewhat generically distinct: hard news, soft ('fancy that/who'd have thought it?') news, features, lifestyle discourse, sports reports, business news, opinion-editorials and so on. These vary in narrativity. But even hard news stories have a structure profoundly unlike oral narratives of personal experience. Most typically, the modern English-medium hard news story is oriented around the opening sentence, which will include the most tellable and critical world-disrupting event of the story that it introduces. Thereafter, orientational and complicating action reports will follow, in an order that often has more to do with salience relative to the lead and headline than with chronology. Or as Allan Bell puts matters:

> Perceived news value overturns temporal sequence and imposes an order completely at odds with the linear narrative point. It moves backwards and forwards in time, picking out different actions on each cycle.
>
> (Bell, 1991: 153)

In fact, a news story's reordered telling exploits and relies upon the reader's ability to reassemble events in their experienced order insofar as the reader feels the need to do this. But the relayed version clearly privileges news value, or 'salience of latest outcome', over chronology – presumably judging that modern readers do, too. The headline is often composed last, a simplified and highly-evaluated version of part of the lead sentence, and usually by a different, editorial, hand. While it would be hard to maintain that headlines are neutral or impartial, this has often been claimed of the body-copy of hard news items, particularly in the English-medium press. Journalists pride themselves in their objective reporting, and eschewing of opinion and subjective evaluation. As White (1997) has shown, the typical news story of English-medium western journalism has a lead-dominated and orbitally-organized generic structure, these contributing to the effect of establishing an impersonal authorial voice, that purports to convey impartial and objective common sense. By orbital structure, White means the way in which successive segments of reported action, or orientation, or comment from story-participants are not so much linked to each other in series, but separately linked (by longer, weaker loops) back to the lead sentence which, each in its own way, they explicate. He identifies five broad kinds of satellite, each directly attached to the lead and supporting of its content: Elaboration; Cause and Effect; Justification; Contextualization, and Appraisal-Attribution. The lead sentence is thus the nucleus of the news story, carrying the event that is represented as the most acute departure from and greatest threat to ordinary life as we readers know and cherish it: White calls this nucleus a *constructed* 'peak of social-order disruption' (1997: 112).

In reflecting upon these news structure choices it is important to bear in mind that, for all their 'naturalness' for us today, these are cultural choices that could be otherwise: hard news items *could* be told chronologically, with headlines that only introduced the story without divulging the outcome, as they were in the past. What, then, is the motivation for the lead-dominated and orbiting-satellite structure? It has often been explained in terms of repetitive amplification of the previously-selected lead: but more recently it has been suggested that it also helps 'naturalise and portray as commonsensical the ideology which informs' the selection of just this story, handled in just this way (White, 1997: 111). More generally proponents of Critical Discourse Analysis (Fairclough, 1989; 1992; van Dijk, 1988; 1993) emphasize the power that dominant social groups wield through their discourses. Those controlling discourses construe and project what counts as common sense, ordinary and reasonable, often in subtly partial ways, effecting degrees of exclusion or marginalization of subordinated social groups. The construal and projection may be calculated and considered; but quite often it is unconscious and seemingly invisible to those beneficiaries who enact or sanction it (cf. presupposition, in 8.5): it is usually all the more effective for being so.

In summary, newspaper hard news stories have developed a distinct narrative structuring, quite at variance with the Labovian high point oral Narrative or indeed Recount, Anecdote or Exemplum. In being one of the most powerful articulators and representers of its proprietor's and readers' world (especially of that world's 'new' or emergent culture), functioning as mirror, lamp and lens, the newspaper is a powerful ideological instrument. It is not that the newspapers carry 'more ideology' than most other processes and participants in our world; but rather that the ideology is exceptionally widely disseminated, influential and inspectable. With the lead sentence of hard news items established as the 'nucleus' of the story, and the headline as pithy paraphrase of the lead, there is a powerful warrant for directing critical narrative analysis particularly at those elements.

## 8.3  Political narratives in the news

A particularly influential linguistic study of the covert and even unconscious ideological pressures on the hard-news story was conducted by Tony Trew (1979), who applied a kind of linguistic criticism of text that was in some respects a precursor of Critical Discourse Analysis, using the Hallidayan system of linguistic description (sketched here at 4.9; see also 3.7 and 7.5). Trew's thesis was that mainstream newspapers typically espouse and legitimate some version of the dominant ideology that operates in a society, and must do so even in the course of reporting news that is 'awkward' for that ideology. Trew writes:

> Often one can see over a period of days a sequence in which something happens which is awkward from the point of view of the newspaper reporting it, and this is followed by a series of reports and comment over the succeeding days, perhaps culminating in an editorial comment. By the time the process is finished, the original story has been quite transformed and the event appears as something very different from how it started.
>
> (Trew, 1979: 98)

Trew supports these claims in a comparison of two British newspapers' divergent reports (in June 1975) of a single incident in pre-independence Rhodesia (now Zimbabwe). Below are the openings of those stories, from *The Times* and the *Guardian* respectively:

From *The Times*:

## RIOTING BLACKS SHOT DEAD BY POLICE AS ANC LEADERS MEET

Eleven Africans were shot dead and 15 wounded when Rhodesian police opened fire on a rioting crowd of about 2,000 in the African Highfield township of Salisbury this afternoon.

and from the *Guardian*:

## POLICE SHOOT 11 DEAD IN SALISBURY RIOT

Riot police shot and killed 11 African demonstrators and wounded 15 others here today in the Highfield African township on the outskirts of Salisbury.

Despite similarities of content, *The Times* report is in the passive voice, while the *Guardian* is active; and while *The Times*'s headline mentions the agent of the killings (*by police*), this agent is deleted, as passivization commonly allows, in the lead sentence, and has to be retrieved by inference from the subordinate temporal clause (*when Rhodesian police* ...). Trew notes a number of differences, of grammar and vocabulary, between the two reports, many of these contributing to a picture (in *The Times*) of the rioters and even the ANC (African National Congress) as chiefly responsible for the deaths, or instead (in the *Guardian*) of the police as chiefly responsible. But he more particularly focusses on the daily revisions to the story of the Salisbury killings in subsequent issues of *The Times*, and how the killings are incorporated into allusions to *Salisbury's riots* and these, in turn, become mere backcloth or precursor to *ANC rifts*. By means of subtle and quite possibly unconscious retroactive re-casting, the larger narrative that emerges is one of tragedies and disorders ultimately caused by violent 'tribal' factionalism among black Africans, 'with the whites concerned merely to promote progress, law and order' (Trew, 1979: 105–6). At some point, press 'reformulation' no doubt becomes misrepresentation and even defamation (where individuals are named), with attendant legal liabilities. But even where these are not involved, a more general process operates: over time, and in the hands of intermediaries, one story turns into a different story.

The specific incident reported occurred twenty-five years ago, but there are a number of respects in which the topic and sub-genre is anything but dated. Even as I write, within and beyond Harare (formerly Salisbury) there are demonstrations and acts of public disorder, sometimes ruthlessly put down by government forces and sometimes noticeably not, as a power-struggle involving the ruling party (ZANU PF), the opposition party (MDC), landholding white Zimbabweans and landless black Zimbabweans, unfolds. Stories and headlines in several respects cognate with those discussed by Trew are quite likely to appear.

Other contentious incidents, as distant in time, in which demonstrators were shot and killed by security forces, continue to reverberate in our media and in the public conscience – most notably the 'Bloody Sunday' shooting and killing, on 30 January 1972, in Londonderry, Northern Ireland of 13 unarmed civil rights marchers by British Army paratroopers who claimed to be returning fire on terrorists. A new commission of inquiry chaired by Lord Saville, is even now (2001) in the process of gathering evidence; it is charged with getting nearer the whole truth than the report prepared by Lord Widgery in 1972 (a report increasingly regarded as, at best, unreliable).

The public march, demonstration, or protest, because it involves some effort and discomfort on the part of protesters and invariably attracts media attention, is in a democracy or quasi-democracy one of the most powerful resources available to the marginalized and one of the threats most feared by the powerful (significantly, in contemporary Britain, policing of public protests is increasingly guided by statutes, such as the Public Order Act of 1986). In a democracy the powerful are assumed to rule with the consent of the governed; but a sizeable public march makes exceptionally clear that the consent of some of the governed is withheld. So more recently in Britain we have had the 'Countryside Alliance' demonstration in London, and the failed mass demonstration against high fuel prices; and internationally we have seen the range of articulate and organized dissent during the World Trade Organization summit in Seattle, in December 1999.

Compare the treatment of those Seattle 'manifestations' in the *Independent* and *The Times*, both of 1 December. In the *Independent*, the headline, subhead, accompanying graphic and opening body-text are reproduced opposite.

# Spirit of the Sixties returns with a vengeance to harass capitalism

WORLD TRADE TALKS Riot police fire tear gas as chanting protesters form a human barricade to stop delegates attending the summit in Seattle

*[large photograph of stationary protesters linking arms, no police or opposed group apparent, one (female) prominently centred, wearing a white shirt emblazoned with the message 'This is a Peaceful Protest']*

Tens of thousands of protesters, cheering and whooping, thronged into downtown Seattle yesterday to form a human barricade blocking delegates from the World Trade Organisation, turning the opening of the much-contested ministerial meeting into a colourful and passionate "carnival against capitalism".

In *The Times,* headline, subhead, graphic and opening are as follows:

# WTO protesters wreck start to talks

Police fire gas as carnival turns sour, Bronwen Maddox reports from Seattle.

*[large photograph, long shot, of crowded city intersection, with baton-wielding police in riot gear centred and in focus, accompanied by an armoured vehicle and with smoke/gas in the further distance, between the police and a large throng of protesters; upper bodies of other protesters also in the near distance, at bottom of photograph; one or two placards – 'Profit at what cost? No to WTO' – in focus.]*

Demonstrators forced the World Trade Organisation to postpone and then cancel its opening ceremony yesterday. Police firing pepper spray and rubber bullets waded into ranks of steelworkers and costumed environmentalists as the demonstration's carnival atmosphere turned to menace, threatening severe embarrassment for President Clinton.

There are a number of ways in which these two versions of events diverge: to focus solely on the processes in the headlines, where the *Independent* talks of a *returning* and *harassing, The Times* unequivocally reports that the protesters *wrecked* the start to the talks. And both papers, intriguingly, invoke the process of one state *turning (in)to* another state as what crucially happened; but while the *Independent* reports that the opening of the talks turned into a carnival, *The Times* asserts that an initial carnival atmosphere turned to menace (or turned *sour,* as the subhead runs).

Why is *The Times* so evidently decided that the protestors' disruptions of the WTO talks lead to a 'turning sour' or 'menace'? The reason must be that *The Times* underlyingly presupposes the legitimacy of those WTO talks: the newspaper has (and expresses) no doubts that in a normal and ordered world the WTO talks would commence smoothly, and that this in itself (as distinct from anything the delegates decided) would be no more tellable than if a parliamentary session scheduled to begin at 2 p.m. on a certain day did indeed begin at that time. By contrast the *Independent* reports the actual events with no such entrenched commitment to the assumption that the talks commencing on time is simply normal, reasonable and ordinary. It treats the carnivalesque disruptions as legitimate and as reasonable as the WTO gathering (possibly more so). So the *Independent* tells the story of the talks-disruption in a way that implies that, as far as the newspaper is concerned, it would not be a disaster or a great threat to the social order if the WTO talks collapsed entirely (and had to be re-opened on some quite different basis, perhaps much more responsive to the various interests of those protesting here). The *Independent* is not at all sure that the protesters are endowed with less legitimacy, and are not expressive of a better emerging social order, than the WTO delegates. Perhaps they have *more* legitimacy. Similar uncertainties of construal and legitimacy-assigment shadow some of the media coverage of other contentious issues where two partly-reasonable but counterposed world-views vie for support: e.g. divergent responses to the BSE/CJD crisis, or to experimental planting of genetically-modified crops.

## 8.4 The unfolding news story: a contemporary example

For the purposes of a more extended analysis of the political and ideological determinants of a hard-news story (and of the narrativization of politics), I will turn now to a very recent British news story, and five newspapers' treatment of it. The news item concerned comments made by the leader of the opposition Conservative Party, Mr Hague, about crime and policing, soon after the brutal killing in London of a black child by still-unidentified individuals. Offering a synopsis of 'the background' to an ongoing hard news story is inevitably contentious, but it is also essential. I shall try to be neutral in recording the following facts:

1    On 28 November, 2000, a ten-year-old boy called Damilola Taylor bled to death from a stab wound in his leg, after reportedly being attacked by three teenagers, possibly black. Damilola was Nigerian-born and black, and had lived in England for less than a year. The attack and death occurred in an acutely run-down housing complex in London, reportedly haunted by drug addicts, drug pushers, and petty criminals.

2    In the weeks that followed this tragic death, a good deal of public anguish and soul-searching ensued, particularly since the police were unable rapidly to identify, arrest and charge any suspects. Why and

how had this happened? Where had society gone wrong? Was this a failure of the schools, of parenting, of social provision, of policing; did such outrages (social workers on the estate said that stabbings and violence were routine, not exceptional) follow from a profit-driven 'selling' of violence by the media and the larger culture? While the chattering classes obsessed about the new Human Rights Act, how had Damilola Taylor's rights been protected?

3   The 'frontline' agency in crime prevention is the police. Since the early 1990s, during both Conservative and Labour governments, recruitment to the police has failed to keep up with numbers departing (retirement, resignations). The police forces, particularly the London (Metropolitan) one, have been been widely described as 'demoralized' in the aftermath of the MacPherson report. The MacPherson report was a government-commissioned enquiry, chaired by a senior judge, into the mishandling, by the Metropolitan police, of the investigation of the murder of Stephen Lawrence, a black teenager, allegedly by one or more of a gang of known racist white youths. The eventual, belated trial of those youths failed to secure any convictions due to lack of corroborating evidence. Among many other observations, the MacPherson committee concluded that there was 'institutional racism' (unwitting or unconscious race-based differential treatment) in the Metropolitan police force and that this needed to be addressed immediately. This conclusion was praised in some quarters as a facing up to reality, denounced in others as a slur on all decent police officers and bound to damage further the public trust.

4   Partly as a consequence of the MacPherson sentiments, London police officers on the streets began using their powers to 'stop and search' individuals acting suspiciously much more infrequently (statistics showed that those subjected to 'stop and search' treatment – other nouns used here include *indignity*, *harassment*, and *provocation* – were disproportionately members of racial minorities). Therefore, in a sense, post-MacPherson race-sensitivity may have caused more defensive policing, and less interventionist vigilance over street crime. This is summarized in certain quarters as 'race-sensitivity (political correctness) impeding the fight against crime'. At the same time it is also widely recognized that, for example, male black youths are disproportionately the victims as well as the perpetrators of street crime.

5   It was suggested by some that the combination of lower police numbers, demoralization and a 'retreat' from the pro-active stance of routine stopping and searching, made it more easy or more likely for opportunist street crime, against property or the person, to go undeterred and undetected.

6   Police numbers in many regional forces have begun to rise in recent months, and the decline in numbers in London has ceased. All agree that pay as much as conditions is a factor hampering recruitment to public service professions in London (e.g. the high cost of living).

All the above are only *part* of the background, but they are a necessary contextualization for the newsworthy items, duly reported by most national newspapers, below. In essence these were a series of widely-publicized statements made in the days following Damilola Taylor's death, by Mr William Hague, leader of the main party opposed to the Labour government, the Conservative Party. In answer to some of the questions listed under 2 above, he declared that the Labour government were in part to blame, for presiding over conditions which made tragic deaths like Damilola's more likely to happen.

Now at last to the news items, all taken from reports of Mr Hague's intervention published on one day (Tuesday, 19 December, 2000). Consider first just their headlines:

| | |
|---|---|
| *Guardian* | 1. **Hague race jibe angers ministers** |
| *Independent* | 2. **Race and policing: Hague's defiance inflames the anger** |
| *Telegraph* | 3. **Tory leader 'won't be gagged on crime'** |
| *Mirror* | 4. **CRAZY HAGUE DEFIES DAMI DAD'S PLEA** |
| *The Times* | 5. **Hague links Labour with murder rise** |

The differences between these headlines suggest that these papers are not even telling entirely the same story. Judging by references to him in all five headlines (four times by family name, once via his political position), it is agreed that the story is 'about' Mr Hague. But thereafter divergences appear: only the two centre-left broadsheets (*Guardian* and *Independent*) mention *race* in their headlines. By contrast the centre-right broadsheets (*The Times* and *Telegraph*) mention *crime* or *murder* (but not race), while the *Independent* headline alone invokes a distinct issue which, it implies, lies at the tellable core of the story: *policing*. The tabloid *Mirror* is different from all the above in its acute personalization of the story, as a clash of a crazy, defiant Hague and 'Dami's pleading Dad'.

Simply by lining up these five headlines, it is easy to see which account is relatively sympathetic to Mr Hague or, conversely, unsympathetic to him, and which reports tend to be at least not unsympathetic to Labour or 'ministers' or those feeling 'anger'. Without further analysis it is possible to categorize the *Guardian* headline as unambiguously critical of Hague, respectful of ministers, the *Independent* as more neutral but mildly critical of Hague, the *Telegraph* as approbatory of Hague, the *Mirror* – the only tabloid here – as sensationalist in its anti-Hague sentiment, sympathetic to Damilola's dad, and *The Times* as uncritical of Hague, and undeclared or guarded in its criticism of Labour. The crucial openings to these five contrasting news treatments will now be briefly discussed in series, but contrastively. Due to space limitations, nearly all commentary is directed to the headlines, but occasional brief mention is also made of the following bodycopy, which certainly warrants further analysis. Hard-news story headlines (as distinct from those – often oblique or trivial or merely witty

– that accompany 'soft news' or human interest stories) are invariably of particular importance, by virtue of their prominence and careful composition. The headline is the narrative's Abstract, with the complication that it has been composed *after* the preparation of the body-copy. They are a kind of 'text-bite' that emerged long before sound-bites were recognized: pithy, crucial, viewpoint-shaping encapsulations.

From the *Guardian*

# Hague race jibe angers ministers

**Nicholas Watt and Nick Hopkins**
**Tuesday December 19, 2000**

William Hague yesterday raised the stakes in the row over law and order when he ignored a plea for restraint from the parents of Damilola Taylor to issue a blunt warning that a Labour election victory will lead to more tragic murders in Britain's inner cities.

Hours after the Taylors had accused Mr Hague of using their son's death as a "political football", the Tory leader went on the offensive to declare that politicians could not bury their heads in the sand over crime levels.

Only the *Guardian* and the *Mirror*, the most clearly anti-Hague and pro-Labour of the five papers canvassed here, specify in their headlines a particular affected human as recipient of the verbal process (a jibe in the *Guardian*, defiance in the *Mirror*) initiated by Mr Hague. That human recipient is *ministers* in the *Guardian*, and *Dami's dad* in the *Mirror*. And there is nothing to suggest that either the *Guardian* view of *ministers*, or the *Mirror*'s of *Dami's dad*, is at all negative. By contrast the *Independent* is unspecific about who exactly is made angry by Mr Hague's defiance, and in the *Telegraph* and *The Times*, in the implicit matrix clause in each case, there is really only one stated participant: Mr Hague, who won't be gagged (in the *Telegraph*) or who projects an entire claim, that Labour is linked with murder increases (in *The Times*). So only in headlines 1 and 4 above is there the most direct representation of a human-to-human confrontation. In the *Guardian* something Mr Hague has said has 'angered ministers'. And it is striking, to say the least, that what he has crucially, tellably said according to the *Guardian* is so different from what, according to *The Times*, he has said. For in the latter he has linked Labour with a rise in incidence of murder; but in the *Guardian* he has uttered a 'jibe' about race.

Here the key and powerfully evaluative term is *jibe*: nothing remotely similar occurs in the headlines or copy of the other newspapers surveyed. Standardly a jibe is a wounding and negative, even destructive remark, typically about something of relatively minor importance. Often the source of the jibe, in being so represented, is also regarded as frivolous, playful, or non-serious, while the target or addressee of the jibe suffers embarrassment or humiliation. But a jibe is not a critique, it is not balanced, fair or reasonable, it is a 'scoring points off' someone – 'a rude or insulting remark about someone that is intended to make them look foolish' (according to the corpus-based Cobuild dictionary). On several scores, then, *jibe* is a marked and therefore informative choice here. If we do not ordinarily make jibes about really serious matters – religion, death, cancer – then a 'race jibe' implies a kind of deepseated inappropriateness in Mr Hague's way of broaching the topic; besides, as the dictionary indicates, we standardly jibe at a person, not an abstract category such as race. The newspaper is perhaps suggesting – but again only tacitly – that Mr Hague is underlyingly intent on embarrassing particular individuals (the Home Secretary and other Labour ministers), under cover of protesting that he is concerned only with 'the issues' (crime and policing).

From the *Independent*:

# Race and policing: Hague's defiance inflames the anger

By Paul Waugh and Andrew Grice
19 December 2000

William Hague rejected a plea yesterday from the parents of Damilola Taylor to stop using their son's death as a "political football" and even suggested that voting Labour would lead to similar tragedies in future.

Richard and Gloria Taylor accused the Tory leader of seeking to use the killing of the 10-year-old boy for political advantage when he said that a fall in police numbers was partly to blame.

But Mr Hague was unrepentant and warned that he would not be "bullied" into dropping the issue of low police morale and numbers. He triggered further condemnation by suggesting a second Labour term would result in more crime and "more tragedies" similar to that of Damilola.

The *Independent*'s headline somewhat clumsily reports that Mr Hague has 'inflamed the anger'; on the assumption that 'inflaming' or causing increase in anger is invariably undesirable and ill-advised, it is implicit in this representation that Mr Hague has acted in regrettable ways.

From the *Daily Telegraph*, Tuesday, 19 December 2000:

# Tory leader 'won't be gagged on crime'

**By George Jones Political Editor**

WILLIAM HAGUE claimed last night that another Labour government would mean more tragedies such as the murder of Damilola Taylor.

Despite criticism from the boy's parents that he was using their son as a "political football", he said he would not be bullied into silence on inner city crime, falling police numbers and morale. Mr Hague said he was "very sorry" for Damilola's parents but refused to back down or apol-ogise for talking about the implications of the murder. No areas of public debate on crime should be off-limits, he said.

Labour described the Tory leader as "a desperate man who has made a terrible mistake". Jack Straw, the Home Secretary, refused to apologise for suggesting that he was a racist. "I believe the Leader of the Opposition is playing the race card," he told MPs.

The *Telegraph* headline is one of the more ingenious reworkings of events, using passive voice which enables the teller to dispense with prominent naming of who it might be who is intent on gagging Mr Hague. But notice the direct speech representation of Mr Hague's words; actually this is pseudo-direct speech, common in newspaper headlines: it is not a faithful record of Mr Hague's words since, judging by the body-copy that follows, he never used the word *gagged*; it seems that he did, however, say that he would not be 'bullied' into silence (see also bodycopy in the *Independent*) about low police morale and rising crime. Using *gagged* in a passive construction with agent-deletion is probably judicious for the *Telegraph*, in view of the fact that Mr Hague was urged not to speak further by two quite different parties: Damilola's grieving parents, and the Home Secretary and other Labour ministers. It would be narratorially incoherent for Mr Hague, or a newspaper, to represent the Taylors as in any position to gag or bully a leading political figure.

From the *Mirror*:

# CRAZY HAGUE DEFIES DAMI DAD'S PLEA

WILLIAM Hague last night defied a plea by the parents of murdered Damilola Taylor to stop using his death as a "political football".

The Tory leader astonishingly ignored the request by dad Richard and mum Gloria and predicted "more tragedies" from another term of Labour government.

Mr Hague was rounded on by all sides as he insisted police numbers had contributed to the stabbing of Damilola, 10, three weeks ago.

The *Mirror* report uncompromisingly casts Mr Hague in a negative light, from its headline evaluative description of him as *Crazy Hague* – the *crazy* being highly evaluative and 'in excess of' anything in the co-text to warrant this verdict. While Hague is *crazy*, what he has most tellably done is *defy a plea* – a significantly unidiomatic collocation (compare *ignore a plea* or *defy critics*: in the second sentence of the report he *ignores the request*, but again how the reader is to take this is not left to chance, since we are told that he *astonishingly ignored the request*). Standardly, those who plead are weak and vulnerable, so that Hague's contraversion of the plea earns him no credit (compare torturers ignoring the pleas of victims), despite the use of the potentially approbatory verb *defy*. Indeed someone who defies the pleas of others is being represented enacting rather an odd procedure, since pleas are far too weak and subordinate (compare *defying a threat*) to warrant being defied: hence, perhaps, the attribution of craziness, bolstered by the following characterization of this behaviour as *astonishing*. In addition, Mr Hague is represented as in conflict, in the first instance, not with the Labour government but with the father of the murdered boy, Damilola, or *Dami's Dad* (notice the gender bias here, which 'promotes' just the father as opponent, from the couple cited in the bodytext: *dad Richard and mum Gloria*). The intimacy or solidarity reflected in the informal naming of the Taylors is clearly in contrast with the distanced (*The Tory leader*) or even hostile (*crazy Hague*) namings of Mr Hague. Consistently, across headline and all the quoted copy, Mr Hague is Subject and Theme; in the *Mirror* the text is unequivocally *about* Mr Hague and his defying, ignoring, predicting and, finally, being rounded on. Consistently he is presented as acting in ways that are mildly absurd, if not *crazy*. Thus he is said to have insisted that 'police numbers contributed to the stabbing of Damilola': here the paper has used a nominalization – *police numbers* – of a potentially quite misleading kind. Anyone reading this who was unversed in the ongoing debate could be forgiven for thinking that Mr Hague had absurdly claimed that by their numerousness the police had facilitated the crime; whereas *police numbers* is a kind of contracted nominalization, denoting the relative *decline* in police numbers in the last few years.

From *The Times*:

# Hague links Labour with murder rise

### BY PHILIP WEBSTER AND TOM BALDWIN

WILLIAM HAGUE inflamed the growing political tensions over crime and race last night by suggesting that the re-election of a Labour government could lead to more tragedies such as the murder of the schoolboy Damilola Taylor.

Hours after being accused by the parents of Damilola of using their son's death as a political football, a defiant Conservative leader said he would not be "bullied" into letting the issue of police numbers and morale drop.

In a series of interviews organised after the parents' criticism, Mr Hague voiced his personal sympathy for them. But he pitched straight into more controversy when asked in a BBC interview if Labour's crime policies would lead to more cases such as Damilola's. "There would be more crime if police numbers and police morale continue to fall," he said. "It will mean, yes, that there are more tragedies we will end up discussing."

*The Times*'s headline, although it makes Mr Hague Theme and Subject, also makes him the source of a projected proposition, which has been complexly grammatically transformed; the 'congruent' and spelled-out sense is something like:

> *Mr Hague has said that government by the Labour party has indirectly caused a rise in the incidence of murders.*

But, in newspaper discourse, to *link* carries associations and insinuations entirely missing from more neutral projecting verbs like *say, allege* and *claim*. The difference is partly reflected by the lexicogrammatical fact that you cannot write a coherent counterpart headline that runs:

> **Hague alleges/claims Labour with murder rise*

This is because *link*, unlike *allege*, has incorporated into it the sense that the following nominal phrases 'go together': so to *link* is not merely to name two or more entities, but also to assert their connection (possibly causal). Furthermore, where the verb *link* is used with a human agent and two inherently human objects, it seems to have a negative 'semantic prosody'. By a negative semantic prosody I mean that despite its seeming neutrality, in particular contexts of use the word usually carries and spreads to the co-text a negative connotation – but this usage tendency is sufficiently subtle that it has not become codified in dictionary definitions as 'part of the meaning' of the word. *Link* can be used neutrally, or even positively, particularly when the two entities linked are inanimate; but with human agent and one or more human objects, as corpus research confirms, the linking is of suspects with crimes or, in situations of actual or simulated scandal, adulterous sexual partners or shady business dealings: to detect a link is to uncover a suspectly-concealed connection.

Even quite preliminary scrutiny of the Cobuild corpus confirms these observations. On the assumption that *Hague links* is 'headlinespeak' for *Hague has linked (Labour rule with rise in violent crime)*, I selected and list below the first instances of *linked* I found in the corpus. (This sort of selectivity is necessary so as not to be distracted by all the occurrences of *links* as a noun, references to the organisation *Link*, and so on). When *link* is used as a verb, it is overwhelmingly past tense, and here are the first five such random and unrelated examples that the corpus offered me:

> *Fat ... particularly saturated fat, has been linked to coronary heart disease and other diseases ...*
> *discovering the mechanism that linked India's monsoon with Peru's El Niño – ...*
> *Your addiction to laxatives may be linked to fears about growing up.*
> *They ... [pre-cognition and telepathy] ... They are strongly linked in some meaningful way ....*

*his Christian Democrat power base is linked to the Sicilian Mafia. . . .*

Three of these five are unequivocally 'negative' linkages – saturated fat with heart disease, laxative–addiction fears, and a power base and the mafia, respectively. The other two here are not noticeably negative – but they are also different structurally from our target construction, namely where *link* is used with at least one human-reference object. Again, outside of newspaper headlines, past or perfective constructions rather than present tense are much commoner in this usage. The following (non-random) example from the corpus is absolutely typical, and again confirms the normally negative semantic prosody of the construction:

> *A study in Canada has linked warm winds – called chinooks – to migraines in some sufferers.*

Notice too that in the corpus the following preposition of choice is *to* and not *with*: it is as if *The Times* is a little uncomfortable with the explicit causality implied by the standard 'directional' preposition (which would also require a change in order of entities: *Hague links murder rise to Labour*) and elects to 'temper' the connection by a semantically weaker and vaguer choice, *with* (weaker yet, and not a preposition at all, would have been *and*).

We have already seen that the small differences between these news treatments are arguably as important as larger ones. To mention another, consider contrasting use here of the phrase *political football*. While all five papers report the phrase 'political football', in four papers the Taylor parents are said to have accused Mr Hague of using *their son's death* (a nominalization) as a political football; but in the *Telegraph*, the only fully Hague-aligned paper in this group, the parents are said to have accused him of using *their son* (a mere nominal entity) as a political football. If that characterization makes the parents' criticism marginally less coherent and retrievable, it thereby makes Mr Hague's position more justified.

Fascinatingly, in News International's other British national newspaper besides *The Times,* the tabloid *Sun*, the Hague/police numbers story does not figure at all on the 19 December: it is as if the furore simply has not happened. And this extraordinary fact serves as a reminder of how these news stories, and the further narratives they give rise to, multiply and spread in complex ways. Thus these stories are not just about crime and policing and race and Mr Hague; they are also 'about' entirely undeclared characters and events, only apparent to the insider–reader, such as the approaching general election and Mr Michael Portillo. Mr Portillo is Mr Hague's chief rival for the leadership of the Conservative Party and, assuming that party's success at some future general election, for the prime ministership. But the pro-Tory press is said to be divided over the competing claims of Hague and Portillo, with the *Telegraph* remaining pro-Hague while the News International papers, *The Times* and the *Sun*, have become more receptive to the idea of a Portillo takeover. This background may explain the way that *The Times* treatment of Mr Hague's intervention is comparatively lukewarm, while as noted, the *Sun* chooses not to feature it at all.

One of the things to conclude is that incremental sociopolitically embedded national stories such as the Hague/policing one are a good deal more nuanced and heterogeneous, incorporating parts of other important ongoing politicized narratives, than news reports of outrages and disasters in distant settings. The average British reader's connection to a Zimbabwe news item, even where this reports actual deaths in a blatantly ideologically-motivated way, remains less direct than in relation to British or European news, in terms of political, social, military, or economic involvement.

A further general conclusion that may be advanced is that detailed linguistic analysis shows the news media *struggling* to narrate the news they relate – particularly where that news concerns political initiatives and responses (rather than, say, accidents and disasters). What *exactly* did Mr Hague say or do, that needed reporting on 11 December? Each newspaper's editorial team has to fashion an answer to this question, in setting about telling the story. Despite or because of their position as privileged witness and narrator, the newspapers themselves grapple with a kind of narratorial and discursive 'turbulence' as they strive both to report with accuracy and at the same time articulate a reasonable evaluative construal of events. The turbulence is reflected in the incongruous usages and idiomaticity tensions of the headlines and lead sentences, where expressions heavy with clashing presuppositions or discordant semantic prosodies are yoked in awkward collocation. There, *despite* the great care and effort expended on word- and phrase-selection, we have found a powerful public figure reported as 'defying a plea', 'inflaming the anger', making a 'race jibe', 'inflaming the tensions', and so on. And, it should be emphasized, these collocational incongruities in headlines and lead sentences are not instances of the intentional or unintentional humour that are often noted. Rather they are Bakhtinian clashings or wrenchings of verbal patterns which it seems reasonable to trace to inconsistency of narratorial stance, or turbulent conjunction of voices and evaluations. They arise as journalists contrive to 'get the story straight' but remain aware that there are always at least two sides to any story.

## 8.5 The linguistic apparatus of political construal: notes on key resources

Here is a brief review of some of the key linguistic phenomena it seems sensible to examine when analyzing the political orientation of a narrative. Most are lexicogrammatical systems where choice of formulation, or 'slant', is possible; they can all contribute to the discoursal variations, transformations, or alternations to be found where different treatments of a news item are compared.

1. *Transitivity*. Following Halliday's account of clause transitivity as the representation of reality (4.9), it is reasonable to look at just which entities are presented as participants in a text's representation of events. Which individuals or groups tend to be cast as agent (sayer, thinker), and which tend to be cast as affected medium, in the text (see also Passivization, below)? What *kinds* of process are particular protagonists reported as initiating? And which relevant parties are scarcely mentioned at all?

Consider the protest against the Seattle WTO talks: was this chiefly a physical battle (as the abundant television coverage of police–protestor confrontations and the now-standard designation as *The Battle of Seattle* would suggest) or a conflict of wills, or more one than the other? Similarly, are protests against foxhunting, or against genetically-modified experimental crops, as essentially physical (as distinct from mental and ethical) as they are often represented? The media, in their pursuit of exciting copy and a more dramatic portrait of the day's happenings, are surely likely to represent matters in a more material and less mental way than might be the case. The success or failure of various campaigns (political, military, commercial) may have even more to do with winning hearts and minds than we tend to think. And it may be that the dominant party seeks to reinforce whatever physical/material advantage they have, by their emphasis on that advantage in their statements (= stories) to the press, so that mental (and verbal) opposition is worn down. These are highly speculative comments, but they seem to be important issues to do with textual presentation – and they are issues that a Hallidayan anatomy of transitivity enables us to explore.

Besides the processes and participants of transitivity analysis, it is often crucial to examine that content that a text casts as the third and backgrounded component, circumstantial elements. Circumstances can extenuate or incriminate, and they often have more to do with underlying causes than is first apparent. In the case of the controversial sinking of the *General Belgrano* during the Falklands War (2 May 1982), a number of surrounding circumstances that might have influenced the public's evaluation of the action were absent or variably presented in initial reports. For example, just where was the *Belgrano* in relation to the British 200-mile exclusion zone; in which direction was it steaming; how close to British ships was it at the time of the attack; how near to it were other Argentine naval vessels (which might have rescued the crew); and how long did it take to sink?

Deciding whether surrounding circumstances are ever indirect causes is often difficult, and a circumstance that is actually foregrounded in a headline is definitionally no longer neutral background: at the very least, to highlight a circumstance is to suggest that it is rather less tenuously involved in whatever incident has occurred. All of these implications are strengthened by the use in headlines of such conjunctions as *as.* Recall *The Times* headline discussed by Trew:

## RIOTING BLACKS SHOT DEAD BY POLICE
## AS ANC LEADERS MEET

*As* rarely explicitly expresses a causal connection in headlines, usually serving as the most succinct means of reporting temporal connection or simultaneity; but since it does elsewhere express causal relation, readers may attribute a residually causal emphasis even while assuming that the 'declared' interpretation is temporal.

2. *Passivization*, especially with agent-deletion. Passive voice sentences are a significant representational variant, which need to be seen alongside their closest counterpart, the active mood sentence. For example, an initial representation of a key event may use a transitive material process clause, that is to say, a clause containing a physical process done by one participant to another. Active voice, the normal and simpler ordering, places the agent as subject, followed by the process undergone, followed by the affected entity as object, e.g.

> *Police shoot Africans*
> *Youths stab boy*

A common variant of this is the complex transitive clause where an attribute or condition of the affected, perhaps arising as a result of the process stated, is also mentioned:

> *Police shoot Africans dead*
> *Youths stab boy to death*

But a further alternative, often with a distinctly different effect, is the passive construction. By passivization the affected participant is brought to the focal subject position in the sequence, and the semantic agent can optionally be deleted:

> *Africans (are) shot dead (by police)*
> *Boy stabbed to death (by youths)*

With reference to informativeness, the reformulation says less: we no longer have an indication of the cause or agent of the process of shooting. But it does thematize (bring to the front) the most affected or changed participants.

3. *Suppletion of agentless passives by intransitive clauses.* An (agentless) passivized or complex-transitive clause can be supplanted by an

intransitive clause relatively smoothly. Typically, both clauses will have the structure S–P–(A), and while there may have to be a change of lexical verb, the new verb choice can be close in meaning to the original:

> *Africans shot dead (in Salisbury riot)*
> → *Africans die (in Salisbury riot)*
> *Boy stabbed to death on crime-ridden estate*
> → *Boy dies on crime-ridden estate*

The affected participant formerly in object position is now the sole stated participant, occupying subject position, and the former description of a causal relation, what *x* did to *y*, is now simply a report of what happened to *y*, or even, of what *y* 'does'.

4. *Nominalization.* A nominalization is a conversion and encapsulation of what is intrinsically a clausal process in the syntactic form of a noun phrase, hence treating the entire process as an established 'thing' – which can then serve as a participant in some other more directly reported and inspectable process. Nominalization 'de-narrativizes' a process, making the process mere background to a product or thing. This formulation:

> *Damilola Taylor died of stab wounds*

is a process and a narrative. But the following equivalent

> *The death of Damilola Taylor from stab wounds*

is a nominalization, assuming a narrative but not telling it. Similarly, in the Salisbury riot story –

> *The deaths of 13 Africans*

– nominalization can attenuate the sense of 'shooting dead' or 'dying' as experienced processes. The reformulations deflect the reader's attention further from questioning whether these deaths were killings or not, and if so who the killers were. Nominalization transformations such as this recast an implicit process into the form of a static condition or thing. This nominal condition or thing can then be used as the agent or affected participant or carrier of some other process, now become the focus of our attention:

> *The Taylors had accused Mr Hague of using **their son's death** as a 'political football'.*

> ***The deaths of 13 Africans** triggered a further wave of violence in Salisbury townships today.*

Nominalization is one of the crucial linguistic resources deployed in news reports. But as the examples above suggest, it can also be exploited and abused: it enables the user to refer without narrating, without clear and explicit report. The teller can be economical with the facts (as they see them). Nominalizations are exploited, used as sword and as shield, by every political and ideological faction or persuasion. In the explicitly political arena, they often serve to contrive implicit or explicit transfers of responsibility – unsurprisingly, in view of the fact that varying answers to the question, 'Who is to blame?' lie at the heart of much political discourse. It is not that nominalization is inevitably 'wrong' or undesirable – it is an invaluable means of textual condensation, e.g. in academic and scientific writing. But it clearly can be used, in barely perceptible ways, to background what arguably should be in the foreground. In some ways nominalization is more threatening than the ultimate kind of backgrounding, declining to report a story at all: nominalizing reformulations are still a kind of reporting of what happened, usually with most of the main participants noted, and the 'hard' facts (numbers, times, places, etc., involved) recorded correctly. Given that degree of accuracy, busy readers may not have the resources to reflect on the lexicogrammatical slantedness of the interpretation.

On the other hand, readers busy or idle are not dupes or stooges: they are often adept at sniffing out the linguistic and communicative manipulations that newspapers perform. Readers of every political persuasion can, given time and motivation, reinterpret the incidents that their newspapers interpret for them. But such reading against the grain is effortful and, in the long run, rather a perverse exercise in indirectness. Even the most active of readers is likely, in the longer run, to be habituated and 'reconciled' to the categorizations and evaluations constantly relayed to them by the news outlets they patronize. Cumulatively, through a lengthy text, and across a series of stories filed over days and weeks on the same issue, and given the likely congruence of a newspaper's treatment of the particular issue with their treatment of a broader grouping of issues, the effect of enforcing and reinforcing a particular view of the world can be almost irresistible. George Orwell's novel *1984* dramatizes these efforts of world-view construction and reconstruction at a tyrannical extreme.

5. *Modality and evaluation* (see 3.7, 6.4 and 6.6). Within systemic linguistics more recently, the systems of lexical resource available for conveying evaluation have been brought together under the cover-term of Appraisal. Appraisal theory postulates that, by means of complex networks of vocabulary expressing various kinds of appreciation, judgment, and affect, speakers can 'encode' their interpersonal evaluations of the subject-matter. For detailed accounts, see Martin (2000), White (2000) and Eggins and Slade (1997).

6. *Namings and descriptions* (see also 4.4). Consider again Trew's news stories about riots and killings (we can note, relevantly, that the *Salisbury,*

*Rhodesia* of the 1970s has become *Harare, Zimbabwe*). Were those who acted *rioters*, *demonstrators*, or *troublemakers*; were they a unified group or was there a ruthless, violent minority amongst the majority; were those actually shot representative of the entire group, or innocent bystanders, or ringleaders, or what? Notice, in passing, the contrasting evaluations carried by the words *leader* and *ringleader*. Were the police ordinary police or special police, black or white or mixed or both-but-stratified. If trained to deal with riots, trained by whom, with what objectives? How many police actually opened fire, were they young, nervous recruits, or hardened old stagers? All the foregoing questions are probing both the facts and, by implication, their proper reported description; and all descriptions carry some interpretative and political charge. Parallel scrutiny of facts, namings and descriptions can be directed at the characterizations of the protesters, delegates and police in the 'Battle of Seattle' story, or indeed of Mr Hague, the police, and Damilola's attackers, in the Hague/policing story. How can or should Mr Hague have been named, for example? In one local South London newspaper's version of the Hague/policing story (SouthLondon Online), Mr Hague is referred to as *the Yorkshireman*, thereby presumably intending to intimate that he is 'an outsider' and perhaps ill-informed. In the most salient areas of political contention, journalists – like the rest of us – have rich inventories of overlapping descriptors to choose from as they sort out which characterization fits their (ideologically contextualized) account of things best. Some sets of variant description are particularly familiar, and often contain noticeably positive or negative evaluation: cf. *terrorist* versus *freedom fighter* versus *gunman* versus *men* [sic] *of violence*; *question* versus *allegation*; *reply* versus *rebuttal*; *answer* versus *refute*; *opinion* versus *allegation*; *opinion* versus *fact*; *answer* versus *justification*; *national security* versus *government cover-up*; *policy* versus *expediency*.

At the same time it is quite possible for there to be lexical 'gaps' in the vocabulary standardly available for describing events and participants. Take the case of workers going on a one-day strike: how might the strike's proponents best describe their action? One common description, 'day of industrial action', seems particularly ill-advised, a kind of ready-supplied ammunition for critics who, quite reasonably, point out that such occasions are days of industrial inaction. Alternatively, nominalizations like 'one-day stoppage' (which gives no kind of purpose to the action) and 'one-day strike' draw some attention to those doing the striking, but fail to implicate any other party or circumstances as underlying causes of the stoppage. Some unionists like the emphasis on workers as powerful, as having some control over production, that phrases like 'industrial action' and 'day of protest' suggest. But that in itself may be bad strategy if your narrative is to be taken up by a hostile press. There really does seem to be something of a lexical-descriptive gap here, with no standard pithy expression that would represent the one-day stoppage as a demonstration, by suspension of work (and remuneration), of a collective sense of deep grievance: perhaps the phrase 'day of hardship' would come close.

Over the past fifteen years, public discourse has become even more self-aware, under the pressures of monitoring by one interested group or another, who wish things to be named (represented) a certain way and are prepared to contest namings in some other objectionable way, and who are furthermore able to wield some kind of 'capital' (publishing house-style; or sociocultural support from liberal-progressive opinion; even legal rulings) to uphold or exclude particular namings. Some of this has (itself) been dismissively labelled as political correctness; but it is a broader and more important process than that tainted phrase suggests: in a thorough study, Cameron (1995) calls it verbal hygiene. Whatever the label, it is a discoursal self-consciousness that is thoroughly characteristic of contemporary Western culture, where 'spin', branding, image, surface, the 'look' (of the model, the Web page, the gesture) is deemed so important in, as before, winning hearts and minds (if not also lawsuits).

Besides considering single lexical points in a text, it is important also to look at the lexis of stories more holistically, and consider what kinds predominate. Is the lexis abstract or concrete, and in either case, which kind of domain is it standardly used to refer to? Matches and mismatches (intentional or otherwise) between the basic message to be conveyed and the language used to convey it can rapidly be uncovered in this way (e.g. advocating peace and reconciliation but using the language of force and conflict – *smashing through ignorance by mobilizing the forces for change*).

7. *Collocational incongruity.* Under this label may be gathered all the demonstrably atypical or infelicitous constructions – clearly having most impact in headlines and leads – of the kind discussed towards the end of 8.4 and thus not elaborated here. By contrast with some of the other discourse-transformative resources discussed in this list, these clashes of idiom or usage may well not be deliberate, even though, ironically, they seem to arise after much careful deliberation over individual word selection. Mr Hague is defiant so that the verb *defies* is selected; the Taylors' request for their tragedy not to be used in a policy debate is nominalized as a *plea*. But the chaining of these in text gives rise to the incongruity of a powerful person *defying a plea*, possibly reflective of ideological and narrative turbulence, amenable to Bakhtinian explanation as a clash of voices.

8. *Presupposition.* This is the term used to describe a speaker's back-grounding, in their utterance, of various kinds of assumptions that are nevertheless retrievable from that utterance. Thus if I say *the car battery is flat again* I presuppose that the battery has been flat before. Even if the sentence is cast in the negative – *Thankfully the battery isn't flat again* – the presupposition remains true (the battery *was* flat before). See Chapter 8 of Toolan (1998) for a simple literary-minded exposition, Simpson (1993) and Levinson (1983) for a detailed linguistic account. The most strategic use of presupposition in public or political discourse is so as to 'insert' into the

record (but in the background, as if they were uncontroversial facts, common ground) propositions that are contestable or slanted. To take two examples from the *Daily Telegraph* story discussed above, when this reports

> [Mr Hague] said he would not be bullied into silence on inner city crime, falling police numbers and morale.

it relays without objection Mr Hague's presupposition that somebody has been intent on bullying him into silence on inner city crime, etc. Notice by contrast that the *Independent* questions Mr Hague's presupposition by using scare quotes:

> [Mr Hague] warned that he would not be 'bullied' into dropping the issue.

On the other political side, the *Telegraph* also reports the Home Secretary as saying 'the Leader of the Opposition is playing the race card' – a formulation which presupposes that there exists such a thing as 'the race card'.

But presuppositions can shape controversial narratives in much less explicitly political contexts, too. Suppose, for example, that someone has tragically bled to death after having been stabbed by unknown assailants; news bulletins might refer to *the brutal murder*. This presupposes that the term *murder* validly applies – but in the circumstances this is prematurely to categorize and in a sense to pre-judge the violent attack: there may have been neither intent to cause life-threatening harm, nor recklessness.

The above are examples of relatively direct, linguistically-encoded pre-supposition. Often as interesting to reflect upon are the cultural or societal presuppositions that can be inferred from what members of a community talk or write about, and from how they do so. The community or culture involved need not be coterminous with nationality, but could be based on a sport, music, a religion, a hobby – every imaginable grouping that might sustain a monthly magazine or an Internet discussion group. Clearly, very different kinds of things will be narratively 'tellable' (being significant, or calamitous, or amusing, or a triumph, etc.) for each of these communities, and strikingly different cultural presuppositions will form a backcloth to the foregrounded tellable material. Here is the headline to an inside-page news item in the latest issue of my university's Library Bulletin:

*Periodicals Information Point Moves*

But in the more 'encompassing' media, such as national newspapers, radio and TV, where single compendious texts contrive to address a relatively heterogeneous audience, a greater degree of guessing about audience interests, and of creation or shaping of audience interests, will be involved. It is quite possible for a newspaper to attempt to 'induce' and nurture certain presuppositions in its readers, which they would not spontaneously subscribe to. Indeed to some extent competing commercial media *have* to 'force' reader presuppositions in this way: with each succeeding publication or broadcast, they have to project the meta-message that the stories they are relaying are highly relevant and tellable.

This section should not end without a reiteration that narratives are enabling props as well as insidious reconstructions. Accordingly, and bearing in mind that ideological perspectivism in language-use is inescapable, we should recognize the good side of news stories in the press. Readers are afforded some interpretation, some halfway coherent construction of what is past, present and to come in the larger world around them. And obviously these constructions are supplied far more rapidly and presented far more effectively than any individual reader could manage on their own.

Hard-news narratives, we have seen, construe and reconstrue newsworthy facts and events (both awkward and convenient) so that these are congruent with the 'macro-story' of a newspaper's broader view of the world. In the case of long-running news items, the stories form a sequence of tellings in which changes of emphasis, over time, are likely. We cannot always safely predict that a particular paper's angle on an issue or story will stay constant – as Trew's example showed. But the world has moved on a long way since the Salisbury killings of June 1975 that Trew discusses, and it would be interesting to chart the shifts in *The Times*'s own broader account of 'the Zimbabwe story'. One might take shifts and revisions in the presentation of just one participant, for instance, by way of illumination.

What sort of character, for example, has *The Times* construed Robert Mugabe to be, over the quarter-century from 1975 to 2000? My impression is that, along with many other conservative journals, *The Times* first cast Mugabe as a Marxist ideologue presiding over senseless terrorist violence, bent on the annihilation of the white factions in Africa, and impervious to conciliatory dialogue. After the Whitehall conference, however, in which ZANU (PF) participated – and especially after the substantially free and fair democratic elections (1980) in which, to the surprise of many Western commentators, Mugabe emerged a clear victor over his rivals – it was, quite literally, a different story. Now Mugabe appeared reasonable after all, educated and religious: his two Western degrees were emphasized, as was his devout Catholicism. In the decades thereafter, there was a steady cooling towards Mugabe and the new order in Zimbabwe as more stories emerged of inter-tribal persecution and sharp control of political opposition. (Notice the use of nominalizations here, for events that undoubtedly have agents and affecteds.) Present-day *Times* narratives depict an ageing and unstable, quasi-dictatorial figure, presiding over economic chaos and failure, fomenting racism in his attacks on political opponents, intent on maintaining a one-party state within a democratic shell. All these shifts in characterization suggest that either Mugabe has changed rather radically, or *The Times* has, or – and this is the most likely – both have, in ways that complexly interact. But insofar as it is true that *The Times* (the teller) has changed its mind about Mugabe over the years, notice how different this is from literary narration where, for example, we might expect Joyce's Gabriel or Nabokov's Pnin to change and develop (drop some attributes and gain others), but do not expect the author, in the course of the telling, to change their mind. If Mugabe were a character in a novel, we would regard such drastic shifts in presentation as reflecting an incompetent or negligent narrator, who didn't seem to know their own story (incompetence different in kind from the 'uncertainty' of Simpson's negative-modality narrators). But this is one major way in which press narratives differ from literary ones.

President Mugabe is still in power as I write; he is one of those extra-ordinary political survivor–endurers, like Presidents Castro of Cuba, Moi of Kenya, and Mandela of South Africa, Senior Prime Minister Lee Kuan Yew of Singapore and former Prime Minister Thatcher of Great Britain, General Pinochet of Chile and – a Mandela still awaiting release from her Robben Island – Aung San Suu Kyi of Myanmar. A careful tracking of the narrative construction and re-construction of any of these figures over the years, in and out of office, is always likely to be revealing.

Unlike a literary narrative, press narratives are never 'finished': there is always tomorrow's edition, which may have to assimilate new and awkward events, even to the extent of revising the newspaper's back-ground construction of events. So *caveat lector*: let the reader beware. Newspapers – like governments – often do not know what they are talking about. They may know no more than Bertha at the end of 'Bliss' wondering what is going to happen now; but unlike her they must at once provide a satisfactory account. Their macro-narratives are interpretations of the past and 'authoritative' predictions about the future, but the future is a foreign country, ill-understood, so that reading newspapers for the truth is a bit like religious belief – an act of faith. At the present time in Britain, perhaps no narratives so confirm this as those fumblingly related, by politicians and journalists alike, concerning the gradual but much-resisted development, by federation, of these United States of Europe.

## 8.6  News stories online

Over the last ten years or so, a profoundly important development with respect to print or text news media has emerged which must be factored into any analysis of news narratives: the Internet, which, besides many other things, is taking the paper out of newspapers. Increasingly, people are accessing their newspapers – especially the broadsheets – via their computer screens rather than a paper copy. The online version of any newspaper is inevitably different in content (including fewer and different accompanying advertisements) and format and reading experience than the print version. It is likely, too, that the sequence in which a reader 'samples' the linked screens of text, of the online version, is different, and less linear or even 'orderly', than in the case of the newsprint copy.

Equally important are all the hypertext possibilities of online media. I will mention here only their simplest forms, involving hotlinked *text*, but increasingly hypermedia allows the possibility of, for example, a text story about the Prime Minister's latest pronouncement to be accompanied by an audiovisual file carrying a forty-second cache of the relevant speech; similarly, reviews of music recordings, concerts, plays and new books can, in principle, be accompanied by brief samples (audiovisual where applicable) of the material being discussed. Sites such as BBC Online have been doing this for some time, and were traditional newspapers to move in that direction in their online sites, it would be no surprise in this postmodern culture of consumerist infotainment, and discoursal plenitude or excess (the informational plenitude that Chatman noted in the traditional narrative film – 4.8(j) – can be seen as quite modest and manageable by comparison).

At its simplest, then, hypertext possibilities mean that where, for example, the *Guardian* runs an article on harassment of the MDC opposition party by the Government and ZANU (PF) in Zimbabwe, the editors can choose to embed, within the article, hotlinks to a range of directly-related, or more background items, which the reader can surf to. Equally commonly, a menu of such links can be displayed in a sidebar running alongside the news item. And those linked items *themselves* may contain links to numerous further reports, profiles, opinion pieces, government documents and so on. In view of which, several related questions arise: what is the sequential *structure* of the online news report: should one 'jump' to linked pages – particularly if these are linked pages within the same day's edition of the newspaper – at precisely the point where that link is offered in the body of the report, subsequently jumping back to the original text? And if one does pursue some of the advertised links, at what point do you *know* that you have reached the end of the news item? For our experience of any of the larger news services' online materials is that in practical terms these are, as the *Guardian* site explicitly declares, 'Unlimited'. For such reasons it is quite possible to conclude that the Internet, like a multi-purpose library and leisure complex, is in many respects an anti-narrative device, exploiting the technology that banishes several desiderata of narrative listed in Chapter 1: teleology, a critical high-point, an individualized agonist, a palpable teller, and closure.

There are, of course, 'more narrative' (in the adjectival sense) places on the Internet, such as the individual's Web pages, particularly where these have remained stolidly unmodified for months: here we do sense individualization, a depicted teller, and closure, but no teleology or genuine crisis point. And every 'complete' online edition of a newspaper would appear to provide closure for that day at least, just as the purchased newsprint version does: but even that 'temporary' closure is undercut by the online newspapers' increasing provision of 'breaking news' items, posted on the site as soon as possible: thus, checking the *Guardian* at 10:50 a.m., I find a new item of breaking news has been added as recently as 10:46: the ants in the discourse colony that is the online news site are always coming and going (but are not the same ants).

The emergence of a huge array of competing TV channels in Britain and elsewhere is representative of a greater diversification and, importantly, confusion of the media that shape public opinion and sentiment. The diversification and confusion take many forms. One example concerns newspaper-allegiance: in the past someone might subscribe to the *Daily Telegraph* and have it delivered to their door every day, as a result deriving their picture of, say, Zimbabwe or the leader of the Opposition's statements solely from this consistently conservative source. But the contemporary online reader of the *Telegraph* is in a very different position: by means of a few clicks and without moving from their seat, their computer can jump to the *Guardian* news pages, or the *Mirror*'s, or CNN or indeed Zimbabwe's *Daily News* (http://www.dailynews.co.zw).

As noted, online newspapers today are far from offering merely the 'bare text' of the news item: even where it does not offer audio or video links, the online page will bristle with panels and sidebars, carrying commercial advertisements (usually more colourful) of all kinds – sometimes grotesquely at odds with the content and mood of the news story – as well as the previously-mentioned links to other parts of the current online issue, or to items in past online issues of the newspaper, or to external websites. In the *Telegraph's* version of the Hague/police numbers story, a sidebar on the left offers links to a number of external sites (listed below), and arguably these contribute to the evaluation or 'uptake' of the story they frame. The editorial teller intimates that these pages are part of the background to the narrative, tellable if the addressee believes they need to be told about them: in a sense, each offered hotlink of this kind approximates an Abstract, a point at which, by clicking or not clicking, the addressee can be told the supporting narrative, or not. But from the point of view of the 'centered' story, items in these sidebar menus are, even when not clicked on and expanded upon, highly evaluative. Consider the selection, and presentational order, of the organizations listed as links in the online *Telegraph's* story, including the preponderance of police organizations:

> Conservative Party
> Labour Party
> The murder of Damilola Taylor – Metropolitan Police
> Racial and Violent Crimes Taskforce – Metropolitan Police
> Police – Home Office
> Metropolitan Police Federation
> Police Services of the UK
> Police Federation of England and Wales

## 8.7  Stories of class and gender

Besides race, the other two most universal axes along which division, exclusion and ideologically-motivated discrimination proceed are gender and class. To put this starkly, in Western culture and elsewhere, narratives of all kinds have tended to 'tell' a story about the inferiority or subordination of women to men, and of the working class to the middle class. In a sense that outcome is an inevitable corollary of a culture embracing and putting store by these gender and class categories: part of the reason for subscribing to the categorization of people into working class and middle class is so that you can tell stories that assert differences and asymmetries between these two groups. So classist and gendered narratives performatively sustain the class- and gender-oppositions which their tellers and addressees wittingly or unwittingly endorse and live by.

If class- and gender-oppositions were genuinely ones of identities that were merely 'different but equal', like, perhaps, a person's preferring tea to coffee, the consequences might be slight. But in sociocultural practice, gender and class differences are robustly hierarchical, contriving to empower one group by dint of disempowering or marginalizing others. As countless stories imply. Again using a Hallidayan analysis to specify the choices of process and participant that have been made in relevant narratives, we can ask with whom lies the power to do, to cause, and to affect? Asymmetry will soon be apparent, whether the texts studied are nineteenth-century British fiction or Hollywood blockbuster action movies of the last twenty years or contemporary television commercials. These trends do not hold true for all narratives, of course, and they have probably weakened as tendencies over the last few decades; but they remain powerfully present.

To the extent that the above generalizations hold, it seems that such narratives simply replicate mainstream reality and main-stream ideology. But there are numerous departures – and ways of departing – from the narrative-ideological norms, whether we are looking at published novels or personal stories embedded in conversation over lunch. Such ideologically non-standard narratives are like 'minority reports' on the way things are (or were, or might be). They express a local sub-group's preferences as being at some degree of variance from the larger society's assumed dominant norms. And although such local contestings of the sociopolitical orthodoxies are not the norm, still they may occur anywhere; but they may fail to be sharply visible because those contestings are themselves heterogeneous syntheses of normative positions on some issues and radical positions on others. For example, a story might contest orthodoxies of class and race discrimination and yet remain covertly sex-discriminatory (or patriarchal), and so on: using the list of linguistic features in 8.5 as a guide, it is possible to identify the aspects of a discourse which represent one position, and those which articulate a perhaps conflicting one. Limitations of space prevent a fuller exploration and demonstration of these issues here.

Such limitations also forestall discussion of the various other respects in which we can talk about gendered narratives, and the desirability of a feminist narratology (Lanser, 1986; 1995; 1999; Warhol, 1989; Mills 1998a, b; Fludernik, 1999b). Is the Labovian 'high point' narrative structure, with a mounting action rooted in conflict and leading to an abrupt climax a 'masculinist' format? If so, can it be contrasted with a preferred feminist story structure, equally 'valid': an unfolding of events, in waves of progression, that more clearly brings the story and its audience back to its point of departure, in a more circular fashion? From time to time analysts have speculated along these lines, and various individual narratives can be adduced in support (one might cite Michelle Roberts' *Une Glossaire/A Glossary*, briefly discussed at 1.3; or stories by contemporary writers such as Margaret Atwood, Grace Paley, Jeanette Winterson, Ann Beattie, Carol Shields, Jane Smiley, and Alice Munro – see discussion of her 'Circle of Prayer' in the Notes and exercises below). In the modern period of English literature, much 'structurally female' writing can be traced to Virginia Woolf; Cather, Chopin, Richardson and Mansfield may also be mentioned.

Different again are questions of gender 'in' the written narrative. For example, where the gender of a story's author or third-person narrator is unknown, to what extent do readers like to determine this, or simply make assumptions, and if the latter, on what textual bases? Or where a first-person narrator figures within the text, with gender references excluded or suppressed, again how important is this to the addressee and how do they go about 'resolving' the ambiguity by reference to textual content? As indicated earlier, race and gender and class are some of the most ingrained categories that we live by, but all these and others are now widely recognized to be culturally-created and contingent, rather than biological essences inherited at birth. Accordingly, in literary narrative especially, contemporary authors often challenge or deny any expectations readers may have that a character will be unambiguously presented as female, middle-class, heterosexual, and black (or, in each separate respect, not).

## 8.8  Prejudice in ethnic narratives

The sociopolitical partiality of certain types of everyday discourse emerges very vividly in van Dijk's (1984) studies of ethnic prejudice in cognition and conversation. Again, limitations of space prevent a proper treatment, but this work is widely reported elsewhere. Suffice it to say that, in the discourses of mainstream European cultures, minority ethnic groups (like homosexuals, immigrants, refugees, asylum-seekers, and possibly religious fundamentalists) are construed in the way that the male middle-class construes women, only much more so. In Holland, van Dijk found that the conversational stories involving minority ethnic groups told by majority-group members characterized these 'foreigners' as culturally and even physically threatening, alien and strange, incomprehensible, irrational, untrustworthy, irreligious and prone to criminality. Such crude and consistent stereotyping means that a Proppian folktale analysis, even without much amendment, fits the negative stories told about minorities:

> The Dutch people are the heroes or the victims, and the outgroup members are the villains. Even the events and the actions involved may be drawn from a limited repertory. Minorities cause us trouble of various kinds: they make noise, cause dirt in the street, take our jobs or houses, or are engaged in crime. Minority stories are becoming a specific genre of the folklore of ingroup prejudice.
>
> (van Dijk, 1984: 81)

Amidst this dreary predictability of content, one unpredictability of structure was interesting: fully half of van Dijk's corpus of stories lacked a solution or resolution to the problems raised in the complication.

> And that is precisely how the ingroup storyteller sees the social conflict: minorities cause problems, but we cannot do anything against that. Instead of a heroic success story, we then have a complaint or accusation story.
>
> (90)

If such narratives are, indeed, geared to generalized complaint, then they have some of the properties of what systemicists distinguish from Labovian narrative as exempla (see 7.6). As exempla they facilitate negative evaluations that can, if needed, be cast in generic sentence form – 'they can't be trusted'; 'they send all their money back home' – and these in turn can be grounds for deontic prescriptions about what should be done (with them).

The power of the prejudice in ethnic narratives persists today in Western Europe and beyond, in diverse forms. Important studies continue to appear on the racialization of political discourses, narrative or otherwise (e.g. van Dijk, 1991; 1992; 1993; Blommaert and Verschueren, 1998). In recent years, Wodak and her co-researchers have turned their attention to a critical discourse analysis of European discourses on immigration, and the virulently anti-immigrant far-right political discourse of Jorg Haider and his Freedom Party, currently part of the government coalition in Austria (see e.g. Wodak *et al.*, 1999; van Leeuwen and Wodak, 1999). In Britain, arguably, the acceptable (at least, legal) face of racism today is the 'europhobia' to be found in some of the tabloid newspapers' treatment of European Union stories.

## 8.9 Stories in court

A final arena in which I want to draw attention to the political dimension to assessments of tellers and their stories is that of the law. That, contrary to official assumptions, not all tellers are equal under the law is highlighted in the work of O'Barr and his co-researchers. Lind and O'Barr (1979), for example, report the findings of a detailed analysis (using actual US court transcripts) of the different kinds of language used by witnesses. Their first finding was that

Many of the most common and important dimensions of variation in court speech seemed to carry information about the power, status, and control of the speakers.

(Lind and O'Barr, 1979: 70)

In particular, speakers seemed to divide rather noticeably into two camps: those who used a way of speaking with most or all of the features of what has been called 'women's language' but is better termed 'powerless language', and those who adopted a way of speaking that is socially recognized as 'powerful language'. Powerless language style, first identified in Lakoff (1975), is marked by the following features:

a high frequency of intensifiers like *so* and *very*; of 'empty adjectives like *cute* and *charming* and *ghastly*; hyper-correct grammar; polite forms (*would you like to . . .?*); higher frequency of accompanying gestures; more hedges (*well, I guess*); rising (question-type) intonation in declarative sentences; greater pitch range and more rapid pitch changes (heard as more dramatic than the powerful male's drone).

(Powerful language is defined negatively, as speech that is largely devoid of the above features). Correlation of social position with use of powerful versus powerless language was unmistakeable: witnesses who were professionals, people in authority, of either sex, used few or no powerless language features; but low social-prestige witnesses, including the unemployed, did. The researchers now re-recorded actual powerless-speech testimonies in four versions: versions with and without the powerless-speech features, and with male and female actors as speakers. When these versions were presented to judges under controlled conditions, they found that for both the male and female witnesses, the power speech produced perceptions that the witness was markedly 'more competent, attractive, trustworthy, dynamic and convincing than did the powerless speech testimony' (Lind and O'Barr, 1979: 72).

Lind and O'Barr went on to observe that witnesses' testimony tended to vary in another, immediately evident, way: in the length of a witness's response to a lawyer's question. Some witnesses supplied (and were allowed to supply) lengthy narrative answers to relatively few lawyer questions, while others produced fragmentary testimony – brief answers to numerous lawyer questions. Both intuition and courtroom manuals (which advise lawyers to have their own witnesses give them narrative answers but to restrict opposition witnesses to fragmentary ones) suggest that narrative answers imply trust in a witness. That trust and evaluation is of course the lawyer's, but there seems to be plentiful evidence that subjects in the role of jurors will, to some extent, accept and adopt a lawyer's assumed evaluation of a witness. And, of course, this encapsulates a major goal of a lawyer's examination of witnesses, in the adversarial system: that *this* witness be accepted as truth-telling, that *that* witness for the opposing side be discounted as dishonest or unreliable, and so on. In short, as barristers have long known informally, the manner in which witnesses and attorneys speak in the presentation of testimony – the manner and format of narratives in court – can affect social and even judicial evaluation of them by jurors.

It is possible to treat criminal cases, in particular, as situations in which two pre-eminent tellers, the counsels for the prosecution and the defence, are the architects of two extended and partially conflicting narratives. Each of those narratives is a collaborative effort, with attempts at validation and corroboration from perhaps a number of witnesses, and each is also a fragile and threatened narrative, in that witnesses' assertions may be challenged and probed under cross-examination. But the two leading counsels are undoubtedly chief narrators – particularly during cross-examination, where both sides are so intent on 'putting their case' as a coherent narrative that witnesses' denials are largely disregarded by the lawyer involved: a semblance of question-and-answer dialogue frames what is essentially narrative monologue (see Heffer, in preparation). See also the work of Atkinson and Drew (1979), which shows how subtle can be the negotiations of description, evaluation and inferrable intention during cross-examination of tribunal witnesses.

The upshot of hearing both the case for the prosecution and that for the defence is that judge and jury are presented with two clashing narratives, possibly with partially divergent sequences of events, and contrasting claimed motivations, resolutions and evaluations. Judge and jury have to attempt a sifting of these two narratives, a merging which may involve rejecting very many of one party's assertions regarding the events, characters, setting and motivations. The particular goal that will delimit these activities of sifting and merging is that of upholding or rejecting a specific charge that certain individuals are guilty of criminal wrongdoing. Matters are not quite this straightforward, however, since, as Heffer (adopting Bruner) shows, somewhat orthogonally to the sequential, discursive, everyday narrativizing of the facts of a case lie the legal rules and principles, which form an equation or paradigm. Thus theft is the (a) dishonest (b) appropriation of (c) property (d) belonging to another (e) with intention permanently to deprive them of it, and if those five elements fail to be established, then the narrative is not a 'theft' narrative and the criminal charge will fail (even if some other narrative, such as 'transfer of property using undue influence', seems to fit). Broadly, the law applies paradigmatically; but lay jurors, it is postulated, proceed syntagmatically or narratively. In the course of their 'narrativizing' of the case, barristers and the judge (who in English courts provides a summing-up), must negotiate a difficult integration of the paradigmatic and the narrative (see Heffer, in preparation).

One interesting feature to notice is the way witnesses are required to state only those things they know to be the case, and to avoid airing opinions or judgments (except when specifically asked to do so, as in, for example, 'Did the defendant appear troubled or anxious at that time?'). In other words, judicial procedure attempts a separation of what Labov has distinguished as the referential and the evaluative: witnesses are to provide unevaluated referential reports; lawyers incorporate these in their submission of evaluated, point-laden narratives; and judge and/or jury decide whether to accept those narratives, in part or in whole. The persuasive but inherently suspect narratives (suspect given that, as everyone is aware, they cannot both be true) that opposing lawyers weave are always constructed with the end in view of compelling either assent to or dissent from the conclusion that the jury 'are sure that the defendant is guilty' of the crime. Permeating these narratives are complex attributions of blame, responsibility, and negligence. What applies to courtroom narratives applies to a large degree to coroner's inquiries and legal tribunals as well (one may predict that a rich array of kinds of narrative inequalities and disvaluations are likely to be found in the discourses of employment, immigration and mental health tribunals).

Like the analyses of O'Barr and his co-researchers, those of Ruth Wodak (1985) address the question of the glaringly different consequences – for example, in terms of sentence – that different strategies of self- and testimony-presentation may have in, for example, trials of motorists for dangerous driving – where 'different modes of class- and sex-specific socialization' (1985: 184) and narrative 'effectiveness' militate against female working-class defendants of limited education.

And what local or extended metaphors are invoked to give shape and vividness to narrative representations in the criminal court? I will cite just one that span the wrong way. The prosecution lawyers in the O. J. Simpson criminal trial, in their final summing up to the jury, drew heavily on the 'jigsaw' metaphor, suggesting that over the preceding months various witnesses had brought 'pieces' of the puzzle to court, and that the complete picture could now be assembled (Cotterill, 2000). The defence team very effectively 'turned' this metaphor by reminding jurors that in a typical jigsaw puzzle, the player is guided by the picture on the front of the box, available *in advance* of all efforts to put the pieces together. And that, they contended, was precisely how the prosecution had preceded: first they decided on the picture, one in which Simpson was pre-judged as the murderer, and then they sought the pieces to 'fit' that picture. This rejoinder may have had only minor impact in this most atypical of trials, but it could only strengthen the defence case.

Finally, linguistic analysis of narratives in the (chiefly criminal) justice system has most prominently established itself as part of 'forensic linguistics', one of the fastest-growing new fields of linguistics (Coulthard, 1994, 1996, and in preparation). When in 1952 the state convicted and later hanged Derek Bentley, a learning-disabled young man, on the grounds that he was the knowing accomplice of Chris Craig, a minor, who shot and killed a police officer, were there irregularities and reasonable doubts about the written narrative statement of events that the police took from Bentley? Was Bentley's narrative all his own words, without police additions or 'scaffolding' via leading questions? Making proper allowance for the stressful circumstances in which such narrative statements are made and taken, and with due consideration for whatever may be distinctive about a particular detained person's narrative idiolect, are there reliable indicators in structure, word-choice, and so on, that can distinguish genuine and uncoerced statements from those where there may have been interference and fabrication? In the Bentley case, on posthumous appeal in 1997, the 1953 conviction was ruled unsafe (largely on the grounds of the original judge's biassed summing-up, but the forensic linguistic evidence concerning Bentley's statement was not discounted). Linguistic analysis of the narrative portions of suspect documents – statements in custody, witness statements, suicide notes, anonymous blackmail or threatening letters, etc. – is becoming increasingly robust and reliable, and the courts' growing attention to it reflects this. The stakes could hardly be higher. Nowhere is it more palpably evident that, individually and collectively, our narratives are our life stories.

## Further reading

An excellent place to begin with is Fowler *et al.* (1979) which includes the work by Trew that I have discussed; Bolinger (1980) is a similarly invaluable general treatment. Thereafter, specifically on Critical Discourse Analysis, see Fairclough (1989; 1992; 1999); Caldas-Coulthard and Coulthard (1996); and special issues of the journal *Discourse & Society* (e.g. 1992). On the language of the news media, especially of hard news narratives, see Fowler (1991), Bell (1991), White (1997), van Dijk (1988) and Bell and Garrett (1998). Theoretical commentary on the Internet, hypermedia and their implications is voluminous; see Aarseth (1997) and Murray (1998) for a taster. On gender, feminism and narrative, a beginning can be made with Lanser (1986), Warhol (1989), Mezei (1996), Mills (1998a), Fludernik (1999) and Bucholtz (1999). On the political aspects of ethnic stories, see Sykes (1985), van Dijk (1984; 1991; 1992; 1993), Wodak *et al.* (1999), Blommaert and Verschueren (1998). And on the political consequences of courtroom discourse, see Lind and O'Barr (1979), O'Barr (1982), Atkinson and Drew (1979), Bennett and Feldman (1981) and Wodak (1981; 1985). On stories in US Supreme Court proceedings: Amsterdam and Bruner (2000). Kress and van Leeuwen (1996) is a rich and multi-stranded account of the semiotic import and logic of multimodal texts, particularly those that include graphics. This study is full of contributions towards the development of a systematic understanding of what is involved in visual literacy. On all these overlapping areas there is now a host of journals to consult, including *Discourse & Society*, *Forensic Linguistics*, *Journal of Pragmatics*, *Text* and *International Journal of the Sociology of Language*.

## Notes and exercises

1 Hodge (1979) offers an analysis of the processes and participants that appear in the headlines of one British broadsheet's foreign news coverage on just one day. The broad trends are as follows:

    1 Public persons say and tell, they do not otherwise act and are not acted on.
    2 Private persons only exist if they are the subject of violent action, but what they say or feel does not exist as news.
    3 The world outside Britain is unrelievedly a world of conflict, usually between states, or within states, or between governments and subversive forces. The conflict is occasionally resolved, temporarily at least, but is more usually the motive for the reported action.

4  Since they are mediated through public persons, conflicts exist mainly through statements and attitudes.

5  Since public figures predominate over private, words and feelings predominate over actions.                                                  (Hodge, 1979: 161–2, slightly abridged)

Extract the headlines of the foreign news stories of any newspaper you have to hand. Analyze these headlines, in terms of their transitivity (4.9) and draw up lists of the agents and mediums in material processes, the sayers and sensers in clauses of verbal or mental process, and so on. To what extent do you find Hodge's claims still valid, nearly twenty-five years later? Attempt a similar analytical exercise on the same newspaper's headlines for (a sample of) its domestic news stories. Which – if any – of Hodge's generalizations need amending if they are to apply to this rather different sample? Do any amendments have to do with domestic journalism's greater attention to 'human interest' stories? In fact, can we use a Hallidayan transitivity analysis to uncover some of the basic ingredients of what newspapers count as 'human interest' or soft-news stories?

2  Using the critical discourse-analytic 'toolkit' set out in this chapter, analyze and comment upon any current newspaper account of President Mugabe, and events in Zimbabwe.

3  If one wants to make the case for a female or feminist story structure, the short story by Canadian writer Alice Munro called 'Circle of Prayer' may be as good a test-case as any (a quite different alternative would be Angela Carter's 'The Company of Wolves'). Only a few preliminary observations can be offered here, possible pointers to rather than defining criteria of feminist structuration. To begin with temporal sequencing, in my analysis, 'Circle of Prayer' comprises eighteen distinct temporal segments (which I label 'a' to 'r'), which are presented in an order quite at variance with their reconstructible chronology. Thus the chronologically earliest segment, about how Trudy and her now ex-husband Dan met, is eighth to be told. The discoursal telling begins with the account of how Trudy throws a jug across the room at or at least towards her teenage daughter, Robin (the jug, made some time ago by Dan in a pottery class, formerly held a necklace, a precious keepsake to Trudy, which she has just discovered that Robin in a grand gesture has dropped into the coffin of a tragically-killed school acquaintance). What is told first in the discourse is chronologically the eighth episode. But even this episode, which falls into three subparts, is told achronologically: first we are told that Trudy threw the jug, then we are told the history of the jug and where it sits and what is kept in it, and then we are told how Trudy came home from work, got the jug down, found as she expected that the necklace was missing, confronted Robin in her room, and threw the jug. But it is not simply the anachrony of the telling that sets this structuring at a remove from typical 'high-point', crisis-and-resolution narration. It is more broadly the sense that *no single particular* crisis is available, as it were, to be resolved: Trudy's complex of concerns is not that simple, that it can be cast as a linear narrative with trajectory and endpoint. In these respects, a couple of brief textual segments are particularly striking. They are brief, remarkably similar and symmetrical segments, which I reproduce here:

b  You threw a jug at me that time. You could have killed me.
   Not at you. I didn't throw it at you.
   You could have killed me.

q  You threw the jug. You could have killed me.
   Yes.

As far as chronological sequence is concerned, these, in the order presented here, are unquestionably the 'latest' moments in the story. In fact they record two scenes or episodes that may have occurred indefinitely long after the entirety of the story proper – even ten or twenty years later. And it seems reasonable to treat them as temporally distinct from each other since by the time that (q) arises, but only then, Trudy is prepared to admit she might have killed Robin. But as far as narrational sequence is concerned, as my labelling indicates, episode (b) is the very second scene to be told, right after the jug-throwing episode discussed above; and episode (q) – and here is the symmetry – is the penultimate scene to be told. In a long and complex story, these belated moments are told prematurely but separately, in counterposed positions.

The story is also feminist in its eliding of a straightforward answer to the 'about-ness' question. It is hard to say what the story is chiefly about, and even harder to say 'what finally happens': these feel like the wrong questions to dwell on. 'Circle of Prayer' is substantially about Trudy's strained relations with her infuriating independent-minded daughter (or housemate?). At least they are talking again by the end of the story proper, when Robin – a running champion – phones her mother at the end of Trudy's workshift and asks, 'Can I run over and ride back with you?': a simple form of constructive circularity or recurrence. But the story is also about Trudy's feelings for and resentments of her ex-husband Dan and his infidelity; and it is about how she now lives, her work, her friends. These include her friend Janet, who has joined a Circle of Prayer, and explains to Trudy:

> 'What the Circle is really about is, you phone up somebody that is in it and tell them what it is you're worried about, or upset about, and ask them to pray for you. And they do. And they phone one other person that's in the Circle, and they phone another and it goes all around, and we pray for one person, all together.'

With due allowances for differences, this is not so far removed from being a fair description of the entire story, which seems at core to dwell, therapeutically, on what Trudy is worried or upset about. As a therapeutic narrating cure, there is no mas-culinist 'triumph' at the close of the story, although it does end with a kind of male triumph. The final narrated episode, (r), involves learning-disabled Kelvin, a young male resident in the Home that Trudy works at; Kelvin has worries of his own, about other residents and how he relates to them. But when Trudy asks him if he ever prays and if so what he prays for, Kelvin has an answer:

> 'If I was smart enough to know what to pray for,' he says, 'then I wouldn't have to.'

In context, Kelvin's observation is remarkably powerful, and shows Kelvin has an insight which his self-description (not smart enough) denies. Not knowing quite what to pray for applies not just to Kelvin but to Trudy too, and is perhaps a liberation as much as a problem. While Bertha in 'Bliss' wonders what will happen *now*, Trudy – like Kelvin – seems not to know what she would *want* to happen now or next, and the cyclical trajectory-less structure of the story in a sense validates this, even making the narrative with beginning, middle and end seem simplistic. The Trudy-focalized narra-tive reflects on what it calls Kelvin's 'halfway joke':

> It's not meant as comfort, particularly. Yet it radiates – what he said, the way he said it, just the fact that he's there again, radiates, expands . . .

If the case is to be made out for an alternative, feminist structural format or tendency in some literary (and non-literary) narratives, then evidence from a variety of facets of text-construction, including those exemplified above, are likely to be relevant. Other facets likely to be of relevance will include focalization, narrational mode and speech- and thought-representation. Calibrating a story's deployment of all these ele-ments, in combination, it may be possible to identify tendencies which might warrant classifying the story as 'more feminist' or 'more masculinist', without needing – or wanting – to specify two well-defined categories, 'feminist' and 'masculinist' struc-tures. But the starting-point remains literary competence and cultural judgment, and mine is that 'Circle of Prayer' contrasts with 'Barn Burning', the jug-throwing so dif-ferent from the rug-throwing, in ways which might conceivably be related to femin-ism and masculinism. The challenge is to spell out those ways.

# Bibliography

Aarseth, E. (1997) *Cybertext: Perspectives on Ergodic Literature*, Baltimore: Johns Hopkins University Press.

Ahlberg, J. and A. Ahlberg (1979) *Burglar Bill*, London: Collins.

Amsterdam, A. and J. Bruner (2000) *Minding the Law*, Harvard: Harvard University Press.

Atkinson, M. and P. Drew, (1979) *Order in Court*, Atlantic Highfields, NJ: Humanities Press.

Austin, J. L. (1962) *How To Do Things With Words*, Oxford: Clarendon Press.

Bakhtin, M. M. (1981) *The Dialogic Imagination: Four Essays*, M. Holquist (ed.) Austin: University of Texas Press.

Bakhtin, M. M. (1986) *Speech Genres and Other Late Essays*, Austin: University of Texas Press.

Bal, M. (1985 [1997: 2nd edition]) *Narratology: Introduction to the Theory of Narrative*, Toronto: University of Toronto Press.

Baldry, A., P. Thibault, *et al.* (2000) *Multimodality and Multimediality in the Distance Learning Age*, Campobasso: Palladino Editore.

Bally, C. (1912) 'Le style indirecte libre en francais modeme', *Germanisch-Romnanisch Monatsschrift*, 4, 549–56, 597–606.

Bamberg, M. (ed.) (1997a) *Oral Versions of Personal Experience: Three Decades of Narrative Analysis* [special issue of the *Journal of Narrative and Life History*], Mahwah, NJ: Lawrence Erlbaum.

Bamberg, M. (ed.) (1997b) *Narrative Development: Six Approaches.* Mahwah, NJ: Lawrence Erlbaum.

Banfield, A. (1982) *Unspeakable Sentences*, New York: Routledge & Kegan Paul.

Baron, H. (1998) 'Disseminated consciousness', *Essays in Criticism*, 48, 4, 357–78.

Barthes, R. (1970) *S/Z*, Paris: Seuil.

Barthes, R. (1977) 'Introduction to the structural analysis of narratives', in *Image–Music–Text*, London: Fontana.

Bauman, R. (1986) *Story, Performance, and Event: Contextual Studies of Oral Narrative*, Cambridge: Cambridge University Press.

Bayley, J. (1963) *The Character of Love: A Study in the Literature of Personality*, New York: Collier Books.

Beaman, K. (1984) 'Coordination and subordination revisited', in D. Tannen (ed.) *Coherence in Spoken and Written Discourse*, Norwood, NJ: Ablex.

Bedient, C. (1969) '*Middlemarch*: touching down', *Hudson Review*, 22.

Bell, A. (1991) *The Language of the News Media*, Oxford: Blackwell.

Bell, A. and P. Garrett (eds) (1998) *Approaches to Media Discourse*, Oxford: Blackwell.

Bennett, G. (1983) ' "Rocky the police dog" and other tales', *Lore and Language* 3, 8, 1–19.

Bennett, W. and S. Feldman (1981) *Reconstructing Reality in the Courtroom: Justice and Judgement in American Culture*, New Brunswick, NJ: Rutgers University Press.

Bennett-Kastor, T. (1983) 'Noun phrases and coherence in child narratives', *Journal of Child Language*, 10, 135–49.

Bennett-Kastor, T. (1986) 'Cohesion and predication in child narratives', *Journal of Child Language*, 13, 353–70.

Bennett-Kastor, T. (1999) Predications and nonreferential cohesion in Irish-speaking children's narratives', *Functions of Language*, 6, 1, 195–241.

Benveniste, E. (1966) *Problemes de linguistique generale*, Paris: Gallimard.

Berendson, M. (1981) 'Formal criteria of narrative embedding', *Journal of Literary Semantics*, 10, 79–94.

Berendson, M. (1984) 'The teller and the observer: narration and focalization in narrative texts', *Style*, 18, 140–58.

Bhaya, R., R. Carter and M. Toolan (1988) Clines of metaphoricity, and creative metaphors as situated risk-taking. *Journal of Literary Semantics,* 17, 1: 20–40.

Bickerton, D. (1967) 'Modes of interior monologue: a formal definition', *Modern Language Quarterly*, 28, 2, 229–39.

Bissex, G. (1981) *Gnys at Work: a Child Learns to Write and Read*, Cambridge, MA., Harvard University Press.

Blommaert, J. and J. Verschueren (1998) *Debating Diversity: Analysing the Discourse of Tolerance*. London, Routledge.

Bloor, T. and M. Bloor (1995) *The Functional Analysis of English: a Hallidayan approach,* London: Arnold.

Bolinger, D. (1980) *Language, the Loaded Weapon*, London: Longman.

Bolinger, D. (1981) *Aspects of Language*, New York: Harcourt Brace Jovanovich.

Booth, W. (1961) *The Rhetoric of Fiction*, Chicago: University of Chicago Press.

Bordwell, D. (1986) *Narration in the Fiction Film*. London and New York: Routledge.

Bronzwaer, W. J. M. (1970) *Tense in the Novel*, Groningen: Wolters Noordhoff.

Brown, G. and G. Yule (1983) *Discourse Analysis*, Cambridge: Cambridge University Press.

Brown, P. and S. Levinson (1987) *Politeness*, Cambridge: Cambridge University Press.

Browne, A. (1983) *Bear Goes to Town*, London: Arrow Books.

Bruner, E. (ed.) (1984) *Text, Play and Story: The Construction and Reconstruction of Self and Society*, Washington DC American Ethnological Society.

Bruner, J. (1986) *Actual Minds, Possible Worlds.* Cambridge, MA: Harvard University Press.

Bruner, J. (1990) *Acts of Meaning,* Cambridge, MA: Harvard University Press.

Bruner, J. (1992) The narrative construction of reality, in H. Beilin and P. Pufall (eds) *Piaget's Theory: Projects and Possibilities.* Hillsdale, NJ: Lawrence Erlbaum, 229–48.

Bucholtz, M. (1999) '*You da man*: Narrating the racial other in the production of white masculinity', *Journal of Sociolinguistics*, 3: 4, 443–60.

Burton, D. (1982) 'Through glass darkly: through dark glasses', in R. Carter (ed.) *Language and Literature*, London: Allen & Unwin, 195–214.

Butt, D. *et al.* (1995). *Using Functional Grammar: an Explorer's Guide*, Sydney: National Centre for English Language Teaching and Research.

Caldas-Coulthard, C. and M. Coulthard (eds) (1996) *Texts and Practices: Readings in Critical Discourse Analysis*, London: Routledge.

Cameron, D. (1995) *Verbal Hygiene*, London: Routledge.

Carter, R. and P. Simpson (1982) 'The sociolinguistic analysis of narrative', *Belfast Working Papers in Linguistics*, 6: 123–52.

Carver, R. (1989) 'A Small, Good Thing', in *Cathedral and other Stories,* London: Vintage Books.

Carver, R. (1994) 'Little Things', in *Fires: Essays, Poems, Stories*, London: Harvill.

Cazden, C. (1981) *Language in Early Childhood Education*, Washington DC: National Association for the Education of Young Children.

Chatman, S. (1969) 'New ways of analysing narrative structures', *Language and Style*, 2: 3–36.

Chatman, S. (1978) *Story and Discourse*, Ithaca: Cornell University Press.

Chatman, S. (1990) *Coming to Terms: the Rhetoric of Narrative in Fiction and Film*, Ithaca: Cornell University Press.

Chomsky, N. (1957) *Syntactic Structures*, The Hague: Mouton.

Chomsky, N. (1965) *Aspects of the Theory of Syntax*, Cambridge: MIT Press.

Christie, F. *et al.* (1984) *Children's Writing: Reader*, Victoria: Deakin University Press.

Christie, F. and J. Martin (eds), (1997) *Genres and Institutions: Social Processes in the Workplace and School*, London: Cassell.

Clark, H. (1977) 'Inferences in comprehension', in D. Laberge and S. J. Samuels (eds) *Basic Processes in Reading*, Hillsdale, NJ: Erlbaum.

Cohn, D. (1978) *Transparent Minds: Narrative Modes for Presenting Consciousness in Fiction*, Princeton, NJ: Princeton University Press.

Colby, B. (1970) 'The description of narrative structures', In P. Garvin (ed.) *Cognition: A Multiple View*, New York: Spartan Books.

Cook-Gumperz, J. and J. Green (1984) 'A sense of story: influences on children's storytelling ability', in D. Tannen (ed.) *Coherence in Spoken and Written Discourse*, Norwood, NJ: Ablex, 201–18.

Cotterill, J. (2000) Representing Reality in Court: Power and Persuasion in Trial Discourse, unpublished PhD dissertation, University of Birmingham.

Coulthard, M. (1994) 'Powerful evidence for the defence: an exercise in forensic discourse analysis', in J. Gibbons (ed.) *Language and the Law*, London: Longman, 414–42.

Coulthard, M. (1996) 'The official version: audience manipulation in police records of interviews with suspects,' in C. Caldas-Coulthard and M. Coulthard (eds) *Texts and Practices: Readings in Critical Discourse Analysis*, London: Routledge, pp. 166–78.

Coulthard, M., in preparation, *Language as Evidence*, London: Routledge.

Crawford, P., B. Brown and P. Nolan (1998) *Communicating Care: the Language of Nursing*, Nelson Thornes, Cheltenham.

Crossley, M. (2000) *Introducing Narrative Psychology: Self, Trauma, and the Construction of Meaning.* Buckingham: Open University Press.

Culler, J. (1975a) *Structuralist Poetics*, London: Routledge & Kegan Paul.

Culler, J. (1975b) 'Defining narrative units', in R. Fowler (ed.) *Style and Structure in Literature*, Oxford: Blackwell.

Culler, J. (1981) *The Pursuit of Signs*, London, Routledge & Kegan Paul.

Culpeper, J. (2000) 'A cognitive approach to characterization: Katherina in Shakespeare's *The Taming of the Shrew*', *Language and Literature*, 9:4, 291–316.

Culpeper, J. (forthc.) *Language and Characterization: People in Plays and Other Texts*, London: Longman.

Dijk, T. van (1984) *Prejudice in Discourse: An Analysis of Ethnic Prejudice in Cognition*, Amsterdam: John Benjamins.

Dijk, T. van (1988) *News as Discourse*, Hillsdale, NJ: Lawrence Erlbaum.

Dijk, T. van (1991) *Racism and the Press*, London: Routledge.

Dijk, T. van (1992) 'Discourse and the denial of racism', *Discourse & Society*, 3:1, 87–118.

Dijk, T. van (1993) *Discourse and Elite Racism*, London: Sage.

Dillon, G. and F. Kirchnoff (1976) 'On the form and function of free indirect style', *Poetics and Theory of Literature*, 1, 3, 431–40.

Docherty, T. (1983) *Reading (Absent) Character: Towards a Theory of Characterization in Fiction*, Oxford: Clarendon Press.

Dry, H. (1995) 'Free indirect discourse in Doris Lessing's "One off the short list",' in P. Verdonk and J. J. Weber (eds) *Twentieth Century Fiction: from Text to Context*, London: Routledge, 96–112.

Duchan, J., G. Bruder and L. Hewitt (eds) (1995) *Deixis in Narrative: A Cognitive Science Perspective*, Hillsdale NJ: Lawrence Erlbaum.

Dundes, A. (1968) Introduction to Propp, *The Morphology of the Folktale*, Austin: University of Texas Press.

Eaton, J., G. Collis and V. Lewis (1999) 'Evaluative explanations in children's narratives of a video sequence without dialogue', *Journal of Child Language*, 26(3), 699–720.

Edwards, D. (1997) *Discourse and Cognition*, London: Sage.

Eggins, S. (1994) *An Introduction to Systemic Functional Linguistics*, London: Pinter.

Eggins, S. and J. Martin (1997) Genres and registers of discourse. In T. Van Dijk (ed.) *Discourse as Structure and Process*, London: Sage, 230–56.

Eggins, S. and D. Slade (1997) *Analysing Casual Conversation*, London: Cassell.

Ehrlich, S. (1990) *Point of View: A Linguistic Analysis of Literary Style*, London: Routledge.

Ely, R., J. Bleason and A. McCabe (1996) '"Why didn't you talk to your mommy, honey?": gender differences in talk about past talk', *Research on Language and Social Interaction*, 20, 7–25.

Emmott, C. (1997) *Narrative Comprehension: A Discourse Perspective*, Oxford: Oxford University Press.

Fairclough, N. (1989) *Language and Power*, London: Longman.

Fairclough, N. (1992) *Discourse and Social Change*, Oxford: Polity Press.

Farr, M. (ed.) (1985) *Children's Early Writing Development*, Norwood, NJ: Ablex.

Faulkner, W. (1942) *Go Down, Moses*, New York: Random House.

Faulkner, W. (1950) *Collected Stories of William Faulkner*, New York: Random House.

Ferguson, F. (2000) 'Jane Austen, *Emma*, and the Impact of Form', *Modern Language Quarterly*, 61:1, 157–80.

Fillmore, C. (1974) 'Pragmatics and the description of discourse', *Berkeley Studies in Syntax and Semantics*, 1, Chapter 5.

Finegan, E. (1994) *Language: its Structure and Use*, New York: Harcourt Brace.

Fish, S. (1980) *Is There a Text in this Class?*, Harvard: Harvard University Press.

Fleischman, S. (1997) 'The "Labovian model" revisited with special consideration of literary narrative', in M. Bamberg, (ed.) *Oral Versions of Personal Experience: Three Decades of Narrative Analysis*, Mahwah, NJ: Lawrence Erlbaum, pp. 159–68.

Fludernik, M. (1993) *The Fictions of Language and the Languages of Fiction*, London: Routledge.

Fludernik, M. (1996) *Towards a 'Natural' Narratology*, London: Routledge.

Fludernik, M. (1999a) 'Defining (In)Sanity: The Narrator of *The Yellow Wallpaper* and the Question of Unreliability', in W. Grünzweig and A. Solbach (eds) *Transcending Boundaries: Narratology in Context*, Tübingen: Gunter Narr Verlag, 75–95.

Fludernik, M. (1999b) 'The genderization of narrative', *GRAAT*, 21, 153–75.

Fowler, R., (ed.) (1975) *Style and Structure in Literature*, Oxford: Blackwell.

Fowler, R. (1977) *Linguistics and the Novel*, London: Methuen.

Fowler, R. (1981) *Literature as Social Discourse*, London: Batsford.

Fowler, R. (1986) *Linguistic Criticism*, Oxford: Oxford University Press.

Fowler, R. (1991) *Language in the News*, London: Routledge.

Fowler, R. *et al.* (1979) *Language and Control*, London: Routledge & Kegan Paul.

Fromkin, V. and R. Rodman (1978) *An Introduction to Language*, New York: Holt, Rinehart & Winston.

Frow, J. (1986) 'Spectacle binding: on character', *Poetics Today*, 7, 2, 227–50.

Gee, J. P. (1991) A linguistic approach to narrative, *Journal of Narrative and Life History*, 1, 15–39.

Gee, J. P. (1996) *Social Linguistics and Literacies: Ideology in Discourses*, London: Taylor & Francis.

Genette, G. (1980) *Narrative Discourse*, Ithaca: Cornell University Press.

Genette, G. (1988) *Narrative Discourse Revisited*, Ithaca: Cornell University Press.

Georgakopoulou, A. and D. Goutsos (1997) *Discourse Analysis: An Introduction*, Edinburgh: Edinburgh University Press.

Georgesen, J. and C. Solano (1999) 'The effects of motivation on narrative content and structure', *Journal of Language and Social Psychology*, 18(2), 175–95.

Ginsberg, M. P., (ed.) (1982) 'Free indirect discourse: a reconsideration', *Language and Style*, 15, 2, 133–49.

Greimas, A. (1966) *Sémantique Structurale*, Paris: Larousse.

Grice, H. P. (1975) 'Logic and conversation', in P. Cole and J. Morgan (eds) *Syntax and Semantics 3: Speech Acts*, New York: Academic Press, 41–58.

Hagenaar, E. (1996) Free Indirect Speech in Chinese. In T. Janssen and W. van der Wurff (eds) *Reported Speech: Forms and Functions of the Verb*, Amsterdam: Benjamins, 289–98.

Halliday, M. A. K. (1971) 'Linguistic function and literary style', in S. Chatman (ed.) *Literary Style: A Symposium*, London: Oxford University Press, 330–65. Reprinted in J. Weber (ed.), *The Stylistics Reader*, London: Arnold, 56–86.

Halliday, M. A. K. (1978) *Language as Social Semiotic*, London: Edward Arnold.

Halliday, M. A. K. (1994) *An Introduction to Functional Grammar*, 2nd edition, London: Edward Arnold.

Halliday, M. A. K. and R. Hasan (1976) *Cohesion in English*, London, Longman.

Halliday, M. A. K. and R. Hasan (1985) *Spoken and Written Language*, Victoria: Deakin University Press.

Harré, R. (1998) *The Singular Self: an Introduction to the Psychology of Personhood*, London: Sage.

Harris, R. (1981) *The Language Myth*, London: Duckworth.

Harris, R. (1998) *Introduction to Integrational Linguistics*, Oxford: Pergamon.

Hart, C. (1969) 'Eveline', in C. Hart (ed.) *James Joyce's Dubliners*, London: University of California Press.

Harvey, W. J. (1965) *Character and the Novel*, Ithaca: Cornell University Press.

Hasan, R. (1984) 'The nursery tale as a genre', *Nottingham Linguistic Circular*, 13.

Hawthorn, J. (ed.) (1985) *Narrative: From Malory to Motion Pictures*, London: Edward Arnold.

Heath, S. B. (1982) 'What no bedtime story means: narrative skills at home and school', *Language in Society*, 11, 49–76.

Heath, S. B. (1983) *Ways with Words*, Cambridge: Cambridge University Press.

Heffer, C. (in preparation) *Making a Case: Narrativization and Categorization in the Courtroom Language of Legal Professionals*. Unpublished PhD dissertation, University of Birmingham.

Hemingway, E. (1964) 'Indian Camp', in *The Essential Hemingway*, Harmondsworth: Penguin, pp. 279–83.

Herman, D. (1997) Scripts, Sequences, and Stories: Elements of a Postclassical Narratology, *PMLA*, 112:5, 1046–59.

Hernadi, P. (1972) 'Free indirect discourse and related techniques', appendix to *Beyond Genre*, Ithaca: Cornell University Press, 187–205.

Hickmann, M. (1985) 'Metapragmatics in child language', in E. Mertz and R. J. Parmentier (eds) *Semiotic Mediation: Sociocultural and Psychological Perspectives*, Orlando, FL: Academic, 177–201.

Hickmann M. (ed.) (1987) *Social and Functional Approaches to Language and Thought*, New York: Academic Press.

Hirose, Y. (2000) Public and private self as two aspects of the speaker: a contrastive study of Japanese and English, *Journal of Pragmatics* 32, 1623–56.

Hodge, R. (1979) 'Newspapers and communities', in R. Fowler *et al.*, *Language and Control*, London: Routledge & Kegan Paul, 157–74.

Hoey, M. (2001) *Textual Interaction: An Introduction to Discourse Analysis*, London: Routledge.

Hoover, D. (1998) *Language and Style in The Inheritors*, New York: University Press of America.

Hummel, M. (1999) 'Polyphonie, Appell und Perspektive bei erlebter Rede: Franzosisch, Portugiesisch, Spanisch', in S. Grosse and A. Schonberger (eds) *Dulce et Decorum est Philologiam Colere, I–II*, Berlin: Domus Editoria Europaea, 1633–49.

Hunston, S. and G. Thompson (eds) (2000) *Evaluation in Text: Authorial Stance and the Construction of Discourse*, Oxford: Oxford University Press.

Hymes, D. (1972) 'Models of the interaction of language and social life', in J. Gumperz and D. Hymes (eds) *Directions in Sociolinguistics*, New York: Holt, Rinehart & Winston.

Hymes, D. (1982) 'Narrative form as a "grammar" of experience', *Journal of Education* 2, 121–42.

Iser, W. (1978) *The Act of Reading: a Theory of Aesthetic Response*, London: Routledge and Kegan Paul.

Jahn, M. (1999) 'More aspects of focalisation: refinements and applications', *GRAAT* 21, 85–110.

James, H. (1963 [1884]) 'The art of fiction', in M. Shapira (ed.) *Henry James: Selected Literary Criticism*, Harmondsworth: Penguin.

James, H. (1966 [1888]) *The Portrait of a Lady*, Harmondsworth: Penguin.

Jameson, F. (1972) *The Prison-House of Language*, New York: Princeton University Press.

Jaworski, A. and N. Coupland (1999) *The Discourse Reader*, London: Routledge.

Jefferson, A. (1981) 'The place of free indirect discourse in the poetics of fiction: with examples from Joyce's 'Eveline', *Essays in Poetics*, 5:1, 36–47.

Jefferson, G. (1978) 'Sequential aspects of story-telling in conversation', in J. Schenkein (ed.) *Studies in the Organization of Conversational Interaction*, New York: Academic Press.

Johnson-Laird, P. (1981) *Mental Models*, Cambridge: Cambridge University Press.

Johnstone, B. (1990) *Stories, Community, and Place: Narratives from Middle America*, Bloomington: Indiana University Press.

Johnstone, B. (1996) *The Linguistic Individual: Self-expression in Language and Linguistics*, New York: Oxford University Press.

Johnstone, B. and J. Beam (1997) Self-expression and linguistic variation, *Language in Society*, 26, 221–46.

Jones, C. (1968) 'Varieties of speech presentation in Conrad's *The Secret Agent*', *Lingua*, 20, 162–76.

Joyce, J. (1956 [1914]) *Dubliners*, Harmondsworth: Penguin.

Joyce, J. (1960 [1916]) *A Portrait of the Artist as a Young Man*, Harmondsworth: Penguin.

Kennedy, C. (1982) 'Systemic grammar and its use in literary analysis', in R. Carter (ed.) *Language and Literature*, London: Allen & Unwin, 83–99.

Kermode, F. (1967) *The Sense of an Ending : Studies in the Theory of Fiction*, New York: Oxford University Press.

Kernan, K. (1977) 'Semantic and expressive elaboration in children's narratives', in S. Ervin-Tripp and C. Mitchell-Kernan (eds) *Child Discourse*, New York: Academic Press.

Kress, G. and T. van Leeuwen (1996) *Reading Images*, London: Routledge.

Kullmann D. (ed.) (1995) *Erlebte Rede und impressionistischer Stil: Europaische Erzahlprosa im Vergleich mit ihren deutschen Ubersetzungen*, Gottingen: Wallstein, 528 pp.

Labov, W. (1972) *Language in the Inner City*, Philadelphia: University of Pennsylvania Press.

Labov, W. (1981) 'Speech actions and reactions in personal narrative', *Georgetown University Round Table on Languages and Linguistics*, 219–47.

Labov, W. (1997) 'Some further steps in narrative analysis', in M. Bamberg (ed.) *Oral Versions of Personal Experience: Three Decades of Narrative Analysis* [special issue of the *Journal of Narrative and Life History*], Mahwah, NJ: Lawrence Erlbaum.

Labov, W. and J. Waletzky (1967) 'Narrative analysis: oral versions of personal experience', in J. Helms (ed.) *Essays on the Verbal and Visual Arts*, Seattle: University of Washington Press.

Lakoff, R. (1975) *Language and Woman's Place*, New York: Harper Colophon.

Lanser, S. (1981) *The Narrative Act: Point of View in Prose Fiction*, Princeton: Princeton University Press.

Lanser, S. (1986) 'Toward a Feminist Narratology,' *Style*, 20, 341–63. Reprinted in R. Warhol and D. Herndl (eds) *Feminisms: An Anthology of Literary Theory and Criticism*, New Brunswick, NJ: Rutgers University Press, 1997, 674–93.

Lanser, S. (1995) 'Sexing the narrative: propriety, desire, and the engendering of narrative', *Narrative*, 3, 85–94.

Lanser, S. (1999) 'Sexing narratology: toward a gendered poetics of narrative voice', in W. Grunzweig and A. Solbach (eds) *Transcending Boundaries: Narratology in Context*, Tubingen: Gunter Narr, 167–83.

Lawrence, D. H. (1955) 'Odour of chrysanthemums', *The Complete Short Stories*, London: Heinemann.

Leech, G. and M. Short (1981) *Style in Fiction*, London: Longman.

Leeuwen, T. van and R. Wodak (1999) 'Legitimizing immigration control: a discourse–historical Analysis', *Discourse Studies*, 1:1, 83–118.

Levinson, S. (1983) *Pragmatics*, Cambridge: CUP.

Lind, E. and W. O'Barr (1979) 'The social significance of speech in the courtroom', in H. Giles and R. St Clair (eds) *Language and Social Psychology*, Oxford: Blackwell, 66–87.

Linde, C. (1993) *Life Stories: the Creation of Coherence*, New York: OUP.

Linde, C. (1999) The transformation of narrative syntax into institutional memory, *Narrative Inquiry*, 9:1, 139–74.

Lodge, D. (1977) *The Modes of Modern Writing*, London: Edward Arnold.

Lodge, D. (1981) *Working with Structuralism*, London: Routledge & Kegan Paul.

Longacre, R (1983) *The Grammar of Discourse*, New York: Plenum Press.

Lothe, J. (2000) *Narrative in Fiction and Film*, Oxford: Oxford University Press.

Lubbock, P. (1973) *The Craft of Fiction* [1921], New York: Viking Press.

Luelsdorff, P. A. (1995) 'A grammar of suspense', *Journal of Literary Semantics*, 24:1, 1–20.

Lyons, J. (1977) *Semantics*, 2 vols, Cambridge: Cambridge University Press.

McCabe, A. and C. Peterson (eds) (1991) *Developing Narrative Structure*, Hillsdale, NJ: Lawrence Erlbaum.

McCabe, A. and C. Peterson (1996) Meaningful mistakes: the systematicity of children's connectives in narrative discourse and the social origins of this usage about the past. In J. Costermans and M. Fayol (eds) *Processing Interclausal Relationships in the Production and Comprehension of Text*, Hillsdale, NJ: Lawrence Erlbaum, 139–54.

McConnell-Ginet, S. and P. Eckert (1995) Constructing meaning, constructing selves: snapshots of language, gender, and class from Belten High. In K. Hall and M. Bucholtz (eds) *Gender Articulated; Language and the Socially Constructed Self*, London and New York: Routledge.

McHale, B. (1978) 'Free indirect discourse: a survey of recent accounts', *Poetics and Theory of Literature*, 3, 249–87.

McHale, B. (1983) 'Linguistics and poetics revisited', *Poetics Today*, 4, 1, 17–45.

McHale, B. (1985) 'Speaking as a child in U.S.A.', *Language and Style*, 17, 351–70.

McKay, J. H. (1978) 'Some problems in the analysis of point of view in reported discourse', *Centrum*, 6, 1, 5–26.

McKay, J. H. (1982) *Narration and Discourse in American Realistic Fiction*, Philadelphia: University of Pennsylvania Press.

Mandler, J. and N. Johnson (1977) 'Remembrance of things parsed: story structure and recall', *Cognitive Psychology*, 9, 111–51.

Mansfield, K. (1981) *The Collected Short Stories*, Harmondsworth: Penguin.

Margolin, U. (1989) 'Structuralist approaches to character in narrative: the state of the art', *Semiotica*, 75, 1–24.

Margolin, U. (1996) 'Characters and their versions', in C. Mihailescu and W. Hamarneh (eds) *Fiction Updated: Theories of Fictionality, Narratology, and Poetics*, Toronto, University of Toronto Press, 113–32.

Martin, J. (1983) 'The development of register', J. Fine and R. Freedle (eds) *Developmental Issues in Discourse*, Norwood, NJ: Albex, 1–40.

Martin, J. (1992) *English Text: System and Structure*, Amsterdam: Benjamins.

Martin, J. (2000) Inter-feeling: gender, class and appraisal in *Educating Rita*. In S. Hunston and G. Thompson (eds) *Evaluation in Text*, Oxford: Oxford University Press.

Matthiessen, C. (1995) *Lexicogrammatical Cartography*, Tokyo: International Language Sciences Publishers.

Mezei, K. (1996) 'Free indirect discourse, gender, and authority in *Emma*, *Howards End*, and *Mrs. Dalloway*', in K. Mezei (ed.) *Ambiguous Discourse: Feminist Narratology & British Women Writers*, Chapel Hill: University of North Carolina Press, 66–92.

Mezei, K. (ed.) (1996) *Ambiguous Discourse: Feminist Narratology & British Women Writers,* Chapel Hill: University of North Carolina Press.

Michaels, S. (1981) ' "Sharing time": children's narrative styles and differential access to literacy', *Language in Society*, 10, 423–42.

Michaels, S. (1985) 'Hearing the connections in children's oral and written discourse', *Journal of Education*, 167:1, 36–56.

Michaels, S. and J. Collins (1984) 'Oral discourse styles: classroom interaction and the acquisition of literacy', in D. Tannen (ed.) *Coherence in Spoken and Written Discourse*, Norwood, NJ: Ablex, 219–42.

Mihailescu, C. and W. Hamarneh (eds) (1996) *Fiction Updated: Theories of Fictionality, Narratology, and Poetics*, Toronto: University of Toronto Press.

Mills, S. (1998a), 'The gendered sentence'. in D. Cameron (ed.) *The Feminist Critique of Language: A Reader*, London: Routledge, 65–77.

Mills, S. (1998b) 'Post-feminist text analysis', *Language and Literature*, 7:3, 235–53.

Mitchell, T. (1975 [1957]) The language of buying and selling in Cyrenaica. In T. F. Mitchell, *Principles of Neo-Firthian Logic*, London: Longman.

Muhlhausler, P. and R. Harré (1990) *Pronouns and People*, Oxford: Blackwell.

Murray, J. (1998) *Hamlet on the Holodeck*, Cambridge, MA: MIT Press.

Myers, G. (1999) 'Functions of reported speech in group discussions', *Applied Linguistics*, 20, 3, 376–401.

Nabokov, V. (1957) *Pnin*, Harmondsworth: Penguin.

Neisser, U. and R. Fivush (eds) (1994) *The Remembering Self: Construction and Accuracy in the Self-narrative*, New York: Cambridge University Press.

Nelles, W. (1984) 'Problems for narrative theory: *The French Lieutenant's Woman*', *Style*, 18, 2, 207–17.

Nicolopoulou, A. (1996) Narrative development in social context. In D. Slobin, J. Gerhardt, A. Kyratzis and J. Guo (eds) *Social Interaction, Social Context, and Language: Essays in Honor of Susan Ervin-Tripp*, Mahwah, NJ: Lawrence Erlbaum, 369–90.

Nicolopoulou, A. (1997) Children and Narratives: toward an interpretive and sociocultural approach. In M. Bamberg (ed.) *Narrative Development: Six Approaches*, Mahwah, NJ: Laurence Erlbaum, 179–215.

Norrick, N. (2000) *Conversational Narrative. Storytelling in Everyday Talk*, Amsterdam: John Benjamins.

Nünning, A. (1999) Unreliable, compared to what? Towards a Cognitive Theory of *Unreliable Narration*: Prolegomena and Hypotheses. In W. Grünzweig and A. Solbach (eds) *Transcending Boundaries: Narratology in Context*, Tübingen: Gunter Narr Verlag, 53–73.

O'Barr, W. (1982) *Linguistic Evidence: Language, Power, and Strategy in the Courtroom*, New York: Academic Books.

Ochs, E. (1979) 'Transcription as theory', in E. Ochs and B. Schieffelin (eds) *Developmental Pragmatics*, New York: Academic Press, 43–72.

Oltean, S. (1993) 'A survey of the pragmatic and referential functions of Free Indirect Discourse', *Poetics Today*, 14:4, 691–714.

Onega, S. and J. Garcia (eds) (1996), *Narratology*, London: Longman.

Ong, W. J. (1975) *Orality and Literacy*, London: Methuen.

Palmer, J. (1978) *Thrillers: Genesis and Structure of a Popular Genre*, London: Arnold.

Pascal, R. (1977) *The Dual Voice*, Manchester: Manchester University Press.

Payne, M. (2000) *Narrative Therapy: an Introduction for Counsellors*. London: Sage.

Peer, W. van and J. Chatman (eds) (2001) *New Perspectives on Narrative Perspective*, Albany: State University of New York Press.

Perez, C. and H. Tager-Flusberg (1998) 'Clinicians' perceptions of children's oral personal narratives', *Narrative Inquiry*, 8(1), 181–202.

Peterson, C. and A. McCabe (1983) *Developmental Psycholinguistics: Three Ways of Looking at Child's Narrative*, New York: Plenum Press.

Peterson, C., B. Jesso and A. McCabe (1999) 'Encouraging narratives in preschoolers: an intervention study,' *Journal of Child Language*, 26(1), 49–67.

Piaget, J. (1959 [1926]) *The Language and Thought of the Child*, London: Routledge & Kegan Paul.

Plum, G. (1988) 'Textual and Contextual Conditioning in Spoken English: A Genre-Based Approach', unpublished PhD thesis, Department of Linguistics, University of Sydney.

Polanyi, L. (1978) The American story: cultural constraints on the structure and meaning of stories in conversation, unpublished doctoral dissertation, University of Michigan.

Polanyi, L. (1981) 'Telling the same story twice', *Text*, 1, 315–36.

Polanyi, L. (1982) 'The nature of meaning of stories in conversation', *Studies in Twentieth-Century Literature*, 6, 1–2, 51–65.

Polanyi, L. (1985) *Telling the American Story: From the Structure of Linguistic Texts to the Grammar of a Culture*, Norwood, NJ: Ablex.

Pratt, M. L. (1977) *Toward a Speech-Act Theory of Literary Discourse*, Bloomington: Indiana University Press.

Price, M. (1968) 'The other self: thoughts about character in the novel', in M. Mack and I. Gregor (eds) *Imagined Worlds*, London: Methuen, 279–99.

Prince, G. (1973) *A Grammar of Stories*, The Hague: Mouton.

Prince, G. (1982) *Narratology: The Form and Function of Narrative*, The Hague: Mouton.

Prince, G. (1991) *A Dictionary of Narratology*, Aldershot: Scholar Press.

Propp, V. (1968 (1928]) *The Morphology of the Folktale*, Austin: University of Texas Press.

Redeker, G. (1996) 'Free indirect discourse in newspaper reports', in C. Cremers and M. den Dikken (eds) *Linguistics in the Netherlands*, Amsterdam: Benjamins, 221–32.

Reilly, J., E. Bates and V. Marchman (1998) 'Narrative discourse in children with early focal brain injury', *Brain and Language*, 61(3), 335–75.

Rifelj, C. (1979) 'Time in Agatha Christie's novels', *Language and Style*, 11, 4, 213–27.

Riffaterre, M. (1973) 'Interpretation and descriptive poetry', *New Literary History*, reprinted in Young (ed.) (1981).

Rimmon-Kenan, S. (1983) *Narrative Fiction: Contemporary Poetics*, London: Methuen.

Roberts, M. (1994) *Une Glossaire/A Glossary*, in *During Mother's Absence*, London: Virago, pp. 131–81.

Romaine, S. (1985) 'Children's narratives', *Linguistics*, 23, 83–104.

Rothery, J. and J. Martin (1980) Writing Project, Papers I (Narrative: Vicarious Experience) and 2 (Exposition: Literary Criticism), Sydney, Department of Linguistics, University of Sydney.

Rubin, M. (1999) *Thrillers*, Cambridge: CUP.

Rumelhart, D. (1975) 'Notes on a schema for stories', in D. Bobrow and A. Collins (eds) *Representation and Understanding*, New York: Academic Press.

Rumelhart, D. (1977) 'Understanding and summarizing brief stories', in D. Laberge and S. J. Samuels (eds) *Basic Processes in Reading*, Hillsdale, NJ: Erlbaum.

Ryan, M.-L. (1981) 'The pragmatics of personal and impersonal fiction', *Poetics*, 10, 517–39.

Said, E. (1982) *The World, the Text, and the Critic*, London: Faber.

Sauerberg, L. O. (1984) *Secret Agents in Fiction*, London: Macmillan.

Saussure, F. de (1983) *Course in General Linguistics*, trans. R. Harris, London: Duckworth.

Schank, R. and R. P. Abelson (1977) *Scripts, Plans, Goals, and Understanding*, Hillsdale, NJ: Erlbaum.

Schiffrin, D. (1981) 'Tense variation in narrative', *Language*, 57, 1, 45–62.

Schiffrin, D. (1994) *Approaches to Discourse*, Oxford: Blackwell.

Schlesinger, P. (1987) *Putting 'Reality' Together: BBC News*, London: Methuen.

Scholes, R. and R. Kellogg (1966) *The Nature of Narrative*, New York: Oxford University Press.

Scholes, R. and A. W. Litz (1969) *Joyce's Dubliners: A Critical Edition*, New York: Viking.

Semino, E., M. Short and M. Wynne (1999) 'Hypothetical words and thoughts in contemporary British narratives', *Narrative*, Fall.

Short, M. (1988) 'Speech presentation, the novel and the press', in Willie van Peer (ed.) (1988) *The Taming of The Text*, London: Routledge, pp. 61–81.

Short, M. (1996) *Exploring the Language of Poems, Plays and Prose*, London: Longman.

Short, M., E. Semino and J. Culpeper (1996) 'Using a corpus for stylistics research: speech and thought presentation', in J. Thomas and M. Short (eds) (1996) *Using Corpora in Language Research*, London: Longman, pp. 110–31.

Short, M., E. Semino and M. Wynne (2001) 'Revisiting the notion of faithfulness in discourse report/(re)presentation using a corpus approach', *Language and Literature*, 10.

Silva-Corvalan, C. (1983) 'Tense and aspect in oral Spanish narrative: context and meaning', *Language*, 59, 4, 760–80.

Simpson, P. (1993) *Language, Ideology and Point of View*, London: Routledge.

Simpson, P. (1997) *Language Through Literature: an Introduction*, London: Routledge.

Sinclair, J. McH. and M. Coulthard (1975) *Towards An Analysis of Discourse*, London: Oxford University Press.

Slembrouck, S. (1992) 'The parliamentary Hansard "verbatim" report: the written construction of spoken discourse', *Language and Literature*, 1:2, 101–19.

Smiley, J. (1988) *The Age of Grief*, London: Collins.

Smith, B. H. (1978) *On the Margins of Discourse*, Chicago: Chicago University Press.

Snell, N. (1982) *Julie Stays the Night*, London: Hamish Hamilton.

SouthLondon Online (icSouthLondon.co.uk)

Spark, M. (1961) *The Prime of Miss Jean Brodie*, London: Macmillan.

Stanzel, F. (1971) *Narrative Situations in the Novel*, Bloomington, IN: Indiana University Press.

Stanzel, F. (1981) 'Teller-characters and reflector-characters in narrative theory', *Poetics Today*, 2, 2, 5–15.

Stanzel, F. (1984) *Theory of Narrative*, trans. C. Goedsche, Cambridge: Cambridge University Press.

Stein, N. and E. Albro (1997) 'Building complexity and coherence: children's use of goal-structured knowledge in telling stories', in M. Bamberg (ed.) *Narrative Development: Six Approaches*, Mahwah, NJ: Lawrence Erlbaum, 5–44.

Stein, N. and C. Glenn (1979) 'An analysis of story comprehension in elementary school children', in R. Freedle (ed.) *New Directions in Discourse Processing*, Hillsdale, NJ: Ablex.

Sternberg, M. (1982) 'Point of view and the indirections of direct speech', *Language and Style*, 15, 2, 67–117.

Sterne, L. (1967 [1760]) *Tristram Shandy*, Harmondsworth: Penguin.

Stubbs, M. (1983) *Discourse Analysis*, Oxford: Blackwell.

Sykes, M. (1985) 'Discrimination in discourse', in T. van Dijk (ed.) *Handbook in Discourse Analysis: volume 4*, London: Academic Press, 83–101.

Tannen, D. (1979) 'What's in a frame?', in R. Freedle (ed.) *New Directions in Discourse Processing*, Norwood, NJ: Ablex, 137–81.

Tannen, D. (ed) (1982) *Spoken and Written Language: Exploring Orality and Literacy*, Norwood, NJ: Ablex.

Tannen, D. (1988) *Talking Voices*, Cambridge: Cambridge University Press.

Tannen, D. (1991) *You Just Don't Understand: Women and Men in Conversation*, London: Virago.

Tannen, D. (1994) *Talking from 9 to 5*, London: Virago.

Taylor, T. J. (1981) *Linguistic Theory and Structural Stylistics*, Oxford: Pergamon.

Thompson, G. (1996) *Introducing Functional Grammar*, London: Arnold.

Todorov, T. (1977) *The Poetics of Prose*, Oxford: Blackwell.

Toolan, M. (1988) 'Analyzing conversation in fiction', *Poetics Today*, 8, 2, 393–416.

Toolan, M. (1998) *Language in Literature*, London: Hodder.

Traugoft, E. and M. L. Pratt (1980) *Linguistics for Students of Literature*, New York: Harcourt Brace Jovanovich.

Trew, T. (1979) 'Theory and ideology at work', in R. Fowler *et al.*, *Language and Control*, London: Routledge & Kegan Paul, 94–116.

Tyler, S. (1978) *The Said and the Unsaid: Mind, Meaning and Culture*, London: Academic Press, 1978.

Umiker-Sebeok, J. D. (1979) 'Preschool children's intraconversational narratives', *Journal of Child Language*, 6, 91–110.

Uppal, G. (1984) 'Narratives in Conversation', unpublished MA thesis, National University of Singapore.

Uspensky, B. (1973) *A Poetics of Composition*, Berkeley: University of California Press.

Verdonk, P. and J. J. Weber (1995) *Twentieth-Century Fiction: From Text to Context*, London: Routledge.

Vestergaard, T. and N. Schroder (1985) *The Language of Advertising*, Oxford: Blackwell.

Vincent, D. and L. Perrin (1999) 'On the narrative vs. non-narrative functions of reported speech: a socio-pragmatic study', *Journal of Sociolinguistics*, 3(3), 291–313.

Voloshinov, V. N. (1973) *Marxism and the Philosophy of Language*, trans. L. Matejka and I. R. Titunik, New York: Seminar Press.

Vuillaume, M. (1998) 'Le discours indirect libre et le passe simple', in S. Vogeleer, A. Borillo, C. Vetters and M. Vuillaume (eds) *Temps et Discours*, Louvain: Peeters, pp. 190–201.

Vygotsky, L. A. (1962 [1978]) *Thought and Language*, Cambridge, MA: MIT Press.

Wall, K. (1994) '*The Remains of the Day* and its challenges to theories of unreliable narration', *Journal of Narrative Technique*, 24, 18–42.

Warhol, R. (1986) 'Toward a theory of the engaging narrator', *PMLA*, 101, 811–18.

Warhol, R. (1989) *Gendered Interventions: Narrative Discourse in the Victorian Novel*, New Brunswick, NJ: Rutgers University Press.

Warren, W. H., D. W. Nicholas and T. Trabasso (1979) 'Event chains and inferences in understanding narratives', in R. Freedle (ed) *New Directions in Discourse Processing*, Hillsdale, NJ: Ablex, 23–52.

Watts, R. J. (1984) 'Narration as role-complimentary interaction', *Studia Anglia Posnaniensia*, 17, 157–64.

Waugh, L. (1995) 'Reported speech in journalistic discourse: The relation of function and text', *Text*, 15, 1, 129–73.

Weinsheimer, J. (1979) 'Theory of character: Emma', *Poetics Today*, 1, 185–211.

White, P. (1997) 'Death, disruption and the moral order: the narrative impulse in mass-media hard news reporting', in F. Christie and J. R. Martin (eds) *Genres and Institutions: Social Processes in the Workplace and School*, London, Cassell, 101–33.

White, P. (2000) 'Media objectivity and the rhetoric of news story structure', in E. Ventola (ed.) *Discourse and Community: Doing Functional Linguistics*, Tübingen, Gunter Narr Verlag, 378–97.

Wodak, R. (1981) 'Discourse analysis and courtroom interaction', *Discourse Processes*, 3, 369–80.

Wodak, R. (1985) 'The interaction between judge and defendant', in T. van Dijk, (ed.) *Handbook of Discourse Analysis: volume 4*, London: Academic Press, 181–91.

Wodak, R., R. de Cillia, M. Reisigl and K. Liebhart (1999) *The Discursive Construction of National Identity*, Edinburgh: Edinburgh University Press.

Wolf, D. (1984) 'Ways of telling: text repertoires in elementary school children', *Journal of Education*, 167, 1, 71–87.

Wolf, G. *et al.* (1996) 'Pronouncing French names in New Orleans', *Language in Society*, 25, 407–26; reprinted in R. Harris and G. Wolf (eds) *Integrational Linguistics: A First Reader*, Oxford: Pergamon, 324–41.

Wolfson, N. (1976) 'Speech events and natural speech', *Language in Society*, 5, 189–209.

Wolfson, N. (1978) 'A feature of performed narrative: the conversational historical present', *Language in Society*, 7, 215–37.

Wolfson, N. (1979) 'The conversational historical present alternation', *Language*, 55, 1, 168–82.

Wolfson, N. (1981) 'Tense-switching in narrative', *Language and Style*, 14, 226–30.

Wolfson, N. (1982) *CHP, The Conversational Historical Present in American English Narrative*, Cinnarminson, NJ, Foris Publications.

Yacobi, T. (1981) 'Fictional reliability as a communicative problem,' *Poetics Today*, 2:2, 113–26.

# Index